Australia[illegible] on

A GENEALOGY C[illegible] NTS

Alan McKee

OXFORD
UNIVERSITY PRESS

OXFORD
UNIVERSITY PRESS
253 Normanby Road, South Melbourne, Victoria 3205, Australia

Oxford University Press is a department of the University of Oxford. It furthers the University's objective of excellence in research, scholarship, and education by publishing worldwide in

Oxford New York

Athens Auckland Bangkok Bogotá Buenos Aires Cape Town Chennai Dar es Salaam Delhi Florence Hong Kong Istanbul Karachi Kolkata Kuala Lumpur Madrid Melbourne Mexico City Mumbai Nairobi Paris Port Moresby São Paulo Shanghai Singapore Taipei Tokyo Toronto Warsaw with associated companies in Berlin Ibadan

OXFORD is a trade mark of Oxford University Press in the UK and in certain other countries

First published 2001

National Library of Australia
Cataloguing-in-Publication data:

McKee, Alan.
Australian television: a genealogy of great moments.

ISBN 0 19 551225 1.

1. Television broadcasting—Australia—History.
2. Television programs—Australia—History. I. Title.

384.550994

Edited by Lucy Davison
Cover designed by Racheal Stines
Typeset by Promptset Pty Ltd (Stephen Chan)
Printed through Bookpac Production Services Singapore

Contents

Acknowledgments

This book is dedicated to Frances Moore, who tried to teach me how to argue. And to Marc Brennan, who showed me that academic life can be a lot of fun, and other things are even better.

Thanks to John Hartley, who introduced me to cultural studies and to the excitement and delight of writing about popular culture, and without whom I would be far less interested in writing about television.

I am grateful also to Ian Craven, who got me started on the whole thing, and whose skill in avoiding Grand Unified Theories I only appreciated in retrospect.

I owe a debt of gratitude to everyone who helped with the research for the book: above all, to Chris Keating, whose encyclopaedic knowledge of Australian television is matched only by his generosity in sharing that information; Tamara Osicka and Richard Keyes at Screensound; Geraldine Rodwell and all of the staff at the ABC TV News and Current Affairs Library; Sonia Loje at the Grundy Organisation; Marea Burke at CTC Productions; Helen and Penny at the Victorian Branch of Screensound; Carol Matthews at Crawford Productions; Mike Collins and James Davern at JNP; Salvatore Russo at the ABC; Polly Watkins and Michael Hirsh at Working Dog Productions; Len Downes at Channel Nine; and Hal McElroy at McElroy and McElroy.

I also appreciate the contributions of viewers who shared information: all the letter writers, emailers and callers; Diane, Cameron, and David Grant;

Peter Criddle; Darren Gray; Ian McLean; and Gary Gillatt, who writes about television so very well.

I am very grateful to the friends who put up with me during the research trip: Andrew, Craig, Brady, Brad, Dave, and Rachel.

Thanks to the people who helped publicise the book and solicit viewer feedback: Geoff Shearer at *TV Week*, Radio 3AK, Sue Yeap at the *West Australian,* Post newspapers, and Damien, Karen and Jim at 6WF.

I gratefully acknowledge my research assistant, Catherine Breen, and Linda Jaunzems for secretarial support: jobs well done. The staff at the Edith Cowan University library and the Social Sciences and Humanities Library at the University of Queensland have all been helpful above and beyond the call of duty. Patrick Jewell's technical expertise and generosity made the book look much better than would otherwise have been the case.

Many colleagues responded to requests for information: Paul Alberts, John Hartley, Graeme Turner, Toby Miller, and McKenzie Wark. Thank you also to Frances Bonner, Sue Turnbull, Andy Medhurst, Rick Thompson, and Catharine Lumby for support of all kinds, and to Graeme Turner and Chris Keating for useful comments on the first draft.

I would also like to acknowledge everyone in the School of Communications and Multimedia at Edith Cowan University—one could not imagine better colleagues. This research was made possible by study leave and a grant from Edith Cowan University.

Thanks also to Jill Henry at OUP, who seemed to like the project, and to Lucy Davison, who writes English much better than I do.

Finally, thanks to Grania Sexton, who helped to keep me sane while I was writing the book. And, of course, Marc, who is at least as clever as me.

Alan McKee
February 2001

INTRODUCTION

Australian Television: A Genealogy of Great Moments

Watching television

I watch television.

According to the data gathered by the Australian Bureau of Statistics, I fluctuate between being an average and a heavy consumer of television (ABS 1995: 165). On the weeks when work or social life impinge, I can manage only the average Australian viewing time: around two hours and twenty-three minutes a day. Without these distractions, I can manage up to six or seven hours, and even more at weekends. Recently—and oddly enough, while researching this book—I found myself living in a flat with no television, and for two weeks watched nothing at all. It was a dispiriting experience.

For me, television is for watching. I am interested in the programs that are shown: the stories they tell me, the images and the performances they present. I am not particularly concerned by who owns the stations. The legislation that governs broadcasting is of only secondary interest to this viewer, after the fact, as a useful intertext by which to understand the programs better. Production information is similarly fascinating: the kind you can find in *Who Weekly* and *TV Week*, as well as the more detailed information available to an audience in a variety of popular writings and programs about the 'behind-the-scenes' world of television production.

This is only one possible approach to television. Many researchers are interested in quite different ways of thinking about the medium—by studying legislation and ownership of television institutions, for example. And it is entirely legitimate, of course, to take a variety of approaches to the same object of study. However, the perspective of the viewer—of the 'I' who starts this book—is not one that has been given much space in academic approaches to television. Much writing in the area proceeds with the implicit or explicit assumption that questions about what people are watching are not really suitable or important questions for the academic study of television. Research into the forms that these programs take; which ones are popular and which ones aren't; what part they play in the wider Australian mediasphere and semiosphere; and (particularly important for this book) which programs survive as important parts of Australia's cultural heritage—these questions are largely ignored. This book puts forward a modest proposal—that such questions constitute a suitable way to approach Australian television, and that researching them can add important dimensions to our understanding of the medium.

Canons and cultural heritage

When I watch television, I do not simply sit in front of the apparatus and watch whatever 'flows' onto the screen. It is not only the liveness of the medium that seduces me. There are specific programs that I like, whose return to the screen after the summer break gives me particular pleasure. There are programs that I remember long after they have ceased transmission.

I do not wish, at this stage in the book, to generalise from my own viewing experience and to claim that therefore this is how all people watch television, although I think there is sufficient material presented here to suggest that I am not alone in thinking about television in this way. Rather, I wish to use this introduction to explain how this book came to be written. I research and I teach about Australian television and, for me, that means looking at Australian television programs—not simply those that are broadcast now, but at those that have gone before. A book that takes this approach does not currently exist; that is why I had to write it for myself. But as soon as I began, I encountered a problem: there is no established methodology for deciding what programs to look at. Facing many decades of television programming in Australia, just how does an author decide which ones are worth writing about? I did not want simply to repeat the pioneering and encyclopaedic work of Albert Moran and Peter Pinne (1993) or Tony Harrison (1994), which attempted to list every drama series and every program (respectively) ever broadcast on the medium in Australia. I felt from my own viewing that all programs are not equal: some stand out more than others. But how to decide which those were? Even formulating the question was difficult. What language should we choose to describe those programs that have survived, made more of an impact, or been in some way distinctive in the history of the medium: the 'best' programs (suggesting aesthetic criteria)? my 'favourite' programs (suggesting a personal response unconnected to wider social and cultural considerations)? the most 'important' programs (suggesting perhaps an industrial or cultural relevance beyond their own textual existence)? Finally, I settled—still with some hesitation—on the 'greatest' moments in Australian television—a term with a pleasing ambiguity, in that it can cover a variety of criteria for distinction. But even then, the programs that would fit into this book were not immediately obvious. This is because 'greatness' is not a category that has traditionally been used in thinking about television programming. Other media (books, painting, even film) have established and commonsensical procedures for deciding on the 'greatness' of individual texts—the concepts of canon, and of cultural heritage—but television has rarely been thought of in this way. This book thus remains ambivalent about its object—'great moments'. For, even having written it, I find that without the support of the discriminatory apparatus that serves other media, incorporating approaches that are so familiar as to be unthinking, it is difficult to be certain about what the book's object of study actually is. In trying to think this through for myself, I have turned to the canons of other media and examined their usefulness for discussing television.

The 1997 Symposium of the Australian Academy of the Humanities, for example, was entitled *Our Cultural Heritage*. The writers included in the collected papers from this symposium argue that 'we have reason to be proud of our heritage ...' (Bigelow 1998: vii); that: ' ...we should prepare to celebrate and give thanks for all the great and wonderful things which we have achieved as a nation' (Smith 1998: 4). This can include ' "creative arts", especially the "newer" arts such as film' (Bell 1998). They aim to justify the retrieval of 'great moments' in Australian architecture, writing, visual arts, and film.

Television does not get a mention in this collection. It does not even appear in order to justify its exclusion. Television, it appears, does not have an archive: it is, once again, simply an ephemeral flow (see Bianculli 1996: 15 for a similar example in the United States context). The idea that television might be part of Australia's 'cultural heritage' is unthinkable for the symposium collection—or at least, unspeakable. But, other media have established 'canons'—lists of the texts that are commonly assumed to be, in some way, 'great' examples of their form. John Corner notes that 'Study of film ... work[s] often from a canon of established classics ...' (Corner 1991: 2). By contrast, Australian television has no 'canon' of 'established classics'.

In film studies, the decisions about which texts deserve a place in the canon have often been achieved through aesthetic judgments. Television is not a medium that has traditionally invited assessment of its programs in such familiar aesthetic terms as the 'good', the 'beautiful', or the 'true'. Only a small amount of writing in Australia has analysed programs in this way, 'attempt[ing] to elaborate principles of taste as transcendent, going beyond any one period, culture or medium ...' (O'Sullivan et al. 1994: 6), naming programs 'good' or 'bad', 'beautiful' or 'true'. Both Albert Moran and Elizabeth Jacka have enlivened encyclopaedic lists of production with aesthetic judgments on the programs being listed. Moran, for example, is willing to grant that *Return to Eden* was 'wonderful melodrama' and *The Dismissal* is 'a commanding and fascinating series ...' (Moran & Pinne 1993: 381, 146), although it is obvious that he is more interested in ratings and financial means of judging programs. Jacka presents aesthetic judgments about the ABC's drama productions such as *Marion* ('a beautifully filmed screenplay'), *Scales of Justice* ('a landmark of innovative and politically courageous program making') and *The Magistrate* ('aesthetically satisfying') (Jacka 1991: 74, 80, 88). Articles with a similar aesthetic approach can be found in the journal *Cinema Papers*, writing particularly on mini-series in the 1970s and 1980s (Ryan 1977; Burnett 1984; Murray 1984; Mayer 1985).

Such writing tends to ascribe most value to those television programs that most resemble texts of another medium (the more filmic mini-series, or one-off dramas, for example), those that have traditionally invited aesthetic assessment. Even to think of television in such a way seems like a category error. Tom O'Regan notes that there are

> three competing personae for the [film] critic: the cinephile, the critical intellectual and the cultural historian ... [For the first], film is conceived in predominantly expressive terms ... as a performance text to be judged, appraised and considered ... [Secondly t]he film criticism of the critical intellectual institutions are concerned with a film's social and ideological meaning ... [Thirdly, f]ilm histories [treat] ... film as archival record ... [where] curating the past is a public good.
>
> (O'Regan 1996: 341–5)

It is interesting to ask what the equivalent roles for the writer on television programs might be. The cinephile's only obvious equivalent is the 'couch potato'—someone who is rendered a passive zombie by a love of television programs. The critical intellectual might write on television news programs. The cultural historian, finally, is perhaps replaced by the political historian, who can trace the changes in ownership and legislation of the medium over the years. In none of the categories is there a strong tradition in Australia of critical writing interested in television programs (see Marc 1995: 134 for a suggestion that the United States situation is similar).

In a sense, this is an advantage that television has over other media, since aesthetic assessments (universalising claims of 'good' or 'bad' which ignore differing individual responses or criteria for assessment) are now understood by cultural studies writers to be problematic and elitist (O'Sullivan et al. 1994: 6). This requires a writer interested in the 'great moments' of Australian television to formulate and explicitly state the criteria for assessment. So although I sense that underlying the Australian Academy of the Humanities' claims for 'cultural heritage' is an understanding of 'culture' in the sense of 'high culture', my use of the term is informed by the 'culture' of Raymond Williams and of cultural studies more generally: culture as a whole way of life. If this view is accepted, then writing a genealogy of the television programs that can fairly be said to contribute to Australia's cultural heritage is not an impossible project. The 'greatness' of the 'great moments' I am studying here is not an indication of how wonderful they are. I am not insisting that they are 'Of surpassing excellence ... used as a ... rapturous term of admiration: "Magnificent".' Their greatness is rather that they are 'Of more than ordinary importance, weight or distinction; important, weighty, distinguished, prominent; famous, renowned' (*OED* 1989: 797, 798). David Bianculli notes in the introduction to his history of *Television's 500 Biggest Hits, Misses and Events* that 'Memorable doesn't necessarily mean good' (Bianculli 1996: 16), and for the argument of this book, it is not necessary to question whether or not the programs here discussed meet abstract, universalising aesthetic criteria for being 'good' or 'bad'. Rather, the argument is that some Australian television programs are part of the country's cultural heritage, where culture is a whole way of life.

Public archive

If one is not applying aesthetic criteria to the choice of which television programs to include in Australia's cultural heritage, how does one proceed in deciding what belongs in this category? Why, to take an example from this book, should *Neighbours* be included but not *Echo Point*?

There has simply not been enough work in this area to sediment into an unproblematic methodology for making judgments about the relative importance of television programs. Graeme Turner's work on 'transgressive television' in Australia, tracing a genealogy of programs from *In Melbourne Tonight* to *Perfect Match* (Turner 1989), is important to note at this point, as is John Hartley's discussion of the democratisation of Australia's public sphere through television (Hartley 1996). John Docker attempts to understand the importance of popular programs such as *The Price is Right* and *Prisoner* (Docker 1983), and his essay 'Popular Culture and Bourgeois Values' (1988) is another important contribution to writing on Australian television programs. But useful though this work is, there is simply not enough of it to constitute a tradition that can be called upon unproblematically. There is no readily available methodology for making the choice of which programs should be chosen.

Or rather, there is no tradition and no methodology *in academic writing* about television by which to make such judgments. Luckily, if we turn to popular culture itself, we find that much of the work of deciding which programs deserve recognition as part of Australia's cultural heritage has already been done. The Australian media (including but not limited to television) are engaged in a daily process of remembering some television programs while forgetting others, discussing and negotiating what I will call a 'public archive' of the important programs in Australia's television history. The criteria for inclusion are not explicit, and they are certainly not traditionally aesthetic. But there is a remarkable consistency, over several decades, in the archive of television programs that are regarded as making an important contribution to Australian culture. My contention is that this public archive might suitably be included in accounts of Australia's cultural heritage.

This point can be substantiated in the first instance by citation. In the course of my research and writing I came across dozens of examples of the maintenance of an archive of great moments in Australian television and found that new examples are added to the mediasphere on an almost daily basis. On television itself, see for example *30 Years of Television* (1994); *40 Years of Channel Nine Unplugged* (1999) and *35 Years of Television* (1991); *Simply The Best*'s program on 'the best TV Show of the Century' (1999); and *Today Tonight*'s item on 'TV's Top 100 Moments' (1999); *Our Century's* account of television's history (1999); *Homicide: 30 Years On* (1994) and *The Homicide Story* (1970); the last, tribute episode of *Hey Hey It's Saturday* (1999).

In newspapers and magazines, see 'The 25 All-time Best Australian TV Shows' (Elder 1995: 6S) or 'Channel 7: 40 Years of Television' (1999); 'The

50 Most Influential Shows in Australian Television History' (Dale 1998: 5); *TV Week*'s 'What's Your Most Memorable Australian Television Moment?' (1999) or *Who Weekly*'s 'The 100 Greatest Moments in Television' (1999); and the publications of the Australian Television Appreciation Society, including its magazine, *TV Eye* (Keating 1993).

In advertising, take the examples of television 'promos' presenting 'Perth's own TVW Channel 7—40 years in the making' (1999); and an advertising series for Harvey Norman promoting 'Great Moments in Television' and featuring such moments as '*A Country Practice*: Lucy and Matt's Wedding' (Norman 1999: 29).

The writers who have paid most attention to television programs are consistently those writing in more journalistic or popular modes: Adrian Martin, for example, writes about 'indelible TV memor[ies]' (Martin 1994: 57), a concept almost unimaginable for those interested in legislation and the adequacy of news coverage of political events. Similarly, Morris Gleitzman's account of Australian television is focused on its programs (Gleitzman 1992).

Simply citing this material is not enough; we must also decide what to do with it. The relationship between academic and non-academic forms of writing on culture can be an uneasy one. Much writing in media studies and cultural studies emerges from a desire to condemn popular culture, and to turn it into an *object* of study to which academic ideas and theories are applied, rather than viewing it as a source of ideas with which the academic writer might engage. So, for example, Simon Frith and Jon Savage, commenting on *The Modern Review*, describe this magazine's construction of television's archive as 'self-serving nostalgia' (Frith & Savage 1997: 14).

But it is not necessary to think of popular culture in such a way, as an adversary engaged in projects completely unrelated to those of cultural studies. This book rather follows the work of Thomas McLaughlin and his discussion of 'vernacular theory' (McLaughlin 1996). McLaughlin argues that the living of everyday life—including the work of the popular media—involves the practice of philosophy, in the sense of asking questions about, and making sense of, individual and social existence. He distinguishes this work from that of academic research by degree, not by kind, and argues that academic thinking and writing is distinguished from 'vernacular theory' by certain standards of 'rigour' and 'decorum' rather than by virtue of being involved in a completely different project. It is possible, if such an argument is accepted, to take the archiving work of popular culture seriously, rather than dismissing it for the ways in which it fails to live up to academic standards.

Of course, such an argument will be anathema to some potential readers of this book. If popular culture is seen as an intellectually unworthy object of study, there can be little interest in examining the ways in which it establishes television as part of Australia's cultural heritage. But if McLaughlin's arguments are accepted, then we open up a new area of study, and discover that Australian popular culture insistently wants to archive certain television programs—to create a sense of the medium's part in Australia's cultural heritage. The process of creating and maintaining this archive I call 'collective memory'.

Collectively remembering a public archive

Several media historians have attempted to make sense of the way in which some texts survive beyond their initial circulation. Mark Jancovich uses the term 'cultural memory' (Jancovich 1996: 169), and Paddy Scannell speaks of 'social memory' (Scannell 1996: 91); Michael Gitter and his co-authors refer to the 'collective television unconscious' of the nation (Gitter, Anapol, and Glazer 1999: back cover), while David Bianculli writes about 'shared television memories' (Bianculli 1996: 16). I prefer to use the term 'collective memory' to describe the process whereby certain texts are remembered and accorded a place in a public archive of the most important moments in Australian television.

'Knowledge of the past is generally referred to as memory', states John Nerone (1989: 89). What we think of as 'history' is one particular kind of memory, a subset of knowledge about past events that emerged in the nineteenth century and is sanctioned by particular professional practices involving 'standards of documentation and attention toward matters of historical significance' (Nerone 1989: 96–7). Professional history, however, 'is as much a fabrication as popular memory' (Nerone 1989: 98) and tells stories about the past for particular reasons, just as much as do other forms of memory (see also Lipitz 1990: 31; Spigel & Jenkins 1991: 117; Popular Memory Group 1982: 206). Given the paucity of 'professional' historical work on the importance and survival of Australian television programs, it is reasonable to look to other accounts of television's past—other kinds of memory—for a project such as this one.

As the writers gathered in the book *Collective Remembering* claim, memory is always a social process. It does not simply occur 'inside the heads of individual human beings', because expectations of what will be remembered, and how it will be remembered, are always cultural: 'remembering and forgetting [are] inherently social activities' (Middleton & Edwards 1990: 1), and 'memory [is] a socio-culturally constituted process ...' (Cole 1990: viii–ix). In societies where mass media exist, these media play an important part in the process of remembering about a culture: as a 'repository of collective memory' (Lipitz 1990: 5), where 'memories of the past' are 'evoke[d] and shape[d] (Spigel & Jenkins 1991: 119). Indeed, 'we are forging through the media a common recollection' of past events (Nerone & Wartella 1989: 85). This is not history in the professionally sanctioned sense, but it is a form of memory about past events that is no less useful or powerful.

For many writers who draw on the concept of collective memory—or synonyms such as 'popular memory ... public memory and social memory' (Nerone & Wartella 1989: 86)—such accounts of the past are set up in binary opposition to official history in order to celebrate the greater 'truth' of the excluded voices of oppressed groups. Mary Jo Maynes suggests that the idea of collective memory became important for historians through the 'radical historiography' of the British New Left movement (Maynes 1982: 5). In the work of the Popular Memory Group, for example, 'popular' is employed in a socialist sense to mean the memories of 'the people', in binary opposition to the 'dominant memory' of official histories by powerful groups in society: 'the governmental and parliamentary systems ... [and] BBC pomposity' (Popular Memory Group 1982: 207, 208). Some media historians draw on such a binary, placing 'popular memory' in opposition to 'official history' (see Spigel 1995: 22; (Lipitz 1990: 20, 43). But such a binary is not useful for this book: this is not an attempt to recover the 'reality' of people's experiences of Australian television programs in opposition to the bourgeois accounts of official history. Indeed, as noted above, there is little official history of this topic. But more than this, it is important to understand that 'the opposition ... between popular and official pasts ... is not absolute' (Spigel 1995: 21–2). Indeed, there is more than one official account of any aspect of the past, just as there is more than one collectively memorialised account. It is more useful to 'think in terms of pluralities: there are social memories, and rarely 'A [single] social memory for whatever event, practice, epoch or symbolic entity which is the subject of recollection' (Nerone & Wartella 1989: 87). In writing this account of the television programs that are collectively remembered in Australia—the public archive of programs that might fairly be added to accounts of 'our cultural heritage'—I have drawn on a variety of sources. These include television's own accounts of itself that it broadcasts to audiences, the memories presented in other media, the academic and industrial accounts of the past that are collected in books, monographs, and articles, and the individual memories of audience members. These all contribute to a collective remembering of Australian television's archive that is far from homogenous or simple: some programs are more remembered by some segments of the population than by others (some primarily by academics, some by journalists, some by individual audience members), but all these memories might be understood to make up the public archive of Australian television.

Populist histories

The existence of the public archive reassures me that the project of attempting to write a genealogy of Australia's 'great' television programs, in the absence of traditional criteria such as aesthetics, is neither a foolhardy nor an impossible one.

It is worth taking a moment here briefly to address the question of populism, simply because academic writing that discusses elements of popular culture without condemning them is always open to charges of being 'populist' (see, for example, McGuigan 1997). It should be obvious by now that this book does not set out to reduce popular culture to a homogenous landscape of identical moments, all of which must be discussed and celebrated equally. Indeed, the point of the book is to identify those moments that have survived in a public archive of Australian television programs. It is true that the tone of the book is not condemnatory, and for some writers, this in itself might constitute populism.

However, it seems to me that many academic writers who worry about populism are, as Leon Hunt has argued, 'sweeping aside a huge and diverse cultural output which has … only been studied cautiously and highly selectively' (Hunt 1998: 161). Studying elements of popular culture is not the same as studying 'popular culture' as a whole (I'm not even sure what that mythical entity consists of), and to study elements of popular culture without a predetermined condemnatory agenda is not the same thing as celebrating the mythical totality of 'popular culture'. Behind many charges of populism seems to lie a real distaste for popular culture: an incredulity that it can support sustained critical study, and an 'itching to get back to more "serious" matters' (Hunt 1998: 161). This project merely suggests that Australian television supports a public archive, and that an attempt to map that archive is of interest to media and cultural studies in Australia.

Methodology

In analysing the public archive of the way in which Australian television's programs are remembered, I have triangulated information from a variety of sources:

- popular histories of Australia's television programs
- mentions (usually brief) in academic histories of television
- contemporary coverage of television in other media
- my own experiences as a television viewer in Australia
- suggestions from other media academics
- letters solicited on radio and in newspapers from viewers asking them to answer a general question about their favourite television memories
- fan coverage of programs on the internet and in fanzines.

From this material, I have attempted to produce an account of programs that have been important in Australia for a variety of reasons. The book then proceeds as a genealogy, structured not so much by a single linear argument as by an account of a series of moments. To the extent that I do wish to make an argument, it is simply to demonstrate that a public archive of Australian television programs does exist, and that they are remembered and archived in a variety of ways. Whether the point that for me follows logically on from this—that these Australian television programs can be added to 'our cultural heritage'—is acceptable to readers will depend on the preconceptions that they bring to this book. I demonstrate that television is not a homogenous flow, and that audiences employ discrimination in their accounts of the programs that have been broadcast on the medium. This contradicts common academic conceptions of television as a 'flow', with everything broadcast on it melding into a single endless text (Gripsrud 1998). However, to prove this point will not be enough to convince all readers of this book that these texts therefore deserve to be accorded any importance in accounts of Australia's cultural heritage. Surprisingly, despite thirty years of writing in the cultural studies tradition, many academics writing on popular culture still see it as trivial, judging it aesthetically and finding it worthless. There is no argument I can offer up to counter this: belief or disbelief in the value of aesthetic judgments are not positions with which one can engage rationally. As with all forms of belief, atheists and believers will find themselves speaking from such different paradigms, and relying on such incompatible principles, that the possibility of useful dialogue is minimal. All I can say is that if one accepts the view that traditional aesthetic judgments of 'good' and 'bad' are not a useful way to make sense of culture (O'Sullivan et al. 1994), then this book offers enough evidence to show that many of the programs broadcast on Australian television are of sufficient importance to justify inclusion in 'Australia's cultural heritage'.

The 'importance' of the programs varies. All have survived in the mediasphere, many of them beyond the moment when they ceased production: they are still cited, mentioned, remembered, and circulated. They linger, years after they were first broadcast. Some of them have changed the forms taken by television. Others are representative of general trends in Australian television programs. Some contain particular moments that have strongly cemented themselves into the 'collective memory' of Australian culture. Of course, I do not wish to claim that I know how audience members have 'really' interpreted these programs. Indeed, as I have argued elsewhere, such a proposition—that we ever know exactly what happens in a viewer's head about anything, never mind television programs, outside of acculturated representations—is a meaningless one (McKee 1999b). With Lynn Spigel, I believe that 'While the media discourses do not directly reveal how people responded to television, they do reveal an intertextual context—a group of interconnected texts—through which people might have made sense of television and its place in everyday life' (Spigel 1992: 2). It is for precisely this reason that I have attempted to triangulate information from a variety of sources about the importance of the programs in this book.

Having gained some sense of their importance, I have then returned to the programs themselves. This book is, after all, about those programs that have supplied 'great moments'. It is the texts of those programs in which I am interested. The contextual research suggests possibilities for interpreting those texts in ways that are not completely alien to the cultural context in which they first circulated, and in which they continue to circulate as part of the public archive of Australian television.

However, the return to the texts of the programs proved sometimes to be a haphazard procedure. Very little early television programming was recorded; much of that was never archived; and of the material that does still exist, not all is available for study (see Cunningham & Turner 1993: 39, 40). Some of the programs no longer survive, and it has been necessary to rely on secondary accounts; in other cases, specific episodes have vanished, but others give a sense of the program. Some programs are inaccessible, not held by Screensound (the federal government's audiovisual archive) but by private production companies, who rarely allow access to them, and never without a good deal of careful negotiation. Other programs do exist, and I have given details for students of Australian television interested in following up these accounts of how these programs can be accessed.

Partial accounts

This book is a genealogy, and as an account of Australian television 'greatest moments' it is explicitly partial. It does not claim that this must be, 'inevitably', the only approach to the medium, nor that these are the only programs that might be placed into this archive. I take the meaning of the term from Foucault's writing: 'genealogy is gray, meticulous and patiently documentary. It operates on a field of entangled and confused parchments ... it rejects the metahistorical deployment of ideal significations and indefinite teleologies. It opposes itself to the search for origins' (Foucault 1991 [1971]: 76, 77).

I cannot claim to come up to Foucault's own rigorous standards for what a genealogy, or a genealogist, should be: 'Genealogy ... depends on a vast accumulation of source material ... [and it] demands relentless erudition' (Foucault 1991 [1971]: 76, 77). Rather, I wish merely to draw upon the sense he gives the term of escaping from attempts to write totalistic, unifying, and final accounts of what has gone before in culture—accounts that insist that the history of Australian television 'must' be written from only one perspective. There are many other programs that could have been chosen for this project, and other ways in which they could have been organised. And, of course, no chapter addresses every possible aspect of interest about a particular program—it would be impossible to do so—but each chapter focuses rather on one or two areas that collective memory identifies as particularly important about them.

Indeed, some of the decisions taken in ordering this archive may be contentious. I have not, for example, included imported programs in this book. In a way, this is unfair—as some of the most important programs on Australian television have undoubtedly been those imported from the USA and the UK. There are two reasons for this decision. First, I wanted to retain at least some commonality between the 'Australian television' constructed as an object of study in this book and the 'Australian television' of previous works. Writing on the political economy of Australian television's legislation, ownership, and institutions has tended to focus, of course, on Australian-produced examples. This book still has at least something in common with the objects of study of previous writing on the medium.

Second, I suspect that the question of imported programs in Australia's television history might better be served by a separate work. Tom O'Regan notes that Australian television has a 'double-face' (O'Regan 1993: 59): imported and Australian-made programming. In the Australian mediasphere, these two faces are presented in quite different ways. Recent work has begun to trace the ways in which imported programs function quite differently in the Australian mediasphere from those made in this country (Cunningham & Jacka 1996); (Nixon 1998). Australian television works hard to distinguish between imported and Australian programming, insisting on the 'Australian' provenance of homemade programs in promos and advertising. The television ratings circulated in popular culture suggest that audiences are also very aware of this difference: it is almost always Australian current affairs, lifestyle, and drama programs that are the most popular of their genres in Australia.

I have also excluded moments that are vitally important to the development of television, but are not specifically Australian: moments such as the moon landing and the funeral of Princess Diana. Other accounts of television's greatest moments, both journalistic and academic, have tended to include these ('The 100 Greatest Moments in Television' 1999; Bianculli 1996). Again, I feel that they function quite differently from television's other programming, and their international nature makes them suitable for separate study.

Further, I have chosen to focus on programs that were important nationally. This excludes programs that were particularly important in only one state and whose reach did not extend to other parts of the country. In Australia, this is a particularly contentious decision. Important differences still remain between states. Despite the fact that the commercial stations are now fully networked in urban areas, travelling across state lines in Australia can still be a disorienting experience. Programs move across the schedules in disturbing ways, and the fact that many states are at different stages in broadcasting the same program means that a favourite character can suddenly die in one state, only to be resurrected when arriving in another. Sports programs appear and vanish. And you can never be entirely sure who will be reading your news: a familiar national face, or some local upstart you've never seen before. Many of the programs in this book were particularly popular in one state—*In Melbourne Tonight*, of course; *The Sullivans*; even *Neighbours*—but all of these also achieved some level of national importance. The nation remains an important level of analysis of Australian culture, and I have chosen to retain that focus in this book.

Unfinished business

I watch television, and I watch it because I enjoy the programs it presents. Similarly, I write about television programs because I enjoy them, and such research seems to me to provide an important perspective on the medium. This book draws on evidence for collectively remembered elements of Australian television's programming history in order to map the public archive of 'great moments' on the medium, and to propose that the evidence that these moments exist—rather than vanishing into an ever-moving flow of homogenous items—means that they might fairly be included in accounts of Australia's cultural heritage.

But the lack of previous work in this area—even given that there is a remarkable degree of consistency over the years, as we shall see, in which moments should be included in this genealogy—means that the project is necessarily provisional. This book can only begin the process of studying the cultural heritage of Australian television programs; it cannot rely on a substantial and agreed canon of programs with which it engages. Given this fact, it is to be expected that readers may have many disagreements about the moments I have included in, and excluded from, this book. What about *Skippy, the Bush Kangaroo*? *The Norman Gunston Show*? *The Gilles Report*? *Sex with Sophie Lee*? *Vietnam*? *Chances*? *Power Without Glory*? *Pick-a-Box*? *Perfect Match*? *This Day Tonight*? Or *Blackout*? All of these programs could justify a place in the genealogy. I do not think this is a failing of the book; it is rather part of its purpose. Those writers who have tried to write on television programs have often found themselves in a similar position: strongly aware of the disagreements that might emerge when attempting to write an archive of a medium that cannot make appeal to a familiar and standardised canon. David Bianculli closes the introduction to his *Dictionary of Teleliteracy* with the challenge 'if you become incensed that I could include *The A-Team* yet exclude *Absolutely Fabulous*—that is an argument and a debate, it is my pleasure, as well as my intention, to instigate' (Bianculli 1996: 16). As Morris Gleitzman puts it in his account of Australia's television programs in 1987, 'Best mini-series: *The Life and Loves of A She Devil*. That's what I think and if you don't agree, tough. Nobody's stopping you from writing to the *Herald*'s Letters Page with your choice and mentioning my name several times' (Gleitzman 1992: 37).

It may be that, in some years time—after much research, writing and publication in this area—it will be obvious that I am wrong in every instance. I look forward to the situation in which I can be convinced of this by other researchers who take a genuine interest in the Australian television programs that have lasted, have made an impact, have been important—the programs that are collectively remembered in the public archive of Great Moments in Australian Television.

1

In Melbourne Tonight/ *The Graham Kennedy (Channel Nine) Show*: Advertising Transgression

1951–70, 1972–75

On 3 March 1975, Graham Kennedy did an impression of a crow on live Australian television, and it sounded very like the word 'fuck'. For this, he was punished by the Australian Broadcasting Control Board: they banned him from broadcasting live. This was to be the end of an era for Australian television—an era that had begun with the first broadcast of the variety program *In Melbourne Tonight* on 6 May 1957 (in only the second year of regular television broadcasting in Australia), and an era during which Graham Kennedy was, to quote the cover of the *TV Times* in 1958, 'Mr Television' in Australia ('Mr Television' 1958). In the years from 1957 to 1975, Graham Kennedy's television show—variously titled *In Melbourne Tonight, The Graham Kennedy Show*, and *The Graham Kennedy Channel Nine Show* (depending on which year we discuss, and in which state you were living)—was one of the most important programs in the Australian media.[1] (For the rest of this chapter, I will refer to this program by the common shorthand of its first incarnation: *IMT*.) Kennedy's official reprimand by the Australian Broadcasting Control Board in 1975—and the chain of events it set in motion, which led with amazing rapidity to Kennedy leaving the chair of the program in which he had become legendary—are symptomatic of the way in which variety programs have existed as an object of extreme discomfort and annoyance for bodies of the state in Australian television history. The debacle over the (possible) use of the word 'fuck' on Australian television sums up a certain hysteria in television's early years—hysteria around programs such as *IMT*—on the part of the government's appointed watchdog, the Australian Broadcasting Control Board. This program is an important part of Australia's public archive of television, and one central aspect of its archived image is the concept of subversiveness, and its relation to television as a medium. This chapter traces the place that *IMT* holds in the public archive of Australian television programs, and the ways in which it can be understood as part of Australia's cultural heritage.

Advertising Kennedy

According to one correspondent for this book:

> I am 73 years of age, and can honestly say that in my lifetime the person who gave me the most pleasure and laughter … is Graham Kennedy, *In Melbourne Tonight*. What he used to do with advertisements was hysterical and they stuck in your mind—still do actually.

Another identifies as a specific moment, 'The dog piddling against the desk in Graham Kennedy *In Melbourne Tonight*'. Advertorials broadcast several decades ago are still remembered as important parts of Australian television's heritage.

Indeed, Graham Kennedy and the variety programs he presented are a strong place to begin an account of the public archive of Australian television, not just because these programs are some of the earliest Australian examples to be collectively remembered, but because of the consistency with which Kennedy appears in accounts of the medium. He and his programs are regularly listed in television's accounts of its own history—in programs such as Channel Nine's *Our Century* (1999), the series *The Australian Image* (1989b; 1989c; 1989d; 1989e), and the Channel Nine documentary, *Graham Kennedy: King of Television* (2000). They also appear in histories of the medium in newspapers, magazines, popular books, and academic writing, where he consistently appears as a 'legend' (Johnson & Smiedt 1999: 140); a 'star' (Hutchinson 1986: 255); and 'Australia's first television personality' (Hutchinson 1986: 257; *The Graham Kennedy Story* n.d.: 5). Indeed, he is Australian television royalty: 'King Gra-Gra … the most famous man in Australian television and, after 35 years, its longest reigning and most victorious protagonist' (O'Grady 1989: 22).[2]

Such accounts give a strong sense of the importance of Kennedy and his programs in the public archive, but say little about the particular importance of his star image, and of the programs. If he is a 'legend' and a 'star' and 'television royalty', what is he legendary for? What kind of star, or royalty, was he?

Kennedy and Newton break the rules of performance and decorum in an advertorial for Raoul Merton shoes

In Melbourne Tonight was an example of the 'tonight show' variety format, which originated in the USA, with Pat Harrington's *Broadway Open House* in 1950 (Jones 1999: 31).[3] Its structure was a simple one. The host of the program is its star. He presents a variety of acts—including comedy sketches and star turns (singers and comedians). The host and star of *In Melbourne Tonight* was Graham Kennedy. He presented comedians and singers, dance sequences performed by the Channel Nine dancers, and comedy sketches—in which he sometimes appeared. As viewers remember, the program also featured regular advertorials—short segments of advertising copy read or presented by Kennedy himself. This is the first point at which we can consider the survival of *IMT* in the public archive.

The advert for Pal dog food, mentioned above, has been remembered in other media spaces. During the course of this segment, Kennedy's own dog, Rover, ignored the food that was offered to him and set off on a quick tour of the studio, culminating in his urinating on one of the studio cameras. This moment—along with several of the other subversive advertorials in *IMT*—is included in the 2000 documentary *Graham Kennedy: King of Television*. This is one way in which *IMT* survives in the public archive, as a site of subversive, spontaneous performance. This documentary also includes a fight between Graham and sometime sidekick Bert Newton, which degenerates into throwing Raoul Merton shoes at each other across the set, and an advertorial for Colvan Potato Chips.

In this, Kennedy holds up a bag of the product: 'Well, it's nearly got a quarter of a potato in it …', he says, folding the bag in half to show how empty it is,' … and they've got the hide to charge twenty cents. Now that's terrible. If you mashed all that down, there'd only be the tiniest, tiniest …'. Suddenly, as if spontaneously inspired, he shouts, 'I'll do it, I'll do it. I want to show you something. I love Colvan; they're going to love me for this'. He pours the crisps out on to his desk and says, 'Now that looks a lot, but you watch …', and crushes them into crumbs, pours them back into the bag, and folds it over and over to show that the potato product fills barely one-eighth of the bag. The audience screams with delight and bursts into applause as Kennedy goes on: 'It's down to there—where the hell's the potato? [pause] I'm in the mood to lose them all tonight' (*Graham Kennedy* 2000).

Kennedy's physical disrespect to products he was employed to advertise

With both correspondents for this book and television itself promoting Kennedy's subversive approach to advertorials as an important and (collectively) memorable aspect of *IMT*, returning to the programs themselves provides many more examples of this tendency. Although very few of the early editions of *In Melbourne Tonight* are available for public viewing, those that do survive testify to the importance of this subversive and cheeky performance of advertorials in the program. 'If it weren't for Raoul Merton shoes,' Kennedy says in one 1960 example, 'my feet would not be in the condition they are now', he says, breaking into laughter as he adds:

> Truly, it's only because of Raoul Merton that I have ingrown toenails, for instance. No, that's a load of rubbish. It's only because Raoul Merton shoes are not expensive, they're only ... they're only ... I've forgotten how much they are ... there's a lady in the front row who knows ... 99 and 11 ... Now doesn't that look good? [pause] No, it's not the best, but for the price ...
>
> (*GKC9S* 1960)

It is obvious from these examples that the advertorials for which Kennedy is remembered by both individual viewers and media texts are examples of a cheeky form of subverting generic expectations about what advertorials should be. This is certainly an important part of *IMT*'s survival in the public archive, and of what the program contributes to Australia's cultural heritage.

Transgressive behaviour

The public archive of Australian television has presented Kennedy's advertorials as a central part of his importance. It thus positions him as spontaneous and willing to break the rules for a laugh: in short, cheeky.[4] And the advertorials are not the only way in which Kennedy's performance in these early programs is transgressive. Graeme Turner's contribution to discussion of Australian television's public archive suggests it was 'the deconstruction of the variety show that gave Graham Kennedy's *In Melbourne Tonight* its enormous audience ...' (Turner 1987: 90), and watching early Kennedy, his transgressiveness is obvious. The programs feature not only advertorials that do not follow the rules of how advertorials should work, but also an apparently calculated refusal of everything that should make good television.

To start with, Kennedy is not good looking in any traditional sense: with his big eyes, pointy nose, and small chin, he does not have classically attractive looks. Further, in his early shows, Kennedy's performance is one of incredible informality. He does not appear professional in the traditional sense. Indeed, he comes across as profoundly ill at ease. His performance doesn't flow. His delivery is littered with pauses, with 'ums' and 'ahs', as he looks off to the side of the set. Much of his performance is silence—looking around, apparently deciding what to say next. At one point, the sound of scenery shifting behind him can be heard. He stops talking, looks behind him, looks back at the audience and makes faces. He seems to be inviting the viewer to be conspiratorial with him, offering neither jokes nor entertainment, but the fact of sharing the knowledge that both he and the audience are watching a television program being produced. He doesn't seem to take the whole thing very seriously (*GKC9S* 1960).[5]

He is conspiratorial, but he is not particularly funny. Presenting one program, he starts by reading out a series of jokes, which are, generously, only mildly amusing: 'Did you hear about the pirate who thought the crow's nest was a cabin for his wife?' (*GKC9S* 1960). Importantly, though, his performance style is predicated precisely on these jokes *not* being funny; Kennedy makes this not only an advantage, but almost an art form. When the audience groans at this previous joke (obviously it is not the case that its humour has diminished with time—it was not very funny in 1960 either), and then start to laugh slightly, Kennedy immediately comes to life: 'No!' he snaps at them, 'Don't get carried away ... It's not worth clapping; you mustn't. We might get better than this.' He pauses. 'We have to get better than this.' This is Kennedy's trademark, and he returns to it throughout his career. He continually apologises for jokes, for example when telling '... a funny story. This is so new that it was only made up about half an hour ago by one of our writers who drinks a lot'. He tells the joke and then says, 'That's possibly one of the reasons why Alan Hopgood [presumably the writer] is leaving ...' (*GKC9S* 1960). Introducing one advertorial, Kennedy makes a silly joke about tiaras. There is a long pause. The audience starts to laugh a little bit. Kennedy slowly turns to the camera, raises his eyebrows, and says (not laughing, but speaking): 'Aha. Aha. Ahahahahaha'.

Much of Kennedy's material is neither vulgar nor funny. It is simply Kennedy chatting, rather aimlessly it appears, to the camera or to the audience, or undercutting his jokes with a refusal to find them funny.[6]

Dangerous suggestiveness

IMT holds an important place in Australia's public archive of television programs. It is remembered particularly for elements of subversiveness—as evidenced by the advertorials that are so strongly remembered, the transgressiveness that Graeme Turner identifies, and the persistence of the crow call that opens this chapter. Bringing such a perspective to bear on the contemporary reception of the program is telling: for a historical perspective suggests that such subversiveness—or 'suggestiveness'—was particularly upsetting to a number of viewers at the time of *IMT*'s original broadcasts.

IMT and its descendents featured comedy sketches as well as advertorials.[7] These comedy sketches exhibit a level of suggestiveness that is familiar from variety theatre and other cultural sites of the period—the *Carry On* films in the United Kingdom, for example. And these comedy sketches seem to have been regarded at the time as being rather more subversive than the advertorials for which the program is now more commonly remembered. Tracing the reaction of a certain set of contemporary viewers to this aspect of *IMT* demonstrates the parameters of the program's importance in the public archive. It also explains why the crow call was not simply the end of an era for Kennedy's broadcasting, but an entirely logical and consistent extension of tendencies that were publicly identified with *IMT* throughout the period of its broadcast, and for which it is remembered and written into the public archive today.

The contemporary comments I wish to draw on here are those of a particular group of expert viewers of early *IMT*—the members of the Australian Broadcasting Control Board. The members of this government body—set up in 1949 to administer the federal government's *Broadcasting and Television Act 1952* (Cwlth)—were careful viewers of *IMT*, and the terms of their discontent with it, outlined in the Board's *Annual Report* of 1958, are telling:

> Televising of objectionable matter … there have been occurrences in which regular programme personalities have introduced jokes, comments or actions capable of bearing a double-meaning; that the less desirable meaning had not been missed was made evident by the audience. These matters have been brought to the notice of the stations concerned, which have undertaken to avoid recurrences. It appears that insufficient rehearsal and a tendency to indulge in unprepared 'patter' are often the cause of the trouble.
>
> (ABCB 1958: 44)

The Board is bothered by material that is 'suggestive' as much as it is with outright 'vulgarity' (ABCB 1961: 49; ABCB 1963: 64; ABCB 1966: 50). And *IMT*—although the Board is scrupulous in not naming names—seems to have been dangerously 'suggestive' in its double entendres, as well as the subversion of generic expectations in Kennedy's advertorials.

Of course, to examine such discourses does not tell us what all viewers at the time 'really' thought of Kennedy. Nor does it tell us exactly how public debate was undertaken at that time. It does, however, provide an interesting intertext: a set of pronouncements by some very public—and possibly influential—viewers of Kennedy's variety programs. For it appears that the Board really did not like variety programs on Australian television. And it seems it was the humour of the programs that particularly offended these expert viewers.

A few examples can be found of the tendency towards 'suggestiveness' and 'double entendres' in surviving and available copies of early *IMT*. One sketch, set in an art gallery, involves a woman singing about how many famous historical figures have given their names to everyday objects: 'Alexander is crème de cocoa mixed with rum/Edgar Hoover is a vacuum'. One line goes 'Venus de Milo is a pink brassiere'—and she holds up a woman's undergarment to illustrate this point (*GKC9S* 1960). (Given that women's 'foundation garments' were a source of some concern to the Board,[8] their dislike of comedy sketches such as this one—see below—is not surprising). Later in the same sketch, as a female museum visitor bends over, an attendant fluffs her bottom with a feather duster and she asks, 'What are you doing?' to which he replies, 'It's my job to clean the seats'. Suggestiveness indeed. A similar level of vulgarity can be seen in a Western sketch in which a woman walks in wearing a low-cut dress:

> 'I call this my atomic bomb dress.'
> 'Why atomic bomb?'
> '90 per cent fallout.'
>
> (*The Graham Kennedy Show* n.d.)

In the early years of television, we can see a real concern in public discussion about what this medium is, how it functions, and how it will fit into Australian society. Particularly worrying for those entrusted to monitor the nation's morals is the accessibility of television. It is a medium that must be monitored particularly closely for moral standards. The Board notes in 1963 that:

> From the earliest days of television in Australian, the Board has been aware of the tendency of performers to play to the few people in the studio audience and forget that the real audience is a family circle in many thousands of homes. There is a considerable difference between material that is suitable for the revue theatre or nightclub and that which is suitable for television.
>
> (ABCB 1963: 64)

But it is not enough merely to state this once. The Board finds this medium so worrisome that almost every year it must make the same point: that 'television programmes are received in the homes of all types of citizens' ... (ACB 1967: 84); that television programs 'have a largely uncontrolled entry into the home, are in a different category from entertainment at theatres and other places where the audience must make a conscious effort to attend the performance' (ABCB 1964: 71); that 'the medium is one which penetrates intimately and indiscriminately into the life of the family' (ABCB 1968: 79–80); that it

> reaches a great number of persons of all ages in the privacy of their homes. It is an intrusive everpresent medium which by its nature tends to be used in a less selective manner than that dictated by the conscious decision to purchase a ticket for a theatrical performance, night club or other out-of-home entertainment.
>
> (ABCB 1973: 106–7)

The Board had tools at its disposal to control explicitly blasphemous or obscene material. Part of its function was explicitly censorious and moralistic: ensuring that section 118 of the Broadcasting and Television Act was not breached. Section 118 'prohibits the televising of any matter which is blasphemous, indecent or obscene' (ABCB 1960: 39). But what really posed a problem for the Board—and made it necessary that it should make the point about the dangerous and indiscriminate 'penetration' of television every year, rather than simply stopping offensive practices—was the fact that Graham Kennedy's variety shows (and the other programs these expert viewers were so worried about) were not, in fact, explicitly obscene or blasphemous. Rather, they employed double entendres and suggestiveness in order to speak to two audiences at once, presenting language that was on one level clean enough for the family circle at home but was simultaneously dirty enough for those adults who could go to the Tivoli theatre if they wanted to. It was, in short, *suggestive*—and this was not acceptable.

The expert viewers of the Board are particularly bothered because the material in question is not, technically, breaching the guidelines under which television must operate. It is sticking to the letter of the law, and still managing to be rude. When the art gallery attendant offers to dust a 'seat', the viewers of the Board worry that some people might realise there is a pun being played on the posterior, or that 'fallout' might relate to a potential fate of breasts as much as to the dangers of atomic power. Annual reports repeatedly make comments such as:

> During the period to which this report relates, some of the live programmes presented by commercial television stations were the subject of complaints concerning dances, lyrics and comedy sketches which were considered to be of a suggestive nature ... In most cases the Board felt that the complaints were justified, and although they did not constitute a breach of section 118 of the Broadcasting and Television Act 1942–1960, which prohibits the televising of any matter which is blasphemous, indecent or obscene, they were of sufficient importance for the Board to take action to ensure that they would not be repeated ... brought to the notice of station managements, which usually welcome the information [as] all stations have shown a desire to maintain high standards ...
>
> (ABCB 1960: 39; see also ABCB 1963: 64; ABCB 1964: 71)

The material is not 'obscene'; it is not 'indecent'; it is not 'blasphemous'. It is particularly dangerous because it can be—as Kennedy's advertorials appear to be—unscripted and spontaneous. This is indeed dangerous for a moralistic government body—for it can lead to uncontrollable broadcasting. It can be 'suggestive': it can employ double entendres, and it can say more than it appears to. And the fact that these expert viewers complain every year about suggestiveness, also stating, every year, that they have told the station managements to control it more strongly (with the station managements apparently assuring the Board, every year, that they welcome the information as they have 'a desire to maintain high standards') suggests just how little power the Board had in controlling the output of television stations in the 1950s and '60s.

IMT, then, survives in the public archive particularly for advertorials that appear spontaneously to challenge generic expectations. And during the period of its run, it seems to have contributed to Australia's cultural heritage an admirable use of suggestiveness and double entendres in order to avoid official attempts to control the uses to which the then-new medium of television could be put. These two aspects of the program then lead us to the moment that opens this chapter—a moment that is strongly present itself in the public archive, and that strongly demonstrates both of these tendencies in *IMT*: the crow call.

Public archive of the crow call

In Melbourne Tonight/The Graham Kennedy (Channel Nine) Show finished its first incarnation in 1970.[9] It returned—renamed *The Graham Kennedy Show* in all states—on 19 September 1972, lasting only until 1973. It returned again, briefly, on 3 March 1975. 'On the first night, during an advertisement for Cedel soap', writes Hutchinson, providing a level of detail that suggests the importance of this moment in the public memory of Australian television, 'Kennedy uttered what was to be known as the "crow call"—FAAAAARK.' Indeed, Hutchinson's account tells not only of the moment itself, but also its reception and institutional conditions, into collective memory, as he notes that 'this bit of larrikinism outraged all right thinking persons, including the Broadcasting Control Board. He was banned from live television on 18 March' (Hutchinson 1986: 264). The Board's comments about this performance included the suggestion that Kennedy had 'overstepped the bounds of good taste for a variety programme' and 'had made deliberate use of an expression which the Board had previously ruled as totally unsuitable for television' (as quoted in Hutchinson 1986: 264).

This 'crow call', as it is known, was the beginning of the end for the first era of Graham Kennedy on Australian television. From that point on,

Kennedy's show had to be prerecorded. When Channel Nine took advantage of this fact in order to edit out some comments Kennedy made about the Minister for the Media, Kennedy left the program and never returned (Hutchinson 1986: 264).[10]

This crow call survives in the public archive of Australian television as a lasting moment of transgression. Several correspondents for this book name it a 'Great moment in Australian television'. By 1979, a biography of Kennedy notes that this has become 'the famous "crow call" ...' (Parsons, Scott, & Robertson 1979: 37), and its infamy continues into later decades. When television personalities are asked by *Who Weekly* in 1999 to nominate their own personal favourite moments, Mikey Robins turns to the crow call as well: 'Graham Kennedy's crow impersonation. At the time, one of the great misjudgments of Australian taste. In retrospect, still not a great gag' (Robbins 1999: 95).

The crow call is an example of Kennedy's wider presence in the public archive of great moments in Australian television: appearing to be cheekily spontaneous and being suggestive to the point of upsetting the expert viewers of the Government's watchdog body.[11] Here is how the Board's *Annual Report* describes this moment:

> Following an incident in the edition of *The Graham Kennedy Show* televised by GTV in Melbourne on 3 March 1975, the Board ordered on 18 March 1975 that Mr Graham Kennedy's appearances on radio and television were to be restricted to performances that were recorded in advance and approved by a responsible station executive ... The Board had carefully examined a tape recording of the incident and was convinced that Mr Kennedy deliberately made use of an expletive which it had previously ruled as totally unsuitable for use on the family medium of television ...
>
> (ABCB 1975: 122–3)

This moment ties in to questions of both spontaneity and suggestiveness. It is Kennedy's spontaneity—his liveness—that the Board identifies as the source of his danger and thus takes away from him by forcing him to prerecord. But this punishment did not come about because he had actually been 'obscene' or 'blasphemous' on Australian television. Even though the Board is 'convinced' that it hears 'an expletive', what it in fact heard was a crow call with suggestive possibilities. As one correspondent for this book comments of 'Graham Kennedy's "crow call" ', 'This surprisingly inoffensive little noise (which to my ears still sound[s] nothing like the word "fuck" and to which the audience failed to react ...)' (Keating 1999a).[12] It was, after all, only suggestive. It was not convincing obscenity. It was this combination of spontaneity and suggestiveness that created the archetypal moment of *IMT*'s survival in Australia's public archive.

The crow call survives as a benchmark, against which public profanity can be judged. For example, writing in 1999, Phillip Adams noted his concerns about a new television program by suggesting that '... nothing in [Channel] Nine's history—including Graham Kennedy's notorious crow impersonations—came within a bull's roar of [Mick] Molloy's first program [of his new series]' (Adams 1999: 29). Similarly, in the same newspaper, a comedian's description on radio of ex-Prime Minister Paul Keating as a 'fuckwit' is compared with Kennedy's moment of glory:

> *Sunday Age* columnist Kate Langbroek this past week called former Prime Minister Paul Keating 'a f—-wit' on community radio station 3RRR and not a soul rang to complain about it. The response was in stark contrast to that which greeted Graham Kennedy's far more oblique use of the f-word on television in 1975.
>
> (Martin 1999: 6)

This article then goes on to interview Kennedy about his views on the place of 'fuck' in entertainment; over two decades later, this moment still qualifies Kennedy as Australia's expert on profanity in the media. This is reinforced on 26 September 1999, when a story on *Sixty Minutes* dealing with a magistrate's ruling that the word 'fuck' could not be considered offensive language featured clips from Kennedy, noting the controversy that was started by his innuendo (see also Melloy & Partridge 2000). In recent accounts, the moment becomes part of a teleological narrative of the liberalisation of the Australian public sphere: discovering that it is now possible to say 'fuck' without being thrown off television. Kennedy's 'faaaark' is remembered as, simultaneously, transgressive and yet somewhat old-fashioned. He is naughty, with all of the safe cosiness that the term implies.

Kennedy's career

The Graham Kennedy Channel Nine Show ended in 1975, and with it, an era of Australian television stretching back to the beginning of the form. Variety programs were, by this point, a far less important part of Australian television:

> The popularity of local drama series resulted in an equally dramatic downturn in variety programs. From 1965 variety production effectively ceased in Brisbane, Adelaide and Perth. Fewer shows came out of Sydney and Melbourne and Graham Kennedy and Bobby Limb, the biggest stars of the variety cycle, were seen infrequently.
>
> (Moran 1997a: 117)

In 1990, however, the Seven Network revived the tonight show format with Steve Vizard's *Tonight Live*. Throughout the 1990s, variety remained an important part of Australian television production. Meanwhile, since leaving *The Graham Kennedy Channel Nine Show*, Kennedy's television career had become been sporadic. In his appearances, he consistently presented cheeky almost-vulgarity as his defining characteristic, most notably in his *Blankety Blanks*, which stands as a perfect metaphor for the function of Kennedy's star persona: replacing the vulgar with the censored, and making fun of the censorial attitude. A revised and Kennedy-less version of the show in 1999 prompted a nostalgic account of Kennedy's suggestiveness, still surviving in the public archive:

> This is not the classic Graham Kennedy version ... In its day, the sassy double entendre was entertaining, leaving you listening in disbelief that such sauciness was going to air in primetime, but since we're all grown up enough for the F-word to be occasionally uttered on TV, it's just not the same.
>
> ('Review of *Blankety Blanks*' 1999)

Kennedy's performance in *Blankety Blanks* continues to refuse the expectations of the television personality; he continues to use the spoken 'Ahahahaha' to draw attention to the unfunny nature of jokes in the program.

Kennedy also presented '*Graham Kennedy Coast to Coast*, an innovative late-night program … that mixed news, accompanied by its conventions of seriousness and frequent urgency, with comic traditions drawn from centuries of carnival and vaudeville, a hybridising of genres usually considered incompatible' (Docker 1997: 878).

Throughout this career, Kennedy worked to ensure that the crow call survived as part of the public archive of Australian television. In one edition of *Graham Kennedy Coast to Coast*, he tells a biblical joke: 'Noah went up the hill, and he said, "God—there's a flood coming. Should I build an a-aaaaaaaahrk?" And do you know what? Noah didn't do live television for a long time' (*Graham Kennedy* 2000).

Similarly, an appearance at the *25 Years of Television* celebration in 1981 gave Kennedy the opportunity to remark that if he had his time over, he'd do it all exactly the same—'but a different crow call'; while on an episode of the children's program called *Shirl's Neighbourhood*, he referred to it again (one of the program's characters being Claude the Crow) (Chris Keating 2000, pers. comm.). His final regular television job was hosting *Graham Kennedy's Funniest Home Videos* (ABT 1991: 20).

Kennedy's star image—condensed in and often metonymically referred to by the crow call—remains an important part of Australian television: 'Graham Kennedy returned to his home town of Melbourne last Friday to air his News Show on Channel 9 ... During an ad-break, television's veteran larrikin bared his buttocks to the audience of 300' ('Flash of the Old Gra-Gra' 1988: 18). He may bare his buttocks during a television program, but it is during the ad-break. And there is nothing the Australian Broadcasting Control Board (or its later incarnations, the Tribunal and then the Authority) can do about such instances. Suggestiveness, vulgarity, but not obscenity—not quite obeying the rules of what television should, so the authorities say, be about—this is what Kennedy and Kennedy's FAAARK are about, how they are remembered in the public archive, and what they have to contribute to our cultural heritage.

Availability

The only publicly available copies of *IMT/The Graham Kennedy Show* that I have found are two episodes (one of which is incomplete) held at Screensound. Screensound is the federal government's National Collection of Screen and Sound, based in Canberra. Its catalogue can be accessed through the web (http://www.screensound.gov.au/). Screensound also has offices in each state's capital city. The terms and conditions of viewing material at these offices vary from state to state.

Notes

1 Kennedy's program was originally known interstate as *The Graham Kennedy Show*, the title being changed to *The Graham Kennedy Channel Nine Show* following the GTV-9/TCN-9 affiliation. *The Graham Kennedy Show* in 1973 was the first time Kennedy was genuinely broadcast for a national audience; the earlier interstate programs had merely been special editions of the basic Melbourne program.

2 See also Kemp 1971: 23; Parsons, Scott, and Robertson 1979: 37; Docker 1997: 878-9; Moran 1997a: 117; O'Grady 1989: 24; Bolton 1978: 8; Jones 1999: 20, 23. There is some disagreement over when Kennedy became a national celebrity—Australia's 'King of Television' rather than simply Melbourne's. Rob Johnson suggests that Kennedy was already well known in Sydney by the end of 1958 (Johnson & Smiedt 1999); Graeme Turner by contrast suggests that Kennedy didn't become a national star until *Blankety Blanks*. It is certain, though, that by the time of writing this book, Kennedy was written into the public archive as the King of Australian Television, and that his early variety shows were being claimed as part of that national heritage (see particularly Channel Nine's 2000 documentary *Graham Kennedy: King of Television* (2000).

3 Steve Allen was the first successful tonight show host in the USA, working until 1957. *In Melbourne Tonight* began on 6 May 1957 as an Australian-produced variety program, shown only in Melbourne. It was not the first variety program in Australia—that honour goes to *Sydney Tonight* with Keith Walshe, which began on 3 December 1956 (Jones 1999: 16). Neither was it the first example of the format in Victoria (which was the *Late Show*, which debuted on HSV-7 at 9.30 p.m. on Friday, 3 May 1957. Noel Ferrier hosted the program until late 1957, when Bert Newton took over (Jones 1999: 20; Chris Keating, pers. comm., 17 May 2000). However, it was to be the most successful variety program ever produced for Australian television.

4 It is an interesting fact, although not directly relevant to this argument, that some commentators remember Kennedy's spontaneity as being entirely, and strictly, rehearsed—see Mike McColl Jones, Ken Sutcliffe, John Mangos, and Harry M. Miller in the documentary *Graham Kennedy: King of Television* (2000).

5 It should be noted that this is to say nothing of Kennedy's own attitude towards television production—only that this is what his performance communicates.

6 It is not clear to what extent this performance of disbelief in the performance of television was distinctive or typical of television at the time. By the end of the twentieth century, such an approach was the dominant one in variety and chat programs in Australia: *Good News Week Nite Lite*, *O'Laughlin*, *Rove*, *Club Buggery*, *Molloy*, *Mulray*, *Denton*, and *Live and Sweaty*, to name only a few 1990s examples, have specialised in deconstructing the variety form, the television format, and the very studio in which they are recorded. Some writers claim that Kennedy's performance was unique for the time: 'While others in those early years were treating their TV appearances with dignity and even pomposity, Kennedy's spontaneous irreverence had the whole of Melbourne talking' (Murphy 1981: 63). Others, however, see this kind of performance as typical of the time, either pointing to other examples of similar performance, such as Ernie Sigley (see Hall 1976: 92), or noting more generally that 'early television' was 'sloppy ... ruptures and discontinuities [were] the norm' (Caldwell 1995: 45). This position is supported by the observation of a contemporary commentator that 'there is still a feeling of improvisation in a lot of the programmes' (Casson 1959: 23). Chris Keating feels that *IMT* was 'unique in its particular content and Kennedy's on-air demeanour, but that in fact the *program* itself was very typical in the overall format of "Tonight" shows to that point' (Chris Keating 2000, pers. comm).

7 While it is true that dances and songs were also a part of the program, these do not seem to have survived in the public archive. For example, Graeme Blundell claims that 'He would announce the ballet and his audience would get a beer, the art and culture bits of the shows really being the commercial breaks' (Blundell 2000: 28).

8 'To reduce the possibility of future unacceptable advertisements, the Board has collaborated with the Australian Association of Advertising Agencies, and the Australia Association of National Advertisers in the development of a statement of guiding principles ... [for the] preparation of advertisements for foundation garments and other products which may give rise to problems of judgment and taste ...' (ABCB 1967: 100).

9 At this point *IMT*, after 3005 episodes, changed its title to the *National Tonight Show*; it was hosted by Ugly Dave Gray, who had been guest hosting *IMT* before this.

10 The material that was cut was an opening monologue by Kennedy about Doug McLelland: 'He has failed and he knows it too, and the public know it. This misguided minister took credit for a mythical boom in television production. There is no boom. Employment in television production is down this year by over 30 per cent. His point system has proved utterly ineffective ... We are all suffering from the lack of local content at the moment ... We can't compete with the price of [imported] shows ... This is a $6000 a night show ... We've been through this before and Face Up Comes Kennedy ... I'm just thinking of those initials [slow, building laughter]'. Kennedy then does his crow call again—'aaaaaarkh!'—which gets a round of applause, before attacking 'the inane carrying on of the Australian Broadcasting Control Board' and going on to 'demand, here nationally tonight, that Senator McLelland be dismissed from office, and I would suggest most strongly that the portfolio itself be dropped ... That's all I want to say'. Later in the program, we hear his voice on the surviving tape, during the commercial break: 'I wonder if they'll cut the opening. Do you think they'll cut the opening? Because if they do, I'll do it live here on *This Day Tonight* tomorrow night, because I have that arrangement with Peter Couchman. I'll be live and I can go "faaark", because it doesn't come under the authority of those stupid people.' Later in the show, he asks Bert Newton, 'Did you see my piece at the start of the show? ... I said that Senator McLelland should be sacked ... I said that local production is down by 30 per cent', and he ends the episode by singing 'for all we know, we may never meet again'. Many thanks to Chris Keating for this information.

11 In relation to the questions raised in note 3, it is interesting to note that at least one television historian believes that Kennedy's crow call was a deliberate attempt by Kennedy to be forced to prerecord—which the station did not want—so he could get home from work earlier (Keating 1999b). Chris Keating cites an interview in the 7 May 1977 edition of *TV Week*, in which Kennedy claims that this was his intention (p. 63). Again, it is possible that the spontaneity that forms part Kennedy's contribution to the public archive is a carefully rehearsed one.

12 Although it should also be noted that Keating, from various items of textual evidence, believes that the clip that is often included in compilations as 'the' crow call is not in fact the moment that upset the Broadcasting Control Board. He wonders if 'the actual "Faaark" is still too close to a full-blooded "Fuck" for Nine to screen with comfort' (Chris Keating 2000, pers. comm.).

2

Four Corners: Convincing Bias

1961–

On 31 August 1963, *Four Corners* presented an item on the Returned & Services League (RSL)—including shots of members of the League drinking beer in an RSL club, songs mocking the institution, and very aggressive interviews with RSL members. As a result of that program, the Executive Producer—Mr Allan Ashbolt—was sacked from the ABC.

This moment produced intense public debate—in newspaper stories, in letters to the press and to politicians, and even within parliament itself. The object of discussion in this heated debate was the notion of 'objectivity': what does the term mean, and what is its relevance to current affairs journalism? In relation to this topic, this moment is an emblematic one for understanding Australian television and its archive. It points to one of the most prominent ways in which Australian television has been discussed in the public sphere.

The archive of *Four Corners*

The importance of *Four Corners* is of a different kind from that of *The Graham Kennedy Show*. It is only in one area of the public archive that *Four Corners'* importance and glories are carefully memorialised. Kennedy was one of the most popular television performers in Australia for many years, and his show was at the centre of the Australian mediasphere for much of that time. By contrast, *Four Corners* is not so important in terms of its demographic reach. It has never been a regular 'top ten' program in Australia.

However, for academic and industry commentators (rather than for the wider public sphere), *Four Corners* is a vital part of the archive of Australian television.[1]

Four Corners is a weekly ABC current affairs program that began on 19 August 1961. It was not the first such program in the world: it was modelled on a British program called *Panorama* (Moran 1997a: 116; Blain 1977: 122). In Australia, though, it was a first: the first national space in which current affairs could be discussed. At that time, Australia had no national daily newspaper (Inglis 1983: 217), and most current affairs television was state-based. The early episodes of the program were presented in a magazine-style format, consisting of a series of short items. The first host of the program was Michael Charlton (Hall 1976: 102).

Many academic and journalistic writers have placed *Four Corners* at the centre of Australia's mediasphere. It is 'the flagship of ABC public affairs sessions' (Semmler 1981: 156), and 'Nothing since has matched the profound effect on production attitudes or the nation's viewing habits' (Courtis 1981: 98). It is 'The prototypal Australian television documentary (or current affairs) program' (Breen 1997: 128).

For many of these writers, the moments that make *Four Corners* so important are those that have resulted directly in changes to the practice of governments in Australia. The program is often celebrated—both by academic and journalistic writers—for those moments that 'caus[ed] Royal Commissions and result[ed] in public figures being jailed ...' (Masterson & Patching 1990: 189–90). For example, a 1985 program on indigenous deaths in custody resulted in a Royal Commission (Pullan 1986: 152; Mickler 1998: 174), and the 'most frequently cited example' (Gibson 1997b: 628) of *Four Corners*' reach in party politics is the effect of the 1987 episode, 'The Moonlight State'. This led to the Fitzgerald Inquiry, the jailing of Queensland's police commissioner, and the National Party government losing power after more than twenty years in office (Bowden 1990: 72, quoting Gerry Teekman; Schultz 1998: 215; Breen 1997: 128; *35 Years of Television* 1991). These are great moments as much in politics as in television's history, and this, I think, explains their survival in the academic version of Australian television's public archive.

The great moment that opens this chapter has also been remembered in the academic version of the public archive. It did not result in a Royal Commission, although it did lead to questions in parliament, and no public figures were jailed as a result of its broadcast, although the producer was sacked. And the episode led to a heated public debate about how a public sphere should function:

> A 1963 program on the Returned Serviceman's League (RSL) ... stirred controversy for showing members of the organisation in casual dress drinking at a bar, rather than exclusively in the context of formally structured studio debate ... The story on the RSL directly challenged the organisation on its claim to political neutrality.
>
> (Gibson 1997b: 628)

This moment has certainly been remembered in Australia's public archive. On the flyleaf of his autobiography, Ashbolt highlights 'the famous *Four Corners* report on the RSL' (Ashbolt 1974); Clement Semmler notes that the 'item critical of the Returned Serviceman's League ... evoked fierce public and political controversy ...' (Semmler 1981: 24); Ellis Blain notes that it 'brought about [Ashbolt's] removal' (Blain 1977: 123); and the documentary *Four Corners: 25 Years* (1987) proudly covers the controversy with a series of clips. What was this 'controversy' about?

RSL controversies

The *Four Corners'* item on the RSL was one segment, running around twenty minutes, in a 1963 episode of the program. Looking at it in the 1990s, it is obvious that the program is putting one side of an argument—that the RSL is a partisan, rather than politically neutral, organisation—very strongly.

Following a brief introduction by compère Gerald Lyons, the segment opens with shots inside an RSL club, showing old men in hats, sitting with beers. From the very opening, the RSL is presented as a group of beer drinkers. Following this scene-setting section, we cut to the studio, and a presenter wearing a suit and tie, speaking to the camera (ABC archives do not record his name). There is no voice-over at this point to explain what the thrust of the segment will be. This presenter gives a monologue that is explicitly subjective, explaining his own history and feelings:

> Yes, I'm wearing my RSL badge now, but I don't always wear it ... I have had it [the badge] on, and younger people have said, 'What's that?' ... they seem surprised ... they don't recognise it, and they don't want to ... And why should they? ... In those days [when he was younger] ... if you saw an RSL badge coming, you dodged. You didn't want that sort of beery sentimentality that was thrown at you ... I remember being in uniform at a school Anzac Day ceremony—and I couldn't have been more embarrassed. And today, I think for

> young people particularly, the same thing applies ... their image of the RSL ... [is the] poker machine, Sunday afternoon concert party and beer-drinking men ... We talk about wearing your badge to honour the dead—well, we remember what the dead thought about it. They were the ones we went to school with, we served with them, they were the ones who with us dodged all this sort of thing ... It is useful, this badge, it's a status symbol that still impresses a lot of people, that section of the population, middle-aged and over ... but to the largest section of the population, the young people ... it doesn't matter at all. And why should it?
>
> (Ashbolt 1963)

This introduction does not present the audience with what we will later discover is the thrust of the segment: it does not mention the question of whether or not the RSL is a political institution, the supposed point of the item. It is rather a personal viewpoint, attacking the relevance of the RSL. After the opening shots of beer-drinking, its presenter twice refers to beer as a defining feature of the RSL. This articulation continues throughout the segment.

Allan Ashbolt is the reporter in the filmed sequence. At one point, he presents explicitly subjective and personal musings on the RSL—'[D. H.] Lawrence sensed a jingoistic, super-patriotic strain in some Australians, and he thought it very dangerous'—and while he talks, we are shown shots of the Caulfield Central RSL club. Again, this sequence of shots includes many images of beer-drinking: close-ups of beer being poured into jugs, people passing beer along, pouring it into each other's glasses. These are the images that illustrate Ashbolt's discussion of the history of this RSL branch.

Later in the segment, RSL members are interviewed about the organisation. This is loosely linked to the argument of the piece: most of the interviewees state that the organisation is about comradeship and support (thus, implicitly, not about politics). The first of these is framed so that his glass of beer is in shot.

Later still, the program includes, in a very long segment, a film of a satirical song in a revue club. The entire song is shown—several choruses—and Ashbolt's voice-over suggests that it 'reflects' the views of 'the younger generation'. The song is all about how drunk RSL members are: 'We walk to the bar through slops on the floor, through the empty schooner jungle that's keeping us poor', sings the performer: 'Roll out the barrel, let's have one more while the barman is pulling a fast one'. He puts on a slurred, drunken voice as he sings, 'Who gives a damn if there's another war? We're still fighting the last one'. This is presented without any interrogation; it is claimed simply to be what 'the younger generation' feels.

This segment works hard to make its case against the RSL. The use of interviews takes full advantage of the possibilities for hectoring and lack of respect. The presentation of interviewees in the program is structured to make those attacking the RSL appear far more convincing than those defending it. The first such speaker is 'a Canadian scholar at the Australian National University ... Gerry Kristianson'. He is filmed talking directly to the camera, giving what amounts to a speech—he even has his notes in his hand: 'The Returned Serviceman's League has always been a pressure group,' he begins, speaking for several minutes without interruption. The next witness for the prosecution is 'prominent university student spokesman, Dr Peter Willensky'. Again, he speaks directly to camera, again, reading from notes: 'While everyone would support the welfare activities of the RSL, a lot of people show a lot of disquiet about the way it has entered the political arena'. The third critic is 'Alec Robertson, editor of the communist newspaper *Tribune*'. Again, he talks to camera, and again seems to be looking down at his notes as he makes his speech: 'We had enough of the iron hand during the war ... The real danger [to Australia] lies in the possibility that in backroom negotiations, this kind of group can panic a government'. This entire polemic is presented unedited and uninterrupted.

By contrast the 'Minister for Repatriation, Mr Schwartz', and the RSL Deputy President, Sir Raymond Huish, are both interviewed by Allan Ashbolt, and both are interviewed aggressively and asked difficult questions. In the interview with Mr Schwartz, Ashbolt keeps asking similar questions, over and over, until he receives an answer he is happy with: 'I have often heard the Minister for Repatriation described as the "Minister for the RSL". Is that a fair description?' 'Is the RSL a "pressure group"?' 'Does it "lobby" the government?' 'Does it have much influence on issues other than returned servicemen?' The Minister admits freely that it does have access and influence, but refuses to name it a pressure or lobby group—'Lobbying is not a very pleasant term'. Unsatisfied with the Minister's position, the interviewer keeps probing, refusing to accept on face value the answers that are given. This approach is even more obvious in the interview with Huish. The entire interview takes the form of Ashbolt setting Huish up, in a long-winded logical trap, to contradict himself. Starting by asking, 'Is it still part of the RSL pledge not to take part in politics?' and receiving an affirmative answer, Ashbolt then asks a lengthy series of questions about hypothetical situations, in which he asks Huish to imagine the RSL, for example, opposing a possible Labor government's position on the Communist Party: 'You would be campaigning against the Labor Party in fact, and you would be taking part in party politics!', he exclaims delightedly, with the air of one who has won a particularly exciting game of chess. Huish looks very uncomfortable as he admits that 'If that happened we would be doing that, if that were the case, yes'. Much skilled rhetoric goes in to establishing this position; Ashbolt takes full advantage of the possibilities of the interview format.

Ashbolt's voice-over completes the item.

> If the RSL is then ready to become involved in party politics on one issue, it would probably be prepared to go in on other issues. This would lead to a basic change in its philosophy, its function, and its power structure in the Australian community. An important question facing the RSL is whether the rank and file of members would accept such a change. But more important is the question of whether the Australian people as a whole would accept it.

This is an astonishing prediction and extrapolation from what has been shown on screen, presented as fact by the reporter in the segment.

It is obvious, then, that the program is working hard, using a variety of rhetorical tools, in order to convince the audience that the RSL is indeed a partisan organisation—and one that is flawed in other ways, from being unrepresentative to being associated with drunkenness. But in order to understand why this item might be remembered in academic and industry recollections of Australian television's public archive, it is necessary to understand something of the status of the RSL in the late 1950s and early 1960s in Australia, and the nature of current affairs television in the same period.

Power and beer

At the time of the program's broadcast, the RSL was a potent force in Australian public affairs, and had been for many years. As the cover of the official history of the League notes with some pride, the organisation is 'the envy of ... other interest groups' because of 'the influence on the League on governmental policies' (Sekuless & Rees 1986). Arlene Sykes claims that 'the power and influence of the RSL' in the early 1960s was an important part of Australian public life: 'though we tend to forget this today, [the RSL] wielded very considerable influence, even having—though it was theoretically non-political—direct access to cabinet' (Sykes 1994: 17–18). Much of the League's political work involved lobbying for 'adequate repatriation facilities' ('The RSL' 1965: 179)—a term describing 'the whole scheme of compensation and benefits provided for ex-servicemen by government' (Kristianson 1966: xxiv). But as well as political interventions in this area, the organisation also lobbied on 'matters of importance to Australia' (Kristianson 1966: xxiv). The RSL was strongly involved in conservative lobbying to protect what it saw as important Australian traditions, central to a conservative idea of what Australia was and should be. For example, the League claimed 'custodianship' of Anzac Day ('The RSL' 1965: 178), lobbying governments to ensure that 'entertainment facilities for the general public remained closed by law' on that day (Sekuless & Rees 1986: 140), while RSL members could drink in their clubs on the day. '[T]he preservation of Australian security' (Kristianson 1966: xxiii) was another matter on which the RSL took it upon itself to represent the nation, strongly arguing for anti-communist activities in Australia's public sphere. Indeed—in a move reminiscent of American blacklists—during the early 1960s, the League was receiving lists of suspected communists in Australia from Melbourne Law School (Sekuless & Rees 1986: 138).

Despite the League's powerful presence in the Australian public sphere and governmental workings, the RSL insistently portrayed itself as a politically neutral organisation. As the official history of the organisation proudly puts it, in all of its anti-communist activities 'the League was at pains to preserve its party political neutrality' (Sekuless & Rees 1986: 138). G. L. Kristianson—the researcher who appeared in the *Four Corners* item—notes in 1966 that, even though 'the RSL has also always been a political pressure group, deeply involved in attempts to influence the decisions of Australian governments', it has also 'tried to be a "non-partisan" body, avoiding involvement in the party process or attempts to take over the reins of government' (Kristianson 1966: xxiii). A similar logic is used by an anonymous writer on the League in 1965:

> The RSL has always been a strong proponent of ... 'national conservatism' ... because of the stand taken by sections of the Labor movement on questions which the RSL has seen as vital to Australian security—notably conscription and anti-Communism—the League has often been aligned on important issues with the political right. But in fact the League's conservatism has had no economic or industrial overtures, and is exemplified by the organisation's ability to take a stand which aligns it with one or other of the major political parties, while sincerely maintaining that it is neutral in party politics.
>
> ('The RSL' 1965: 188)

It is obvious that the League's claims to politically neutrality were an important part of its potency in the Australian public sphere. So long as the organisation could argue that it was not aligned with any political party, it could claim to represent 'Australia' rather than one particular group of Australians. The distinctions involved in this argument remain unconvincing: the League is obviously partisan in its very commitment to an idea of Australia that is socially conservative. Given the disparity between its potency and its claims about its own status, it is unsurprising that the RSL during the early 1960s was 'controversial' and 'the subject of ... much interest and ... many conflicting points of view' ('The RSL' 1965: 178). But as long as the argument that a commitment to social conservatism was not, in fact, a form of bias, was convincing—that it was rather common sense that all Australians would want to defend traditional values and that stating this was simply repeating objective facts—the RSL could lay claim to a privileged place of neutrality, objectivity, and common sense in the Australian public sphere.

One of the central aspects of the 'conflicting points of view' that challenged the RSL's claim to represent the interests of Australia was the use of humour, and particularly the mocking of RSL members for their consumption of beer. In this, the opening shots of the *Four Corners'* item on the League, and the continued emphasis on beer-drinking throughout the piece, are not outlandish or unexpected attacks on the organisation; rather, they draw on wider public discourses of the time that attempt to discredit the work of the RSL.

By 1960, the idea that the RSL was a haunt of drunkenness was a common one. Before this time, the official history of the organisation notes, the RSL faced 'a series of attacks by critics, who painted the organisation as outdated, introverted, drink-sodden and militaristic' (Sekuless & Rees 1986: 140). The most controversial episode in this history—before *Four Corners* entered the public archive—was a stage play by Alan Seymour entitled *The One Day of the Year.*

This play centred on the question of what was becoming known as 'the generation gap'. Its central focus was the RSL, standing as a symbol of older Australia. One of the young characters in the play states at one point that Anzac Day is 'just one long grog-up ... a lot of old has-beens getting up at the local RSL' (Sekuless & Rees 1986: 140).

The play was banned from the Adelaide Festival in 1960: obviously, such attacks on a supposedly neutral and undoubtedly powerful political organisation such as the RSL were not acceptable. But the idea that the RSL was drink-sodden continued throughout the 1960s—indeed, '[t]he attacks snowballed' after the play was banned (Sekuless & Rees 1986: 140).

Throughout the 1960s, these allegations continue: that 'the League is primarily oriented towards self-indulgence—beer-swilling and poker-machine playing' ('The RSL' 1965: 187). Indeed, it is a 'common view', says Kristianson in 1966, that 'the RSL [is a] drink-sodden militaristic pressure group' (Kristianson 1966: xx). This public discourse attacking the RSL continues to the end of the 1960s—when 'Edna Everage' (Barry Humphries) is interviewed in the 1969–70 Australian sexploitation mockumentary *The Naked Bunyip* (directed by John B. Murray), she comments that she does not get much sex as her husband Norm sleeps a lot—'particularly after he's been at the RSL', she says, making a drinking motion with her hand.

It is obvious that the *Four Corners* item was drawing on an important public counterdiscourse in order to challenge an organisation that was powerful in Australian public life but that did not open itself to the normal process of political debate at the time, claiming rather that it was a non-political, neutral body.

Response to the RSL piece

The controversy surrounding the broadcast of this item emerged quickly and visibly. Members telephoned branch officials demanding that protests be made. By the Sunday afternoon of the second screening, these officials demanded an official protest by the organisation, and some Victorian sub-branches had sent telegrams to the Prime Minister (see Kristianson 1964: 22).

This response quickly found its way into the newspapers where, on the following Monday, 'several sub-branch leaders [of the RSL] were quoted as saying that they had sent telegrams of protest to the prime minister, and one added that the feature had been "crude and really got into the gizzards of the returned men"' (Kristianson 1964: 22). The state presidents or acting presidents of the RSL in Victoria, South Australia, and Tasmania were quoted in newspapers around the country, condemning the program as 'offensive' and as presenting a 'false image' of the RSL. New South Wales State President Mr Yeo appeared in the following Monday's newspapers 'complain[ing] of the "false image" that had been created and expressed dismay at the fact that an avowed Communist should have been given uninterrupted time on the feature while his interview [done for the program] had been deleted entirely' (Kristianson 1964: 22–3). This controversy 'dominated letters to the editor pages for more than a week' (Pullan 1986).

Late on Monday, 3 September 1963, the Acting National President of the RSL released a statement to the media, complaining about 'the lack of reference on the programme to the welfare work of the RSL, the deliberate deletion of statements by League spokesmen and the giving of uninterrupted time to the critics of the League while subjecting the Acting National President to a cross-examination'. The general tone of the complaint was that the item had given a 'thoroughly distorted and uninformed view of all that the League represented' (Kristianson 1964: 23). The League also complained in writing to the Chairman of the ABC (Kristianson 1964: 23), and several sub-branches of the RSL complained directly to the Prime Minister, making charges about the program being, as the Vice President of the Kew sub-branch put it, 'deliberately planned, misleading, slanted, vicious and sneering' (Sekuless & Rees 1986: 139). Huish also complained to the press and the Prime Minister that 'the program presented a completely distorted picture of the league' ('Menzies Called for Script of "Four Corners"' 1963: 10). The issue went as far as Parliament: 'In Canberra yesterday, more than 20 Government backbenchers saw a special screening of the ... program on the RSL ... [and] were unanimous in the opinion that the program was "loaded" against the RSL' (*Sydney Morning Herald*, 12 September 1963). And Allan Ashbolt, the Executive Producer of the segment, was sacked by the ABC. For Kristianson, there is little doubt that 'his dismissal was in part attributable to RSL complaints' (as quoted in Sekuless & Rees 1986: 139), even though—despite requests by many RSL sub-branches and some state branches for political intervention—'it must be understood that none of these RSL complaints were "official" ... [and] there is no [explicit] evidence that political intervention did occur' (Kristianson 1964: 25, 26).

The public debate that followed on this topic for several years (Sekuless & Rees 1986: 140) continued within the terms set by *Four Corners*. Some religious groups condemned the RSL for the immoral behaviour with which it was charged. Hector Harrison, 'Moderator General of the Presbyterian Church in Australia', wrote to the RSL that in order to 'win' over communists, the good folk had to live good lives: 'we need to reform ourselves and a poker-playing, excessively drinking community needs a moral and spiritual jolt' (as quoted in Sekuless & Rees 1986: 138). The *Anglican* newspaper ran an editorial saying that the RSL was 'more interested in grog and gambling than high idealism' (Sekuless & Rees 1986: 138). Several political cartoonists presented similar accounts. For example, the Perth *Daily News* on 3 September 1963 featured a Paul Rigby cartoon showing a group of 'diggers' in suits throwing up their hands in horror and carrying placards: 'Us? Beer drinkers?' and 'Help stamp out television!' (Kristianson 1966: 151). Similarly, a 1965 cartoon by Bruce Petty 'depicted the League as an elderly sot, beer glass in hand, watching the luring of Australian soldiers to their deaths and calling for "more" '('The RSL' 1965: 184).

As noted above, the terms of the RSL's attack on the piece tend to revolve around the idea of objectivity, and this is the way in which the debate about the program was largely carried out in the days following its transmission. Kristianson describes the RSL's attacks on the program as being concerned with 'the problem of balance ... the bitterness of the debate about the programme [raised] several important points regarding the role of publicly-owned broadcasting facilities and the limitations under which such facilities must operate were raised' (Kristianson 1964: 28, 20).

As a current affairs program on public service television, what freedoms did *Four Corners* have? At the time of this public debate, some Federal Labor MPs attacked the RSL, accusing it of trying to override freedom of speech. In response, the Federal Secretary of the League wrote to James Darling (the Chairman of the ABC) stating that: 'the ABC does not have freedom to present a distorted viewpoint ... the freedom is to present an ... objective case' (quoted in Sekuless & Rees 1986: 139).

It was the lack of 'objectivity' that most offended the League. While some complaints were of factual inaccuracies—for example, the program's claim that most League members did not support the views of its leadership (Sekuless & Rees 1986: 138, 140; 'The RSL' 1965: 190)—most were about the lack of 'balance' in the story. The first official reaction from the RSL, from National Secretary A. G. W. Keys, worried that the item had not presented a 'broad picture of the League's activities', having instead 'selected the most controversial questions' (Kristianson 1964: 22). Rather than denying the existence of some social aspects of the RSL—the beer-drinking—members of the organisation alleged that other parts of its work should have been shown to provide balance. A sub-branch president claimed that 'we saw no shots of the true picture—no war veterans' homes ... no contingents of blood donors' ('The RSL' 1965: 183). Letters to the press from RSL members accused the item of being a 'cockeyed, political piece of propaganda', 'slanted', and 'not a balanced program' (*Canberra Times*, 4 September 1963):

> it is evident that the program lacked balance in its treatment of the RSL. The League critics were given uninterrupted time to develop their views but Sir Raymond Huish, while closely questioned, was given no opportunity to reply to criticism. Indeed, he was never at any time aware of criticism that was to be voiced.
>
> (Sekuless & Rees 1986: 139, quoting G. L. Kristianson)

It is ironic that *Four Corners* was accused of not being objective precisely because it was, in turn, accusing the RSL of not being objective. The claim to neutrality and balance was obviously a powerful one in the Australian public sphere in 1963. Looking at the current affairs programs that had come before *Four Corners*, the centrality of this concept—and what it actually meant in terms of television's representations of public life—becomes clear.

Prehistory of current affairs

Four Corners entered into an already existing genre of current affairs in Australian television. Current affairs were not a central part of the early Australian mediasphere, but they did exist (Cunningham & Miller 1994: 47). Indeed, the first program to be aired on Australian television was a documentary: *This is Television*, a behind-the-scenes look at Channel Nine (Cunningham & Miller 1994: 42), and a few current affairs shows appeared in the early years of the medium. Often credited as Australia's first current affairs program is *Seven on Seven*, a thirty-minute ATN 7 program that played after the 6.30 p.m. news bulletin, starting on 3 December 1956 (Beilby 1981: 9; Chris Keating, pers. comm. 17 May 2000); it included studio interviews and magazine-style features. Other examples in the 1950s included Channel Nine's *Nightwatch* in 1959, a police 'reality' show, following ambulances and police cars (Keating 1999b), and *Meet the Press* (Moran & Pinne 1993: 13).

Looking back at this genre, and the ways in which it was discussed in the public sphere, it is notable that there was an expectation that these programs would be absolutely 'objective'—a term that seems to have been synonymous with formality. There was to be no suggestion that reports on public events in early news and current affairs programs were originating from a subjective, human viewpoint; they were, rather, to present a supposedly simple and objective 'truth'. One element of this charade was to deny that it was human voices that were presenting stories. The words that were read out were not associated with any one person; they were the 'voice of God', presenting a universal 'correct' point of view, rather than only one possible, individual, interpretation of events. For example, when ABC radio first started, announcers were not allowed to give their names. Even more than this, they had to wear dinner jackets when doing evening shifts—even though, of course, the listeners could not see them. As Bill Peach explains this apparently bizarre behaviour, 'It was part of the old ABC culture that objectivity and impartiality were somehow achieved by anonymity' (Peach 1992: 35). When television made reporters visible, the instructions concerning correct behaviour became even more strict. W.A. Hamilton, the ABC's Controller of News, gave instructions that interviewers were 'not to move a muscle—nod, smile or react in any way that could be interpreted as a result of an answer or an indication of a barb in a question' (Davies 1981: 153).

The presenters were not to be human; they were simply representatives, the conduits through which the 'truth', the single correct viewpoint on any given situation, could be spoken.

Similarly, the people who were interviewed in early current affairs television—public figures and experts—were not human. They did not have opinions or personal feelings. They were not embodied. They were, again, seen to be neutral conduits through which facts would pass. Public figures did not have bodies, or the entire field of emotions, personal preferences, and prejudices associated with them. They were to be presented as rational thinking machines. As Robert Pullan points out, in these early days of television most of the Australian public did not even know what their own Prime Minister looked like, as 'debate, opinion makers believed, was not about trivia like five o'clock shadows, it was about issues of public moment' (Pullan 1986: 12).

So, speakers were to be experts; the opinions or thoughts of those not holding an institutionally sanctioned position were not only of no interest; they were also possibly controversial, and must be controlled: 'It never occurred to us [producing a radio show in 1956] how frightening it was to top management to find people ... giving their own personal views on a subject they chose, without recourse to experts' (Blain 1977: 69). These experts were chosen simply for their sanctioned status. Other considerations—such as an ability to entertain the audience—were unimportant (see Blain 1977: 67)

The relationship between the objective interviewers and representatives of sanctioned institutions was naturally to have no messy emotional or partisan elements; it was to be a simple communication of incontrovertible facts. For example, discussing the period 1956–64, Albert Moran describes Channel Nine's *Meet the Press*, an early current affairs program, as:

> a discussion-cum-interview between an eminent visitor to Australia, or distinguished guests, and senior newspaper executives of Consolidated Press. The discussion was usually polite and dignified, the questions were never probing or uncomfortable, and the general atmosphere was usually one of exclusivity and smugness.
>
> (Moran & Pinne 1993: 13)

Discussion should be 'polite' and 'dignified', not 'probing' or 'uncomfortable'. It was necessary for early current affairs to be absolutely respectful towards politicians and other public figures. The point of current affairs was not to engage with these interviewees, not to provide a meeting of different points of view or ideas. The program itself would not have any ideas or opinions of its own; it was merely to be a conduit through which public figures could disseminate to the viewing public what they wanted to say. The way in which such programs were regarded by the authorities can be seen in an early report of the Australian Broadcasting Control Board. The 1957 report has a section entitled 'Controversial Matter'. It is in this section that it discusses current affairs programming, stating that 'stations have made a cautious beginning with ... session of the *Meet the Press* type' (ABCB 1957: 46). The very fact that politicians might appear on television is, in itself, 'controversial' for the authorities, no matter how polite and dignified the questions they might face. This is stated explicitly in a later report: four years after *Four Corners* has begun, and two years after the 'controversial' report on the RSL, the Board reminds broadcasters that Paragraph 6 of the Broadcasting Standards, which all commercial broadcasters must follow (although not the ABC), requires 'the observance in television programmes ... of respect for ... social institutions' (ABCB 1965: 61). So the governing body of broadcasting in Australia specifically requires respect for 'social institutions': governments, police, the court system. Television current affairs are explicitly banned from being anything other than polite. So complaints about the behaviour of television reporters could be made during the 1960s specifically in terms of bad manners.

> MP COMPLAINS OF BAD MANNERS OF TV INTERVIEWERS ... 'They are rude and brash—they cause acute distress to people watching and the people they are interviewing' Mr Bate accused the interviewers of trying to put themselves above the people they interviewed. 'It was bad manners, not bad politics, that got *Four Corners* into trouble'
>
> ('MP Complains of Bad Manners' n.d.)

Refusing to be objective

Placing the *Four Corners* item on the RSL into this context, it is obvious that it was challenging basic understandings of what current affairs should be and, more than this, understandings of what the public sphere was and how it should operate. Kristianson summarises the public debate about the item in precisely these terms. He notes that some participants in this discussion claimed that all ABC programming should be 'purely objective'. However, this was not accepted by all participants, as theoretical debates about the public sphere and the function of the media in democracies progressed. Other discussants, for example, argued that 'controversial material cannot be presented in a perfectly balanced fashion without becoming dull', thus defending *Four Corners* for its presentation. According to this argument, the program's bias was admitted, but was seen to be an acceptable way to 'promote discussion' (Kristianson 1964: 27).

By drawing on prominent public counterdiscourses about the RSL (regarding drunkenness, for instance) in order to humanise the organisation and suggest that it was not a neutral and objective public entity, *Four Corners* itself refused to accept the objectivity that was claimed for participants in the public sphere. It demonstrated this itself—by presenting a partisan account of the organisation in the public sphere—and made the same claims about the RSL.

In this, the RSL story is representative of long-running trends in *Four Corners*. Mark Gibson notes that in *Four Corners'* stories 'The narrator has generally appeared on-screen, a significant break with the off-screen "voice-of-God" narration which was the dominant convention in 1950s documentary' (Gibson 1997b: 628). More significant than this, 'The involvement of the narrators-reporters with their subjects, usually on locations … open[s] up subjective points of view' (Gibson 1997b: 628). The inclusion of unscripted material represents a further challenge to tenets of absolute control and respect (Gibson 1997b: 628).

Robert Pullan notes that the first producer of the program 'liked the director's technique of focusing entirely on the subject's face, believing that the look on a subject's face at the moment he heard a question often revealed more than his rational response moments later' (Pullan 1986: 15). This represents a direct challenge to authorities' prohibition of the visual, the personal, and the probing.

Quite against the desires of the ABC authorities, and perhaps because of the intimacy of the medium, the first presenter of the program, Michael Charlton, became the ABC's 'first star' (Hall 1976: 102), 'the first Australian celebrity of television journalism' (Pullan 1986: 24). He was voted 'most popular personality of 1962' by the readers of *TV Week* (Inglis 1983: 217; see also Blain 1977: 122).

And *Four Corners* used interviews. Now that the interview has become the 'dominant mode of conveying information in the broadcasting media', it is odd to remember that the mode is 'a recent and culturally specific invention' (Bell & Leeuwen 1994: 1, 2). But in the earliest days of television, interviews were regarded with a great degree of suspicion, since the format challenged precisely the tenets of formality discussed above: 'When television was first introduced ... [i]nterviews were not to be allowed ... They belonged to the more "showbusiness" approach of public-affairs journalism' (Bell & Leeuwen 1994: 38). When the interview format emerged in nineteenth-century journalism, it was immediately associated with the personal, the trivial, the intimate—even with the visual (Bell & Leeuwen 1994: 32)—in short, everything that the authorities wished to censor in Australia's television current affairs.

Not only did *Four Corners* 'interview' public figures, but it also 'interviewed' non-experts: passers-by in the street, whose only qualification for speaking in the public sphere was their randomness—vox pops. The very first episode of *Four Corners* closed with 'the ABC's favourite street interviewer, Keith Smith, asking people what they were worried about' (Hall 1976: 102): 'In 1961, people weren't used to seeing ordinary people on television—all they had seen were celebrities, politicians at election time, overseas people, newsreaders and sporting commentators. You hadn't seen ordinary Australians saying anything' (Pullan 1986: 22, quoting Keith Smith).

Four Corners was breaching most of the protocols set down by the authorities for current affairs coverage. Of course, it was not the first program to do this, either in Australia or in other countries: Bell and Leeuwen (1994) suggest that the informal interview came to Australian broadcasting with Dorothy Vautier, presenter of women's programs on 2GB (Corner 1991: 7–8 discusses British examples; Pells 1997: 88 looks at American ones). But *Four Corners* was an important part of this reformatting of public affairs in Australia. And examples such as the controversy over the RSL story suggest the ways in which this alteration took place.

Given this, it is telling that the terms of public discussion about the RSL story—debates over objectivity and balance—have been the terms in which public debate about *Four Corners* has continued throughout the program's history (Aitken 1972: 14; Inglis 1983: 281). Indeed, a stable genre exists of academic and journalistic articles 'discovering' bias in *Four Corners*, or defending the program against such charges (Shipp 1971; Arndt 1986; Manning 1988). Some academics have found other ways of denigrating the move away from inhuman objectivity in current affairs: Murray Masterson and Roger Patching worry about the move from 'serious' to 'popular' current affairs television (Masterson & Patching 1990: 189–90). Philip Bell, Kathe Boehringer, and Stephen Crofts similarly worry about 'the ideology of personalisation' and the way in which current affairs programming replaces 'issues' with 'personalities' (Bell, Boehringer, & Crofts 1982a: 82, 103).

However, it is also possible to understand the controversial aspects of the RSL item in more positive ways. Stuart Cunningham and Toby Miller argue that it is precisely its bias that has made *Four Corners* so important in Australia. It has, they state, 'a certain public interest partiality that takes our biggest step toward a significant television political culture' (Cunningham & Miller 1994: 58). The move towards the private, intimate, emotional modes of communicating employed in the controversial RSL segment need not be viewed with dismay. Indeed, it can be seen as a necessary part of a public debate that challenges a powerful institution whose authority rests precisely on claims of neutrality and objectivity. In Australia, the traditions of journalism that began with the publication of the Sydney *Gazette* and New South Wales *Advertiser* in 1803—the latter a newspaper publishing government-approved reports about the government's activities, which the *Advertiser* said were *not political*—have meant that the practice of journalism supporting the status quo has not been thought of as political, biased, and suspect (Pullan 1986: 10). Indeed, Pullan argues, 'support for the status quo ... has been thought of as non-political' throughout the history of Australian journalism (Pullan 1986: 42). This was the context into which *Four Corners* was born. When it first started, Charles Moses, the ABC's General Manager, 'was firmly against the idea that *Four Corners* should "expose" anything. It should inform without taking sides, he said, it must not set out to expose' (Pullan 1986: 46).

So, in a dehumanised, institutionalised, non-entertaining, respectful, objective mediasphere, *Four Corners* broadcast a story about drinking and political desires in the RSL, and it is collectively remembered for doing so. It attempted to challenge the idea that dominant political institutions were neutral precisely by not being neutral itself. In a mediasphere where the demands of objectivity and respectfulness supported political organisations that made their own claims for neutrality, *Four Corners* broadcast an account that drew on powerful counterdiscourses in order to personalise and humanise the RSL. It is an important part of the public archive of Australian television. It contributes to Australia's cultural heritage a turning point in the televising of public affairs, and a healthy disrespect for objectivity and authority.

Availability

Most episodes of *Four Corners*—including the RSL item—are available for purchase from the ABC's Archives and Library Services in Sydney.

Note

1 Although it should be noted that the 2001 Logie Awards featured a special celebration of '40 Years of 4 Corners' that brought the program's archive to an audience of over 2.5 million Australians.

3

Homicide: Life on the Melbourne Streets

1964–77[1]

On 20 October 1964, the first episode of the Australian cop show *Homicide* was broadcast and rated 33 per cent of the viewing audience.[2]

For an Australian cop show to be broadcast was not a first: on another medium—radio—cop shows such as *D24* had been running for ten years (O'Regan 1991: 11–12). But for a *television* drama with Australian lead characters to be *popular*—that was unusual. Indeed, although it was by no means the first drama series in Australian television—it is possible to list half a dozen before this date, not to mention hundreds of one-off television plays[3]—*Homicide* was the first drama series to be really important to the Australian audience. *Homicide* was the series that made it possible to imagine Australian drama as a regular part of television scheduling.

Homicide is a police show, shot in Melbourne. It centres on the homicide squad of the Victorian police, and each episode deals—as the title suggests—with a murder. The first three stars of the program—fifteen detectives appeared in the program's thirteen-year run (Harrison 1994)—were Detective Sergeant Frank Bronson (Terry McDermott), Detective Rex Fraser (Lex Mitchell), and Inspector Jack Connolly (John Fegan).

Homicide has survived well in the public archive. Documentaries such as *Homicide—30 Years On* (1994), *The Homicide Story* (1970), *ATV Thirty Years of Television* (1994), and *Thirty Five Years of Television* (1991) have written it into Australian television history. It is remembered as the first successful Australian drama series, the germinal moment that made possible a tradition of Australian television drama, and the popular drama program that allowed

Australian actors to use their own accents 'for the first time in their careers' (*Homicide: 30 Years On* 1994).

In order to understand the importance of *Homicide*'s Australian provenance, and why the program's debut is remembered as such a germinal moment in the public archive of Australian television, it is useful to consider the cultural context in which it first appeared.

Dramatic context

During the years 1956–64 Australian television was dominated by American programming. In 1960, up to 70 per cent of each station's programming was imported drama (that is 70 per cent of all programming, not just 70 per cent of the drama) (ABCB 1960: 38). About 80 per cent of that imported drama was American: the rest was British (Cunningham & Turner 1993: 2). In the late 1950s, it was American cop shows that were the favoured genre for Australian television audiences: *Perry Mason, 77 Sunset Strip*, and *The Untouchables* (Jones & Bednall 1980: 22).

These facts did not go unnoticed at the time. Cultural critics such as Robyn Boyd could complain in 1960 that 'As every producer knows the mass audience rejects the possibility of any Australian entertainment being entertaining' (Appleton 1988: 2). Meanwhile, Hector Crawford—the head of Crawford Productions, who would go on to make *Homicide*—was engaged in a one-man crusade to convince politicians and television stations that Australian drama was a moral necessity. In a self-published pamphlet of 1959, he describes the dominance of American drama programs in Australia, and thunders:

> Do these programmes stimulate among Australians a consciousness of national identity and pride in our nation and a regard for our own cultural ideas and patterns? Do they typify Australian attitudes and institutions, Australian habits and customs, Australian manners, speech and dress? Do these programmes help to enrich the life of Australian families? Do they stimulate the life of the nation by offering opportunities for the artistic and creative abilities of Australians to develop and to be appreciated and shared in by other Australians? Do they enlighten Australians as to their own country's history and traditions, its national life and the achievements of their fellow-Australians? Do these programmes help Australians to know and understand one another and bring to them a wider knowledge of those areas of their own country which they may never have the opportunity to visit?
>
> (Crawford 1959: 14–15)

Presumably, the answer is no. Presumably, *Homicide* would do all of these things.

But what did *Homicide* do for the Australian mediasphere? How was it taken up? What were the discourses and discussions that took place around this, the first successful Australian drama series on television?

Quiet debut

Given its retrospectively remembered germinal status, there is a distinct lack of excitement in the Australian mediasphere regarding the first broadcast of *Homicide*. This can be explained with reference to institutional factors. One group of magazines and newspapers in Melbourne at the time—*The Listener-In TV*, the *Sun*, and the *Herald*—were produced by the Herald and Weekly Times organisation, which was a majority shareholder in HSV-7—the television station that broadcast *Homicide*. The Melbourne *Age* newspaper, by comparison, was affiliated with GTV-9, while the *TV Times* was produced by the ABC. It is to be expected, then, that only the HSV-7-affiliated publications would give space to the broadcast of this new Australian drama series. The others, understandably, show little interest in the programming of a rival television station. For example, the cover stories for the Melbourne *TV Times* during this period are entirely about American programs: *Dr Kildare* has the cover on the week that *Homicide* debuts; later in the year, the closest that the *TV Times* get to an 'Australian' cover is the story that 'Lorne Green [star of *Bonanza*] may buy Australian property' (2 December 1964).

A preview article on *Homicide* in *TV Week* is hidden at the back of the magazine (17–23 October 1964); the cover story is 'Zorro Unmasked'—again, an American show. And the covers for *TV Week* for the rest of the year also feature American programs and stars: *Bonanza*, *The Beverly Hillbillies*, Paul Newman, *Doctor Kildare*.

During this period the *TV Times* and *TV Week* do have regular articles on Australian *variety* shows, such as coverage of *IMT*, particularly in the Melbourne editions. Indeed, the only comment in *TV Week* about *Homicide* in the weeks after its first transmission is to lament its effect on variety production ('*Homicide*—Sudden Death to New Show Hopes' 1964). Indeed, the program seems almost invisible to *TV Week*. In a series of articles on 'TV Trends of 1965' (1964)—by which point *Homicide* was already a successful and unique program on Australian television—there is no mention of the program. Similarly, the Melbourne *Age* has little interest in *Homicide*; it is mentioned, in the week of its first broadcast, in a small article in its *TV*

Guide, which tends to focus most strongly, again, on variety shows (the cover story for the week of *Homicide's* first episode is that *IMT* is moving to a new studio). The rest of the *Age*'s television coverage during this period focuses on *Four Corners*. During the weeks of *Homicide*'s first broadcast, the cancelling of a *Four Corners* special on capital punishment features on the news pages of the *Age*, and leads to letters to the editor on the need for freedom of the ABC (see, for example, *Age*, 5 November 1964). This is serious discussion of serious television in a serious newspaper; *Homicide* does not rate much interest.

The HSV-7-affiliated *Listener In-TV* and the *Herald* are much more positive and excited about this new television program. The former features Australian production much more strongly than other television magazines—again, focusing on variety programs, and often giving cover stories to these. This magazine does present reviews of *Homicide*, and viewers' letters about the program. And for each of the first three weeks of *Homicide*'s run, it is the major story on the *Herald*'s TV page; the paper also features a news story after the program's first broadcast and reviews each episode.

The launch of *Homicide*, then, was not an immediate bombshell in the Australian press. It did not, overnight, push Australian drama to the centre of the mediasphere. Rather, it crept in gradually, displacing neither American drama nor Australian variety from the front pages of the television press.

There is *some* sense of the program's importance for Australian TV: as *TV Week* states in its introductory article, '*Homicide* has to be good—it represents a long awaited re-awakening in the industry and failure would hamper any Australian production for a long time to come' ('*Homicide* Strips Melbourne Naked' 1964: 79). But this importance does not push it onto the front cover of any magazines or newspapers.

But what about the coverage the program *did* receive? How was *Homicide* placed in the mediasphere? What issues were raised for the audience? And how do they relate to the program that was broadcast in 1964?

Places and chases: locating *Homicide*

A small article introducing *Homicide* appears on 14 October 1964 in the *TV Times* (it is a single column, compared with the two-page illustrated spreads on programs such as *The Addams Family* and *Bonanza* in the same issue). The article acknowledges the importance of this 'eagerly awaited step by Australian commercial television studios into the world of live drama production on a big scale', and notes that 'Its heroes will be three "fair dinkum" Australian policemen based on Melbourne's Russell Street headquarters' ('*Homicide*—New Local Series Bows in on HSV' 1964: 3). The article then goes on to suggest what will be, for the media, one of the most important aspects of *Homicide* for a Melbourne audience: the specificity of *place*.

The *TV Times* article begins with a sensational promise of 'car chases down St Kilda Road'. St Kilda Road is a well-known Melbourne street. The point the *TV Times* attempts to make is that this combination—St Kilda Road and car chases—is an improbable one. It is a combination of everyday places with the fantasy world of car chases. And, looking at the slight coverage that the debut of *Homicide* received, it is apparent that an important part of the program's introduction to Melbourne viewers is to teach the audience about how they should react to having what has previously been only fantasy—car chases—happening in their own, real, 'local' area.

The term 'local' has been often used in debates about Australian television. Critics and government bodies alike have insisted that it is necessary to have 'local' production of Australian television (see Hector Crawford's comments above). But as Toby Miller has pointed out, the term has often been abused (Miller 1990: 130). Often it is used in such a way that it in fact means 'national' (in the sense that 'local' production is 'Australian' production). Such a use of the term continues in cultural theory to the present day (McKee 1999a). But this use is misleading: it is not clear how a production made in one part of Australia is necessarily 'local' to audiences watching it around the country. (How local is Melbourne to a viewer living in Perth? Darwin? Hobart?)

At first, this was not an issue: *Homicide* was both made and broadcast in Melbourne. And to show familiar spaces on television—the same physical locations in which its audience might walk—was indeed one of *Homicide's* breakthroughs, and one for which it is well remembered (see Murray 1973: 18; Moran 1982: 95; Flew 1997: 786; Moran 1997a: 117). For an audience that might regularly go to the city centre, the locations the program showed might be understood as *geographically* local: these were sites that viewers might indeed visit for themselves, might already be familiar with. This is indeed how the program is positioned in the Australian mediasphere by contextual discourses when it is first introduced. Its very practical kind of localism is seen to be something new, something exciting, but also slightly problematic. For an audience unused to television drama production in their own city had to be tutored in how to react to it.

For example, a *TV Times* article in November is headlined 'The Fake Cop Caper' (1964: 12). It begins: 'My assignment: to investigate reports about a bogus team of detectives seen in various parts of Melbourne over the past few weeks'. The idea that there could be actors playing policemen in Melbourne is so strange that it is worthy of a story, in which readers can be advised on how to react should they encounter such an outlandish situation: ' "Pick the fake policeman" is getting to be a popular pastime in Melbourne these days', the author notes, before suggesting that even the real police have been confused by this situation—quoting one who says: 'We offered to help out, but they seemed to have things under control' ('The Fake Cop Caper' 1964: 12, 13).

This is a popular approach for introducing *Homicide* to the Melbourne audience. A *TV Week* article similarly focuses on the strangeness of Melbourne being the site for such televisual fantasies.

> The powder blue police car skidded to a halt in busy Bourke St, Melbourne. Even before the wheels stopped rolling, the doors flew open and out jumped two men, closely followed by the driver. As the three men sprinted across the pavement and dived into one of the stores, the crowd automatically stepped aside. Just as hundreds of shoppers, lunchtime strollers and motorists thought they were going to see a real live police drama, a voice boomed above the roar of the traffic. 'Cut!'
>
> ('*Homicide* Strips Melbourne Naked' 1964: 76)

The Melbourne audience is the 'hundreds of shoppers' who thought they were going to see a real-life crime; they—like the readers of this article—must learn how to react to television production on their doorstep. The *Listener In-TV* is similarly pedagogical in its article headlined 'On the Street Where You Live':

> if you should come across what looks like a robbery, brawl, police chase or accident in the streets of Melbourne or in your own suburb, don't jump to conclusions. Before you barge in to help, or race to phone for the police, look around for a red sign nearby that reads '*Homicide* filming'. If it's there, you are witnessing an incident being enacted by the cast of the first Australian crime drama TV series, *Homicide* ... Unlike previous [Australian] dramatic shows, which were staged mostly in the TV studios, *Homicide* goes out into the streets to film actual locations in Melbourne.
>
> ('On the Streets Where You Live' 1964: 2)

If you should come into this strange situation, this is how you should react—a guide to etiquette for those who are unused to having drama filmed in their own city. And it is now, the article suggests, likely to be part of readers' everyday lives.

> You could come across a *Homicide* film unit anywhere in Melbourne, at any time of the day or night. Film director Ian Jones and his crew are quite happy for you to watch the filming, but please remain in the background and don't wander in front of the cameras.
>
> ('On the Streets Where You Live' 1964: 2)

The wondrous simplicity of 'Don't wander in front of the cameras' suggests an audience completely unused to 'local' production.

This is the 'local' in the most literal sense: local production as production in the audience's locality, production that they might 'wander' into. This is a localism of geography: it is 'On the Streets Where You Live'; on 'St Kilda Road'; on 'Burke Street'. It might even be filmed in your house (Hood 1964: 20). The program encourages such a feeling of familiarity: watching episodes now it is notable how keen it is to give out street names and addresses (and although the residential street names used in the program were all fictitious, the suburbs were real). Where did the murder take place? 'Barker Street' (*Homicide* 1964b). Where does the suspect live? '87 Cartwright Avenue, Balwyn' (*Homicide* 1964a). And the sex worker who is providing an alibi? 'Pecker Street, St Kilda' (*Homicide* 1964c).

As well as insisting on particular locations by naming them, the program also *visualises* Melbourne's locality. The filmed location sequences of *Homicide* present a variety of Melbourne sites. The title sequence presents the city centre as an 'urban jungle', with the recognisable vista of Russell Street and a familiar building—the police headquarters there. A story set in the suburbs provides shots of suburban Melbourne streets (*Homicide* 1964b). The houses are familiar to a Melbourne inhabitant: the veranda, the ironwork around the top. Later, a drive into a local patch of forest presents familiar species of trees.

At the beginning, then, *Homicide* is set in a very specific locality: this is 'your' locality, the places known by a Melbourne audience. Of course, when the program was broadcast in Sydney the next year, and in other states in later years, this initial localism was lost, submerged into a more generalised 'Australian' national recognition. But at the time of its initial broadcast, it was its presence 'on the streets where you live' that formed a strong part of its appeal.

Accenting *Homicide*

'Viewers may have some trouble', says the *Listener In-TV*, 'in accustoming themselves to Australian accents in a crime series. Our children by now are probably convinced that all detectives speak with an American accent' ('*Homicide* Gets Off to a Good Start' 1964: 9). This concern is raised by other writers on *Homicide*'s first broadcast. 'TV cops and robbers with *Australian* accents', says the *TV Times* with a tone of wonderment ('*Homicide*—New Local Series Bows in on HSV' 1964: 3).

This is another important aspect of *Homicide's* contribution to Australia's cultural heritage. The program is well remembered as the first drama series on television that allowed actors to use their own Australian accents (although *Consider Your Verdict* had also done this to some extent). Ian Jones, a director with the program, claims that 'a lot of the actors ... were using an Australian accent for the first time in their career' (*Homicide: 30 Years On* 1994). This claim seems to be supported by other accounts of early Australian drama production. Reg James, from Grace Gibson Productions, remembers that in making radio drama 'We used mid-Atlantic accents, because we had to sell programs overseas, and a local accent wouldn't have been acceptable ... we didn't use Australian accents because at the time we didn't believe they were acceptable to Australians' (*The Australian Image* 1989c). Leonard Teale, who would later become a star of *Homicide*, also remembers that

> One occasion I was working for the ABC ... I had to say something about 'It's about time we were going home', and having been born in Queensland, and knowing how people speak there, I quite naturally said [it with the Queensland accent] ... No, no, no [said the director], Australian stockmen do not drop final gs and do not drop the first h, and straight out of southern England, this Australian stockman had to say [with a received pronunciation accent] 'It's time we were going home'.
>
> (*The Australian Image* 1989c; see also Peach 1990: 19)

Homicide, then, was one of the first television drama series to allow Australian accents to be heard in a fictional context. And contemporary press coverage was concerned about how audiences would react to this.

According to some histories of Australian television, audiences hated hearing such an accent on television. Many accounts claim that viewers were disturbed by hearing the Australian accent in *Homicide*. A nostalgic newspaper account, for example, claims that

> When Australia's first police drama went to air 30 years ago this week, the TV station was deluged with complaints: 'Why on earth do you make your actors put on those shocking Australian accents?' infuriated callers asked after watching the first episode of *Homicide*. 'They sound absolutely ghastly' ... [Ian Craw-

> ford says that] 'All our actors were talking in their normal voices. It's just that the public wasn't used to hearing an Australian accent on television. They heard either American shows or British shows, or their own Australian actors talking in the kind of English accents everyone in theatre was encouraged to use in those days. People ended up assuming that was an Australian accent. They'd never heard real Australian accents before'.
>
> (Williams 1994c: 29)

There is little contemporary evidence to support this popular memory of public reaction: available accounts suggest that audiences were quite happy to hear the Australian accent on television. Indeed, as one news story (in the *Herald*, of course) puts it, 'Immediately after the first program finished at 8.30 last night, the HSV-7 switchboard was jammed with congratulatory calls' (Salt 1964: 30).[4] However, given the importance that is granted *Homicide*'s Australian accents in the public archive, it is interesting to look at the way in which these accents are used within the program.

Each of the early episodes of *Homicide* opens with a voice-over (supplied by John McMahon). This deep, authoritative 'voice-of-God' introduces the situation that will develop during the episode: 'Monday, September 21—Pelham Street Railway Yards, Jollimont. A young boy happily trespassing on Railway Property' (*Homicide* 1964c).

McMahon's voice-over recurs throughout each episode, explaining what is happening in each filmed sequence. This aesthetic may be influenced by the program's origins as a television version of the Crawford's radio series *D24*, but it also had a practical rationale: in the early days of the program, the *Homicide* production crew did not have the technology to shoot broadcast quality sound on outside scenes, tending to use the sound recorded there only as a guide track for post-synch dubbing (although occasionally the sound was judged good enough to be used in the broadcast episode). This voice-over is intrusive and all-knowing, defining the roles of characters that we might otherwise not know about. For example, the voice-over in one episode comments over a scene of two men in conversation: 'From the guest house, Colin Tait drove to a house in Elsternwick, and there he met the man who had kidnapped his wife' (*Homicide* 1964b).

In an aesthetic decision reminiscent of its radio heritage, the program does not trust us to make sense of even the most obvious visuals without spoken explanation. In 'The scent of death' (episode 7), as we see Detective Sergeant Bronson call in at a factory on his way to meet a dog handler, the voice-over tells us that 'On his way to meet the dog handler at the Star junkyard, Detective Sergeant Bronson called at the factory of the Pinnacle Shirt

Company'; in the same episode, while we watch the tracker dogs leading the police to the railway yard, the voice-over tells us that 'The tracker dog led the police to the railway yard'. This voice-over is given absolute authority to understand the narrative and explain it to us. And although John McMahon was Australian, his upper-class accent sounds to me almost American—although an American audience I played it to thought it sounded British. It is certainly not a broad 'Strine' accent.

In the hierarchy of authority in the program, next to the 'voice-of-God' narrator is Inspector Connolly (John Fegan). His accent in the first few episodes is a strange and malleable thing. It fluctuates to the extent that in some episodes (for example, in 'The Stunt', and particularly in the final courtroom scene of that episode), he sounds as though he is playing an American character; in others, it is Irish-Australian.

The two characters who are the centre of the drama—Bronson and Fraser—have recognisably Australian accents. They are not strong, but they are Australian. The witnesses to some of the crimes have Australian accents that are slightly stronger than the policemen's. And the really rough criminals—for example, the men who kidnap a suburban housewife in episode 5, or the layabout youth in episode 1—have the broadest Australian accents in the program. They even get to use Aussie colloquialisms ('Fair go', says one of the crims in episode 5). A hierarchy is established in which the broader the Australian accent, the less trustworthy the character.

Nevertheless, *Homicide* does feature Australian accents, and it seems that this was, in itself, revolutionary for a drama series on Australian television. One of the most relaxed and casual ways in which it appears is when it should not—when it slips in by accident. For example, in episode 7, many of the main characters are Irish. The actors playing them are obviously Australian—for their Irish accents are badly done, and Australian accents show through in a kind of palimpsest. It is the appearance of the accent in such unexpected ways that emphasises its importance in *Homicide*.

Comparing *Homicide*

Homicide is well remembered as the 'first' popular Australian drama at a time when United States imports dominated television. It is interesting to examine the way in which it was compared with imported programs at the time: sometimes to celebrate its Australian specificity and sometimes to condemn its poor production values.[5] This is distinct from the discussion of 'localness' that focuses on the presence of the everyday, familiar, physical spaces of Melbourne in the program. This is more of an attempt to celebrate 'Australianness', to accept the terms presented by Hector Crawford's demand for Australian content, and to discuss the program in terms of national identity.

Some of the introductory articles explicitly compare *Homicide* to the familiar form of imported cop shows: '*Homicide* will be Australia's answer to America's *Naked City* and England's *Z-Cars*. It is an hour-long thriller which will be compared with such imports as *The Detectives* and *San Francisco Beat*' ('*Homicide* Strips Melbourne Naked' 1964: 77). The short article introducing the program in the *Age TV Guide* notes that

> The first Australian-made one-hour crime detection series will be launched ... on Tuesday. It is considered a bold venture into a field where smooth, sophisticated American crime series have excelled ... [The characters] are not the knock-down drag out type of characters so often portrayed ... on the screen ... They are ... the fellow next door budgeting to pay off his double-fronted home.
>
> ('Melbourne Challenge to TV Detective Imports' 1964: 3)

The difference between this Australian production and the imported cop shows (particularly the American ones) is emphasised in media coverage of *Homicide*. Its Australian provenance is a cause for celebration:

> Wonderful to see a local show 'murder' the opposition on the ratings hit parade. Yup, *Homicide* made it ... it's the top 'live' [that is, Australian] show, and [number] three against all imports!
>
> (Marsha 1964: 8)

> HSV's introduction of *Homicide* to Tuesday night viewing proved that local television can stand on its own feet for entertainment value. The first edition whirled onto the screen with a flash of action ... Production of *Homicide*, particularly the outside filmed sequences, was of the highest standard yet displayed in Australia.
>
> ('*Homicide* Gets Off to a Good Start' 1964: 9)

> *Homicide* ... a healthy comeback for Australian television ... there appears to be too much competition between channels to satisfy viewers with overseas crime programs.
>
> (Wilgeosher 1964)

Indeed, its Australian provenance is given as a reason for not criticising those aspects of the program that are inferior to American examples of the genre (principally production standards). A rare news story (as opposed to a television comment) in the *Herald* the day after the first episode claims that

> Mr Vic Arnold [said that] ' ... the program compared favourably with overseas shows of the same type' ... Inspector F. W. Woonton ... said he felt the show would come up to overseas standards ... An officer of the Australian Broadcasting Control Board said that the program had prospects. 'It has some rough edges to be smoothed out', he said 'We have seen a lot worse American films which have been lapped up by the public'.
>
> (Salt 1964: 30)

Letters to *Listener In-TV* presented similar arguments, emphasising Australian provenance as a way of comparing the program to imported cop shows:

> A choice orchid [that is, congratulations] to *Homicide* for its excellence in acting, photography and general set up. To suggest any improvement along the lines of *Naked City* [as one letter writer had done in a previous issue] is the thought of someone looking for faults instead of enjoying the picture. It is a better show than any imported one because it is local and we know, or have heard of the suburbs where it is being acted. Without being too one-eyed I think we can supply the talent, good photography and beautiful scenery equal to anything which any overseas company can offer, and it has the added attraction of being Australian. It has been proved now that Australia can give viewers A1 entertainment, so why go outside for it.
>
> (Satisfied Viewer 1964: 45)

> I would like to send a large orchid to *Homicide*. Those who find fault are mostly those who would find fault with anything Australian. *Homicide* is good entertainment and the leading characters are as good as plenty of overseas detectives. Also it is good to see our own local suburbs and police cars.
>
> (Wilgeosher 1964)

Even those who want to criticise the program—as Frank Thring does in his review in *TV Week*—are aware of the need for deference to Australian production. 'I have avoided criticising *Homicide*, because one knows the usual cry of crucifying the local product is going to echo down the streets', he remarks—before going on to crucify the program's scripts, dialogue, and acting (Thring 1964: 24).

In contemporary discussion of the program, then, its low production values were almost celebrated, as defining its 'Australian-ness'. Indeed, this schema—Australia versus America; glossy high production values versus slower pace and more amateurish production—survives in the public archive, and continues to be used in critical and academic accounts of the program in the following decades (see (Anderson 1972c: 36; Murray 1973: 16; Davies 1981: 96; Dale 1998: 4).

Watching the programs now, the most interesting thing about its production values is the difference between its filmed and its videotaped sequences. As one of the commentators above notes, it is the 'outside filmed' sequences that have good production values; it is the studio videotaped sequences that have particularly 'rough edges'.

The film sequences are very visual in their language. They delight in presenting spectacle. The first episode—'The Stunt'—opens with a wide panning shot over the Melbourne skyline, moving down and zooming in to the tiny figure of a student running through a park. This is followed by a sequence of students driving flash cars through the streets of Melbourne. This sequence—with its jazz soundtrack—is reminiscent of the 'swinging sixties' in London, evoking a British youth aesthetic.[6] Indeed, throughout the early episodes there are many scenes of driving—extended shots that serve little narrative purpose and that are obviously intended to provide visual interest. These early episodes also present visually interesting locations such as a railway yard; an investigation later leads the heroes to 'the hills', where a chase takes place across the countryside (*Homicide* 1964a).

The swinging sixties aesthetic reappears in the character of Detective Rex Fraser—the youngest of the detectives—whose investigative technique includes chatting up 'dolly-birds', while offering them cigarettes and flirting with them. In the first episode, in order to find out more about the students who are under investigation, he goes undercover to a car rally. 'So as I won't be conspicuous,' he says, 'I'll take a beautiful girl with me.' He picks up the phone: 'Hello Sandra? Grrrrrr. Homicide squad here.' This is followed by

Visual spectacle: the first shot of *Homicide*

scenes of Rex Fraser driving a sports car along a country road with an attractive blonde woman sitting beside him: an almost Bondian scene. This leads to an extended filmed sequence at a Templestowe sports car racing event. This sequence is several minutes long, showing several vintage cars racing while Rex and his woman sit and watch, smiling at each other. This sequence climaxes in a sequence in which the student under investigation reveals his bad temper and jealousy: after losing the race, he drives his car into the side of the winner. This is all very visual storytelling: show it; don't tell it (*Homicide* 1964a).

Bondian aesthetics in *Homicide*

Throughout this sequence, there has been no conversation. As noted above, early in the production of *Homicide* the crew did not tend to record broadcast quality sound on location. This allows the program to take on the 'flashy' visual look of imported productions—indeed, almost demands that it does so. A loudspeaker commentary on the car race is dubbed over this particular sequence, so it is not entirely devoid of words. But in many of the external sequences, the Australian accent is entirely lacking: this is perhaps as convincingly 'American'/'British' as *Homicide* can be.

The cut to the next scene of this episode is a huge jump. It is a videotaped scene in the homicide squad offices. Having just watched a film sequence—which visually and spectacularly communicated a good deal of information—it is now necessary to have all this information presented again—with Australian accents. Frank Bronson and Rex Fraser discuss what happened: how the student hit another car and whether it could have been an accident. We already know from the film sequence that it was not, but we now have to discuss it at length: 'He said his foot slipped off the brake ... For an experienced motorist, that's not very likely', and so on.

The interior shots in the early episodes are crude and very stagy. The lighting is flat. The sets have no detail: most of them consist of the same walls (this is particulary obvious because they are all the same colour) with a small number of props placed in front of them. When the actors actually have to speak (as opposed to appearing in the film sequences), many of the performances are as convincing as those of a cheap porn film. The framing often breaks the conventions of television: characters facing right and speaking to

The courtroom set in *Homicide*

the right are framed on the right hand side of the screen, with an empty expanse filling the left hand side of the screen. There are no extras in the background of most scenes. There is no diegetic sound, and the absolute silence in the background of many scenes becomes quickly oppressive. Mistakes are retained, as actors fluff their lines: 'We won't need you any more now ... just now, Mr Bickford', says Bronson (*Homicide* 1964a).

Some scenes are spectacularly amateurish. One example, exhibiting many of the characteristics noted above, is the scene in episode 5 in which a woman who is about to be murdered telephones a friend. The friend stands awkwardly in front of a blank wall, with no other scenery. A wide mid-shot, from directly in front, reveals plenty of this blank wall. We hear only the friend's side of the conversation as she repeats everything the intended murder victim says; her performance is incredibly stilted.

The courtroom scenes that end each of these early episodes of *Homicide* have even cheaper production values. In these, there is amazingly little visual interest. Everyone is shot in medium close-up, with blank walls behind them. There are no establishing shots of the courtroom, or of the spatial relationships between the characters. Indeed, there is no shot of the courtroom set at all—presumably there isn't one. When we see the magistrate, we see his chair back behind him, the blank wall—and nothing else.

Of course, all of these points can be explained simply: cost. *Homicide* was produced very cheaply. It is interesting, however, from the point of view of the audience for this first successful Australian drama series, to see how the concern with imported competition fits so neatly into the binary nature of the broadcast text itself: filmed sequences that look imported; video sequences that look crude and cheap. American/British: Australian.

The legacy of *Homicide*

Homicide is one of the most influential programs discussed in this book. At its simplest, it created an audience for Australian drama that had not previously been visible (Flew 1997: 786; Moran 1985: 101). It ensured that the production of Australian drama series—previously sporadic at best—would continue uninterrupted from that point on (Moran 1985: 31). It led directly to the creation of two other Crawford's cop shows—*Division 4* and *Matlock Police* (Moran 1985: 101)—and to the dominance of the police genre in Australian drama production (Dale 1998: 5). It also, Chris Keating suggests, gave a boost to the drive for Australian film production (Chris Keating, pers. comm. 17 May 2000). Australian television has never been dominated by Australian programs. It has always retained a large percentage of imported product: in 1968, even after the success of *Homicide* and the appearance of two other one-hour Australian drama series, *Hunter* and *Contrabandits*, Australian drama constituted less than 3 per cent of all drama on Australian television (MacCallum 1968: 67, 68). Nevertheless, *Homicide* made it possible for Australian drama—with Australian accents, local settings and production values that did not quite match up to the imported fare—to survive on Australian television.

But more significant than such industrial considerations, the program continues to be remembered as part of Australian television's public archive. Its legacy contributes to Australian worries about imported programming, and to pride in any 'local' product that succeeds against it. It is part of a narrative of a move away from cultural cringe to a recognition that Australian accents might fairly be heard in Australian drama. It is a breakthrough moment in Australia's cultural heritage.

Availability

Episode 1 of *Homicide* has been commercially released on the tape *Homicide: 30 Years On* (available from Screensound), and episode 376—the first in colour—as part of *The Homicide Story*. Most of episodes 2–509 are held by Screensound, although a small number (for example, 165, 428, 462) are missing. Most are not available for general access. However, a small number—particularly of early episodes—are available, and can be viewed through local Screensound offices. A complete description of every episode of the series can be found on the *TV Eye* website.

Notes

1 *Homicide* ceased production in 1975, but new episodes were aired sporadically until January 1977.

2 According to the Anderson ratings.

3 The first drama program produced in Australia was the pilot episode of *The Adventures of Al Munch*, starring Bud Tingwall (1952), produced for the United States market. *Long John Silver* was made in 1955, again for the USA. These were followed by programs such as *The House on the Corner* (1957), *Take That* (1957), *Autumn Affair* (1958), *Emergency* (1959), *Stormy Petrel* (1960), *Consider Your Verdict* (1961), and *Whiplash* (1961) (Keating 1999b; Moran 1985: 77). During the period 1956–66, the ABC produced 'nearly 400 plays' (Davies 1981: 98).

4 The only voice I can find complaining about the Australian accent is that of a rather snobbish drama critic, who writes in 1978 that 'On principle the Crawfords stuck to using Australian themes, characters, settings and street dialogue (however monotonous this "Strine" might become)' (Rees 1978: 386).

5 It should be noted that I am here discussing only the early episodes of *Homicide*, and the public discussion that took place around them. Chris Keating argues strongly that the program underwent a 'quantum jump in technical quality when the series went to all-film colour in 1972. From that point, the program achieved a far more cohesive look, each episode was presided over by the one director'. Also, he notes that 'the introduction of colour film gave the opportunity for a more experimental style: hand-held cameras, rapid cuts, fantasy sequences to depict psychosis or derangement, and so on' (pers. comm. 17 May 2000).

6 Thanks to the delegates at the 1999 MIT Media in Transition Conference for this insight.

4

The Mavis Bramston Show: Popular Politics

1964–68

On 21 July 1965, *The Mavis Bramston Show* rated over 50 in Sydney, and became the number two rating program of the year nationally (Beilby 1981: 1), thus becoming a 'sensation' that is well remembered in journalistic areas of the public archive (Murphy 1981: 70; Johnson & Smiedt 1999: 169; Jones & Bednall 1980: 24; Davies 1981: 125). *Homicide*, the popular Australian cop show, was rating remarkably well, but even it did not reach the top five programs in Australia until later in its run; *Mavis*, by contrast, once rated a previously unheard-of 59 in Sydney (Davies 1981: 126). It is remembered not only as being 'important in the development of Australian comedy on television' (Herd 1988: 6), but also as 'the first Australian show to use social and political satire as the main source of its humour' (Harris 1994: 113), the program that 'ma[de] it OK to give politicians the disrespect they deserved' (Dale 1998: 4).

It is possible to argue that the importance of *The Mavis Bramston Show* lies in its introduction of the sketch comedy format to Australian television, a format that would continue throughout the decades, producing such spectacular successes as *Fast Forward* (Keating 1999b). However, looking at the program now, its format—a mixture of comedy monologues to camera, sketches, and musical numbers—seems to have much in common with the variety shows that made up such a large part of Australia's early television scheduling. What seems to have been more revolutionary is what *Mavis* had that these later programs did *not* have: political commentary, entertainingly told. It included sketches that commented on politics, on the news of the day, and on important social issues. Devoting a program entirely to such a form of entertaining social commentary—this had not been done before on

Australian television, and explains why its satirical content is an important part of the way it is collectively remembered in Australia.

Mavis's place in television history

The program debuted on 11 November 1964. Presented by three hosts—Carol Raye, Gordon Chater, and Barry Creyton—its format was a mixture of comedy sketches and songs, performed by the stars and a variety of guests. Many of these sketches and songs commented directly on political and social issues of the day. The first episodes were shown only in Sydney. From the sixth episode, it was also shown in other cities.

As noted above, *Mavis*'s format is similar to that of the variety programs that had dominated the first years of Australian television. Indeed, some of the moments from the program that have best survived in the public archive are very similar to elements of preceding variety shows. Gordon Chater used the word 'bum' in *The Mavis Bramston Show*—several times—and this became something of a cause célèbre in a similar way to Graham Kennedy's later 'fuck'. Another fondly remembered moment is almost traditional sketch comedy: the 'Flower arrangement' sketch. This

> became a short-lived legend … [reading from] an innocent book on flowers … Gordon Chater and Carol Raye wrung every last double entendre and risque nuance from the book's instructions on how to arrange flowers, from stamen to stem, from pistil to bloom.
>
> (Davies 1981: 126)

The sketch goes as follows:

> 'I don't like this book', says Chater—'*Floral Arrangement* by Constance Spry … you know what I say, if its popular, its filthy'. He reads from the book. 'Before starting an arrangement, the longest stem should be selected, first making sure that it is strong enough to act as a centrepiece in the display. Take the stem and place it in a bowl of water, then dip it in wax to preserve the bloom for a period.'
>
> (*35 Years of Television* 1991)

Chater pauses over words such as 'stem' and 'bloom', reading them as though they were filth—and it does, indeed, sound very dirty.

Such moments, however, are not what I wish to focus on in this chapter. In their own right, they resemble more a risqué version of *In Melbourne*

Tonight's comedy sketches than a complete change from what had gone before. It is true that sketches such as these used innuendo and double entendre far more scandalous than that appearing in earlier shows, but this is a difference of degree rather than of nature.

What interests me rather more are those moments on *Mavis* when the comedy is not about lewdness, or about challenging boundaries around language and sexuality, but more a satirical attempt to engage with politics and other social issues of the time. This is what *Mavis* offered that had not previously been available on Australian television. True, some commentators find elements of satire—commentary on topical political and social issues—in programs such as Ray Taylor's *Sydney Tonight* (Johnson & Smiedt 1999). And it could be argued that *In Melbourne Tonight* occasionally makes topical comment, with Graham Kennedy, for example, making jokes about the cricket tour of the West Indies. However, as one *IMT* writer remembers:

> There was far more comedic value in joking about Ron Barassi's injured knee or the price of beer going up than in some obscure political issue, unless of course it was an issue like an increase in the price of beer.
>
> (Jones 1999: 46)

By contrast, the degree to which *Mavis Bramston* featured topical issues—even to the exclusion of humour, rather than as a focus for it—seems to be what marks it as a turning point in Australian television.

The Mavis Bramston Show is commonly referred to as a 'satirical' television program. Such a description implies two things about the program: first that it is comic, and second that it makes social comment (Paulson 1967: 3). The term, as with all such descriptions, is necessarily a loose one. The program is not strictly satire, for example, under the precise description offered by the *Oxford English Dictionary*, which would make it more of a 'lampoon' (*Oxford English Dictionary* 1989: 500). Nevertheless, the term is a useful one for drawing attention to the way in which *The Mavis Bramston Show*—as well as showing the comedy that can be drawn from saying the word 'bum'—was involved in a project of 'socially oriented moral and intellectual reform' (Connery & Combe 1995: 2), by 'identifying and condemning behaviour and men [*sic*] [it] regards as vicious' (Pollard 1970: 1).

Placing *Bramston*

The Mavis Bramston Show was the first Australian television program to make it into the country's top five most popular programs. But as in previous chapters, the question of what this might mean in terms of national identity is raised by the fact that this is another program explicitly modelled on an overseas example.

Although satire itself is not specifically a British form, it does have a long history in Britain, both in literary and popular forms (Elkin 1973; Sanders 1995: 237). And it was in Britain that satire moved into television: in 1962, with the appearance of *That Was the Week that Was* (popularly known as *TW3*), a satirical television program that 'brought politics and show business closer together' (Hewison 1986: 30). And *Mavis Bramston* was explicitly modelled on this show. As Carol Raye, creator of the program, says of the invention of *The Mavis Bramston Show*:

> The most popular program in Britain at that time was the satirical, news-oriented *That Was The Week That Was* … 'We weren't doing anything like that in Australia … We had big musical shows, but nothing satirical' … She suggested the idea to James Oswin [general manager] who wasn't impressed … 'I'm not sure that Australians are ready to laugh at themselves.'
>
> (Johnson & Smiedt 1999: 161)

Mavis—like *IMT*, *Four Corners*, and *Homicide* before it—was modelled on an imported example. But unlike these previous programs, *Mavis* applied its satirical approach to the very question of the relationship between Australian and British national identities in television programs.

In the first episode of the program, we are told by Gordon Chater that the station management has insisted on having an English star in order to guarantee televisual success—and that one 'Mavis Bramston' has been chosen (she is in fact a fictitious character, invented for the program). We are told this in the very first filmed sketch in the first episode, where Gordon Chater begins by telling the audience that 'You all must be desperate to meet the star of the show' and explains that, while the station was keen to have Miss Bramston, her performance turned out to be so bad that the production team would not let her appear on the show (*The Mavis Bramston Show* 1964). Chater then presents her audition tape, a performance of English upper-class idiocy in which 'Mavis' herself, with the kind of English accent that can cut glass, talks about her 'mummy' and her desires to come to Australia: 'It sounds so dinky. I absolutely adore the wide open thing'. We then see her performing a musical number, where everything about the shooting and performance conspires to make this supposed star look ridiculous: silly hair, silly frock, silly dancing, a very dodgy deep voice that doesn't hit many of the notes, and an over-expressive performance style with lots of very quick movements, big lip action, and eye-rolling. The program's very title, then, is a commentary on the cultural cringe, on the over-reliance on imported stars in Australia, and a lack of trust in the ability of Australian stars to interest the Australian population. It might be based on a British example, but the program explicitly and satirically insists that this does not make it a culturally cringing example of downplaying Australian talent.

Given this project, it is odd to note that the program's stars are—either literally, or in performance—all English. As Grahame Bond—the man who gave us Aunty Jack—noted years later, 'Gordon Chater was English, Carol Raye was English and Barry Creyton wasn't, but he wanted to be ... It was all terribly British and Noel Coward' (Johnson & Smiedt 1999: 184). Again, the program did not ignore this slightly difficult fact. Also in a sketch in the first episode, it is the subject of a comic song. Carol Raye (the English star) and June Salter (the Australian guest star) sing a song of comparisons. June starts with 'I'm an Aussie and you're a pommy', and the song goes on to list a series of antinomies associated with this binary: 'You're so Harpers, you're so Manchester Guardian, and I'm so Pix and Pose'; lemon squash/shandy, OBE/RSL, Benson and Hedges/roll your own, ending with the consensual statement that 'We'll be partners' and 'We belong together'. It is interesting, considering *Mavis*'s relationship to the cultural cringe, that when June Salter is singing her part in this song, she puts on a very broad Australian accent, which only serves to draw attention to the fact that the rest of the time her cultured accent sounds little different from Carol Raye's pom. There is little unashamed Australian accent in *Mavis*, despite its critical attention to the cultural cringe. The relationship of *Mavis* with England is certainly an ambivalent one.

Mavis in Australia

Despite its lack of claims to world-beating originality, *Mavis* was immensely important in Australian television—for making satire a popular and central part of the Australian mediasphere. As noted above, it is remembered in the public archive as 'the first Australian show to use social and political satire as the main source of its humour' (Harris 1994: 113), and its impact can be seen in the comments of the Australian Broadcasting Control Board in its report of 1965:

> A type of programme relatively new to Australian television came into prominence during the year in the form of locally-produced topical revue, consisting largely of satire ... the emergence of this type of programme was not foreseen

> in 1956 when the Board's Programme Standards were determined. Often only a fine line divides acceptable matter from that which fails to stand the test of ordinary good taste and common sense ... Nowhere is this more evident than in the field of satire ... After consideration of some examples of 'adult' programmes, the Board found it necessary to express its views in a letter sent to all commercial television stations:
>
> > "The avowed object of these programmes is to deal frankly, satirically and facetiously with a number of subjects, some of which, in the first few years of television in this country, would have been regarded as unsuitable for the medium in the social climate of that time. This development seems to be world-wide, and to represent a basic change in attitudes ... The Board regards the maintenance of good taste in television programmes as basic, and is concerned at the use of words and phrases and the discussion of topics which are not even now generally acceptable in mixed company ... the Board thinks it should say that it is possible for adult programmes to be facetious, satirical and sophisticated without necessarily containing vulgarity or indecent suggestions, or employing socially undesirable words, phrases and exclamations" '
>
> (ABCB 1965: 60–2)

For the Board, then, the success of *Mavis* had radically altered the mediasphere they were attempting to police, to the extent that it demanded direct intervention. And it is not simply 'vulgarity' and the use of inappropriate language that so worried the Board. There was also the problem that satire just didn't take public events *seriously* enough, with the reverence and rationality that, surely, they demanded (see Chapter 2):

> The development of Australian topical revue programmes ... led to an unusually large volume of correspondence from viewers. This mainly took the form of adverse criticism (often in very general terms) ... Discussions of current moral or social issues often occur in panel programmes. Complaints received by the Board suggested that serious topics had been treated with ill-considered levity. Stations were advised that it is essential to avoid ... appearing to give irresponsible comment
>
> (Board 1965: 73)

'Ill-considered levity' about 'serious topics'—the refusal to treat political issues, institutions and figures with reverence; the desire to blend genres, to render public affairs entertaining—these might be *Mavis*'s gifts to Australian television. The idea of using comedy as a way to interrogate serious issues of social and political moment had not previously been a part of Australian television. The sudden emergence of such an approach in the Australian mediasphere had the guardians of television's morality concerned.

Knowing what is funny

There is a wonderful sequence before the title sequence of the first episode of *Mavis*'s second season. Two of the stars—Carol Raye and Gordon Chater—are dressed up as a middle-aged couple, sitting in front of the television. Gordon starts the conversation.

GC	'What's on now, love?'
CR	' ... that *Mavis Bramston Show* starts again tonight.'
GC	'That rubbish? We're not going to watch that.'
CR	'Too subtle for you ... all those political jokes and skits, way over your head.'
GC	' ... subtle? They said "bum" one night. What's subtle about that?'
CR	'It had satirical content.'

(*The Mavis Bramston Show* 1965)

The interesting part of the sketch for my argument is that Carol Raye takes it upon herself to tutor Gordon Chater as to how he should be watching the program. He is not a good enough viewer; he fails to understand that 'political jokes and skits' can be funny. This idea of teaching the audience how to react to the program is interesting—they must be taught how to know what is funny. *Mavis* refuses generic distinctions: current affairs versus sketch show; solemn issues versus amusing performances. The 'ill-considered levity' of the program is not its only disturbing aspect. Just as noticeable is *Mavis*'s refusal to limit itself to 'levity'. Watching the program now, it presents some very awkward moments when the audience in the studio obviously do not know if they are meant to be laughing. Satire is not simply about challenging the ways in which 'serious' issues might be discussed. It also—at least in the case of *Mavis Bramston*—challenges the very distinction between the serious and entertaining, the comic and the disturbing.

Tony Fitzgerald suggests that 'Although not essential, humour is a common component of satire' (Fitzgerald 1999: 14). This is worth emphasising: humour is not essential in satire. Indeed, the fact that satire often lacks humour is one of its most interesting characteristics. Anyone who has ever read a copy of the satirical British magazine *Punch* will know that satire is often profoundly unfunny. It is interesting that *Mavis Bramston* takes advantage of its generic status as satire to say things that would otherwise be unsayable. It can use the excuse of being entertainment and comedy, even when it is not being funny. In a mediasphere where *Four Corners* producers could be sacked for showing any kind of 'bias', *Mavis* gets away with making very pointed comment—often without any perceptible humour—simply on the basis of its generic status as 'satire'. The uncomfortable effects of this can be seen in the reaction of a contemporary audience—the studio audience—to the program. The audience in the studio for television programs often tells us how we should react to what we see on television: we know that a joke has been made because the studio audience laughs (in many sit coms, this is the only way that we know that something is meant to be funny). The audience in the studio for *The Mavis Bramston Show*, our guides as to how we should react to this program, often seem confused by what is happening in front of them. They just don't know what to do.

Sketch comedy

The program mixes a variety of different kinds of sketch. As noted above, it is at some times a typical sketch comedy. In one justly famous sketch (which ends the very first episode of the program), Gordon Chater enters the studio, dressed in a suit, and stands on a piece of plastic. He proceeds to sing a song, while abusing himself in various ways: squirting himself in the ear with a soda siphon; squashing tomatoes in his own face; breaking eggs over his head; shoving cake in his face. He finishes doing this and then does it all again, faster. The studio audience are in hysterics. It is an impressive piece of physical comedy, performed with perfect timing, and I found it very funny (*The Mavis Bramston Show* 1964). An item like this could, perhaps, have appeared on *In Melbourne Tonight*. It is not satire; it is not topical revue; it is a man squashing a tomato in his face.

Similarly, in the same episode, June Salter performs a comic song, 'I lost him in the autumn leaves at Loura', a song about a lover lost in a park: 'Our picnic was a failure—now he's food for an azalea'. There is no topical comment in this (*The Mavis Bramston Show* 1964).

Topical comedy

As well as such items, *Mavis* also features comedy sketches that do in fact deal explicitly with social and political issues of the time. For instance, in the first episode of the program, Carol Raye appears, dressed up like a fairytale princess, to sing a song about the legislation that controls the airlines owned by Reg Ansett:

> Reg Ansett has control of all the air … and there's no legal limit to his power here, in Canberra … Monopoly is Reg's favourite hobby … he muscled in on Brisbane's television … Reginald knows who his good friends are … he knows the kind of way to make his venture pay … from Canberra
>
> (*The Mavis Bramston Show* 1964)

After repeated viewings, I am still uncertain about why this song is delivered while dressed like a fairytale princess, but it is obvious that it is an accusation of insider dealing on the part of the government, delivered in a song, sung in the style of music hall, with some jokes in it.

This is an example of the topical comedy in *Mavis*: its topicality can perhaps be measured by the extent to which it is now incomprehensible. For example the lyrics of the theme song from the first episode of the program are now mystifying to the uninitiated: 'We're sure you adore Harry Jensen/ For keeping our pretty city clean./We won't mention books obscene/or even the pill machine!'

Topical comment

The third kind of segment in *Mavis Bramston*, however, is the most disconcerting: These are the sketches—particularly common in the first few episodes, but surviving throughout its run—which are suddenly, crushingly not funny.

This is not the unfunniness of a failed joke or a badly done routine. It is rather speeches and comments that have no place in them for humour. Their positioning in this sketch show is odd, and they signify the importance of *Mavis Bramston* in defining a genre that was unlike anything that had gone before.

Each episode of *Mavis Bramston* starts with 'The headlines from *Oz Magazine*', a series of short jokes on topical issues. The tone of these is often extremely ambivalent. In the sixth episode of the first season (the first episode of *Mavis* to be transmitted outside of Sydney), Barry Creyton's headline is the following: 'In England it is said to be better that nine guilty men go free than one innocent man die. Mississippi can do better than that. They let nineteen guilty men go free and three innocent men die' (*The Mavis Bramston Show* 1964). As Creyton delivers this line, there are some very uncertain titters from the audience, quickly stifled. They are not, apparently, sure if it is meant to be funny. This is a satirical comedy show—they seem to suspect that it *should* be funny. But it is also obvious that stating that three innocent men have been allowed to die by a corrupt legal system is not, in itself, very funny. Creyton goes on: 'It may not seem very just, but it is what the white people want, and in Mississippi, white is right'. This is the punch line. We know this because when he finishes saying it, an amusing noise (a 'boing' from a large drum) is added to the soundtrack. The audience laughs, presumably out of relief: this is a comedy show, after all. But it is not, really. There is no joke in what Creyton says. It is not funny.

In the first show of the 1965 season—the moment when *Mavis* began to climb the national ratings so spectacularly—there is an item named 'The Mavis Bramston Viewpoint'. This is a regular segment in the show. It is introduced by a caption, giving this title, and a photograph of the character of Mavis posing beside it, holding her spectacles, pouting and posing in an affected manner. Already there is a double coding: this may be the equivalent of a newspaper editorial, but it should not be taken entirely seriously. After all, there is Mavis, the figure of fun in the program, standing right beside it.

In this episode, the 'Viewpoint' is about warfare and conscription. It takes the form of a poem, recited by June Salter. The sketch starts with June standing in a suburban living room, looking at a photograph on the mantelpiece of a man in an army uniform. She is speaking to the photograph:

> Just twenty-one long years ago, for us the world stood still
> That sacred year when love was life and you were sent to kill
> Officially that's not the term, t'was in the line of duty …
> I wonder if you knew the years of loneliness it meant?
> I wonder if you knew the stilted telegram they sent?
> When I held Johnny in my arms and wished that you were there …
> It's hard to assess values; I'm confused to know what's right.
> Is there only one solution: that we have to live and fight?
> How do I know that next year our boy will be alive?
> Will politics and patriotism and worldwide peace campaign
> Mean that Johnny has to be a soldier just the same?
> Indonesia and Malaysia, what if war they must declare?
> If I have to face another parting darling, this year—please be there
>
> (*The Mavis Bramston Show* 1965)

The sketch finishes without a single laugh and fades to black. There is a brief delay, and the audience bursts into applause. The segment is not a sketch—it is not funny in that sense. The audience obviously knows that it is not meant to be funny. Even though the program is satire, even though we have heard Chater saying 'bum' and seen him breaking eggs over his own head, the genre of satire does not demand that everything is funny. If we were to see a recitation such as this on *Fast Forward*, we would not know how to take it. It would seem out of place. But for satire, it is more acceptable.

It is notable that the controversies that are most commonly remembered from *Mavis Bramston* are those that feature bums and flower arranging. It might have been thought that those segments that are not funny, but deliberately comment on national policy in a way most critical of the government of the time, would have been more provocative. But apparently this was not the case. As noted above, at this time *Four Corners* was being publicly upbraided for being biased—indeed, in the week that *Mavis* was first broadcast, several staff members of that program were sacked for such reasons. And yet *Mavis*'s blatantly unbalanced political commentary seems to have avoided such public recriminations.

There are other moments that are even more confronting, and even less amusing. The very first episode of *The Mavis Bramston Show* features poetry by Kath Walker (later known as Oodgeroo Noonuccal). Again, the segment is 'The Mavis Bramston Viewpoint', and it is introduced by Gordon Chater. He talks about 'a coloured friend of mine' in the USA, 'a very famous Negro entertainer'. His friend refuses a tour of Australia because of 'the colour problem'. Chater states that he realises there is indeed a colour problem, but he has not seriously thought about it before because the Aboriginal population are 'all locked up on reservations'.

We then see a series of shots of an indigenous fringe-dwelling settlement—images now familiar to us from programs such as *Four Corners* and *Sixty Minutes* (so familiar, in fact, that they have become one of the dominant ways of representing indigenous Australians in the media)—showing shanty huts and the ragged clothes worn by children as they play. We then cut back to Chater, looking very serious: 'Here are three poems by Queensland Aboriginal writer Kath Walker', he says. He is shot in close-up, against black. There is nothing here to suggest that this is comedy, and the audience is certainly not laughing as Chater goes on with his monologue: 'The Aborigines can't forget the past, the mass murders, the slave dealers, and the crimes of our early dealings with the blacks. But Kath Walker writes about them with compassion and pride, never self-pity. She writes with hope for the future and says Let us judge the white man by the best of his race'. Each of the three presenters then reads, in close-up and shot against black, one of Kath Walker's poems.

From a perspective of several decades on, it is easy to critique the content and presentation of these poems: they present an evolutionary account of culture, whereby indigenous people are understood to be more primitive than the settlers and, given time, will develop to become more like them and assimilate. There is also something very odd about having three white personalities reading the poetry, Gordon Chater stating: 'I am black of skin among whites, and I am proud', with no indigenous faces appearing in the studio to comment. But none of this should deflect us from considering that this is an entertainment comedy program, and the most sensationally popular Australian program of 1965. This item is not comedy. The audience does not laugh but sits through the segment in total silence. After Chater finishes the poem, there are, again, several moments silence—and then the audience bursts into applause.

This is 'satire'. We then cut straight to a parody of *Pick-a-Box*, where the panellists have to guess what a viewer's problem is. When this sketch begins, the audience can once again laugh heartily. The comedy is certain again.

Other examples show the audience really uncertain about what it is they are watching, and how they should react to it. Again, in the first episode of the program, an entirely jokeless segment celebrates the anniversary of the end of the First World War. Chater and Creyton perform a medley of songs from 1918. They are dressed in uniforms from the war, wearing false moustaches. The audience at first seems uncertain what to do with this. As the songs progress, a single female audience member can be heard laughing, alone and uncertainly, from time to time. Then the performances begin to get more excessive. They sing in different voices. By the time they have reached the final song 'Australia will be there'—a nationalistic song, with the Australian flag superimposed over them—they are laughing while they sing, and the audience is beginning to laugh more heartily. This is, perhaps, comedy. They are, perhaps, taking the piss out of nationalism. The clues are there—but they are only clues—and the audience is convinced. This is comedy. They laugh at it.

Again, in the first episode, just before Chater begins to pelt himself with tomatoes, Creyton leads a singsong with the studio audience to celebrate the fact that 'the world is currently at peace'. As the audience gets into singing 'Friends and neighbours put a smile on the gloomiest face', a jolly and upbeat song, the camera cuts to a series of still images: soldiers torturing agonised civilians, bodies lying in the street, the Ku Klux Klan, shots of tanks, of Hitler, and of Churchill (these two presented one after the other, with no suggestion that one might be worse than the other). Once again, the audience doesn't know what to do; presumably it's hard to laugh when you're in the middle of a singsong.

Mavis's impact

A few years after *Mavis*'s success, a rather po-faced account of television 'public affairs' in 1968 remembers *Mavis Bramston* as a bad influence on current affairs across Australian television. The writer draws a distinction between first-level public affairs programming (direct reportage of news) and

> The second level [which] is more elastic and allows for an expansion of comment or discussion ... It's of some interest to me to have watched the way in which *The Mavis Bramston Show* paved the way for the widened scope of comment in second-level documentaries introducing a degree of cursing, colloquialism and candour which, having been accepted as amusing entertainment, seeped steadily into areas which had previously been labelled as 'information' areas ... we are entirely accustomed to being informed, visually and verbally, about the lives and times of nonconformists of all kinds and the acceptance of *Bramston* ... on the local scene ... has been paralleled by the acceptance of documentary material on a much more broad-minded level than most of us would have thought possible a few years ago.
>
> (Denton 1968: 47)

Kit Denton is here as obsessed with the issue of coarse language as the Australian Broadcasting Control Board. But it is perhaps *Mavis*'s transgressive bringing together of the serious and the entertaining in its satire that can be seen to have the most lasting impact on the Australian mediasphere, and for which it is well remembered. So, although Nick Herd can note that *Mavis* 'did not immediately spawn any shows of similar format', and that 'It was another ten years before commercial television again attempted revue and sketch comedy with *The Naked Vicar Show*' (Herd 1988: 6), it may be that this is the wrong place to look. Comedy sketch shows may not have immediately become central to Australian television, but it is possible to see *Mavis* influencing other forms of television. As David Dale remembers the program in his 1998 article on 'The 50 Most Influential Shows in Australian Television History', '*The Mavis Bramston Show* let us celebrate our tall poppy syndrome, making it OK to give politicians the disrespect they deserved (and preparing us for the irreverence of our first national current affairs show, *This Day Tonight*)' (Dale 1998: 4).

In particular, when the ABC started the daily current affairs program *This Day Tonight* in 1967, it contained a satirical element that previous current affairs had not highlighted. Many commentators have described this program as 'hard-hitting journalis[m]' (Moran 1997a 117; see also Lloyd 1988: 238). But in accounts of the program by its makers, this is not what is foregrounded. Stuart Littlemore, for example, recalls having Peter Cook and Dudley Moore—the former a central figure in the development of satire in the United Kingdom with his club The Establishment—on *This Day Tonight* doing a satirical sketch about interviewing politicians (Littlemore 1996: 86–8). He also remembers using a parody of the theme song from *The Adventures of Barry McKenzie* to make fun of the Prime Minister, Gough Whitlam. For Littlemore, '*TDT* had built its success on assaulting the conservative values of postwar Australia ... through aggressive interviewing of complacent politicians, tendentious filmmaking in documentary form, [and] satire' (Littlemore 1996: 110–11).

Similarly, Bill Peach's memories of the program suggest that one of its most important aspects was its satirical content (Peach 1992: 208). He recalls a performance of a political commentary to the tune of 'John Brown's Body' by a barbershop quartet; a 1973 government raid on ASIO filmed as an episode of the American detective show *The FBI*; inviting Graham Kennedy to work as guest compère on the program (Peach 1992: 198); and giving the world the animated character of Talbot the Worm, 'who became our mascot and occasionally entered the program to comment on the action or merely to offer a knowing wink ... Talbot ... became a cult hero ... and intruded more and more into the show' (Peach 1992: 200).

Nevertheless, and despite *Mavis*'s popularising impetus, satire remained a troubled form on Australian television. In 1972, the ABC was forced to cancel *Our Man in Canberra*, a satirical drama similar to *Yes Minister*, reformatting it as *Our Man in the Company* (Chris Keating, pers. comm., 17 May 2000). In 1977, ABC management pulled Grahame Bond's *Off Show* just before transmission because 'senior executives' were worried that it contained 'political references': 'Bond said the ABC had told the *Off Show*'s producers that they could not include jokes about Australian politicians' ('ABC Axes Parody on Politicians' 1977). As late as 1985, transmission of the satirical program *The Gillies Report* on the ABC could make headline news: 'Aunty Dares to Be Scandalous' (1985).

Mavis largely avoided such charges. But in using its generic affiliation to make explicitly partial, irreverent, and downright rude comment about public affairs, it contributed to the process of challenging hierarchies of authority that has remained an interesting part of Australian television. It is remembered for its sensational ratings and for its revelation of satire, and it survives as such in the public archive of great moments in Australian television.

Availability

Screensound holds the first two 1964 episodes of *The Mavis Bramston Show*, all of the 1965 season, many of the 1966 season, nothing of 1967, and various clips and highlights from 1968. All are available for viewing.

5

Play School: Forbidden Pleasures

1966–

Sometime in the early 1970s, Benita Collings appeared on *Play School* without a bra. This event caused something of a minor scandal. It was unsuitable behaviour, and not acceptable for our children.

At least, according to collective memory this is the case. However, formal and official versions of *Play School*'s history do not allow for this particular memory. The possibility that this might be an important part of the public archive of Australian television was first suggested to me by a colleague. There was some controversy, he said, in the 1970s when Benita appeared on *Play School* without a bra. I was fascinated by this: a perfect example of the way in which children's television is policed in order to keep firmly in place the myth that children are innocent and sexless, and that they must be protected at all costs. Other individual and informal sources in the course of the research for this book remembered this, or similar events. Discussing the book with non-academic friends, one was certain that the braless appearance had occurred: 'I remember that—Benita, without her bra on'. Another friend did not remember the braless incident, but noted that Benita 'always seemed to be bouncing around in a bikini'. Viewers who responded to public calls for information for the book remembered similar incidents from the program, although not with Benita:

> Alan, I heard you on RRR *Creative Tension* bemoaning the denial of Benita's sexuality at Auntie ABC. John is one bent host of *Play School*, continually playing to the parents who watch. E.g. following Monica Trapaga up a ladder into the rocket at close distance, to the camera 'I think I saw the moon!'
>
> (Geoff Kirwood, pers. comm., 1999)

Another colleague notes that 'the other great adult moment was Noni Hazlehurst performing "Everybody's jumping", also without a bra and egged on by John Waters to repeat it. One of the great moments, and one of the few that men seem to remember'.

Benita's breasts caused another scandal in 1998. After she appeared at the Australian television Logie Awards in a revealing dress with a see-through top, the satirical program *The Panel* made an issue of her appearance. On 22 April 1998, in the post-Logies episode, one of the panellists, Kate Langbroek, is introduced. The other members of the panel discuss her dress: 'It's *the* dress', says Santo Cilauro, referring to the fact that her dress has two and half million dollars' worth of diamonds sewn into it. 'Oh no', says Rob Sitch, '*the* dress was the one the *Play School* woman wore [at the Logies].' Discussing the Logies ceremony, Benita is the first star they turn to, and the first clip they show. 'She was fully topless', says Tom Gleisner. 'Have a look at that.' 'I was sitting at home', says Santo, 'and I thought, oh my God, I've got X-Ray vision!' 'Benita said she was very excited to win the award', Tom continues, 'but you could tell she wasn't, because … [he gestures to his nipples]. I'm just glad Big Ted wasn't invited along!' (*The Panel* 1998).

Obviously, such an eclectic collection of individual responses and televisual moments cannot be taken as representative of general public attitudes towards and memories of *Play School*. But what is even more interesting than the consistency of these memories of the scandalous moments of *Play School* and its presenters is the consistency of tone in which they are remembered—a cheeky delight in speaking the unspeakable, that Big Ted might see Benita's nipples—and the fact that no one to whom I explained the project, either face to face or in the various public calls for information for the book, disagreed with the suggestion that *Play School* might have a sexual component.

No one, that is, except the official sources of information about the history of the program. Having established that Benita's braless performance on *Play School* was a moment that was collectively remembered and might belong in the public archive of Australian television, I tried to research the moment. But it proved unresearchable. On a general level, the archives of official sources are not set up for analysis of television at all (the Australian Public Affairs Information Service does not index most published items on television, or even the magazines in which they appear—*TV Week, New Weekly, Who Weekly*). The ABC's own newspaper clippings service has no reference to this moment.

Finally, I spoke to the production office of *Play School*, and to the woman who was executive producer on the program for twenty years. I explained my project: Dr Alan McKee, from Edith Cowan University, writing an academic book to be published by Oxford University Press. I explained my interest in *Play School*, in the boundary between child and adult, the line between what authorities thought children should be allowed to see and what they were not allowed to see, and *Play School*'s place in the public archive in relation to this. Then I told her of the specific moment I was interested in: when Benita appeared without a bra and caused a minor scandal. Could she help me with any information about this event? She was not impressed. Yes, she said, of course she remembered this moment (so it *did* happen), but she was certainly not going to speak about it. She suggested that only a 'pervert' would ask something like that and refused to make any further comment on the incident. Benita did appear without a bra; more importantly, this was a matter that was noticed in the mediasphere. But it is an unspeakable event. The moment does not exist in official archives, and it does not exist for the production office of the program. It is only in the non-official and non-written aspects of collective memory—perhaps 'folk memory' is a subset of collective memory here—that the incident survives as a great moment in Australian television, and one deserving of archiving as part of our cultural heritage.

Play School as children's programming

Play School is a children's program—one of the longest running on Australian television[1]—and its presenters are 'national treasures' (Gleitzman 1992: 28). The program has had the same theme tune, and the same basic opening titles, for over thirty years (compare this with the numerous changes in tone and style that have characterised a program such as *Four Corners*) (Keating 1999b). *Play School* was one of four children's television programs—along with *Here's Humphrey*, *Mr Squiggle*, and *Bananas in Pyjamas*—to make it onto the set of commemorative 'Australian children's television' stamps released by Australia Post in 1999.

The program is aimed at preschoolers, under the age of five. It is set in a studio, where two presenters (usually one male and one female) tell stories illustrated using a series of well-known dolls (Big Ted, Humpty Dumpty, and others), demonstrate dances, and introduce basic skills (reading the time) and arts (making dolls out of socks). The focus of the program is the presenters: they must carry the half-hour of television with their performances.

The idea of 'children's programming' is a fascinating one. Philippe Aries has famously argued that it was only in the nineteenth century that the category of 'the child'—as a distinct group of human beings with particular attributes—evolved in the form that we now know it (Aries 1973). Before this time, he suggests, children were basically seen as smaller versions of adults. Part of the special identity that was invented for children at this time, according to his account, was an innocence and naivety in regard to sexual matters. Although it is in one way common sense to acknowledge that children are sexual beings, as all human beings are in some way (see, for example, Jackson 1982; Goldman & Goldman 1988; Martinson 1994), the opposite is equally commonsensical: to deny that children are sexual beings. They are, after all, innocent and pure (it is telling that a library search for this chapter using the keywords 'child/ren' and 'sex/uality' produced nine works on children's sexuality, and over five hundred on sexual abuse of children). The very idea of children's television programming works with the modern ideal of children as a separate class of people, requiring particular programs to be addressed to them, dealing with particular issues in particular ways. Lynn Spigel describes the desire to protect children from television as 'a new skirmish in a much older battle' over defining children's culture (Spigel 1992: 52), citing examples as far back as controversies over dime novels at the turn of the twentieth century.

Children's programming must be suitable for children—which means that it must be educational, morally impeccable, and not sexual. Since the beginning of television in Australia, governmental bodies have been involved in legislating and controlling the medium to make sure that this has been the case. The Advisory Committee on Children's Programmes for the Australian Broadcasting Control Board functioned from 1956 to 1971 (Edgar & Callus 1979: 66; ABCB 1957: 46); it was replaced by the Advisory Committee on Children's Programmes, from 1971 to 1978, and then the Children's Program Committee, from 1978 to 1992. Although these bodies were directly responsible only for commercial channels, the Reports, Guidelines, and Principles they produced regarding what children should be watching on Australian television provide a useful intertext for understanding attitudes towards children's programming that were present in the public sphere. Throughout these prescriptions runs the common thread that, as Wendy Keys puts it, 'Children are seen on the one hand as innocent, natural and in need of protection, whilst on the other hand they are perceived as undeveloped, irrational and incomplete beings who must be disciplined and civilised' (Keys 1999: 9).

Children's programming, at various times in Australia's television history, has been required to 'impart real appreciation of the spiritual values and of the qualities of courage, honour and integrity which are essential to the full development of the individual and of national greatness',[2] and to 'set a good example to children, in … personal standards' (ABCB 1963: 106). Children's programming should not offer 'entertainment', at least not as an end in itself (Children's Television Advisory Committee 1974: 5–6). There should be, according to the 1945 Broadcasting Principles (originally designed for radio programming), 'no profanity or vulgarity', no representations of 'torture … the supernatural' or any 'incident which will create in their minds morbid suspense or hysteria'; there must be no dangerous acts that a child could copy (ABCB 1963. 106). And, it seems, there should be no sexuality, although in 1945 this could not even be mentioned explicitly as an injunction. Rather, the Principles note vaguely that the child must be protected from 'aspects of life' for which he [*sic*] 'is not equipped'. The Production Guidelines released by the second Committee comment—for the first time explicitly in this genre—on matters of sex and violence. '[E]xplicit sexual encounters', they suggest, 'would hold little interest or relevance for children of primary school age.' Children also needed to be protected from the wrong kinds of presenters in their programming; presenters must be well educated and well spoken, and must not 'commit glaring solecisms' in their speech (ABCB 1963: 103).

John and Benita on *Play School*

This is what children's programming should be: educational, innocent, and directed towards the romantic ideal of the angelic child. But, as we have seen, there are moments that are collectively remembered from *Play School* that are about other aspects of the program entirely—moments that are about cheeky sexuality. Returning to episodes from the early 1970s with this possibility of reading in mind, the show emerges as a fascinating palimpsest where the naive and childish performances of the presenters are overlaid with a sexuality and humour that is not countenanced in the strict idea of children's programming desired by governmental bodies.

Episodes 406–410 of *Play School* were recorded in 1975. Each features Benita, although she does not remain 'monogamous' even for a week, appearing with co-presenters Peter, Don, and John Waters in the space of five episodes. In all of them, Benita and her co-stars present a performance that is aimed at children, in the sense that the presenters speak very slowly, avoid complex sentence structures, and smile determinedly all the time. As the Australian comedy program *Full Frontal* puts it in a critique of the way in which *Play School* presenters perform for children: 'Patronising. That's a long word, isn't it children? Do you know what "patronising" means?' It is interesting on the copies that the ABC supplies to see the clapperboard identifications before the programs. In one of these, the presenter Peter can be seen in the background, wearing his spectacles and studying the script. When the episode starts, however, the glasses and the script vanish, and he becomes a man-child (*Play School* 1975b). The only similar performances I can recall outside of the genre of children's programming are in the film *Les Idiots*, where a group of actors pretend to be intellectually challenged. For a viewer outside of the demographic that the program aims to address, the endless smiling and repetition of words is quite disturbing. Peter talks to a roll of sticky tape—'I'll put you back in the useful box, sticky'—and mutters 'pour pour pour pour pour' to himself as uses the jug he has just made. Taking it over to Benita, he offers her some (pretend) orange juice. She giggles with delight: 'Oooh, yes'. He sings as he pours: 'Glug, glug, glug, in Benita's jug, out of the big jug, glug, glug, glug' (*Play School* 1975a). These performances obviously aim for aspects of preschool childish behaviour; watching as an adult, seeing adult bodies performing these actions, is very odd.

Benita and her co-presenters also use their bodies very differently from most adults. They do not relax, rather, they hold themselves very carefully. Whenever they sit next to each other—as when they are singing about the animals you might meet in the bush (*Play School* 1975c), or playing the 'clapping and foot tapping game' (*Play School* 1975d)—they very carefully do not touch each other.

Given this insistence on performing a version of childish behaviour, the clothing of Benita, Don, John, and Peter is slightly odd. They all wear (what was for the time) trendy and surprisingly sexy clothing. Benita's make-up is mid-1970s stylish: blue eye shadow and shiny dark pink lips. Her clothes include a bright green top with big lapels (*Play School* 1975a), a green T-shirt top worn tight on her breasts with no bra, through which her nipples are clearly visible (*Play School* 1975b), and a skin-tight ribbed blue jumper (*Play School* 1975e). Such tight sweaters have definite sexual connotations: breasts do not have to be uncovered to be provocative. Although it was thirty years earlier, it is interesting to note that in the 1940s the Production Code Administration in America refused to certify films that featured ' "sweater shots" that emphasized the women's breasts by way of tight, close-fitting garments'. Indeed, the censors threatened 'to reject any film featuring women in tight angora sweaters' ('the sweater industry immediately protested') (Black 1997: 33). It is true that the program does not push the audience towards these breasts. There are no close-ups of the sweaters; nor are there comments on Benita's looks (see chapter 11), apart from the moment where Benita and Peter have played a dressing-up game and he asks the camera, 'Doesn't Benita look funny?' (*Play School* 1975b). Despite such caveats, it is undeniably the case that *Play School* in 1975 presents a variety of 'sweater shots' of Benita Collings.

It is not only Benita whose dress is stylishly and sexually at odds with a childlike performance. The male presenters are even more sexualised. Peter, for example, is a rugged looking man who appears in episode 406 lying on a shagpile rug, wearing a natty ruffled shirt, which is undone to his navel to reveal a spectacular swatch of chest hair. At one point, he is sitting down and leaning forward so that we can see, inside the shirt, his hairy chest right down to his navel (*Play School* 1975a). A later episode shows his pink shirt open several buttons to reveal not only his hairy chest, but also his gold medallion (*Play School* 1975b). Both Don and John Waters wear their shirts open to the second button, although both of these men are smooth-chested (*Play School* 1975d).

I suggested at the start of this chapter that Benita's sexuality has been an important part of *Play School*'s image in the collective memories of Australian viewers. I was also presented with evidence—again, informal folk-memory accounts—that women remembered the male presenters in a similar way. One female colleague believed that 'John Waters was put on for the mothers ... *Play School* was full of sexual innuendo. I used to think it was a secret contract between the producers and the mothers that the children and the husbands didn't know about'. Another noted that during the early 1970s, his girlfriend would never miss the program when Mr Waters was presenting it. When I was discussing the book with another female colleague, her response to the question of whether she had ever watched it for the male presenters was an enthusiastic 'Oh, yeah!', said in a tone that meant, 'Of course', while female students, on hearing of the project, made similar responses.[3]

Double entendres

The presenters of *Play School* thus provide a curious palimpsest—not just adult bodies, but adult bodies sexualised through clothing (and, in Benita's case, make-up), performing a childish innocence that is slow and physically careful, reveals no kind of flirtation, and, for the most part, eschews physical contact. It is this odd doubled performance—anti-sexual childishness and adult sexuality co-existing—that explains the peculiar scandal of Benita's breasts, Noni's jumping, and John Water's comments about the moon.

Watching these episodes informed by the knowledge that many viewers were watching precisely for the scandalous undermining of anti-sexual innocence proves a fascinating experience.

Having explained the thesis of this chapter to a class of students, I showed them a clip from episode 408 of *Play School*. The segment in question is the first in the program and features Benita using a hula hoop while John eggs her on from behind. Benita is wearing a very tight blouse and tight jeans (apparently with a bra on—at least, no nipples are visible). She is using a hula hoop—'round and round', she says, wiggling her hips to keep it up. John stands behind her and stares at her bottom—a perfectly reasonable thing to do, given that she is using a hula hoop, but one that is rendered open to salacious interpretation by the look of open-mouthed concentration on his face as he stares at her posterior. 'Oh', he grunts, 'oh, yes', in a way that sounds quite suggestive. When the hula hoop falls, he is ready to encourage her. 'Have another go', he says. Benita picks up the hoop, noting that 'I might wiggle my hips a bit faster this time'. He looks expectant. Benita gets it going again, as John provides a commentary from behind: 'Yes, that's how it's done ... there, it's staying up. Come on—keep wriggling', he says. 'Wriggle, wriggle ... ooh, yes', he says. 'It's going down', she says. 'Keep wriggling', he says (*Play School* 1975c). There is nothing in the segment that demands a sexualised reading, but there is much there that is open to such an interpretation. 'Is it just me?', I asked the students, wary of having my expectations lead my interpretations; their ready laughter at the moment suggested that it was not, that in fact there was plenty of space for seeing dirty exchanges going on in this episode of the ABC's favourite children's program.

With such expectations in place, the possibilities for double entendres by these monstrous child-adults multiply. When Benita and Peter play 'blind man's buff' in episode 407, he sneaks up behind her and ties a scarf around her eyes ('What's this?' ... 'It's only me!'). He then guides her to a seat, holding her carefully by the elbow, and gives her each of the *Play School* toys in turn to hold. She has to guess which toy she's holding by talking us through what she can feel. She guesses Humpty Dumpty, and Jemima (although not before sticking her hands up her skirt). And then, saying 'This one you just won't guess!', he points at himself, mouthing to the camera 'Me!', and then leans over, sticking his head onto Benita's lap. He smiles and giggles as she runs her fingers through his hair, and grabs his ears, and then says 'A very big nose'. After she has finished stroking his face, she guesses who it is. Given the studied lack of physical contact between the program's presenters, this physical performance is markedly sexual—these are sexually mature adults, dressed to emphasise their sexuality, sticking their faces in each other's groins. Peter then finishes the segment by sitting up and saying, 'Right, I'm going to give you one more really hard one now', reaching for the hobby-horse he has just made out of a broom. Benita reaches over towards his groin before grabbing the horse and says with a smile, 'It's a big stick!' (*Play School* 1975b).

Other examples just in these episodes include banter about 'things that we can do together', offers to 'give each other rides', Benita offering to 'blow things' for Don, which turn out to be balloons ('mine's pretty big')—all offering the possibility of double entendres as they are performed by sexualised adults on children's programming (*Play School* 1975d; 1975e)—and Benita's enthusiastic and braless invocation of a visit to 'jumping land' (*Play School* 1975e).

Imagining children

Play School appears in the public archive as a site where the very fact of its address to supposedly innocent children makes the scandal of its sexuality particularly naughty, delightful, and memorable. It is interesting, then, to note that the address to children that secures this sense of transgression may exist only in the minds of adults anyway. It seems that children do not like children's programs, and that they are aimed at adults after all.

The third report of the Advisory Committee on Children's Television to the Australian Broadcasting Control Board (1962) notes with some dismay that

> The Committee has been informed that commercial audience-measurement surveys show that a considerable number of children watch a great deal of television which is not intended for them, and which may be beyond their powers of understanding. We have considered many suggestions for reducing the risk of exposure of children to programmes with which they may be unable to cope, but have failed to find any complete solution, short of reducing television as a whole to a juvenile level.
>
> (ABCB 1963: 102)

The fact that children don't like children's programs is regularly rediscovered in research about viewing, and often with a sense of amazement. In 1966, the *Bulletin* notes that

> From October 3 there will be a major reconstruction of television programs from 3.30 p.m. through to the 7 p.m. news … Children's programs will not be so definitely aimed at age groups. The ABC has found that the younger age group … is in fact, 'imbedded' in the larger audiences … small children will watch programs for older children or for adults if they are given half a chance … the ABC is now more or less prepared to admit that what it thought children wanted to watch is not what children will watch.
>
> ('One More Week' 1966: 30)

'Given half a chance', children will watch adult programs. Of course, the work of children's television programming and the authorities who oversee it is to try to ensure that they are not given such a chance. Nevertheless, children continue to watch the wrong programs. The *Bulletin* suggests that these findings signal

> probably the final demise of the sort of program which serious-minded people thought of as desirable children's television and which experience has shown serves no particular purpose. What does it matter how elevated and worthwhile a program is if no one is watching it?
>
> ('One More Week' 1966: 30)

This proved not to be the case. Ten years later, exactly the same discovery is made again. The *Canberra Times* reports that 'Children [are] "not fond of quota TV" ' ('Children' 1976), and the *Telegraph* that 'Australian children are spurning juvenile television programs in favour of night adult shows' ('Kids Switch to Adult Night TV' 1976). *Woman's Day* comments that

> In a survey, youngsters were asked to name their favourite programs; parents were horrified at the results … a cross-section of six to 14 year olds, *Number 96*, with its titillation, nudity, adults only rating and 8.30 p.m. time slot emerged clear favourite.
>
> (Harris & Irvine 1976)

It is important to note the age ranges that are given for 'children'—here it is only six-year-olds and older who are surveyed. It may be that infants under six years old do prefer *Play School* and similar programs, but these children have rarely been included in the surveying apparatus and they are not included in this recurring public debate. The 1976 ratings survey by the Australian Broadcasting Control Board does include these infants, listing the top ten programs watched by Australians aged '0–9' years. There are no children's programs in this list, although there are several 'family' ones, such as *I Dream of Jeannie*, *Happy Days*, and *The Flintstones* (ABCB 1976: 130).

In 1978, when the relevant category in the survey has become 'children 5–12 years', the top program is *The Paul Hogan Show*. Again, there are no specifically children's programs listed (ABT 1979b: 63). The same is true in 1979 (ABT 1979a: 64), 1980 (ABT 1981a: 62), and 1981 (when *Sale of the Century* is the top rating program for 5–12 year olds) (ABT 1981b: 73).

Once again, this is a surprise to the newspapers. As the *Age Green Guide* reports, under the headline 'Kids Spring TV Surprise':

> Children seem to enjoy adult programming more than their own ... Among children aged 12 to 16 *The Sullivans*, which was designed for an adult audience, was top of the polls ... The children weren't very enthusiastic about ... those programmes classified by the Tribunal as suitable for screening during the three hours ... allocated to children's television each week ... The BBC-produced *Blue Peter* was generally disliked for the patronising manner of its three young adult comperes.
>
> (McKinnon 1979)

It is worth noting that the definition of what constitutes a 'child' has changed: twelve–sixteen-year-olds are considered adults in some contexts in some countries; here, they are still 'children', and thus the fact that they might want to watch 'adult' programming becomes, yet again, a 'surprise'.

In 1986, academic research discovers this fact yet again:

> If 'children's TV' were to be defined by this small group of favourite programs, it would not include many of the programs which are now shown specially for them. In particular, 'C' programs and ABC child drama are not listed by children as top favourites.
>
> (Palmer 1986b: 177)

Indeed, when 'children were asked to list three programs which they "hated" ... *Play School* [scored] 13%' (Palmer 1986b: 125). (Patricia Palmer explains this as older children dismissing something they see as childish.) Children are not stupid, the research discovers: they 'know which programs are meant for them on TV' (Palmer 1986b: 117). But their favourite programs—from this research—are soap operas such as *Sons and Daughters*, *A Country Practice*, and *Prisoner* (Palmer 1986b: 177).

In 1987, research on the ratings effects of the introduction of Children's Television Standards to govern C classification discovered a 'decline in viewing during the C hour ... largely as a result of children not being satisfied with the programs being shown.' Indeed, 'the issue of poor ratings has been a perennial one since the introduction of C ... recent ratings figures do not indicate that commercial networks have secured large child audiences for their C programs' (Mencinsky & Mullen 1999: 31, 38).

These programs are made for adults

This leads to an obvious conclusion: children's programs are not made for children at all; they are made for adults, in order to reinforce the adults' ideas of what children *should* be like, and what they should *want* to watch. The performances of childlikeness and earnest happiness of Benita and Peter and Don and John are what some parents would like to think their children should like, and should be watching. In a wonderfully unselfconscious moment, Patricia Edgar and her co-authors remark in passing that '*Play School* is prepared for the kinds of parents who want their children to be bright' (Edgar et al. 1973: 112). *Play School* is prepared for parents, not for children. So, 'while it might be clear to children which programs they prefer to watch, the question of "what is children's TV?" is a vexed one for adults' (Palmer 1986b: 114). Concomitant with this constant rediscovery that children are watching the wrong programs comes research showing that adults are insistent in their belief that those children *should* be watching 'children's programs'. Indeed, 'surveys carried out for the ABC show that parents are just as much astray as the ABC programmers on children's tastes' ('One More Week' 1966: 30). It is adults who are most often asked what children's programming should consist of, as in the 1992 Australian Broadcasting Tribunal survey, *What We Want From Our TVs*:

> Respondents were asked a number of questions in the survey about their attitudes to children's television. In considering the results, it is important to remember that the survey sample did not include people under 18 years of age. As such, the findings reflect adult attitudes to children's programs. There was overwhelming support among adults for children's programs to be an integral part of broadcast television ... When asked their opinions about the kind of programs that are good viewing for primary school children ... most respondents listed education ... programs (62%) or documentaries (23%).
>
> (Nugent et al. 1992)

Comedy and drama both rate less than 10 per cent approval. Game shows are not mentioned. Education dominates. Entertainment is still not conceivable for children.

Ambivalent boundaries

Children's programs, it seems, are made for adults. They reassure adults that children are, indeed, innocent and naive about a variety of matters, including being non-sexual creatures (although, as I suggested at the start of this chapter, common sense in one way tells us that children are playfully sexual creatures). And the very fact that children are supposed to be unable to read the double entendres, or take pleasure from looking at the sexualised bodies of these presenters, seems to render these sexual subtexts even more attractive for adults, as a harmless transgression that is noted and placed in unofficial collective memories about Australian television. But this is an ambivalent pleasure. Benita's braless appearances can be fondly remembered by individual viewers, but the ABC must deny this history and name anyone who might be interested in it a 'pervert'. And even stronger actions must be taken if a presenter breaches the codes of what children are allowed to see, or even to know about. The sexualised body is, despite the way in which Benita and her co-stars are dressed in these episodes of *Play School*, still dangerous. In 1973, 'Miss Judy-Anne' (Judy-Anne Garland)—presenter of the children's program *Romper Room*—was dismissed from her position after wearing a revealing low-cut gown on a late night variety program appearance, while in the early 1990s, Sophie Lee caused a 'furore' as host of *The Bugs Bunny Show* when her revealing and sexy clothing meant that the audience included a large number of adult male viewers (Chris Keating, pers. comm., 17 May 2000).

In Britain, one infamous example involved the sacking of Richard Bacon, a presenter of the archetypal BBC children's program *Blue Peter*, because it was publicly revealed by the press that he had taken cocaine (Davies & Machin 1999: 7).

Linking this with another transgression by a British children's television host, John Hartley describes this as a great moment on British television: 'Richard Bacon sacked from *Blue Peter*/Gail Porter strips for the ladmags: kiddie TV discovers (it still doesn't know how to cope with) drugs, sexiness' (Hartley 1999a).

The role of the children's television presenter is so well known, and so sacrosanct, that *Good News Week* can parody it. On 9 September 1999, the ABC had announced five new presenters as part of a project of 'updating' *Play School*. These included one openly homosexual man (Andrew McFarlane) and another who sings about drugs (Jay Laga'aia). This was mocked in *Good News Week Nite Lite*—'What next? Big Ted dealing drugs?'—because it is so obviously unthinkable. Presenters must be squeaky clean for children's television; anything else is an affront. It is necessary to keep the innocence of children's programs precisely, it seems, so that adults can continue to take pleasure from the naughtiness of spotting the sexuality that is really not meant to be there.

Thus, with *Play School*, the sexualisation of Benita's body is an attractive idea for adults who know that children's programming simply cannot countenance such a thing. Benita taking a simple action (not wearing a bra) upsets the delicate balance that cannot allow such actions in the protected area of children's programming on Australian television. For adults, it is notable and important, and worth a public scandal. It is a great moment in Australian television, remembered in folk memories that are not supported by official histories of the program or the medium. It ensures that *Play School* is part of the public archive of Australian television and thus deserves to be acknowledged as part of 'our cultural heritage'. The irony is that most children probably did not notice: they were too busy watching *Number 96*.

Availability

Many episodes of *Play School* are available for purchase from the ABC's Archives and Library Services in Sydney.

Notes

1 It was not the first children's program on the ABC: the broadcaster has shown children's programming since the first year of television in Australia, starting with *Children's TV Club*. On 27 December 1956, *Kindergarten Playtime* began, running for 15 minutes each day (Keating 1999b). In 1966, this program evolved into *Play School*, based—as with so many of the successful programs in early Australian television—on a British model (Semmler 1981: 156). Neither is *Play School* the longest running children's program on Australian television. *Here's Humphrey* started in 1965, and Humphrey has been on Australian television for longer than *Play School* (Heading & Jones 1996: 78).

2 According to Paragraph 15 of the original Television Program Standards.

3 It is not just *Play School* that inspires such sexual fandom. An informant from a mother's group in Western Australia replied to my comments on the dark-haired presenter on the Australian children's program *Hi-5*: 'Nathan?' she responds immediately. 'Oh yes. This video's good because he dresses up in a tight costume like a superhero. At the mother's group, everyone's jealous when somebody gets a new *Hi-5* video—"What's Nathan doing in it?" '

6

Number 96: Speaking sex and Showing Sex

1972–78

On 18 April 1972 (in Sydney), *Number 96* solicitor Don Finlayson turned to Bev Houghton and stated, calmly and with careful pronunciation, 'But Bev—I'm a ho-mo-sexual'. In a program famous for its obsession with sex and sexuality, this was one of the most important moments, and it survives in Australian television's archive as something great. This is the moment when a central, regular, sympathetic (and cute) character in an Australian television program laid claim to an identity that could previously only be presented with hints, suggestions, and coyness.

Introducing a three-week, twenty-four episode series of 'The Best of Number 96' in 2000, on the Foxtel Channel TV1 ('Television's Greatest Hits'), Andrew Mecardo—'Entertainment reporter and devout Kylie fan' ('Supersonic' 2000: 24)—noted that 'Twenty-eight years ago, on the 13th of March 1972, thousands of Australians sat down to watch what newspaper ads were calling "the night that Australian television would lose its virginity" '. Having established the program's emphasis on sex, Mecardo went on to specify the program's claims to fame:

> *Number 96* eventually set new standards for television censorship ... [and] pushed the boundaries every year that it was on air. An entire generation of Australians, including myself, learned about sex from this show. Even if your parents didn't allow you to watch it, there was always someone in the schoolyard who had snuck downstairs and hidden behind a couch to watch. Sooner or later you had to ask mum and dad, What's a virgin? What's a knicker-snipper? What's a homosexual?

Mecardo pronounces the 'hom' of 'homosexual' to rhyme with 'bomb', rather than with 'home', as Don himself did in the scene cited above. He then throws a very camp look at the camera—and he is a very camp presenter—before adding, 'Don't go away. After the break, it's part one of the pantyhose strangler'.

Public archive

Andrew Mecardo is not the only person to remember *Number 96* and its sex. This nightly half-hour soap opera (in its original format) was a vital part of Australian television in the 1970s (Reid & Groen 1977: 88), and of everyday culture in Australia during this time (Byrell 1995: 92). It was the number-one rating program in Australia in 1973 and 1974 (Jones & Bednall 1980: 32), and number nine in the top ten of most popular programs ever on Australian television, until 1981 (Beilby 1981: 185). And it has survived in the public archive as a program that brought sex into Australian living rooms.

Mecardo's phrase, 'The night television lost its virginity', was coined by Channel Ten's publicity chief, Tom Greer, to launch the program (Oram 1988: 24); this slogan has survived as a description of *Number 96*'s importance, bringing sex to Australian television. Hilary Kingsley introduces her comments on the program using the phrase (Kingsley 1989: 262), as does Chris Keating (Keating 1999a). Indeed, the single aspect of *Number 96* that is most commonly remembered in television's public archive is the fact that it had sex in it. The program was explicitly commissioned to be 'controversial' (Oram 1988: 23). Indeed, 'Sexuality ... had been part of the brief' (Day 1981: 147); it was 'to break new ground' and be 'a bit more sexy' (*The Australian Image* 1989e). It is remembered as 'the first show to repeatedly depict full-frontal nudity' (Keating 1999a; Reid & Groen 1977: vii–viii), and presented 'sex-violence [and] pack rape' (Rees 1978: 237–8). It covered 'such subjects as ... abortion, [and] homosexuality' (Reid & Groen 1977: 88), as well as 'incest ... adultery, attempted rape ... wife and lover-swapping, run-of-the-mill affairs, and for a brief and seamy period, witchcraft culminating in the ritual sacrifice of two naked virgins' (Radic 1973: 8). It 'introduced hitherto untouched moral and sexual limits' (Paul Alberts, pers. comm., 29 June 1999). It presented 'permissiveness' (Jones & Bednall 1980) and included 'sex and humour' in a 'daring' way (Kingsley 1989: 6). It showed 'a see-through blouse with nipples and aureoles on the other side' (Anderson 1972b: 40). In fact, *Number 96* was 'full of sex' (Peach 1992: 152), a 'trailblazer when it came to sex' (*35 Years of Television* 1991); it was, indeed, 'a sex serial' (Moran 1985: 123), or a 'sex show' (Hall 1976: 114). It is no surprise that 'These days people remember it for its nudity' (Kingsley 1989: 262).

Particularly central in the public archive of *Number 96* is the character of Bev, played by the surnameless 'Abigail'. This figure condenses for many writers exactly what *Number 96* was about: 'the big-bosomed Abigail' (Peach 1992: 152). She was 'the actress who just couldn't seem to keep her clothes on' (Kingsley 1989: 262), 'its major star and sex symbol':

> Time was whenever Abigail dropped her bra, half of Australia would sit up and take notice. And if you happened to miss the disrobings of Abigail's Bev Houghton, the newspapers kept you in touch as never before with headlines that captured even more followers.
>
> (Hohensee 1978a: 24)

In all of the sexuality that was unleashed on the Australian television-viewing public in 1972, one particular breakthrough in sexual representation has stayed with *Number 96* in the public archive: the fact that it included a gay male character as part of its central community. In an article in the *Financial Review*, Eric Ellis suggests that the moment that Australian television lost its virginity was not, in fact, the broadcasting of the first episode of *Number 96*; rather it was the moment at which Don Finlayson's homosexuality was revealed:

> In 1972, a young lawyer named Don Finlayson broke down on the landing of a Paddington apartment and announced what a titillated Middle Australia had suspected for 12 weeks. He was gay. It was the moment that Australian popular culture lost its virginity, being partially deflowered a few weeks earlier when Abigail's bare breasts were seen for the first time on television.
>
> (Ellis 1996: 41)

Many other writers—particularly in the academic part of the public archive—have agreed with this assessment of importance, placing the representation of a gay character at the centre of *Number 96*'s importance for the public archive. Elizabeth Jacka and Lesley Johnson note that it was 'very progressive in its politics: one of the leading characters as a homosexual, certainly a breakthrough for Australian television' (Jacka & Johnson 1998: 214). Keith Windschuttle argues that '*Number 96* ran ahead of majority community opinion in the 1970s in presenting positive images of working women and homosexuals, and in contributing to the decline of prejudice and discrimination against such people' (Windschuttle 1988: 190). The program provided 'the first affectionate representation of a homosexual, Joe Hasham [the actor who played Don Finlayson]' (Turner 1989: 30); it had 'a broad-brush approach to sexuality including homosexuality' (Howes 1993: 561). 'There weren't any gay people in my building ... but *Number 96* gave them an existence in public culture and that existence seemed to me like third nature' (Wark 1999: 150). Ien Ang and Jon Stratton list Finlayson's homosexuality as one of the defining characteristics of the program (Ang & Stratton 1995: 124).

In journalistic writing, the presence of homosexuality has also been centred in the public archive of the program's importance:

> *Number 96* didn't cause us to become sex-obsessed in the 70s—it was barely ahead of its time in showing the way we were. But it was the first TV show in the world to feature gay characters as heroes.
>
> (Dale 1998: 4)

Sandra Hall similarly makes Don the most important aspect of the program: 'Except for its homosexual hero ... *Number 96* is television's Melbourne *Truth* or Sunday *Mirror*. Each is dedicated to drawing sensationalism out of sex in suburbia' (Hall 1973: 12). The serial was 'arguably the first Australian TV drama to produce home grown cult figures ... Joe Hasham's homosexual Don Finlayson lasted the distance without accident ...' (Day 1981: 148); 'the 70's supersoap *Number 96* did something genuinely provocative when it presented us with Don Finlayson ... Australia's first realistic gay character, was intelligent, charming and sexually active' (Freeman 1999: 4). In a brief history of television for Australian school children, the program is described as 'one of Australia's most colourful soap operas. Its popularity resulted partly from its willingness to treat awkward social issues such as homosexuality' (Hand 1990: 54).

Number 96 holds an important place in the public archive of Australian television. The markers of that place are the presence of sex and, particularly, of homosexual characters.

Archival importance

Number 96 undeniably had important effects on television production in Australia. It was not the first soap opera to be produced in the country. *Autumn Affair* (1958) and *The Story of Peter Gray* (1961) were earlier examples of the format, although neither of these was particularly successful

(Moran 1989: 246). *Bellbird*, on the ABC, was Australia's 'first long-running soap' (Jacka 1991: 72), but 'rarely won higher than average ratings' (Kingsley 1989: 20; see also Day 1981: 146).

By contrast, the incredible success of *Number 96* showed that an Australian drama serial 'could run five nights a week' (Hall 1976: 47). It demonstrated that ' "interpersonal" drama had a place in peak-time scheduling' (Hall 1976: 117–18; Hohensee 1978a: 24). The program's success 'revived the failing fortunes' of Channel 0/10 (Rees 1978b: 237–8) (although *Matlock Police* had been the network's first successful drama), and it put 'television drama ... on a highly industrialized footing' (O'Regan 1996: 223). It also led to a vast reduction in production—for several decades—of the previously dominant police drama series in Australia (Moran 1989: 247).

But for the purposes of this book, it is the program's contribution to the screening of sex that is more interesting. Australian television history contains a number of moments of controversy around sex and nudity. It is possible to trace in these a progression of what is acceptable and what will constitute a controversy, and thus to see *Number 96*'s contribution to this process.

In 1964, a woman's naked back appeared on Australian television. This body part made a headline story in *TV Times*: 'The camera focuses on the wife's bare back while she is in bed' ('Near Nude Scene in ABC-TV Play' 1964: 8). Three years later the Channel 7 program *You Can't See Round Corners* showed a male character running his hand up his girlfriend's leg. This act also caused a controversy. Christopher Day claims that this act 'made headlines throughout the country' (Day 1981: 146; 'The 100 Greatest Moments in Television' 1999: 57). The Australian Broadcasting Control Board was certainly distressed by this 'brief scene of an attempted seduction'. Not only had it 'caused a large number of complaints', but it was also, they believed, 'a serious breach of the ... Standards ... [and] stations intending to televise the programme were informed that the scene must be deleted' (ABCB 1967: 101).

By 1971, viewers were still complaining to the Board about 'indecent or suggestive elements including bedroom scenes, revealing costumes and over-frank action in boy-meets-girl situations' (ABCB 1971: 137). It must be borne in mind that complainants to the Australian Broadcasting Control Board were a very small sample of the Australian population: never more than a few hundred complaints are received by the Board in a given year. And while the complainants in 1971 were still worried about 'revealing costumes' (shades of complaints about the 'suggestive' elements of variety programs, fifteen years earlier), Australian television was broadcasting its first full-frontal nude shot in a drama series: in the first episode of *Matlock Police*, on 25 February 1971 (Keating 1999b).

As to the representation of homosexuality and gay men on Australian television, no homosexual characters had played a regular part in Australian television before 1972.[1] There were limited appearances of gay men as 'social issues' in current affairs television. For example, Dennis Altman describes a documentary appearing in the late 1960s: an episode of *Chequerboard* (ABC) entitled 'This just happens to be part of me'. The documentary featured

> Two homosexual couples ... all very articulate ... [who] talked about their lives and social and political situations ... They were very clear, very cool and ... relaxed ... Perhaps most important was just to see and hear them on television. Contrary to popular belief, they did not have two heads, did not lisp, mince or have limp wrists, and looked just like you or me.
>
> (as quoted in Anderson 1972a: 39)

Discussing this episode, Don Anderson notes the lack of physical contact on the program, although the gay men involved, Peter and Bonsell, 'did have a perfunctory welcome-home kiss'. It was, he argues, 'a "first" program', which 'start[ed] the public's education at an elementary level' (Anderson 1972a: 39). At this point, homosexuality was still thought to be an unacceptable topic for television coverage. In 1969 and 1970, Australian Broadcasting Control Board surveys asked viewers in Sydney, Melbourne, and Adelaide to rate subjects that they found 'embarrassing or in poor taste'. The topics involved were birth control, prostitution, alcoholism, homosexuality, drug-taking, and premarital sex. In every city, homosexuality was rated as the single most unacceptable topic—'embarrassing or in poor taste'. In Sydney, 56 per cent of respondents claimed to be embarrassed about seeing homosexuality on television; in Melbourne, 54 per cent (Board 1970: 21); in Adelaide, the figure is given as 54 per cent.

Social context

Before *Number 96*, then, representations of sex on Australian television appear to have been limited.

In 1972, this program changed the Australian mediasphere by focusing explicitly on sex. In this, it was not out of step with other aspects of Australian culture in the late 1960s and early 1970s. In fact, what is most notable about *Number 96* is that it took so long to arrive, given what was happening elsewhere in the culture. Barbara Sullivan detects important changes in Australia's sexual cultures as early as 1955. She suggests that from this time 'new norms of sexual conduct, marriage and family life were instituted' (Sullivan 1997: 70). She suggests this came about as a result of contraception, '[t]he demand for labour and consumer goods [which] meant that an increasing proportion of women participated in the workforce', and '[t]he sexological discourse during the 1960s [which placed] increasing emphasis upon the role of sex and orgasm in the construction of good relationships' (Sullivan 1997: 72). Further, she argues, 'Discourses about the importance of sexual pleasure and sexual freedom were also central to the emerging counter-culture of the 1960s' (Sullivan 1997: 73).

One of the most obvious testaments to this change in culture is the way in which questions of censorship and the right to consume sexually explicit material (principally books and films) entered the public sphere during the 1950s and 1960s (Sullivan 1997: 75): 'Changes in the dominant sexual culture meant that "normal" Australians were now also more interested in reading and talking about sex' (Sullivan 1997: 96). The early 1970s saw sex become acceptable entertainment in the realm of books and films, with popular sex manuals such as *The Joy of Sex* (published 1972) becoming best-sellers in Australia, and 'cross-over' pornographic/mainstream films such as *Deep Throat* and *The Devil in Miss Jones* 'attract[ing] mass audiences and, for the first time, a large number of ordinary married couples' (Sullivan 1997: 128). In 1970–71, the federal government 'debated the issue of censorship for the first time in more than thirty years' (Sullivan 1997: 130): 'In October 1970, [Don] Chipp [Minister for Customs and Excise] announced the introduction of a new R (Restricted) classification for films which were deemed suitable for adults only' (Sullivan 1997: 134; Naismith 1997: 18). As Gaye Naismith suggests, in the early 1970s,

> for a brief period [bookended by the invention of the R certificate at the start, and the video boom at the end], the sex-themed films were a vital and immediate expression of one of the defining aspects of the cultural milieu of the seventies.
>
> (Naismith 1997: 44)

Soft-core sex films such as *The Naked Bunyip* (1970), *An Essay on Pornography* (1973), and *Alvin Purple* (1973) were an important part of Australia's film culture in the first part of the 1970s (Naismith 1997: 31).

It was in such a context—of greater circulation of publications inspired by sexology (Bell 1972: 3), public debates about censorship, and the introduction of the R certificate, and more general debates about the liberalising of sexual culture—that *Number 96* appeared on Australian television. If television came rather late to this area of 'permissiveness' in Australian popular culture, it is not surprising. In chapter 1, we saw the Australian Broadcasting Control Board's insistence that television is not like other media. Its 'penetration' into the domestic sphere makes it particularly worrisome for the guardians of public morals. Given this, the fact that the sexual revolution arrived on television some time after it reached books and films is understandable. Its ability to bring such ideas into the domestic sphere makes it particularly challenging. Leon Hunt, discussing the UK context, describes this tendency in a positive way, as he discusses television's role in contributing to 'the infiltration of permissiveness into everyday life' (Hunt 1998: 105). He suggests that, originally, changes in sexual culture were something that, for most television viewers, happened 'out there', to other people in other places (the urban middle class in particular). It was through television that these possibilities finally reached the homes of the majority of the population: '1970s popular culture [was] a negotiation of the 1960s (particularly sexual) revolution. Permissiveness [had] left a lot of people behind, but "trickled down" in the 1970s' (Hunt 1998: 20).

In the context of changing attitudes towards sexuality in the public sphere, *Number 96* was an important part of the trickle down in Australia, bringing the ethos (if not the explicitness) of the R rating into the homes of Australia.

What kind of permissiveness?

If this is the context in which *Number 96* appeared, what contribution did it make to the public permissive culture of Australia in the early 1970s? It may have been aiming to take the virginity of Australian television, but how did it set about this seduction? What counted as sex for *Number 96*?

The first episode of *Number 96* opens with two older characters—Dorrie and Herb Evans—welcoming a young married couple into the apartment block that they own. Dorrie and Herb are quickly set up as comedy figures for the program: repressed and old-fashioned, they are the figures of fun who will disapprove of everything that is happening on the show. Bursting in on the couple, Dorrie finds them cuddling. She disapproves strongly: 'Not two minutes in the place, and canoodling on the sofa'

(*Number 96* 1972a). This could describe *Number 96* itself: it doesn't take long to get down to sex. Its public image as a program about sex is quite justified.

Sex made visible in *Number 96*

In the first episode, the program presents the following characters and situations.

- The young, recently married Mr Eastwood tries to have sex with his unwilling, heavily pregnant, wife. He gropes her breasts, and later tries to climb on top of her in bed: 'God, it's been two months now—you make things so difficult'.
- Bev does a photo shoot with photographer Bruce, who lives upstairs. It is for a magazine called *Mod Photography*, but as her flatmate says to her, 'It'll be *Mod Pornography* if you take that jacket off'. Bev does indeed take her jacket off, showing off her flimsy, sheer, and see-through blouse. We see the entire photo shoot, and every time Bev poses—with her hands held up above her head—her nipples are clearly visible. After fourteen minutes, we have our first shot of women's nipples.
- Rose Godolfus, whose father runs the local deli, is attacked by an ex-boyfriend: he carries her across the room and throws her on the sofa so we can see her underwear. He gropes her breasts

(*Number 96* 1972a).

One producer of the program suggests that 'These days people remember it for its nudity, but there really wasn't any. We had a few bare-breasted girls, that's all' (Kingsley 1989: 262). (It is interesting in light of this comment to note that each episode of the program broadcast in the TV1 'Best of … ' series is prefaced with a warning that the program is rated 'M', for mature viewers over 15, and that it contains 'Nudity', when none of the episodes shown include any more nudity than can be found on an average Australian beach.) In the first few episodes, this is indeed the case. There are no full-frontal shots. What we do see is 'a few bare-breasted girls' (or, at least, Abigail's nipples) and a lot of sexual activity. And this activity—sex—for *Number 96* is largely represented by men groping women's breasts.

This happens twice in the first episode, and continues throughout the early episodes of the program. In episode four, Rose has a date with a man whom her father wishes her to marry. They do some serious open-mouthed kissing, followed by him grabbing her breasts. In episode six, when Bev and her flatmate (Janie) have a double date, Janie's date—Alex, a theatre producer—gets his hands on Bev's breasts and does some massaging. Later in the episode, he arrives again at the flat and immediately grabs and massages Abigail's breast. Sometimes it is buttocks that are grasped (in episode three, Alf Sutcliffe slaps Vera Collin's bum), but it is the groping of breasts that is favoured.

Barbara Sullivan notes the masculine inflection of many 'liberal' discourses of sexuality, which often assume 'the "naturalness" of (hetero)sexual activity and the display of women's bodies' (Sullivan 1997: 95). *Number 96* brings 'sex' to Australian television, and much of that 'sex' is signified by the grasping and massaging of women's breasts.

It also involves *looking* at women's breasts and thighs (mainly Abigail's breasts and thighs). In the first episode, she wears a variety of costumes. As mentioned above, for the photo shoot she wears a see-through blouse that clearly reveals her nipples. When she goes down to the shop, she wears a lace dress; her underwear is clearly visible through it. The dress itself is extremely short. It does not entirely cover her buttocks. In episode three, she comes into the living room of her apartment wearing only her bra and underpants to argue with Janie. In episode four, she strides into the living room after an evening out and starts to unzip her dress (the zip is at the front), revealing cleavage and underwear again. Janie is at this point wearing a miniskirt that barely covers her pudenda. In this episode, when Bev gets the photographs from her shoot with Bruce, we can see that they are fully nude shots; the camera starts on a close-up of these, and we can see her naked body (side on, tasteful, no genitalia visible).

There is little equivalent in terms of male nudity in these first few episodes. We see Alf Sutcliffe in the bath, but he is not a sexual figure in the same way that Bev is (being neither young, nor attractive). Male legs appear in episode six, with Alf and Don in dressing gowns, but again, these seem not to be designed to give pleasure. Apparently, Norman Yemm appeared in a nude scene later in the serial ('role' 1972), but there is no sign of this in the earlier episodes.

The 'sex' of *Number 96*, then, largely involves looking at women's bodies, grasping and massaging them. And this 'sex' is important not just narratively, but also visually. Apart from these breasts and legs and buttocks, there is little

Sets in *Number 96* provide little visual pleasure

else in the way of visual pleasure in the program. The sets are as simplistic as early *Homicide*. The first episodes have no location work at all, and only a very small number of sets, all of which are virtually identical. It is not until episode five that we have the first set that represents a location outside the apartment block (the laundrette where Lucy Sutcliffe works), and in episode six the first location work appears (a brief shot in which Mark Eastwood is outside the Godolfus's deli). There is no sound; we just see him walking into the shop.

The shooting style and performances of these early episodes also give little visual pleasure. They rely largely on long shots. There are very few close-ups, no melodramatic zooms, no long close-ups held on faces engaged in excessive acting. The program presents us with brisk performances and long shots, simple sets, and no locations. The only things the program really gives us to look at—and these are placed at the centre of the program's pleasures—are Abigail's nipples and associated body parts. Luckily for viewers looking for visual pleasure, these are present throughout the program.

Complaints by letter

Unsurprisingly, there was public debate about the presentation of sex in *Number 96*. According to one newspaper:

> Channel Ten was bombarded [given the tendency of journalistic discourse to hyperbole, it is worth asking how many calls constitute a 'bombardment'] with phone calls during the [first episode] and the following day complaining about the program. Viewers were 'disgusted'; one woman said the show was 'depraved' and 'disgusting' and that the channel should be 'damned for showing it'.
>
> (Anderson 1972b: 40)

Channel 0 had already elected to censor itself in the very first episode: 'In Melbourne ... Channel 0 elected to black out the lower half of the screen [where Mark Eastwood grasps a breast] during Mark's attempted seduction of his wife' (http://www.magna.com.au/~lindsay/info/ 1972.html). The Australian Broadcasting Control Board would introduce more explicit censorship over the next three years. In its 1972 report, the Board notes that 'By far the largest proportion of complaints to the Board concerned objectionable remarks and undue emphasis on sex ... in early episodes of a new drama series *Number 96*' (ABCB 1972: 116). This led directly to censorship of the early episodes of the program.

> After the first night, in which three episodes of the series were televised, the Board directed station TEN, which originated the programme, to excise objectionable matter from the video-recordings before they were distributed to other stations. After further incidents in subsequent episodes the Board acted in terms of Section 101 of the Broadcasting and Television Act to examine each episode before transmission until such time as it was clear that the producer had a proper understanding of what was required by the Board's Standards.
>
> (ABCB 1972: 118)

The Board notes that after a number of episodes, it stopped this previewing. But in 1973 and 1974, direct interference resumed.

> In late January 1973, a scene involving a youth visiting a prostitute led to the Board invoking Section 101 of the Broadcasting and Television Act in order to examine each episode of the programme before transmission ... In June, two segments showing practices associated with sexual aberrations were, at the Board's direction, deleted from the programme.
>
> (ABCB 1973: 132)

In 1974, 'Action taken over *Number 96* ... included the deletion of several explicit sex scenes, one of which involved sadism. Offensive expressions were cut from two episodes' (ABCB 1974: 137).

Number 96 managed to upset the Board; this is unsurprising. But the 'complaints' received do not, of course, suggest a widespread concern with the sex in the program. The Board itself recognises the demographics of its complainants when it notes that

> There was an unprecedented increase in the volume of written complaints received by the Board during [1973–74] about programme matters ... Part of the increase in complaints was attributable to the formation of groups whose aim is to encourage members to make known individually to authorities, such as the Board, what they see as unsuitable aspects of television programming, particularly in regard to portrayals of behaviour involving sexual morality.
>
> (ABCB 1974: 136)

Even given the presence of such moral watchdog organisations, the number of complaints received is always very small. In the years from 1975 to 1978, complaints about the sexual representations of *Number 96* (and its generic descendent, *The Box*) are tiny in number: seventy are received in 1975–76, nine in 1976–77, and none in 1977–78 (ABT 1979b: 23). The program has millions of viewers; seventy complain. The Board's actions are interesting in suggesting the governmental regimes of propriety in place at this time, but not in revealing more general attitudes to the fact that a television program in Australia was now regularly bringing female nipples into the lounge rooms of the country.

Presenting homosexuality

In the first few episodes of *Number 96*, the character of Don Finlayson (Joe Hasham) appears. He is not a 'homosexual character' in these episodes. He is rather the solicitor who lives upstairs from Bev and Janie, with his flatmate Bruce. In these early episodes, Bruce is established as a playboy: he is the photographer who takes shots of Bev and her nipples. When he goes to the Godolfus's deli, he comments to Rose that 'Half the fun of shopping here is having tasty titbits served up by a tasty titbit' (*Number 96* 1972b). The major plotline concerning these characters in the early episodes centres on Don sabotaging Bruce's party, because he is worried about upsetting the neighbours (*Number 96* 1972c). In episode six, Don has locked himself out of his flat, so Bev invites him in for a drink while he waits for Bruce to get home with his key. This leads to Bev flirting with him. Presenting her back to him, she asks him to help her out of her dress: 'I'm only asking you to make yourself useful. Just take the zip in your left hand and pull it downwards'. Every other man we have met in the program seems to be unable to keep his hands off her; when we see Don looking uncomfortable, shy, and awkward, we know that something is up. When she sits on the sofa next to him and puts her arm around him, Bruce arrives and Don leaves (*Number 96* 1972d).

It is not until episode twenty-eight that Don's sexuality is mentioned. The final scene of this episode is set in Bev and Janie's flat. Don and Bev enter: they've been out on a date. This episode does not exist at Screensound, but the coming-out clip has been included in several documentaries. The clip in *30 Years of Television* starts with a mid-shot of Bev and Don, sitting on the sofa while she holds his hands and runs them over her body—including, of course, her breasts: 'Oh, touch me, I know you feel the way I do. You must. Oh please, I want you. I've never done this, felt this with a man before'. All of this is said in a big close-up, her eyes half-closed, mouth slightly open, panting and gasping. We cut to a big close-up of Don, looking confused: 'I never knew you felt this way. Honestly, I'd never had ... I thought you knew ... I ... I ... I'm a ho-mo-sexual'. This is the cliffhanger end of episode twenty-eight. The scene continues at the start of episode twenty-nine. As Don continues talking, we cut to another close-up of Bev, curling her upper lip in disgust: 'I thought you knew about Bruce and me', he says (*ATV 30 Years of Television* 1994).

In many ways, the scripts for *Number 96* are even more interesting than the episodes that were finally broadcast. It is a tradition in television that the only way gay characters can be outed is by claiming the identity: 'I'm a homosexual'. It is most unusual for them to be allowed to either claim love for a character of the same sex, or to demonstrate that love physically (McKee 1996). Yet the scripts for *Number 96* show the character engaged in a fully realised, physical homosexual relationship. In the scripts for episode twenty-nine, one scene shows Don and Bruce together—'the former in bed; the latter fully dressed, sitting on the bed'. Bruce is thinking of taking a job in Adelaide. They discuss the effect this will have on their relationship. Straight after the 'issue' scene, they are involved in discussing something quite different about their relationship: 'What's going to happen about us ...?' asks Don. Don then gets into the bed with Bruce: 'They lie together without speaking for a moment. Then Bruce puts his arm around Don ... Don snuggles into him ... Bruce turns in bed, moves across to Don and kisses him long and lovingly on the lips.'

Although it is not possible to consult the transmitted version of episode twenty-nine, it is certain that this element of the script was not filmed. Ian Holmes, the Programme Manager at Channel 0-10 at the time, has stated that

> We set fairly strict guidelines to how far they should go. For instance certainly in the first two years of *Number 96* there should be no physical contact by Don Finlayson with whomever, and he should be a likeable, nice, moral person.
>
> (Day 1981: 145)

Despite these limitations, and the inability of the transmitted program to follow the possibilities opened up in its scripts, its achievement is considerable. Don has been presented as a sympathetic character. He is a central and regular part of the community. And for twenty-seven episodes before this moment, he has been primarily Don, the lawyer, or Don, Bev's friend, rather than Don—'the homosexual'. Felsenthal notes that in early representations of homosexual characters, this is unheard of: 'Initially [in the early 1970s] single-episode gay characters, at best self-destructive and at worst evil, were used as narrative plot devices to create conflict among the regular characters of a prime-time series' (Felsenthal 1997: 1477–8).

Number 96 is the first televisual representation in the USA, Australia, or the United Kingdom of a gay character who is a regular member of the central community of a television program; he is not a social issue, a ' "problem" that needed to be solved' (Felsenthal 1997: 1478). Don is a gay man who is a regular, accepted, central character in a television program. He is a character who is openly homosexual, and who has a boyfriend, but who has elements to his character other than just his homosexuality—a character who has relationship problems that are not simply about being gay, but who nevertheless deals with the 'issues' and problems that arise from being a member of a sexual minority in Australia. And he would eventually get to touch a boyfriend on screen: Simon Carr (John Orcsik).

Don's importance

The accounts that survive of audience reaction to Don suggest that this character was a popular element of *Number 96*. 'Women viewers loved him', says one producer, even if it is true that 'They wrote him letters, all wanting to put him straight' (Kingsley 1989: 262). David Sale, a writer on the program, states that 'I was told that little old ladies on the buses were all talking about whether Don would stay with his boyfriend. His character became an icon' (Williams 1994b: 50; hearsay evidence, but interesting nonetheless). More such hearsay evidence comes from Keith Howes, claiming that: 'solicitor Don Finlayson ... was a popular hero, not only with Australian gays, but also with housewives and old folk' (Howes 1993: 562). Liz Kirby (who played Lucy Sutcliffe) claims that 'Joe Hasham had a great following among the television audience. And they accepted his character completely—and therefore they saw that gay people didn't necessarily conform to the stereotype they'd always expected' (Goddard 1990: 42).

It can be suggested that *Number 96* had a broadly educational effect, ensuring that many among the Australian television audience would know of at least one (if fictional) gay character who was not a child molester or sex addict. Keith Howes, for example, claims that the program 'was a trigger for change, which made viewers feel that prejudice against homosexual men was beyond a joke' (Howes 1993: 561).

The cultural context in which the program appeared also included the emergence of movements for gay and lesbian liberation. Activists involved in this campaign—including the early important Australian figure Dennis Altman—identified Don Finlayson as an important part of their work to change public perceptions of homosexuality:

> As far as the mass public is concerned probably the most significant challenge to the popular mythology is *Number 96*. One of the permanent characters is homosexual, who is obviously meant to be one of the nicest characters on the block. He is indeed so nice as to be sickening. But I suspect that the influence of Don on prejudices and fears out in Padstow and Preston and Petries is much greater than anything the gay movement's been able to achieve ... The fact that Don is apparently so well accepted might suggest that the 'woman in the street' is less narrow than politicians and journalists often claim.
>
> (Altman 1973: 6–7)

Altman further suggests that 'Don was just as important as all of us activists' (Goddard 1990: 41–2). Clinton Kramer—the editor of the gay magazine *Campaign*—similarly 'praises the TV series *Number 96* for presenting a homosexual (played by Joe Hasham) in a sympathetic light. "He has shown him as a normal person"' (Moffit 1977: 90, quoting Clinton Kramer). Certainly, a later writer saw *Number 96* fulfilling such a function when he claimed that

> Australian viewers—who have been conditioned by *Number 96* or *The Box* to accept homosexual activities as part of the everyday scene and who have heard, without undue emphasis or sniggering, the gay members of our society referred to as 'poofters'—are not, I think, likely to share the hilarious reaction of the American studio audience who, in the premiere of [US sitcom] *Soap*, dissolved into shocked laughter at the mention of the word 'fruit'.
>
> (Kennedy 1978: 18)

It is possible to trace this importance more directly through the members of the audience who discovered through Don Finlayson a possible identity for themselves. One article claims that 'his fan mail comes from lonely teenage boys who need help with their problems instead of from the public which can't tolerate sexual difference' (Porter 1975: 26). In the correspondence for this book, as well as in responses for a separate research project on the television memories of gay men, Don proves an important part of many memories. Previous research has noted that for some viewers, 'Joe Hasham ... was seminal. Growing up and seeing that on television was amazing. He was a gay man shown as a well-adjusted, good looking career person on Australian TV' (Freeman 1999: 5, quoting Alan Kirkland). Many more examples can be cited:

> being a 13 year old 'migrant girl' sitting at home watching TV with her Italian parents and what a fabulous thing it was having Don and Lee (from *The Box*) come on TV ... I credit those two characters in those two shows as markers in my thirteen-year-old 'just hitting puberty' self and my family in the way gay/lesbian/bisexual/transsexual issues were never an issue.
>
> (Maria, pers. comm. 5 May 1999)

An interviewee on a previous research project remembers a scene watched twenty years previously on *Number 96*:

> [T]he guy was coming out of the shower, they'd been to the beach during the day, they'd both been sunburnt, and as he's coming out of the shower, there's another guy sort of leaning over, drying himself, and one guy's naked and the other guy's got a towel around him, and they come together really closely, and you don't see anything except feet and faces, and then you just see the scene with both feet, and the other towel dropping to the floor ... I thought, hang on, these are two sort of guys who don't look as if they've come out of *Benny Hill*, or *Carry On* type characters, they both had reasonably normal jobs, they spoke normally, they didn't sort of mince or anything like that .... I can't remember if it was in the same show or the following day, they're in bed together, the morning after reading the paper, sort of dozing and chatting, and I thought, that's nice ... I can remember it quite clearly. I can almost remember the furniture in the room ... It think it was the confirmation that it was OK to be gay and not feminine.

Another interviewee demonstrates the importance of the these images by his recall of a scene, long after the event:

> I can very clearly remember the gay character in *Number 96*, and he was very non-camp, he was very straight acting, they had a very camp gay character as well ... to start with we weren't allowed to watch it ... the gay side of things [in *Number 96*] was a very minor kind of subplot ... I remember this scene where one of the characters got himself into the gay character's bed, and the gay character comes in, and there's this man in his bed, and it was like, 'Oh, he's gay too'. And Don, the main gay character says, 'Get dressed'. I remember that, and a discussion, they used the word 'poofter', and I asked, 'What does that mean?' and we had a discussion.

For some queer audience members, *Number 96* has proven a particularly important resource in making sense of themselves and their sexuality.[2]

Post-coital television

By 1977, one writer could claim that *Number 96* had done its work in desensitising the Australian television audience to sex on the box:

> if all the fuss [about the program] seems a trifle tame today, it is largely because viewing habits and expectations have been to some extent altered by this 'sensational' serial. The Australian viewing public has become somewhat blasé. And who is to blame it, after sitting through more than four years, or one thousand episodes, of the antics of the *Number 96* tenants?
>
> (Reid & Groen 1977: 88)

The program had an immediate effect, in the spawning of a copycat sex-oriented soap opera, *The Box*. This program was different from *Number 96* in being set in a television station, but similar in its interest in nudity and focus on sexual 'issues' such as rape and homosexuality: 'boobs and bums were what the public, and what Channel 0 in Melbourne, wanted' (Johnson & Smiedt 1999: 219; see also Hawkins 1974: 7).

The appeal of nudity for its own sake seems to have waned rapidly. After *Number 96* and *The Box*, some writers claim that 'Their frankness remains available to present-day producers, but none has felt the need to take up the same obsessive interest in titillating sex' (Davies 1981: 109); 'Naked bodies are more likely to be greeted with yawns than gasps these days' (Gersten & Bassett 1991: 14–15). Again, the generalisations of journalism must be treated with some care, but the fact that only one Australian program in recent years has explicitly sold itself on sex in this way—*Chances* (Ang & Stratton 1995)—does suggest that the fact of nudity itself does not retain its initial shock and interest value.

The fact that *Number 96* dealt with sexual issues quite openly has been its most consistently remembered aspect. Certainly censorship and negative reactions to gay characters remained in place in the public sphere: in 1974 the Australian Broadcasting Control Board censored *A Current Affair*, noting that homosexual topics were 'unsuitable for television' (ABCB 1974: 138), and reaction to a 'gay issue' episode of *Cop Shop* in 1979 included a letter to the *TV Times* describing the 'disappointed and disgusted' reaction of the writer who asked, 'Who except the morally sick would enjoy hearing about lesbians and homosexuals?' (Caffrey 1979: 40). Nevertheless, gay characters have retained a place in Australian television. It is disappointing that after nearly thirty years, towards the end of the twentieth century, very few programs have followed the path of *Number 96* in making such characters regular and central. In Australian dramas at the start of the twenty-first century, both *Water Rats* and *All Saints* have regular homosexual characters on the periphery of the central community, but *Blue Heelers, Stingers, Home and Away, SeaChange*, and *Neighbours* lack any such regular characters. When gay or lesbian characters do appear, however, they are not likely to lead to Australian Broadcasting Tribunal censorship, or to vexed letters to the editor. Indeed, Australia reached the point during the 1990s where the Sydney Lesbian and Gay Mardi Gras could be broadcast, first on the ABC, and then on the commercial Channel Ten; returning to the channel on which Don Finlayson had appeared (Searle 1997). *Number 96* was groundbreaking. It has made possible representations that were not possible before. And it is remembered for precisely this, adding gay characters to the public archive of Australian television, and to our cultural heritage.

Availability

Screensound holds scripts for most episodes of the program and a few copies of episodes themselves (although not every copy listed on the database as available actually exists). Other episodes are held privately by Nancy Harmon, but these are not generally available for viewing.

Notes

1 Some commentators have suggested that there were many previous 'gay' actors on television, including Gordon Chater. Although these actors may have been gay in their private lives, however, there is no screen presence of their homosexual identity. There may have been an effeminate performance, but this is not the same thing as homosexuality.
2 Throughout this chapter, it should be noted that I am not celebrating 'straight-acting' gay characters as the only 'positive' or acceptable ones. Rather, I am interested in the way in which *Number 96* opened up the range of possible representations of homosexuality in the Australian mediasphere.

7

Anyhow* ... Have a Winfield: Selling Ordinary Nationalism

1972–76 (television); 1972–80 (cinema)

In May 1980, the Advertising Standards Council banned Paul Hogan from advertising Winfield cigarettes. He had already been removed from television on 1 September 1976, as part of a generalised ban of all cigarette advertising on that medium. Hogan's adverts continued in cinemas and magazines for a further four years, until the Council ruled that Paul Hogan must never be involved in any form of cigarette advertising in Australia. Hogan's success in establishing a popularity that crossed demographics in Australia—particularly those of age—was such that a regulatory body had to intervene to control it.

These adverts are important in Australia's television archive for several reasons: as an example of the way in which adverts in this country have often been strongly linked to the creation and promotion of national identity; as part of the career of Paul Hogan (probably the Australian actor with a star image most strongly linked to national identity); and as an example of the way in which the medium of television can successfully achieve cross-demographic communication in its promotion of such a national identity.

Hogan's 'classic first advertisement' (Webb 1973: 52) for Winfield cigarettes has passed into television's public archive. It is not only remembered, but repeatedly described in histories of the medium. Neil Shoebridge's account is typical in the level of detail offered in the description of this moment. He notes that the advert 'opened with a tuxedo-clad Hogan walking onto a stage in front of the orchestra and choir', before going on to describe the action of this advertisement: 'Hogan sat on a step and delivered his opening lines: "G'day. I've been asked to talk to you, see, and being the suave, sophisticated man about town, I thought I'd do the job with a bit of polish, a touch of class." ' Shoebridge's description includes a complete narrative of the advert as Hogan 'turned to the orchestra's conductor and delivered his soon-to-be-famous line, "Let 'er rip, Boris old son" '. His description makes clear the importance in the advert of the distinction between Hogan's star image and the high culture it was lambasting, as at the end of the advert, according to Shoebridge's account, 'The orchestra then launched into the second movement from Tchaikovsky's Fifth Symphony'.

John McCallum adds to this account: 'As the camera pulled back he was revealed to be wearing, below his immaculate dinner jacket, stubbies (cheap rough beach shorts) and thongs (rubber sandals ...)' (McCallum 1998: 210). The phrase 'Let 'er rip, Boris' is undoubtedly now part of Australia's cultural heritage (Page 1992 [1986]: 116; see also Oram 1987: 84–5).

Adverts have provided 'some of the most memorable moments on Australian television', providing 'phrases and expressions which have gone into common usage' (Keating 1999a). The slogan of Hogan's advertising campaign—'Anyhow ... have a Winfield'—entered public culture (Keating 1999a) and became a national 'proverb inscrutable to foreigners' (Morris 1990: 15). When it became simply too popular, it had to be controlled.

The early Ocker

Paul Hogan is one of the greatest stars of Australian television and cinema, and from the beginning, his 'star image' (Dyer 1998) has been as an 'ocker'.

While working as a rigger on the Sydney Harbour Bridge in the late 1960s, Hogan began his career by appearing on the talent show *New Faces*, 'faking his way onto [the] show and then abusing the judges' (Morris 1990: 15). *Who Weekly*, remembering this and placing it in the top ten of television's 100 greatest moments ('The 100 Greatest Moments in Television' 1999: 153), comments of Hogan's debut that it displayed 'Ocker nonchalance'. From this first appearance, Hogan's 'ocker' credentials are emphasised throughout his career. He was not a typical television star. He was a worker who just happened to get into television. He is characterised by irreverence, cheekiness, and a broad Australian accent.

After the appearance on *New Faces*, Hogan was invited to appear in a comedy slot on *A Current Affair*. His role here was to be the 'man in the street' (Windschuttle 1988: 169). He was a 'larrikin' (Shoebridge 1992: 35–6), who would appear on the show to provide commentary on current issues. He was 'the Ocker philosopher, saying whatever he liked about politicians, unions, beer-drinking or whatever else he had a thought about' (Hall 1976: 134). The tone of this piece was to be a comic undercutting of 'the pretensions of television current affairs conventions themselves ... the authoritative expert commentary and the like' (Windschuttle 1988: 168–9). He was positioned as the average, typical viewer: 'He had become their [the viewers'] voice. In his ocker way he was able to articulate what they thought about subjects ranging from politics to pollution' (Oram 1987: 74). And, as an 'ocker', he was presented as being somehow particularly 'Australian': 'The larrikin from humble beginnings who made good, Hoges typified almost everything that is likeable about the Australian character from his blond good looks to his laconic wit and cheeky humour' (Shoebridge 1992: 35–6).

From his earliest appearances, Hogan's character was understood to be 'Australian' and 'ocker' and 'typical'. Then he moved on to the Winfield adverts, where that Australian national identity of ockerism was promulgated in an even more successful form.

Advertising national identity

It is worth emphasising an obvious point at the outset of this argument. There is no such thing as a 'typical' Australian. There is no such thing as a 'genuine' Australian character. Any attempts to pin down such characteristics involve *creating*, not simply *recognising*, national identities. This is a familiar point, but one that bears restating, particularly in the context of Hogan. In much journalistic writing about Hogan, his 'typicality' and 'Australianness' are presented as obvious. He successfully managed to provide a convincing ocker national identity that appealed to a significant part of the Australian population as a suitable one for themselves to recognise. Nevertheless, that identity *was* created. Hogan's cigarette ads—and other elements in his television career—were part of public discourse about national identity. They were successful and convincing. But that is not the same thing as being simply 'true'.

Australian public culture is particularly keen on trying to find suitable forms of national identity. It is interesting, in the context of this chapter, to note that the genre of adverts has been particularly keen on this topic.[1] Some adverts, and some products, have become a part of Australia's cultural heritage: for example, Shoebridge explicitly suggests that '[t]he "I Like Aeroplane Jelly" campaign is more than a part of Australian advertising history. It is part of Australia's cultural heritage' (Shoebridge 1992: 14; see also Dale 1999: 26). Other products that have become part of Australia's 'consumer heritage' (Adams 1987: 15) include 'Aspro, Arnott's ... Minties, Aeroplane Jelly and Foster's Lager' (Cozzolino & Rutherford 1987: 123), and, of course, Vegemite (Fiske, Hodge, & Turner 1987; White 1993).

But as well as the products that have become part of Australian cultural heritage, there is another link between advertising and national identity. Throughout the history of television production in Australia, the government has placed a legal requirement that a majority of television commercials be produced in Australia (Moran 1997a: 115). More than this, many writers have noticed that Australian television adverts are particularly drawn to discourses of national identity in order to sell products, explicitly creating discourses of the nation, and linking those to the product.

> Advertising is a major site for the deployment of images of the nation; there are whole genres of advertising in Australia which are based on a particular signification of national identity—usually involving 'the holy trinity of men, sport and beer'.
>
> (Turner 1993: 255; see also Cunningham 1993: 129; Appleton 1988: 42; Oost 1993: 57)

Other critics have commented on the link between advertising and a national identity consisting of men and beer. Writing in 1969, John Murray notices this tendency in advertising for Carlton & United Breweries (Murray 1969: 74); Stuart Cunningham spots it in ads for Toohey's Flag Ale (Cunningham 1992: 99), as does Jonathan Dawson (Dawson 1990: 95). This is a national identity of the countryside, of intense physical labour, of a working-class, insistently masculine form of Australian culture. These adverts provide a perfect example of the constructed nature of national identities; this construction obviously does not accurately picture *all* Australians. There are few women, for example, living in this country—the country of Australian beer.

A genre in which advertising has been even more explicitly linked to national identity in Australia is the 'humanity ad':

> [These] portray a large number of people ... who are manifestly 'ordinary people' ... the ad is calculated not to describe a good but to identify a product ... with an imagined community ... the theme, so prominent in these ads, of unity in diversity or of a plural community, is one of the most important discursive figures in the ideology of the nation state.
>
> (Turner 1993: 257 quoting Noel King and Tim Rowse)

The product being sold in these adverts can be national productivity, a television station's identity (Dawson 1990: 94–5), or 'Project Australia' (Sanders 1982: 56).

In the case of Paul Hogan—and the Winfield campaign—the kind of 'Australia' that was constructed was, once again, ocker: male and working-class. More than this, it was a nation of ockers who smoked cigarettes.

The first advert

As noted above, Hogan's 'classic first advertisement' (Webb 1973: 52) for Winfield cigarettes is well remembered as part of television's public archive. At the time of its first broadcast, this representation of an ocker male in a dinner suit caused 'controversy' (Matheson 1984: 28)—a term that, as other chapters of this book have shown, is used as a common journalistic means of describing public debate initiated by media texts. In order to understand the importance of this advert, it is necessary to put it into context, and to understand the generic imperatives of cigarette advertising at the time of its first broadcast. Many television personalities had previously endorsed cigarettes on Australian television. Indeed, associating a known face with the product seems to have been the most popular form of promotion for tobacco products. Graham Kennedy, Ernie Sigley, Alwyn Kurts, Jack Thompson, George Lazenby, Tony Barber, Frank Ifield, and even Norman Gunston have all been associated with tobacco products in the history of Australian advertising (Keating 1999b). Most important for this chapter, however, is Stuart Wagstaff's work on cigarette adverts.

An article in the *Bulletin* in 1967 describes the assumptions of cigarette advertising in the years before Hogan walked in front of the orchestra:

> Cigarettes call for a 'sophisticated' treatment. They are usually shown being smoked by healthy young people ... dining out in luxury, stepping into handsome yachts, spanking along roads to stop for a smoke (in a luxury vehicle, of course) ... Smoking is associated with health, wealth and success with the prettiest girls ... For Peter Stuyvesant, Jackson Wain send teams to shoot their models in all kinds of 'exciting' locations—Paris, London, New York.
>
> (Higham 1967: 25)

The article sets out to question these assumptions: 'Wasn't the image of escapism presented by cigarette commercials sometimes a bit overstressed, suggesting a glamorous life far beyond the average man's pocket? Didn't the commercials lose "identification" this way?' (Higham 1967: 25). But the advertising executive who is questioned does not see that there is a problem:

> I do agree we try to project an image of desirability. And what's wrong with that? There's nothing wrong with Mustangs and speedboats, is there? … everybody likes to feel he can live a little like James Bond' … cigarettes are status-symbols. There is, you must remember, more status in smoking a cigarette than in using detergent … cigarette commercials suggest a very high standard of living …
>
> (quoted in Higham 1967: 25)

Before Hogan, it seems, the genre of cigarette advertising was about sophistication, wealth, and, importantly, an international orientation: jetting off, like James Bond (a British icon) to Paris, London, and New York.[2]

Even more explicitly elitist than Peter Stuyvesant, Benson & Hedges at the same time 'concentrated the use of snobbism by turning Stuart Wagstaff into the Benson and Hedges man' (Hall 1972: 48). Wagstaff's image was that of the ultimate sophisticate: he was 'suave' (Hall 1972: 47); he was 'the king of the sophisticates' (Webb 1973: 52). He 'ponced about in art galleries claiming that he smoked Benson and Hedges "when only the best will do"' (Dale 1999: 25).

This was the context in which Hogan's orchestra advert first appeared. 'British and American accents dominated Australian advertising at the time' (Hertz Walpole, as quoted in Shoebridge 1992: 37); and 'most companies wanted their advertising to look and sound British or American' (Shoebridge 1992: 46). Hogan was not 'suave' or 'sophisticated'. In fact, he was deliberately taking the piss out of such approaches to advertising. The Winfield adverts were directly engaging with these contemporary trends, ridiculing the then-dominant mode of advertising cigarettes. In this, they were part of a more general emergence of what was—even at the time—named the 'ocker advert' (Blanch 1976): adverts such as Rolf Harris's British Paint ads; or the Reverend Barrie Howard's ad for Norman Ross Discount, which used 'casualness' and 'colloquialism' (Hall 1972: 48).

In this context, the Winfield ads deliberately drew attention to themselves as being not-international and not-suave; as being, somehow, deliberately and particularly 'Australian' (Johnson & Smiedt 1999: 206). John Singleton, an advertising executive closely linked with the emergence of 'ocker advertising', explicitly contrasts Hogan's Winfield adverts with those of Stuart Wagstaff for Benson & Hedges. '[P]eople like to see themselves as they really are', he claims:

> The fact is most Australians are ocker, and those who raise up their white hands bleating shock and horror are in the minority ... It's amazing that people will put up with pseudo Yank and pseudo English stuff and not their own Australian thing ... I believe the ocker ad will be here for a long time. In five years, no one will be paying it any attention. The ocker ad will become the norm. The other kind will be the exception.
>
> (Blanch 1976: 132)

These adverts were not simply presenting irreverence as entertaining—mocking the fantasy, elite world of previous cigarette adverts. Rather, this irreverent attitude was presented as distinctively Australian. This is what Australians are 'really' like: 'ocker'. Paul Hogan—so the claim goes—represents Australian national identity. It is 'an Australian campaign for an Australian cigarette—no more jet-setting Stuyvesant internationalism, or world-wide Rothmans king size acceptance, but good honest Australiana' (Webb 1973: 51). The overall slogan of the campaign—'Anyhow★ have a Winfield' is remembered as being 'particularly' 'Australian' (Page 1986: 10). The Hogan character was 'tilting at authority', and that was 'a thing that Australians really did identify with' (Page 1986: 10). Winfields were 'a distinctively Australian cigarette' (Page 1992 [1986]: 117; see also Johnson & Smiedt 1999: 206).

This explicit claim to represent an Australian national identity in these adverts occurred in a context of a more generalised move to create and promote Australianness. Patricia Johnson claims that at this time (during the early 1970s) Australia experienced 'a new surge of nationalism', where products were no longer sold by the 'urbanity' of Stuart Wagstaff, but by an Australian identity she describes as 'the down-to-earth and scratch-yer-nose familiarity of the Australian Ocker' (Johnson 1975: 33).

Links have been drawn to the political climate of the time: 'It's Time' was the slogan for the ALP's 1972 election campaign (Page 1986: 9); and 'around the time of Whitlam's election as Prime Minister, [advertisers] decided that it was "OK to be Australian" ' (Page 1986: 9). '[T]here was a huge wave of nationalism' at the time, and this was linked to politics by the fact that 'There were a lot of ockers around then like Gough Whitlam and Bob Hawke, because being an ocker then meant having your feet on the ground, sort of being down to earth' ('How the Ocker Prince Learned to Straddle the World' 1983: 7).

In other cultural sites, Australianness was becoming acceptable: 'Radio announcers who sounded Australian rather than pseudo-Los Angeles or BBC were finding acceptability' (Page 1986: 9). In this context, 'the emerging success of the "ocker" advertising pioneered by John Singleton'—presenting' the first substantial wave to use a demotic style and the vernacular idiom in a confident and assertive fashion'—was an important part of the construction of a public Australian national identity (Cunningham 1992: 97–8).

Hoges: real, authentic, genuine, true

From a commercial point of view, Hogan's Winfield adverts were immensely successful, helping Winfield to reach 'the number one spot among cigarette brands, a position it still holds [in 1992]' (Shoebridge 1992: x), while a 'research study conducted by Rothmans in the late 1980s discovered that more than 30 per cent of Australian smokers still associated Paul Hogan with Winfield', despite his leaving the campaign a decade earlier (Shoebridge 1992: 33).

But more than simply selling cigarettes, or promoting brand recognition, these adverts were immensely successful in promoting the idea that there could be such a thing as a single, unified, Australian national identity, and that Paul Hogan embodied it. In the discourses that are circulated around the adverts, we see an insistence that in the body and star image of Paul Hogan, we can find an exemplar of what Australians are *really* like. As the audience identifies with Hogan—moving away from the 'fantasy' of earlier cigarette ads—a centre is provided around which a national culture can solidify. Hogan is repeatedly referred to in journalistic commentary as being the already *typical* Australian—what we ('all') supposedly are already like.

The adverts provide 'the first real representation of the Ocker, the working class Australian male' (Johnson 1975: 33). He is 'genuinely Australian … an aggressively, unashamedly honest type of Australian' (Webb 1973: 52). He is 'the man-in-the-street' and 'very Australian' (MacDonald 1973: 54). 'Hogan typifies almost everything likeable about the Australian character' and is 'the average Aussie bloke' (Matheson 1984: 28). He is 'typically Australian' (Page 1986: 11). 'He was … very Australian' (McClymont 1986: 10). He was 'the real thing—not somebody putting on a funny voice and pretending' (Hall 1976: 133). He 'reflected the ordinary Australian' (Murphy 1981: 74). He was an 'authentic' ocker (Byrell 1995: 95), 'the down-to-earth dinkum Aussie, Mr Average' (Barr 1977: 200). He is an 'ordinary Australian' (Shoebridge 1992: 38) and 'truly Australian' (Shoebridge 1992: 32).[3] 'Real', 'genuine', 'typical', 'ordinary', 'authentic', 'very', and 'truly' Australian.

There are a couple of moments in the publicity around Hogan's star image where the problems with this become apparent, for of course, Hogan in the Winfield adverts does *not* represent what all Australians are *really* like. In one interview, Hogan states that 'I'm a typical Australian character', before going on in the next sentence to add that 'there's no such thing as a typical Australian, but there are thousands walking around the streets who are just like me' (MacDonald 1973: 54). This ambivalence suggests the tone of the project of national identity. On the one hand, there is no such thing as a typical Australian—which is to say, there is no Australian 'essence' shared by everyone in the country. But on the other hand, we can ignore that awkward fact as we set about the project of creating a national identity: let's pretend that there is something that 'we' all have in common.

Even more tellingly, when Allan Johnston is discussing a later series of adverts in which Hogan appeared (for Australian tourism), he strives to find a way to articulate Hogan's status in relationship to Australian national identity: 'He is what an Australian ... what you expect an Australian ... what an Australian *should* look like' (Page 1986: 11). This reveals exactly the prescriptive nature of the project of national identity. In fact, Hogan is *not* a 'typical' Australian, but he *should* be. This is not showing the audience what they *are* like; it is rather providing a model around which a community can be formed, behaviour measured, and identity appreciated.

The typical Australian

The consensus of public discussion of Hogan's star image is that it is 'typically Australian'. But what does that mean? It means that it is 'ocker'. But what does that mean? Many commentators on Hogan's image rely on simply repeating the terms 'ocker' or 'dinkum' as though these were self-explanatory (Davies 1981: 135). Some writers have gone further by providing descriptions of the characteristics of the 'ocker', the 'typical Australian' personified in Hogan's performance. John Tulloch suggests that Hogan's image ties into earlier versions of the typical Australian, as discussed by Russel Ward in his book *The Australian Legend* (Ward 1978; Tulloch & Turner 1989: 134–5). The characteristics Ward identifies in this archetype certainly agree with those attributed by commentators to Hogan's image. For Ward, the archetypal Australian is *easygoing*, 'ever willing to have a go, but willing to be content with a task done in a way that is near enough' (paraphrased by Tulloch & Turner 1989: 134–5). Similarly, Hogan is 'easy going' (Tulloch & Turner 1989: 131) and 'willing to "have a go"' (Windschuttle 1988: 168–9). For Ward, the archetypal Australian is *laconic*: 'usually taciturn rather than talkative, one who endures stoically' (paraphrased by Tulloch & Turner

1989: 135). Similarly, Hogan is 'quick to decry affectation … in a droll or laconic rather than a verbose way' (Windschuttle 1988: 168–9). For Ward, the archetypal Australian is *disrespectful of authority*: 'the concept that, as Ward puts it, Jack is not only as good as, but a good deal better than his master' (Windschuttle 1988: 169). Hogan is similarly 'irreverent about authority' (Tulloch and Turner 1989: 131), is 'ever ready to knock the eminent (Windschuttle 1988: 168–9), and spends his time 'tilting at authority' (Page 1992 [1986]: 117).

Easy going, laconic and irreverent: this is 'what an Australian *should* be like'. There is also, it is claimed, something particularly Australian about Hogan's self-deprecating humour. Hogan claims for himself that 'The Australian sense of humour is a very special one … Australians love the leg pull in humour' (as quoted in Johnson 1975: 34). Many writers have claimed that Australian humour is a distinctive part of the national character (what Australians *should* be like). Keith Willey, for example, claims that

> some revival of an indigenous humour [it should be noted here that by 'indigenous' Willey does not mean 'indigenous' in a racial sense but 'Australian'] … has an essential part to play in the shaping of any new and distinctive national identity within which Australians of all backgrounds can still recognize themselves and feel at home.
>
> (Willey 1988: 169)

The specific characteristics attributed to that humour include the fact that, supposedly, 'Irony predominates and individuals manipulated by circumstances or a destiny they are unable to control wryly resign themselves to their own powerlessness' (Jones & Andrews 1988: 60). '[S]ardonic irreverence' and lack of respect for authority have also been claimed for Australia by writers such as Phillip Adams (Turnbull 1996b: 13).

Once again, it is important to bear in mind that there is no such thing as a single national humour and, as Clarke has pointed out, claims for national distinctiveness based on particular kinds of humour are as spurious as those made in terms of other characteristics:

> Most of the things said about particular people's humour are said by practically everybody … If you read books about Canadian humour, you'll find that one of the things that characterises Canadian humour is its laconic quality. And you read about English understatement. You also hear it of Jewish comedy, for example.
>
> (Turnbull 1996b: 13)

This, then, is the Australian national identity offered up as 'real', 'authentic', and 'genuine', by this 'typical', 'average', 'ordinary' Australian: Australians *should* be easygoing, laconic, and disrespectful of authority, with a humour tending towards irony and the leg-pull. These qualities are presented in Hogan's adverts for Winfield cigarettes.

Screensound holds only three of Hogan's Winfield adverts, all later examples made for the cinema. In these, it is still possible to see the characteristics described by writers on his television adverts, from the 'classic' first orchestra advert onward. The first television advert poked fun at high culture by placing Hogan in a dinner suit and thongs, and the later 'Ballet' cinema advert returns to similar themes. It is high culture, rather than 'authority' per se, that is being treated disrespectfully here. The advert opens with a typical ballet scene—a line of female dancers in tutus on stage, performing classical ballet movements. Hogan wanders on to the stage and delivers a speech to camera. 'G'day', he says, opening with the vernacular that was previously not allowed in cigarette advertising, and continues to speak with a broad Australian accent:

> Maybe the ballet isn't everyone's cup of tea, but I know youse Winfield smokers like a bit of class, otherwise you wouldn't be smoking the best cigarette in Australia ... so it's up to fellas like meself, on your behalf, of course, to propagate the finer arts.

Hogan is dressed in traditional male ballet attire, including tights. As he talks, the ballet continues in the background, oblivious to the quite different world appearing in the foreground. The advert does not invite us to laugh at Hogan's claims to represent 'class' and 'the finer arts'; as he is the hero, it is 'class' itself that should appear ridiculous. One of the ballerinas comes towards him, and he breaks off: 'Anyhow, it's time for the party-doo'. He lifts her up, and slowly spins her, places her down, and kneels. 'Anyhow', he says. 'Have a Winfield', she interrupts. He looks at her: 'You're learning fast, love'.

Hogan is obviously out of place here, but he is not awkward. He is intensely casual and relaxed. And he does not become a figure of fun: he executes the ballet move without dropping the ballerina, and she then joins the advert. After the caption—'Anyhow, have a Winfield'—we cut back to Hogan and the ballerina, dressed in normal clothes, sitting in a pub drinking.

It is easy to see that the advert presents a character who is 'easygoing' and 'not afraid to have a go'. The fact that his accent is strongly Australian and he shows no concern about pronunciation suggests, perhaps, disrespect for cultural authority, although this is perhaps hidden by the 'irony' of his claim to represent class. And it may be that his 'laconic' character is revealed by his lack of gushing praise of the ballet. The discourses of nationalism around Hogan tell us how to read this advert—where to look in it for the 'Australianness'.

A second advert returns to the orchestra, again placing Hogan against an icon of high-class culture:

> G'day, well Winfield's done it again, and brought out a new extra-mild smoke, and after months of research, I've managed to come up with a fella who has all the characteristics necessary to impress you as extra-mild smokers. Give him a warm welcome. Anyhow, meet my brother Pat.

The humour here is obviously in building up the 'research' into 'characteristics' before introducing his 'brother'. As they go on to discuss the advantages of new Winfield Blue, poetry is the high-art form that is gently mocked: 'That blue pack will get them in', says Hoges. Pat replies, 'Sort of like the sky on a clear day with a light nor-easterly blowing'. 'A bit of poetry for ya', says Hoges to the audience. Pat finishes with 'Runs in the family'. Again, it is explicitly high culture, rather than authority, that is the focus of the advert's humour.

The third advert held at Screensound—'Hoges and Strop at the Olgas'—opens with a shot of the Olgas, while classical music plays. The composition and music suggest something like *Picnic at Hanging Rock*. Two sets of legs walk into shot, and the conversation takes place over this shot of the legs. This conversation does not make fun of high-culture; it makes fun of Australian national identity:

> Gee—look at that. Ayers Rock.
> That's not Ayers Rock, son.
> Well, whose rocks are they, mate?
> They're Olgas.
> Well, why did she leave them way out here where nobody lives?

We cut to a close-up of their faces, with the spectacular landscape visible behind them as Hoges says:

> Lots of people live out here, Strop. Pioneers of the country.
> Makes you feel proud, mate.
> Yup. And it's up to us to fill them in on Winfield 25s.

The camera pulls out at the end of the advert to show that Hoges and Strop are wandering through the Olgas wearing big sandwich boards with 'Anyhow, have a Winfield' emblazoned on them. In this advert, it is 'pioneers' and landscape—traditional icons of Australian national identity—that are treated in the way in which poetry, classical music, and ballets have been in others. The image of Hogan making fun of high-class culture was not the sole theme of this advertising series: it also featured 'this ordinary Australian doing extraordinary things, or in an extraordinary setting ... Hogan appearing as a skydiver, airline pilot, rodeo horse rider, shearer, marlin fisherman, sculptor, golfer, archer and trapeze artist' (Shoebridge 1992: 39, 38).

Looking at these adverts from a position informed by the discourses of national identity that circulated so insistently around them, it is possible to trace the 'ocker', archetypal-Australian identity that they propose.

How well was that proposed national identity received?

Cross-demographic communication

John Hartley has proposed the term 'cross-demographic communication' as a useful way of understanding the communicative possibilities of television (Hartley 1998: 31; see also Meyrowitz 1985). It broadcasts not simply to a 'mass'; rather, it often manages to speak, amazingly well, to a disparate variety of groups, differentiated by such demographic characteristics as age, gender, sexuality, race, and religion. Indeed, as William Boddy has noted, television has often been appealed to as the perfect medium for promoting a unified national identity beyond such demographic considerations (Boddy 1999). Hogan's Winfield adverts attempt to address just such a national audience—to cross demographic boundaries and construct a single, unified address to 'Australians'. In at least one way, his cross-demographic address worked fantastically well: it was his very success in speaking to different ages of Australians as a unified group that led to his removal from the realm of advertising in Australia.

It should be noted that this is not an ontological imperative of the medium. As chapter 8 argues, some programs on Australian television have specifically addressed discrete age groups in ways that divide the audience. This is not a matter of the medium's ontology, but of the particular ways in which its possibilities are realised by particular programs.

Sandra Hall argues that Hogan appealed to such a cross-demographic audience (although she prefers the more derogatory descriptor 'mass'), including even a youth audience who would previously have been bored 'comatose' by such Australianness (Hall 1976: 135).

Marion MacDonald notes that 'small boys of all varieties love him; his bugger-it style ("Any'ow ...") is their own' (MacDonald 1973: 54). Hogan deliberately, it seems, cultivated such an image: 'He has turned down two comedy roles ... [one] in an R-certificate film, which might have damaged "me family appeal" ' (MacDonald 1973: 55). Perhaps the most convincing argument for Hogan's cross-demographic appeal across age, though, is the fact that his Winfield adverts also proved popular with younger Australians: 'Winfield's share of the adult market reached 28 per cent [during the 1970s, and] ... half of the schoolchildren who smoked preferred Winfield' (Oram 1987: 86).

Hogan managed to provide an imaginary Australian national identity that successfully crossed age demographics. And because he was also associated with—indeed, created himself through—cigarette adverts, this could not be tolerated by certain governmental agencies. This too-successful attempt to unify the Australian nation had to stop.

The advertising of tobacco has long been an annoying issue for governments, being a product that is not illegal, but of which they must at least *appear* to disapprove. In the mid-1960s, 'a conference of State Ministers of Health' decided not to ban tobacco advertising, but rather to 'inform the public of the risks attendant on smoking, attention being directed particularly to young people' (ABCB 1965: 71). It is young people, in governmental discourse, who must be particularly protected from smoking—as from everything else. On 1 January 1966, a voluntary code 'governing the advertising of cigarettes on television [and] agreed upon by manufacturers and the Federation of Australian Commercial Television Stations' stated that, among other requirements,

> 1 cigarette advertising must not be aimed at any non-smoker ...
> 2 Principal characters ... should not be under twenty-five years of age ...
> 5 No advertising for cigarettes may appear containing testimonials from persons who have special appeal to young people ...
>
> (ABCB 1966: 59)

Over the years, the rules on television advertising of tobacco became gradually harsher. On 1 September 1973, cigarette advertising was only allowed after 8.30 p.m., and only two adverts per hour could be shown. The next year, the time slot was moved to 9.30 p.m.; a year later, the number was reduced to one per hour. On 1 September 1976, cigarette advertising was banned from Australian television altogether (Bryden-Brown 1981: 110, 112).

Hogan's ads were removed from television along with all other cigarette adverts. They continued in magazines and cinemas. However, at the start of 1980, a group called Movement Opposed to the Promotion of Unhealthy Products (MOP UP) complained to the Advertising Standards Council about Winfield's adverts. They drew on Clause 4 of the advertising industry's own code of conduct for cigarette advertising, which states that 'no advertising for cigarettes may include persons who have major appeal for children or adolescents under 18 years of age', and argued that the high ratings for Hogan's television specials among teenagers meant he was unfit to advertise tobacco products (Shoebridge 1992: 44).

The complaint was upheld:

> Winfield: A New South Wales organisation alleged that the use of Paul Hogan in Winfield cigarette advertisements breached Clause 4 of the Cigarette Code. Complaint upheld. It was decided that Paul Hogan had major appeal to children and therefore, all Winfield advertisements featuring Paul Hogan were in breach of Clause 4 of the cigarette code.
>
> (Advertising Standards Council 1981: 24)

Hogan's success at providing a national identity accessible to children was celebrated by his being banned from the genre of tobacco advertising. As Sir Richard Kirby, chair of the Advertising Standards Council, put it, 'Hogan was simply too popular with children' (Oram 1987: 86), although the Chair of the Advertising Federation argued that the clause should not apply to Hogan, as he appealed to all age groups rather than specifically to the young. He asked, 'How can you find a popular personality who appeals to adults, but not to five to 17 year olds?' (Harding 1980: 59).

Australian class

Hogan's appeal was certainly cross-demographic. But it was not 'mass'; it did not appeal universally to all Australians.

A telling comment comes in a survey of '4000 schoolchildren' as to their feelings on Hogan. Unsurprisingly, 'males liked him much better than females'—an exclusion that has been oft noted in discussions of Australian national identity (Schaffer 1988). More relevant for a discussion of the Winfield adverts, though, 'public-school children [liked him much] better than ones in private schools' (MacDonald 1973: 54). Both children and adults like this Australian ocker type, but not all children and not all adults. Although, as chapter 15 suggests, representations of class are problematic in Australia, it seems reasonable to make a tentative suggestion that class seems to be an important factor in drawing the limits of Hogan's cross-demographic appeal.

It is interesting that, at the period described above, when 'ockerism' became an important part of adverts, and Australian culture more generally seems to have been moving to the acceptance that 'it's alright to be Australian', there were voices in the public sphere condemning such a move.

From the mid 1970s onwards, the Australian Broadcasting Control Board/Tribunal begins to provide in its annual reports a breakdown of the categories of letters of complaint it has received. From 1975 onwards, one of the categories of complaint is given as 'Taste (including "ockerism" etc.)' (ABT 1979b: 24). In the period 1976–78, this is the category in which the Board/Tribunal receives most letters of complaint—more even than complaints about sex or violence on television. The definition of the category in this report states that it includes 'disgusting manners (over-enthusiastic blowing of bubbles in bubble gum ad, scrunching of chips) rough words ("gutsy" and "damn"), ockerism' (Advertising Standards Council 1978: 7).

The fact that hundreds of letters of complaint were being received about these topics gives us some sense of the way in which 'ockerism' could offend a viewing audience unused to seeing anything impolite on television (although it should also be noted once again that a couple of hundred letters is nothing compared with the millions watching these programs and adverts). 'Ockerism' is—like 'scrunching of chips', or the use of the word 'gutsy'—something that could offend only the most delicate of sensibilities. In the 1981 report, the category remains unchanged: 'ockerism' is still a subcategory of 'bad taste' (Advertising Standards Council 1981: 11).

After Hogan's first appearances on *A Current Affair*, the program's producer claims that 'The program was swamped by both fan mail and hate mail. Concerned citizens demanded that Hogan be taken off air, because the image of an Ocker was not one Australians wanted to see' (Johnson & Smiedt 1999: 197).

Journalistic claims about programs being 'swamped' with letters should always be interpreted with some caution—but the letters to the Board suggest at least some degree of controversy. In the public record, we find much proof of controversy around these adverts and the national identity they suggested. An article in a popular women's magazine discusses the terms of reference:

> The Great Ocker ad debate … began seven years ago [in 1969] ... [with ads for] Norman Ross discounts … [now] the ocker ad is with us. Each night, Jax the Ripper, Jeannie Little, Betty Best and … others screech, whine and grate at us like so many demented cockatoos. They're ugly, vulgar and tasteless—but they work
>
> (Blanch 1976: 130)

ABC current affairs literally turned this into a debate on 'Ockers and Ockerism' (Gifford 1976: 7). There were those—including those children from private schools mentioned above—who did not like this ocker version of national identity. There were those who found it 'tasteless' and 'vulgar' and 'rough'. No demographic evidence exists of the provenance of these speakers, but given their discursive positioning, it is difficult to imagine them as anything other than upper-middle class. Here, the national address breaks down.

After the ads were over

Paul Hogan's 'whole fame is based on commercials [and t]here's no one else like that in the world' (Page 1986: 10; see also Hall 1976: 134; Oram 1987: 68; Windschuttle 1988: 169; McCallum 1998: 210; Davies 1981: 135). After the Winfield ads, he went on to have a remarkably consistent career, presenting the ocker Australian image in a series of different commercials. In 1981, he appeared in Britain for Fosters Lager, again as an ocker. In one of these commercials, he was watching *Swan Lake* at the Royal Opera House—holding, of course, a can of Fosters in his hand. Seeing a male dancer appear on stage, Hogan covered the eyes of the woman sitting next to him, saying 'Strewth, that bloke's got no strides on!' Again, the ocker was successful, with Fosters gaining 6 per cent of London's beer market within eight months of its launch (see Oram 1987: 127–8).

These adverts also appeared in Canada and the USA (Page 1986: 11). Hogan then appeared in a campaign for the Australian Tourist Commission, first at home, and then abroad, appearing in adverts selling Australia as a holiday destination for Americans. Again, these were successful, with over 350 000 calls made to the tourism hotline that the commercials advertised, and an 80 per cent increase in demand for holiday visas. Mainly as a result of this success in selling Australia overseas, Hogan was named Australian of the Year by the *Australian* newspaper, he was awarded the Order of Australia—and was named in a national poll as 'the most popular man in Australia' (see Oram 1987: 139; see also Page 1992 [1986]: 118–19; Shoemaker 1994: 188; Matheson 1984: 31).

Hogan also appeared in *The Paul Hogan Show*, a very successful comedy venture, which 'rated in the mid-to-high 30s, [and] knocked [*Number 96*] back to second place' (Johnson & Smiedt 1999: 217), before going on to international stardom with the success of the film *Crocodile Dundee* (1986).

Meanwhile, according to advertising analysts, by the late 1970s the time of the ocker had already gone. Ockerism could no longer be celebrated—as it was with Hogan's early commercials—as being 'real'. Complaints were already being made that 'The brash, loud ocker of television commercials has had his day. He is being replaced by real people in real situations' (Symons 1977: 52).

This is precisely the language that had been used when the Winfield adverts were introduced—that what had gone before was not 'real' enough, that these would offer something more 'real'. Perhaps the persuasiveness of the ocker as a unifying national force is no longer convincing. Writing of 'Life after Hoges', Chris Adams claims that 'the Australian consumer no longer wants to be identified with the ocker image, but rather a more urbane character' (Adams 1990: 22)—which brings us right back to Stuart Wagstaff. Adams argues in 1990 that 'ocker is out'—'there is no replacement for Paul Hogan'. Whereas, for a period at least, there was public consensus (however hotly contested) that Hogan could embody in an individual all desirable aspects of 'the Australian character', nobody after him is accorded the same privilege. In Adams's terms, 'the ideal Australian' after Hogan would have to be a composite of many people, with 'the brains of Ben Lexcen, Bryan Brown's body, Doug Mulray's humour, Jana Wendt's drive' (Adams 1990: 23).

In order to replace Paul Hogan, it would be necessary to create a Frankenstein's monster of bits and pieces. This was what Hogan, in the Winfield commercials to begin with, so spectacularly achieved: in a single body, he managed to hold together a national vision of what 'Australians *should* be'. He was so successful at it that he had to be stopped. And yet the slogan and the adverts and the Australianness are remembered by many writers, and are part of the public archive of Australian television. To the cultural heritage of adverts identified by Shoebridge can be added the Winfield adverts—which sold not only Winfield cigarettes, but Australianness itself, so successfully to Australia.

Availability

Screensound holds only three of the cinema adverts. These are access copies, and are available for viewing by researchers.

Notes

1 I am interested in the way in which advertisements communicate in public culture; I have not made use of previous writing from a Marxist perspective that simply condemns them using the 'capitalism=bad' paradigm (see, for example, Mills 1978).

2 Note that at least one writer—an anonymous reader of this book's manuscript—would disagree with this claim, stating that 'I (and others!) wrote and directed many ads for fags that featured sporting events and other populist dreams years before Hoges'.

3 A couple of exceptional commentators claim that Hogan is not genuine enough. Exhibiting what Marc Brennan has referred to as the 'I like his early stuff' syndrome, they either bemoan the loss of his initial 'genuine' Australian character on *A Current Affair* (MacDonald 1973: 56) or mourn the loss of earlier comics, who were more authentic than Hogan (such as Mo Rene) (Willey 1984: 137).

8

Countdown: Sex and Drugs and Ambivalent Identities

1974–87

On 8 July 1979, Iggy Pop appeared on the ABC music program *Countdown*—as the Corporation's Archive Guide delightfully puts it, 'under the influence of some substance'. He slurred answers to questions, threw his microphone stand around the studio, and scared the front row of young girls in the audience. It was an iconic moment, and suggestive of many of the elements that made the ABC music program so important for Australian television.

Countdown was Australia's first national music program: a mixture of pop gossip, live studio performances, and video clips, hosted by a variety of musical celebrities and featuring the talents of Ian 'Molly' Meldrum. It has passed into Australia's public archive of television's well-remembered programs. During its run, the program became such an important part of Australia's mediasphere that its final episode made front-page headlines in both of Melbourne's daytime newspapers (the *Age* and the *Herald*). It has also survived since its cancellation. The ritual of a Sunday evening watching *Countdown* is an acknowledged part of Australia's public archive of television programs. Few of the correspondents who contributed to the research for this book mentioned the day of the week on which their favourite moments were broadcast. The only program for which this happened was *Countdown*: 'Sundays … [I] used to watch *Countdown*' is a common refrain, and many viewers remember the program in precisely these terms:

> *Countdown* is on TV. It is a ritual, as much of a constant as there can be … One of the most potent cultural imperatives of young people in the 13 years between

1974 and 1987 was that wherever they were, whatever they were doing, they had to achieve a feat that would enable them to watch the greatest show on television.

(Wilmoth 1993: 5)

So '*Countdown* was the big event of the weekend for most of the early to mid-70s' (Wark 1999: 238, 240, quoting Catharine Lumby). And watching the program is only part of the ritual; gathering to share its contents was another: 'When you weren't watching it you were talking about it' (Darren Tofts, as quoted in Wark 1999: 238); 'it seemed to be all anyone ever spoke about at school the following Monday' (Mark Davis, as quoted in Wark 1999: 238–40).

Several specific moments from the program are remembered in the public archive—for example, 'Molly Interviews Prince Charles', which appears as one of *Who Weekly*'s '100 Greatest Moments in Television' (1999: 63). The presence of British royalty—a group still regarded (although this is changing rapidly) as being untouchable, inhuman, and beyond everyday life—makes Molly's blooper so attractive that it is archived in many places. An account of the program's great moments in *TV Times*, for example, focuses on this unattainable quality of Prince Charles by emphasising that 'Every word of Molly's interview with the Prince, questions and answers, had to be written out and sent to Buckingham Palace for vetting. It was returned with official approval on the understanding that the script be used word for word' (Scott 1979: 10–11). Having established the status of the guest as, literally, 'royalty', this account then describes Molly's inability to follow the rules of television: 'Poor [Molly] started his introduction, which was written out on idiot sheets in front of him. He was terrible, couldn't even get through his opening remarks. Four, five, six takes and Prince Charles was looking on patiently.' Finally, this moment is remembered for Molly's inability to respect the decorous boundaries that separate the everyday from the elevates: 'Molly ended by saying, and I saw your Mum in an open carriage ... The Prince froze and looked very very regal—"Do you mean Her Majesty the Queen?" he said very icily, putting Molly back in his place' (Scott 1979: 10–11, quoting Michael Shrimpton; see also Wilmoth 1993: 40).

For this chapter, though, I have chosen Molly's encounter with a drugged American singer rather than a chilly British royal. This moment (which was repeated in 2000 as part of the late-night ABC music show *Rage*'s programming) is memorialised in Peter Wilmoth's account of the importance of *Countdown* in the Australian mediasphere, *Glad All Over*:

> Many moments are crystallised in the *Countdown* generation's consciousness … a golden *Countdown* moment that echoes down the years: Iggy Pop's live performance and his interview with Molly. 'G'day! G'day!' said Iggy, his eyes popping out like organ stops. He jumped up and down on his chair.
>
> (Wilmoth 1993: 189)

Examining the ways in which *Countdown* was discussed during the period of its broadcast, and the ways in which it has survived in public culture, several points of interest emerge. Questions about control and consumption of popular music are of obsessive interest to many writers on the program, who are concerned with Molly's 'extraordinary influence' (Wilmoth 1993: 15) over the music industry and the tastes of young record buyers (Meldrum 1987: 11; John 1981: 82; Murphy 1981: 89; Scott 1979: 10; Stockbridge 1989: 78). More interestingly for the project of this book though, *Countdown* raises important questions about the formation of communities and identities centred on age, with interesting inflections of space, nation, and time. The program allowed suburban viewers to escape not only to a national space of style, rebellion, and youth culture, but also to an international arena. Iggy Pop, drug-fucked on *Countdown*, represents the emergence of an accessible identity in Australia formed around age, rebellion, transgressiveness, and the uses of geography.

Ritual and identity

As noted above, watching *Countdown* is remembered by viewers as a ritual, and no viewer of the program would be likely to forget the time at which it was broadcast: Sunday evenings, six o'clock. As Wilmoth notes, describing this 'ritual', it was a 'potent cultural imperative' to watch the program (Wilmoth 1993: 5), and both the correspondents for this book and the academics questioned by McKenzie Wark for his work on *Countdown* remember this clearly (Wark 1999: 238–40). Jane Kennedy claims that 'We were OBSESSED with *Countdown* … Every Sunday night at six o'clock we sat there and sang along to our favourite one hit wonders, enjoying Molly's "relaxed" hosting' (Jones 1999: 184).

Indeed, this sense of the ritual of *Countdown*'s performance is placed into the public sphere in a fictional performance by yet another figure who drew together an identity composed of sex, drugs, and pop music: Michael Hutchence.

> [In] *Dogs in Space*, the star, played by Michael Hutchence, drags himself around a dilapidated house in Richmond, an old blanket pulled around his body. The pop singer is being harangued by a concerned visitor to play a concert for charity. With a cavalier shrug he mumbles 'I've got to go and watch *Countdown*'. The scene crystallised a Sunday night ritual which has been firmly in place for 13 years, a ritual embraced on a level which, as the show dies, will probably never again be matched.
>
> (Wilmoth 1987: 8)

The sense of a community—indeed, an identity—formed through this ritual is powerful in many accounts. What kind of identity was it that *Countdown* made available to Australian audiences?

Age and drugs

Public discourses at the time of its broadcast and in the public archive repeatedly insist that *Countdown* is a program for the young. Indeed, if you are not a teenager and you are watching this program, there may be something wrong with you. If you are not a teenager and you are *presenting* this program, then something is very wrong indeed.

So, its audience is composed of '14 year old pop fanatics' (Wilmoth 1987: 8). The program is 'the authorised music gospel of every 15 year old in the country' (McCarthy 1978: 7). It has 'an audience of at least one and a half million youngsters, aged mainly between 10 and 16' (Gawenda 1983: 1). To be older than this and watch the program means that you have not grown up: 'I never stopped watching *Countdown* ... I suppose it means I never wanted to grow up' (Wilmoth 1987: 8). Interviews with Molly Meldrum during the show's run continually suggest that there is something very strange about this man who seems to include himself in this teenager identity. The fact that a grown-up could actually respect and wish to take part in this culture is distinctly unsavoury for many writers, who would obviously prefer a figure in the style of 1960s *Bandstand* presenter Brian Henderson, who wore a shirt and tie to present a program by which he was obviously bemused. Teenage culture is something, these writers imply, that should be disapproved of by proper grown-ups. It is worthless and rather dangerous.

One interview with Molly starts by describing the music of *Countdown*—the music that Molly likes—as 'bubblegum music, teenybopper stuff that most people left behind them by the time they turned 20' (Gawenda 1983: 1). Molly has not left it behind; he has not grown up. Leaving 'bubblegum music' behind is obviously the correct thing to do, moving on to more 'adult' music (whether folk or jazz or classical the writer does not specify).

But it is not just the music that Molly Meldrum is caught up in; it is the teenage lifestyle that goes with it. As Peter Wilmoth suggests of the age identity that goes with pop music, 'The whole point of pop was, surely, to be something that would vaguely irritate your parents. The object of parental disapproval could have long hair ... Or they could be either drug-takers, or suspects thereof' (Wilmoth 1993: 88).

Teenage identity—that which *Countdown* services—links pop music with transgression (sexual, long hair, or involving proscribed substances). The fact that Molly might actually be a part of this community seriously worries his interviewers in the popular press:

> Moll [is] the world's oldest teenager ... Any day at Moll's place in Richmond is bedlam but Mondays are more so. Since his house burned down, he's been holed up in a self-contained room out the back. Today he is surrounded by limp-wristed persons sporting triple earrings in left lobes and a general confusion of people running around in a pink funk ... [the music] is incomprehensible. But Moll bops, intense concentration on his face ... 'I relate to kids very strongly', he said.
>
> (Crisp 1984: 29)

The disdain in this article is clear: the teenage group around Molly is composed of 'limp-wristed persons sporting triple earrings'. 'Limp-wristed'? As a term of abuse? In 1984? It is obvious that, to the writer, this transgressive group are, just like their music, 'incomprehensible'. The fact that Molly will not sit quietly and be interviewed is also mentioned in other articles:

> getting Molly to sit down and talk about himself was virtually impossible. For a start, he was always surrounded by people ... a crowd would turn up and the music would be turned on and that would be the end of it. Some of the people were obviously friends. They answered his phone. They drove him around in his Rolls. They did his gardening. They were very young, perhaps in their early 20s. They didn't seem to work ... 'I haven't grown up. Grown ups are closed-minded. They tend to be bigoted and narrow. I'm still a kid and I relate to all those kids out there who watch *Countdown*.'
>
> (Gawenda 1983: 2)

Molly behaves like a kid, likes the wrong music, hangs out with the wrong people—young people who, this *Age* journalist notes, 'didn't seem to work'. This is a strange, foreign world to the journalist:

> Some of them ... couldn't even read ... Some were probably taking drugs. Some were certainly stealing. [Molly] hated the thought that some of them were on drugs. Drugs were a big problem and nothing was being done. 'I don't judge these kids', he said. 'If they are stealing, can they really be blamed?'
>
> (Gawenda 1983: 2)

This is the audience imagined for *Countdown* in public discourses: young, listening to worthless music, making incomprehensible life choices that involve refusing the work ethic, refusing to get a mortgage and their own house, transgressing with drugs and theft. It is no wonder that the writers are so bewildered by Molly choosing to take such an identity as his own. To them, it is entirely strange.

To old men writing on *Countdown,* its sexuality is also completely baffling: 'how often have we seen the spectacle of a group miming a song and not even attempting to do it properly—too intent on the raunchy image and their own egos to even bother to pretend they're playing' (Dudding 1978: 11).

Given such public knowledge about the *Countdown* audience—that this is a group making irrational choices, choosing inexplicable lifestyles—writers worry that *Countdown* must be to blame for *creating* this constituency. To the befuddled adults trying to make sense of it, rational people could never really *choose* such a life; it must be television that is *making* them do it. This is the logic that informs Michael Willesee when he asks Skyhooks on *A Current Affair* if they are not worried that they are corrupting the youth of Australia by appearing on *Countdown* and singing about things such as 'going to bed together, masturbation, smut and orgasms' (Wilmoth 1993: 123).

This seems to me to explain why, as noted above, so much popular writing on the program has been concerned with the 'power' or 'control' of the program over its audience's music-buying choices: it is part of a more general concern about the audience itself. It is an audience that is making choices that appear—to the old farts writing on it—completely incomprehensible. How could they possibly choose this 'bubblegum music'—or this lazy lifestyle, or queer apparel, or drugs, or sexuality—over the rational, logical, proper choice that *I* would have made?

But it is possible, of course, to put this in much more positive terms: that through sex and drugs and rock'n'roll—or perhaps just sex and drugs and 'bubblegum music'—*Countdown* constructed a teenage identity for Australia in a convincing and compelling way. And Molly's role in this is not a disturbing one, but one to be celebrated, for in doing this, *Countdown* made a break with much of the music programming that had gone before.

Music, age, and identity

Countdown was not the first music program on Australian television. And from the earliest examples—such as HSV-7 [Melbourne]'s *Your Hit Parade*, 1956 (Stockbridge 1992 [1989]: 135)—these programs have addressed a constituency defined primarily in terms of age. That is, pop music is linked to teenagers.

> In May 1954, the *Australian Women's Weekly* discovered 'teenagers'. A new monthly supplement was to be included for this post-war 'demographic', which had been produced by prolonged education, suburbanism, and increased disposable income, motorcar ownership and consumer credit. Dress, behaviour and grooming defined the teenager—who was to be found wherever American brand names circulated.
>
> (Bell & Bell 1993: 165)

In the 1950s, the 'teenager' begins to emerge as a public identity: a category for self-definition whose entry is controlled by age, and whose membership implies both consumption (including consumption of pop music) and a desire to escape the limitations of immediate geographical experience in a turn abroad—particularly to the USA. It is in the development of this identity—age linked with pop music and geography—that *Countdown* plays such an important part. The arrival of television in the mid 1950s, Murphy notes, 'coincided almost exactly with the revolution in popular music which cleaved a chasm between the music of parents and the new music ... of kids' (Murphy 1981: 87). Discussing the attempts of television to create music programming that would address this new, age-governed constituency, he notes that 'much of the early programming was rather patronising'. In this category might be included such programs as *Bandstand* (TCN-9, from 1958), presented by a middle-aged Brian Henderson. Henderson was staid and traditional—a man in a tweed jacket presenting a youth music show. In one memorable clip from the program, he presents the show in a shirt and tie, and apologises to the audience for not wearing a jacket: 'It's a pretty hot afternoon,' he says, 'so no coat, if you don't mind' (*35 Years of Television* 1991).

This is not the stuff of teenage rebellion. The main featured singer on *Bandstand* was Col Joye, a man who 'eschewed exaggerated hip movements' (Waterhouse 1995: 242). Overall, *Bandstand* had a 'sedate, clean cut image' (Murphy 1981: 87–8): 'Pop was from another world, kid's stuff, and while television indulged it, Henderson represented the generation gap and the view that this pop stuff was all a bit of frippery. Adults were encouraged to be befuddled about its attraction' (Wilmoth 1993: 31).

In contrast, starting on 28 February 1959, *Six O'Clock Rock* allowed a quite different kind of presenter onto Australian television: 'its "wild one" Johnny O'Keefe'. The program presented itself as 'blatant and rude' and, Murphy argues, 'gave Australian teenagers something to identify with and call their own' (Murphy 1981: 87–8):

> Of course, previously this had been possible by means of the press and through the cinema newsreels productions, but the television with its much larger coverage and ready accessibility ... represented a quantum leap in access to images drawn from the society.
>
> (Stratton 1992: 11)

It is into this tradition that *Countdown* can be written. The program started in 1974, evolving from *GTK* (*Get to Know*), a magazine program on the ABC that included musical performances as well as general arts features (Stockbridge 1992 [1989]: 136), and drawing on pioneering ATV-0 shows such as *The Go!! Show* (1964–67), *Kommotion* (1965–67), *Uptight* (1967–70), and *Happening 70/71/72* (the middle two of which also featured Molly). *Countdown* began with seven thirty-minute episodes in 1974 (Keating 1999b). Like *Six O'Clock Rock*, *Countdown* addressed and thus helped to create a teenage identity, doing so by means of a language of music, talking about transgression, style, and identity. *Countdown* did not change what music programs were for, but it did succeed in performing that role with unprecedented success. If Brian Henderson 'represented the generation gap', then 'Molly changed that. No longer did a host condescend or feign ignorance. No longer was a special adult language used in an attempt to distance pop music from the real world. Molly was assuredly one of us—a fan' (Wilmoth 1993: 31).

Molly was one of 'us'—an emerging identity consolidated in *Countdown*. It was an identity based on music, of course, and sex—the lithe body of John Paul Young, the 'raunchy performances' that upset the granddads who wrote television criticism, and the 'smut' of Skyhooks that so offended Michael Willessee—and, of course, drugs.

In *Countdown*'s celebratory hundredth episode, Molly Meldrum hosted the program famously intoxicated. Some accounts claim he was drunk, others that he had taken something a little stronger (Scott 1979: 10). According to Wilmoth's description of this event, Molly was 'a little the worse for wear' —leading to speculation that someone had 'slipped a little something in his drink'. Molly 'stumbled' off the stage into the crowd, saying 'Let's go into the *Countdown* audience'. As Wilmoth describes this moment, 'It would have been a warm, human gesture, a lovely touch, except for one thing. Molly was facing the wrong way. He was facing a non-existent camera' (Wilmoth 1993: 153). Leo Sayer in London took over for the rest of the show (Wilmoth 1993: 153).

Molly then staggered around, gave out a couple of awards, and then vanished for the rest of the show. Peter Wilmoth lists the *Countdown* performers who were well known for their drug associations: Debbie Byrne, Stevie Wright, Neil Storey, Paul Hewson, Andy Gibb, and, of course, Iggy Pop, whose appearance is the subject of this chapter (Wilmoth 1993: 189).

Countdown addressed a teenage audience and thus called that audience into being. It gave Australians who identified with this culture of non-conformity to adult goals—this culture of music and pleasure and lifestyles that are alternative to traditional adult goals of career and mortgage—a common meeting place and a set of shared knowledges. And *Countdown* also *visualised* this audience.

Again, *Countdown* was not the first music program to do this. As suggested above, the combination of music and transgression had informed the teenage identity since the 1950s, and writing on television music shows of the 1960s, Hill suggests that 'it was the teenage audience who were "the real stars of the show" ... their role as unofficial guides to the latest fashions in clothes, haircuts, and above all, dancing' (Hill 1991: 95).

However, it is *Countdown*'s great success in this project that makes it particularly notable. As in the earlier programs, this audience is visualised. We know who we are because we can see ourselves, gathered in the studio listening to the Little River Band. For example, in the Iggy Pop episode (episode 201), the program consists of separate segments—video clips, live performances, Molly's Humdrum (music gossip), the charts, short pieces to camera by the guest presenter Glenn Shorrock—and what links them all, makes them into a unified whole, is the screaming of the audience. This is pretty consistent; this studio audience will scream for anyone from Iggy Pop to Kenny Rogers. As well as screaming, the audience can be seen throughout the program. Glenn Shorrock spends the episode sitting isolated on a little set by himself, neither interacting with the bands that are playing nor directly with the audience. But he is framed by a line of audience members' hands reaching up at his feet, waving in front of the camera. For the live performances—as with Mental as Anything's 'The nips are getting bigger'—the audience's hands can again be seen, a sea of them waving during the song. And as each music clip finishes, screaming brings us back to the studio. These are the 'teenagers', the group that is being 'controlled' and 'influenced' by *Countdown*—or, alternatively, the group that is forming a workable age-based identity founded on the materials that *Countdown* is making so readily accessible.

National identity

It is also important that *Countdown* was the 'first Australian ... national TV rock show' (Wilmoth 1987: 8). Commercial television's previous examples of the genre had been largely state-based and, if they were networked, would appear at different times in different states (Stockbridge 1992 [1989]: 140). By contrast, *Countdown* was an avowedly national program (Wilmoth 1993).

This is not to suggest that *Countdown* was obsessed with constructing a sense of Australianness. It is more accurate to say that the program helped to overcome geography—the different spaces of country, suburb, and inner city—*within* Australia for an audience not specifically aligned around 'Australianness'. Sally Stockbridge suggests that the program was 'significant for its access to country viewers' (Stockbridge 1989: 77), and as Peter Wilmoth puts it, '14 year old pop fanatics from Hobart to Darwin saw what Heaven must look like' (Wilmoth 1987: 8).

Several writers make the same point with the regard to *Countdown*'s suburban audience. Daryl Braithwaite says that 'When we toured in the western suburbs or in remote places in the country, we saw that *Countdown* was all they had. It was like "Here is someone from Melbourne". For them it was like the Bible' (Wilmoth 1987: 8). McKenzie Wark argues that the program 'created a virtual space across the nation, within which young people could express their own sensations' (Wark 1999: 81). It 'provided suburbia with a way to distinguish rock from pop [and it had the] advantage of being available everywhere' (Wark 1999: 101). For Peter Wilmoth,

> Watching Molly on *Countdown* meant you were plugged into what was happening, you were as close to the action as a suburban teenager could get ... [the program] illuminated the dots on the map of Australia which indicated how many stations the show was reaching.
>
> (Wilmoth 1993: 30)

For these several commentators, it is important that the 'teenage' identity being addressed by *Countdown* was a 'virtual' one, one that reached nationally, addressing youth audiences that might otherwise feel too geographically distant to participate in the 'teenager' identity. It allowed audience members to be 'close'—even if not physically—to what was going on. This was an identity that was physically transcendental, that desired to escape the suburbs and the country, to get 'close' to the cities where it was centred.

The program does retain some separations within Australia—for instance, in episode 201 Glenn Shorrock refers to the differing fortunes of a band in different states: 'Racing up the charts in Sydney and Brisbane'. But at the end of the program, it is the national top ten that provides the climax to the episode (Shrimpton & Emery 1979).

But the status of 'Australianness' in the *Countdown* identity is still an ambivalent one. On the one hand, it is an important part of the identity offered by the program: it is precisely because the program is Australian that the audience can identify, can feel 'close'. But on the other hand, the very point of the identification that this enables is to *transcend* national identity, to feel a part of an even wider, international community of teenagers, music, drugs, and sexuality.

It is true, as several writers have pointed out, that *Countdown* favoured Australian talent, to the extent that some credit it with creating the modern Australian music industry (Smith 1995: 35). So, for example, episode 201 opens with a voice-over introducing the Little River Band as being composed of 'a generation of Australia's best singer-songwriters'. They perform in the studio; then the program cuts directly to an Olivia Newton John film clip. This is then followed by 'Chartbusters', the segment that introduced hot new releases. This is prefaced by a quick montage of images, including an Australian non-musical icon, Dame Edna Everage (*Countdown* 1979).

On the other hand, however, the music that was being promoted on *Countdown*—even if some of it was Australian—was unlikely to be engaged in any kind of nationalist project of building an Australian identity. While the musical genres of older listeners might favour 'overt Australiana … songs about topical events, local heroes or Australian towns', pop music in the 1970s—and the 'teenage' identity it served—was not strongly articulated to national identity (*The Australian Image* 1989a). *Countdown* features clips from many overseas—mainly British and American—bands: in the Iggy Pop episode, 'Some Girls Do', Sister Sledge's 'He's the Greatest Dancer', Rose Royce's 'Love Don't Live Here Anymore' ('Chartbuster of the Week'), two clips from Wings, David Bowie, and more.

Countdown was reaching a national Australian audience, and inviting that audience to identify with a community. That community was accessible to them, given a recognisable Australian provenance, but was not *about* Australia, or an Australian national identity. It was, more importantly, an internationalised community. These ambivalent appeals can be seen most strongly in the figure at the centre of *Countdown*: Mr Ian 'Molly' Meldrum.

Molly—our man in Melbourne

Molly Meldrum was not the official host of *Countdown*—a variety of guest presenters took on that role. In the Iggy episode, it is Glenn Shorrock who actually hosts the show—giving very short introductions to each segment—and he promises that next week's episode will be presented by Miss Dolly Parton. But even given this, it is obvious—and not just, I think, with hindsight—that Molly is the star of the show. The guest host, Glenn Shorrock, has very little presence in the program. He basically appears in very short segments to introduce each video or performance: 'Now on *Countdown* ... Anita Ward ... a retired schoolteacher until someone persuaded her to give ... uh ... singing a try'. He is on-screen for very little time, provides little information, and his performance is an embarrassed and awkward one. His segues can be as short as 'Thank you, Russell. Here's a band called Eruption'.

By contrast, Molly—appearing each week to do his 'Humdrum' gossip segment—is garrulous, even if not entirely coherent. He gets to provide individual input to the show, interviewing Iggy Pop, for example, providing the gossip, and conveying more than simply 'Here's a band called Eruption'. At the end of this episode, Molly comes on to Glenn's isolated set for a bit of a chat. Molly effortlessly slips into being the host, and starts to interview Glenn about his upcoming work, before finishing the show for him: 'Thanks for coming on the show'. It is Molly's show; the hosts are, after all, only guests. The figure of Molly is at the centre of *Countdown*.

And it is this figure of Molly that perfectly combines the national ambivalence of the program: he is publicly celebrated for being, first, a rather naff, uncool, completely normal, and everyday Australian, and, second, for being on first name terms with the biggest of international music stars. It is perhaps a remnant of the cultural cringe that makes this combination so odd, and perhaps explains the ambivalent national appeal of the program; it is avowedly Australian, but only in order to escape that Australianness to somewhere even more 'central' to the teen identity: the USA.

In the 1950s, as Philip Bell and Roger Bell suggest above, the nascent 'teenager' identity in Australia was particularly focused on the USA. It was the rock music emerging from that country that allowed young Australians at that time to shock their parents effectively. This link between youth and American culture continues in Australia to the end of the twentieth century: Channel Ten, the self-proclaimed 'youth' commercial channel, shows more American programming than any other. The importance of this facet of the teenager identity offered by *Countdown* can be seen in Molly's own star image: 'Molly was terminally uncool, but what a world it was that he moved in … [he was] "just a good normal honest average bloke" ' according to James Reyne' (Wilmoth 1993: 30).

Molly was 'uncool' and a 'normal honest average bloke'. He was Australian enough to make it possible for a community to identify with him and solidify around him, but 'what a world that he moved in': 'Molly had excellent connections with overseas pop personalities, partly by entertaining them so well when they were in Australia … where they would often enjoy a backyard barbecue at Molly's house in Richmond' (Wilmoth 1993: 44). Molly was friends with Elton, Rod, David, Madonna, Michael, Billy—all of the biggest international music names for the duration of *Countdown*'s run. He was Australian enough for the audience to identify with, but what they identified with most was escaping the confines of Australia and moving to an international scene.

Again, the ambivalence of nationality in relation to this teenaged identity of sex and drugs and pop music can be seen in a comment such as Molly's: 'I've always found most major overseas acts to be a delight. The most difficult artists to work with are our own Australian artists … They can be so up themselves that someone should shove a bomb up there' (Baker 1989: 22).

Meldrum is perceived as a champion of Australian music but would prefer to work with overseas stars. It is perhaps his 'Humdrum' that exemplifies this tendency, telling us how various albums are doing in the American (rather than the Australian) charts, while championing local music in the same segment.

Iggy pop music

Which brings us back to Iggy Pop, and the performer who draws together and crystallises the elements of this proffered teenage identity: drugs, sexuality, pop music, and American citizenship.

Iggy appears first in Molly's 'Humdrum' segment of *Countdown* episode 201. Molly is trying to review an album—we do not even know that Iggy is in the studio with him, until he starts talking, out of shot: 'Hello dogface!' Molly stops his review: 'Iggy, how are you?' We cut to a two shot, revealing Iggy, topless, with a very firm, smooth, and defined torso, sitting in pair of tight, golden, satin pants. He is wearing a manic grin, and as Molly tries to start the interview, Iggy interrupts again: 'G'day!' he shouts. 'G'day!' He is looking around him energetically as he speaks, grinning at the cameraman, at people off the set. He looks as though he is on a combination of alcohol and speed (Shrimpton & Emery 1979).

Molly has another shot at interviewing him. 'First time I saw you was a couple of years ago, live in concert.' Ignoring him, Iggy reaches out and touches Molly's shirt button. As Molly looks down, Iggy runs his finger up, and catches Molly's chin. Molly says, 'Don't you send me up there, you behave yourself!' He seems to be slightly annoyed, but he is not panicked or angry about the fact that he is trying to interview somebody who is completely drug-fucked and making no sense. He reaches out and holds Iggy's hand, but by this point Iggy is literally bouncing up and down in his seat, giggling joyfully. 'I've got to ask you some sensible questions', says Molly, and Iggy replies, 'Alright'. But as soon as Molly starts talking, Iggy looks away, at the audience, and shouts 'Awright?' Again, Molly reaches out and touches him: 'Iggy, will you concentrate on the questions?' This continues for a couple of minutes. Molly does manage to coax some sort of sense of out him for one question ('What has he learned from David Bowie?'), and then cuts to a film clip. When we return to the studio, Iggy has left—to go and set up for his performance.

Two things are striking about this segment. The first is that Molly is obviously not freaked out by having to interact with a completely drug-fucked guest. He talks to him gently, makes physical contact, tries to bring him down. He does not panic. This is obviously not something out of the ordinary for him to encounter: although it may have been for some of the 10–16-year-olds in the audience. As he says when we come back to the studio after Iggy has left, 'Don't worry about Iggy, cos he's fine'. Molly knows that he is—he'll come down in a few hours.

Even more notable is that, even after Iggy has demonstrated his inability to complete a sentence, he still goes on to play his song, and most importantly, both it and the interview are played in the program. This is what really marks *Countdown* as different from the Australian television that had gone before. The program was not shown live: it was prerecorded. Had the producers wished to remove either Iggy's drug-fucked interview, or his drug-fucked performance from this episode of *Countdown*, they could have done so very easily, and replaced them with another film clip. They did not. A performance of being drug-fucked, which offered little in the way of coherent information but a great deal of entertainment, obviously courtesy of illicit substances, was regarded as suitable material for an ABC program aimed at teenagers. It was in ways such as this that *Countdown* successfully addressed the 'teenagers' in Australia.

Iggy's performance of 'his new single'—'I'm bored'—is in much the same vein. Topless, in his very tight satin pants, Iggy throws himself around the studio, and throws his mike stand around the studio. At one point, he has the microphone stuck down the front of his pants while he sings—an interesting comment on pop music and the performance of sexuality. He seems to remember most of his lines, but they are of less interest than his hyperactive performance: lunging at the camera, sticking his tongue out, then leaping to his feet. Karate kicks, swinging the mike out over the audience—all while gyrating his very tight buttocks and displaying his very attractive body.

Countdown offered an audience, transfixed by its ritual, an identity that was accessible in its Australian provenance but exciting in its international scope: an identity named 'teenage', which sedimented around an audience of a certain age, but was not limited to them—which, rather, offered an escape to an urban and international virtual space of pop music, sexuality, and drugs. Iggy Pop was all of these. The program is remembered as a ritual, as a central part of its audience's lives and identities, and it is remembered for specific moments of transgression, which pitted its heroes against authorities and expectations: Molly and the Prince, Iggy and the drugs. Once again, it is moments of transgression and challenge that are remembered, become part of the public archive of Australian television, and form part of our cultural heritage.

Availability

Many episodes of *Countdown* are available for purchase from the ABC's Archives and Library Services in Sydney.

9

The Sullivans: Nostalgic Visions of Perfect Women

1976–82

On 18 February 1980, Grace Sullivan—one of the most popular characters ever to appear on Australian television—was killed during an air raid on London. This event has proven a particularly potent one for Australian audiences. When I was researching this book, an initial part of the data gathering was to appeal in radio and newspaper interviews for listeners and readers to write to me with their favourite memories of Australian television. The program mentioned most in letters was *The Sullivans*. And it was the deaths of characters in *The Sullivans* that were the major points of remembrance.

> The death of Grace. Matriarch of the Sullivan family. Grace left her beloved Dave and travelled to London to help son John recover from his war wounds. While there, a buzz bomb hit the hospital. John lived, Grace died
>
> (Keating 1999a)

> Lorraine Bayly's farewell to her family in *The Sullivans*, before boarding the plane to London which was to be her final journey. The farewell was made that much more poignant by the fact she half-expected her plane to be shot down, but kept this to herself ... The disturbing execution of Melina in wartime Crete (played by Chantal Contouri). She had been tortured at length to reveal the whereabouts of her husband Norm but was executed as she remained defiant to the end. The twist was that the townsfolk had to watch the execution, including Norm, who had to watch dispassionately.
>
> ('Martin', pers. comm., n.d.)

> The execution by Nazis of Melina (Chantal Contouri) on the Greek island of Crete because she has been collaborating with Australian soldiers Tom Sullivan and Norm … Grace Sullivan is killed in the London blitz
>
> ('Jim', pers. comm., n.d.)

> The program with the most memorable moments for me is *The Sullivans*. I think the most memorable moments were when Tom Sullivan joined the Army and went overseas to fight in the war, and when he was badly wounded in a grenade explosion in Borneo in the final hours of the war.
>
> ('Janine', pers. comm., n.d.)

Similarly, the archives of letters held by Crawfords suggest continuing viewer reaction to Grace's death, remembered though gone:

> I do wish Grace was still in it. Could you please tell me why she was written out of the show?
>
> I am writing to you, can you explain to me why Grace Sullivan was written out of the series?
>
> I would be most grateful to you if you could kindly tell me why the character of Grace Sullivan was removed from your excellent series *The Sullivans*.

As the Introduction to this book suggests, many theories of television have little interest in the programs. A certain cultural studies tradition discusses television's programming in terms of its 'flow'. This book, tracing the moments that are remembered from Australian television, shows that such a metaphor misses an important aspect of television's programming: that there are moments that are important to people, which are remembered.

> Many commentators have noticed the difference between different kinds of time, not only on TV but 'anthropologically' as it were. Everyday time was measured incrementally as a sequence of 'banal', 'profane' or ordinary events. Special time, on the other hand, was the interruption of such flows by 'fatal', 'sacred' and extraordinary events … In people's lives, some events were of 'life-long' significance rather than belonging to ordinary time. Births, weddings and funerals were obvious examples.
>
> (Hartley 2000)

The moments on *The Sullivans* that can be described as extraordinary are 'fatal' in a double sense: literally so (the deaths of characters) and metaphorically so (the moments that are outside the flow of everyday time). The deaths of favourite characters stop the flow, to the extent that, twenty years after Grace Sullivan perished, the moment of her death is still recalled with clarity by viewers.

Contemporary reaction

The Sullivans was a popular program in Australia (although always more so in Melbourne than in Sydney), and Lorraine Bayly's Grace was an important part of its popularity.

In its first years, it rated in the 30s in Melbourne. By 1979, it was the top-rating program nationally in Australia, and rating 40s in Melbourne (ABT 1988: 57). At the 1977 Sammy awards (voted for by readers of the *TV Times*), *The Sullivans* was the most popular series, and Lorraine Bayly won the 'Best Actress in a TV Series' award for her work as Grace ('Harry's Golden Night' 1977: 5). At the 1978 Awards, *The Sullivans* scored four awards, including Lorraine Bayly getting her second 'Best Actress' award. In an article that puts Bayly on the front cover of the *TV Times* in 1978 (proclaiming that 'I'm not Grace Sullivan'), we are told that 'Lorraine Bayly is perfect as Grace in *The Sullivans*. Critics and viewers alike agree', and that 'Today Lorraine is … Australia's highest paid female star' (Dean 1978: 10, 11).

And this central character in this popular series was blown up.

We can trace reactions to Grace's death at the time. Looking at the archive of production documentation and publicity coverage of Lorraine Bayly's departure from the series, it seems that the producers tried desperately not to draw attention to Grace's death. Lorraine Bayly actually left the show early in 1979. At this point in the narrative, Grace left Australia to go to London to see if her missing son John was there. However, when Bayly left, she also filmed a series of inserts, set in London and including her death. These were not shown for over six months, and all the while the network downplayed her leaving by insisting that they did not know whether she would return to the series (when her death had already been filmed). There is then no build-up to the departure itself. In the *TV Week* article on 9 February 1980—nine days before her death was broadcast—a feature article reintroducing the series states simply that 'Grace (Lorraine Bayly) is in London … With Grace at his side, John Sullivan's (Andrew McFarlane's) health improves steadily. The coming year will be a happy one for him'. This, remember, is when Grace is about to be killed and John Sullivan will return to Australia for her funeral. Similarly, in the *TV Week* dated 16 February 1980—two days before her death—an article on 'the new Lorraine

Bayly' doesn't mention that Grace will die that week: 'What would Dave Sullivan think? … It's none other than Lorraine Bayly, in blonde wig and displaying a pair of shapely legs, in a new role that's a far cry from the demure, motherly Grace Sullivan' (Richter 1980: 2).

The way in which Grace's departure is managed, then, seems to be deliberately avoiding making it fatal: she slips out. It is telling to note that it is difficult to decide exactly which is Grace's last episode: some viewers are upset remembering Grace leaving her family in Australia; others by the bomb blast; others by Dave opening the letter she left with the family; others by the funeral. Many different episodes are recalled; it is as though Grace drifted away. The strange management of the program, whereby scenes for several months ahead were shot when Bayly left the program, is surrounded by a secrecy that leads one story to comment in July 1979 (when Grace's death has already been filmed) that 'The cast of *The Sullivans* is as curious as most viewers about whether Grace is coming back. In fact, there's been quite a bit of espionage on set to find out just what the plans for Grace are' ('Closeup' 1979: 7). Other stories, as late as September, comment that,

> With three years of achievement behind it, *The Sullivans* enters its fourth year with two major questions to be answered: Where does the show go, with on-screen segments now set in mid-1944 … [and] will Grace return? … Lorraine [Bayly] has remained overseas on her world trip for several months now and her plans are the industry's number one mystery.
>
> (Robertson 1979: 6)

There is no sense of build-up to Grace's final appearance, the necessary ritual that would mark it as a fatal part of the television experience. That is, until the very day of Grace's death, when Channel Nine suddenly promotes the moment. A full-page advert in a Melbourne newspaper on the day shows Dave Sullivan (Paul Cronin) in tears, holding his face. The caption is 'Tragic news! Tonight, Dave Sullivan learns the shocking truth about the bomb blast in London' ('Tragic News!' 1980). A television column in the Melbourne *Herald* on the day comments:

> But there's more. Much more. At 7 p.m., oh dear. Remember *The Sullivans* last Friday? Remember the explosions? Well, the Channel 9 publicity people have asked me not to give the game away, but they've done that themselves with their full-page advertisements in this morning's press. Why do YOU think Dave Sullivan is crying? Have a box or three of tissues handy.
>
> (Lockwood 1980a: 2)

With a lack of build-up, it appears that this death still stopped the flow of television. The next day, the *Herald* television reviewer wrote on this moment:

> I hope you took my advice last night and watched *The Sullivans* … it was a little different, wasn't it? We have all known, or feared, for some time that something might happen to Grace. Lorraine Bayly made it clear at the start of last year that she wanted a change. So it was only a matter of time. And if Lorraine did really want to get out permanently, Grace had to die. There's no way such a devoted wife and mother could leave her family So goodbye Grace. And good acting from Paul Cronin, Michael Caton and Susan Hannaford. Was there a dry eye in YOUR house?
>
> (Lockwood 1980b: 2)

Dave Sullivan's tears are obviously presented as the model to be followed by viewers; this reviewer demands to know if any viewer could have avoided them. A review of the series on its conclusion three years later remembers that 'a friend … told me that she had answered the door to a new boyfriend after watching Dave Sullivan learn of Grace's death, and she had mascara streaming down her face' (Wilmoth 1983).

A front-cover magazine story three weeks later presenting 'The Real Story! Why Lorraine Bayly Quit *The Sullivans*' claims that

> Grace Sullivan is dead and millions of fans throughout Australia are mourning the loss of one of television's most loved characters … many bewildered fans are asking why Grace had to die … why Lorraine wanted to leave *The Sullivans* … Lorraine has already received letters from fans who are disappointed and upset about her departure from the show. 'The letters have been very warm and sincere', she says, 'Many people asked me not to leave …'
>
> (MacSween 1980: 5)

Journalistic writing is prone to making claims about such things as 'society', 'the public', 'the people', the 'mood' of society, and its 'zeitgeist', often from limited evidence. Here, as elsewhere in the book, this material is presented not as proof that audiences were 'really' behaving in such a way. It is, rather, meant to suggest the ways in which this media event was constructed and offered to readers: that the fact of Lorraine Bayly leaving *The Sullivans* should be worthy of tears, of letters; that this was a moment of note that stopped the flow of television and was worthy of remembrance.

Making sense of Grace Sullivan

Grace's death is not the only one to have had an impact on the Australian mediasphere. Other obviously relevant moments are the deaths of Charlie Cousens in *Bellbird*, Inspector Fox in *Homicide* (Keating 1999b), and Molly in *A Country Practice* (see Robertson 1972: 15; Lopez 1972; Dearn 1972; *35 Years of Television*). The last of these, 'one of television's greatest tragedies' (Day 1991: 23), also appeared in data gathering for this book:

> [M]y top ten moments in Australian television ... number one—Molly dying on *A Country Practice*: I do not think anyone who saw that last episode could have come away from it not affected. TV drama at its emotive best.
>
> Great moments in Australian television ... Molly's death in *A Country Practice*.
>
> I particularly remember the moment when Molly (*A Country Practice*) passed away ... I'm 31 years old with 2 children ... so it was nearly 16 years ago, I guess ... I still get a lump in my throat as I remember Molly slipping in and out of consciousness (and us slipping in and out of the 'blackness') she is watching her child play, and then one last cloud of darkness and that's it ... she's gone ... (ooh, I need a tissue).

Death is an important part of collective remembering of Australian television. Grace's death was one of the most important. In trying to understand how she died, why she died, and what importance her death might hold, it is worth looking in more detail at the character of Grace Sullivan. Who was she, what did she represent, and what died with her?

In a wonderful *New Woman* article in 1999 entitled '30 Chores to Ignore', which encourages a slovenly attitude in its readership, number twenty-five in this list of things *not* to do is 'pay close and constant attention to your kids'. The article expands on why its readers shouldn't bother doing this: 'You'll never be Grace Sullivan, so don't even try' (Gutfield 1999: 104). Twenty years after the death of the character, she is remembered as an ideal. The readers will never be Grace Sullivan because Grace Sullivan is the perfect mother. She entirely subsumes her own desires to those of the family. She has no existence apart from them. As noted above, a contemporary reviewer pointed out that Grace's death was inevitable: 'Grace had to die. There's no way such a devoted wife and mother could leave her family'. Grace's death becomes particularly important in showing the only way out of the traditional family structure for the perfect mother. She could not, of course, have an affair; could not ask for a divorce; could not follow her own needs, desires, or wishes. She could only be hit by a bomb in wartime London while looking after the welfare of her child.

The family in *The Sullivans* is centred by the very naming of the series, and many articles in the popular press suggest that this program is particularly family-oriented. For the documentary *35 Years of Television* (1991), '[f]amilies have always been at the centre of serial dramas, but never more so than when we followed the Sullivans through the Second World War'. In fact, '*The Sullivans* became the country's best-known family' (Day 1981: 156). And it is indeed, apparently, 'family values' that characterise the public image of this series:

> *The Sullivans* have long been Melbourne's favourite family, and now they have become the city's first Royal Family, for Dave and Grace Sullivan have been named King and Queen of Moomba, and their children part of the royal family ... this is the first time an entire family has been chosen ... it is the characters from the show who have been named, not the actors portraying them.
>
> ('Crowning Glory' 1980: 17)

Similarly, when Lorraine Bayly is being set up for *This is Your Life* in 1979, a story covering this event names her as 'TV's most famous mother, Grace Sullivan' ('Trapping Lorraine Was a Piece of Cake' 1979: 7). At this point she has left the show, but the importance of the perfect mother, Grace Sullivan, is remembered. As one article notes, 'After several months [since appearing on the program, although she has not died at this point], the impact of Lorraine's Grace Sullivan has diminished very little' (Robertson 1979: 6). She is the 'much-loved' Grace Sullivan, 'the matriarch of the Sullivans family' ('Who's Who in *The Sullivans*' 1977: 10). As an article quoted above asks, 'what would Dave Sullivan say?' if he saw Grace showing off her 'shapely' legs, for Grace was resolutely unglamorous. The image that survives of her is of 'mother Lorraine Bayly dispensing advice to her war-torn family and friends over copious cups of tea' (Solomon 1989: 23).

Placing such a character into a genealogy of the female leads in Australia's top-rating programs puts her in some odd company. The number-one-rating program before *The Sullivans* was *Number 96*; the Australian program that took over this mantle was *Prisoner*. This gives us a genealogy that leads us from Bev (Abigail), famous for showing her nipples, getting men to squeeze her breasts, and talking candidly about sex, to Grace Sullivan (Lorraine Bayly), famous for being a mother, self-sacrificing to the point of death, fearless, frumpy, and endlessly considerate, and then on to Franky Doyle (Carol Burns), famous for being a lesbian, a killer, and for trying to seduce other inmates of Wentworth. Grace Sullivan is sandwiched by sex, and her death is a death of the kind of womanhood that reactionaries can only dream about.

It is important that *The Sullivans* is a period piece. This fact can hardly be missed. The program is set in the late 1930s and the 1940s—the period of the Second World War. And this forms the basis for much public discussion of the series: is *The Sullivans* really—properly, authentically, historically—accurate? This appears to be an obsession in much newspaper and magazine correspondence while the program is running. It is sold as being 'realistic' ('The Sullivans: Award Winning Universal Appeal' n.d.) and on its 'authenticity' (Pangallo 1979: 5). It mixes original documentary footage with the drama. (A newssheet released in 1979 celebrating the program's success is similarly produced in newspaper format, and mixes articles on the program with reprints of original news articles from the 1940s.) Various articles insist on the program's documentary qualities:

> The infamous Kokoda Trail, used by Australian troops through the New Guinea Jungle in the Second World War, features in *The Sullivans* this week. *The Sullivans'* producers wedded newsreel film with material shot near Sassafras in the Dandenong Ranges ... The sequences have been carefully researched by *The Sullivans* team and locations in the Dandenongs were recreated using actual Kokoda Trail photographs. Some sequences were shot in the studio using the same photographs and the whole wedded with some of the famous newsreel sequences that came out of that war campaign.
>
> ('Sullivans on Kokoda Trail' 1978: 7)

Letters pages in television magazines question details of military history:

> Why isn't Terry sporting a campaign ribbon for his overseas effort and only Norm Baker is sporting the 1939–1945 star ribbon?
>
> (Levett 1979: 40)

> I have always enjoyed *The Sullivans*, but recent episodes involving incidents with American servicemen in Brisbane have been utterly ridiculous to anyone who lived in Brisbane during the war years.
>
> (Wheeler 1979: 40)

> I am an ardent *Sullivans* fan ... I do remember the rationing. In Queensland we had only a tiny ration of butter each week, but the Sullivans are always spreading it liberally, as well as feeding many guests.
>
> (Boyd 1979: 40)

This turn to history fits well with other trends in Australian culture during this time. In many ways, *The Sullivans* represents a movement between two dominant forms discussed by Albert Moran: the soap opera (*Number 96* had previously been dominating the ratings) and the mini-series form, which would become the television phenomenon of the late 1970s and early 1980s in Australia. The Australian Film Commission genre of film focused on history as a way of promoting national identity. Early, popular mini-series followed the same path, and proved particularly fond of wars and their easy nationalism (Cunningham 1989). *The Sullivans* does the same thing. Indeed, Moran suggests the congruity between *The Sullivans* and these other cultural moments in his analysis of the title sequence of the program. He starts from a discussion of mini-series such as *Bodyline, Cowra Breakout*, and *Vietnam*, which were

> based on historical records and documents (photographs, newspapers and other printed sources, film footage and sound recordings) ... the aim of this strategy is well summed up in the opening credit sequence of *The Sullivans*. This sequence turns on an off-screen photographer taking a series of black and white photographs of the family, while in colour the family enjoys itself between shots. The sequence sets up both a series of oppositions and relations between black and white and colour, still photography and film, past and present and public and private. The black and white photographs represent the past, history, an authentic historical record of ordinary people presenting their public faces and selves to the camera. Colour film (colour transmission had just been introduced into Australian television when *The Sullivans* began on air in late 1976) can dramatise the past, bring it alive, give it movement. We see the family break into laughter and spontaneous behaviour between the photographs before resuming stiffer, more formal poses for the still camera ... *The Dismissal, The Last Bastion, Vietnam* ... [shift] from black and white to colour ... dramatising history without damaging or compromising the truth of that history.
>
> (Moran 1989: 253)

In *The Sullivans*, it seems that the return to history—to a celebration of national identity and unity—includes looking wistfully back to a time when women didn't work, when their only priority was the family, when they were not sexually demanding or even particularly interested in sex. In short, returning to the past allows us to escape from the voracious demands of Abigail, of her see-through blouse, and her pushy demands to have her breasts felt up. In turning to the past—to this wonderful, well-researched, authentic past of national unity and social stability—we can discover women who lived as women should.

Our first sight of the maternal Grace Sullivan

The first scene of the first episode of *The Sullivans* shows us the kind of Grace we should expect from this program: she is introduced by showing her motherly characteristics, deciding which of the children should get the crusts from the bread (*The Sullivans* 1976). The annoying gossip from next door, Mrs Jessop (played by Vivian Gray, who has specialised in such roles, also appearing later as Mrs Mangel in *Neighbours*), pops in, and Grace keeps on smiling. It is quickly established that this is her standard facial expression. Grace smiles. She does not have an internal life, no desires, no needs, no wants, or anything that might cause her to frown. The only thing that will wipe the smile off her face is when one of her family is facing a problem. But in the everyday travails of dealing with an annoying neighbour, Grace will be unfailingly polite. She will continue to smile. Until, of course, Mrs Jessop suggests that Grace's son Tom has been in some sort of trouble. Grace bristles as she replies that gossip does not worry her: 'Just a lot of silly old women with nothing else to do'.

Her dress is not glamorous. Lorraine Bayly is thirty-six at this point, and much is made in magazine articles about how the character is made up to look older than the actor. Her clothing is matronly and drab, worn not to flatter or reveal the body. Indeed, watching the early episodes of *The Sullivans*, it is strange to realise that Grace was to become the star of the program. She does not come across as charismatic. She does not get many lines, and

Grace doesn't smile when defending her family

Grace's glad rags

there is little in the way of characterisation beyond simply being a good mother. This means spending much of her time dealing with other people's problems and not having any herself. This woman, who is loved by the nation, who wins the *TV Times* viewers' awards for her popularity, is someone who says grace promptly before every meal: 'For what we are about receive, may the Lord make us truly grateful. For Christ's sake, Amen'.

Grace does occasionally get to dress up. She spends much of the first few episodes of *The Sullivans* wearing an apron, but when Rose and Harry come around to visit in the first episode, Grace does put on a flowery frock, and even wears make-up (should a good religious girl do such a thing?). But her major role in the narrative is as the peacekeeper, ensuring not only that the problems of individual family members are solved, but also that they are all *happy* together. In the second episode of the program, as the war looms, a discussion starts at the Sullivans' dinner table about the ethics of war. John Sullivan is the spokesman for peace, crying out that 'Everybody's talking as if it's just another Grand Final'. He claims that 12 000 people will be 'butchered', and so on. Dave is not happy about this pacifist stance, particularly given that he himself fought in the First World War. But at the end of this engagement, John apologises not to his father, whom he has insulted and upset, but to Grace: 'Sorry, Mum'. It is Grace who gets upset when anyone in her family fights. She is the peacekeeper and the negotiator. She can only be truly happy when everyone in her family is—an unfortunate quality as you prepare to go to war.

Grace also seems to spend much of her time censoring people. When Tom and Dave start making pro-war comments—'let's have a war and get it over with'—Grace, worried about the impact on families, immediately censors them: 'This [conscription] isn't something to joke about'. She also holds a traditional female censorship role (Summers 1994): stopping her family from using inappropriate language. For example, in the second episode of the series, when Dave suggests that the woman who is taking over ownership of the local pub might be 'rough as guts', Grace goes 'hmm hmmmm', and Dave immediately apologises: 'Sorry, love—not at the table'.

When John and Dave are not talking, Grace tries to mediate: 'Are you sure that you're not using [John going to] university as an excuse—for not making the effort?' she asks of Dave. Of course, he does then 'make the effort' to talk to his son. Another rift threatens to emerge in the third episode of the program. The Sullivan daughter Kitty has lost her father's watch, which she had to pick up from the shop. Grace sits down with each of the concerned family members and talks to them about it, sorting it out once again.

By the second episode of the series, we have found out that Dave has a mysterious past. We know that the woman who has come to run the pub used to have some kind of relationship with him. Given Grace's lack of desire and internal life, it is difficult to imagine such a storyline working for her. When, in the third episode, Kitty runs out of the kitchen, upset because Grace will not let her play with the mysterious old hermit who lives down the street, Dave walks in just in time to see her leave. 'What's wrong with her?' asks Dave. 'Oh, nothing', replies Grace: she does not tell him, for it is not, after all, Dave's problem. It is Grace's work to ensure that the family machine is well managed. Dave is a foreman at an engineering works; Grace is the forewoman at home, engineering the family. The division of labour is perfectly gendered. The final image of this scene sums up Grace: she is wearing an apron, sitting at the kitchen table, framed behind the plate of scones that she has just baked. When Dave reaches for one and burns his hand, she says, 'Serves you right—it's for tea'. Indeed, she is a matriarch, sorting out the family with a plate of scones in front of her.

Despite appealing to a period that is often used to construct easy nationalism, *The Sullivans* presents a variety of viewpoints on the war. The most jingoistic position is reserved for the deeply unattractive busybody, Mrs Jessop. The most pragmatic is given to an even more unattractive visiting character, Bert Duggan (Peter Hehir), who is also a wife-beater, selfish, lazy, and who tries to rape John Sullivan's girlfriend. Mrs Jessop's is mindless, obsessed patriotism; Duggan has none at all. And Grace? Well, of course, for Grace war is about her children. She clutches Dave's arm and leans her head against it, muttering, 'I wish there were some way to show the boys what war is like without them having to suffer through it'. Dave knows how to reassure her: 'They'll be alright'. It is her boys she worries about, not the finer points of international politics, or the ethics of warfare. They define the war for her.

The end of Grace

Fittingly, it is her care for her family—specifically, for her son John, whom she must visit when he turns up in a hospital in London—that leads to Grace's death. How else could it be? In episode 598 of the series, Grace appears in only one scene—one of the scenes that had been prerecorded several months before the rest of the episode was put together (*The Sullivans* 1980). While a series of unrelated storylines carry on in the Australian scenes—Uncle Harry has just been let out of prison and a character called Emile has his sister coming to visit—Norm and Tom are in London, getting ready to pick up Grace. Back in Australia, the build-up to her return has begun. The neighbour Kate comes around to the house: 'I'm beginning to stock up so the family will have plenty of food when Grace and John get back. Everyone's so keen to get everything ready for Grace, with all this cleaning and painting the bedroom'. Geoff asks his dad what he thinks of the paint job he's doing in the house: 'Do you reckon Mum's going to like this?' Dave: 'When she finds out that you've done it, she'll love it'. Dave knows that a character such as Grace would like anything if her son had prepared it for her. 'After what they've been through in London', Dave begins—the perfect cue for a cut to some documentary footage. A caption—exactly as if this were a documentary—states that 'The V1 Blitz on London Begins'. We see footage of military police watching the skies, anti-aircraft guns blazing, another caption ('Thursday 6 July 1944'), aircraft, the Houses of Parliament.

By this point, Grace has become almost a religious figure in the program—like the Virgin Mary, she appears only rarely, but is endlessly talked about. This is obviously a result of the structure—Lorraine Bayly has left and the program must be made around her—but it has the effect of turning her into a kind of goddess. The London scenes continue: we cut to a female officer speaking on a phone: 'Yes, I'll pick up you and your mother … I know she's been aching to get home. Alright, John'. Throughout the episode, we build up to her return. A female army officer picks up family friend Norm and son Tom from the airport. They have flown to London to meet up with Grace and John. As they drive past a ruined brick building, Tom introduces the topic of Grace to the conversation again: 'Tell us about Mum'. The officer sums up Grace perfectly: 'She's just a very happy lady who's found one son and longing to see the others … she'll be home in a few days'. As we see more shots of ruins, the officer begins to talk about: 'Hitler's new toy … the buzz bomb'. Tom is, of course, shocked by this: 'Mum's been here for all this'. We have not as yet seen her in this episode.

Finally—more than half way through the episode—Grace appears, just as it begins to seem that she might not really exist (and given just how perfect she appears to be, this would not be surprising). She is framed through a window, writing in a diary. We hear her in voice-over: 'This will be the last entry in my diary. We are going home. Seven months in hospital, and now at last John is free ... we are waiting to be picked up ... To fly home'.

'Home'—a magical word for Grace, and as we hear it, she looks up to stare dreamily out of the window. Shots of her family appear on the screen beside her face: Kitty doing chores; Tom drinking beer; Geoff smiling; John washing up. They are in the kitchen, being homely. This is Grace's dream. She smiles. In case we have not yet got the message, the word 'home' echoes on the soundtrack: 'Home. Home. Home.' This is Grace's mantra, her centre, what she represents.

John is in the background of this shot, and he now wakes up. She chides him over his snoring. She is not a walkover or a wuss. She is not afraid to make fun of her men. She is just perfect and self-sacrificing. And then they are interrupted by the sound of a doodlebug. Grace looks up, suddenly worried, and we cut to black and white footage of a flying plane. Then there is silence—and footage of a bomb dropping. We cut back to Grace and John and a close-up of her hand grasping his; he covers her hand with his. 'What is it John?' she asks. She is helpless, uncertain. He is the man, of course. He will know what's going on. She is only a housewife, mother, matriarch. The shot holds for beat.

And suddenly, unexpectedly, after less than three minutes on screen, Grace Sullivan is blown up. We have no final shot of her face—simply a shot of the room blowing up. We see Grace and John in front of the window, shot from behind. The window blows out, wreckage falls on them. The credits roll. Grace Sullivan is dead. So dies one of the most popular characters in Australian television—a woman very different from those who had dominated popular television drama for the previous four years, and from those who would rule for the next four.

The Sullivans strives to sell itself as an accurate reproduction of history. It has to, as it would be hard to imagine Grace Sullivan living in the 1970s. For the 1970s, television had discovered, was about permissiveness, sex, and alternative kinship structures replacing the traditional family. In a way, it is the footage of the doodlebugs and the genuine clips from the radio announcements of war beginning that make it possible for Grace Sullivan to exist: a nostalgic account of what women should be like, of how they should love their families, care for them more than for themselves. And the only way out of such a role—one that might seem oppressive to us nowadays—is to die.

It is interesting that in the endless letters about *The Sullivans* that appear in the pages of magazines and newspapers questioning the historical authenticity of medals, rationing, and uniforms, nobody ever challenges the nostalgic vision of women in the program. There are no letters of complaint that the program is centred on a perfect, impossibly idealised mother. Rather, she is elevated to the status of the 'nation's best known mother'. It is this status that makes her death so shocking, and for which she is so well remembered. The public archive of great moments in Australian television holds a place for the death of Grace Sullivan, remembered by viewers as a moment when fatality halted the flow of television's programming, and put perfect femininity to death.

Availability

The first three episodes of *The Sullivans* were released commercially on a tape of the same name in 1989, although this has now been deleted (the same tape was released in the UK in 1999 by Acorn). Screensound holds episode 598, Grace's death, but this is not available to view as an access copy.

10

Prisoner: Unglamorous Heroines

1979–86

On 17 February 1979, during the first episode of *Prisoner*, Bea crushed Lynn's hand in a steam press. The scene is graphic, explicit, and not glamorised. It is an important moment in a program that has an important place in the public archive of Australian television. *Prisoner* is the only Australian television program that has developed a sustained cult following not only in Australia, but also overseas. And it appears that the success of the program can be attributed to the way in which it represents women—to the fact that this is television that presents women crushing each other's hands in steam presses.

Prisoner is, as far as I can make out, unique in Western television (Docker & Curthoys 1997: 1295; Curthoys & Docker 1989: 52). It is not just that the cast is almost exclusively female, although that is notable. It is not just that the program allows women to play a wide range of characters—including physically and emotionally strong and weak; mature and immature; amusing and cold; twisted, perverse, and downright nasty, as well as caring and thoughtful—although that is also important. It is not just that relationships between women are at the centre of every episode of this program's seven-year run, although that is rare enough. Yes, all of these elements are present—but more important than any of these characteristics is the fact that none of the women in the program need to purchase this presence at the heart of the Australian mediasphere by making themselves glamorous. And, even more surprising is the fact that this tale of often ugly—or, at the very least, homely—women was a popular success on Australian television for several years, is remembered by many viewers, and is obsessively remembered and archived by a sizeable minority of them.

The crushing of Lynn's hand is memorialised by Channel Ten in the documentary *Forty Fun Years of Television* as number six in its list of 'Ten's Top 10 Moments'. This moment is representative of the possibilities offered by this program, possibilities that neither *Number 96* nor *The Sullivans* could match.

Correspondents for this book also recall this and other similar moments on *Prisoner*:

> [M]y suggestions ... [include] *Prisoner*, Bea Smith (Val Lehman) placing Lynne Warner's (Kerry Armstrong) hand under the hot steam press ... Bea Smith trying to kill the Freak, the Governor of Wentworth Detention Centre being shot by terrorists.
>
> My top ten moments ... the brave and brutal death of Myra Desmond (played by Anne Phelan) during the siege at Wentworth in *Prisoner*.
>
> *Prisoner* was exciting [but] I don't think I realised that they were lesbians for quite a while.

Prisoner is also one of the few commercial television programs in Australia that has been unabashedly celebrated by cultural critics: Elizabeth Jacka and Lesley Johnson suggest that it has 'fascinated Australian television critics and academics', and that 'Like *Number 96*, *Prisoner* was an innovation in soap opera form and content' (Jacka & Johnson 1998: 214). For John Docker, it is 'a triumph of the Australian television industry' (Docker & Curthoys 1997: 1293). According to Morris Gleitzman, it is 'a TV legend' (Gleitzman 1992: 21).

A third way in which the program's status in the public archive of Australian television is confirmed is through its cult following, a following that is unique among Australian television programs. This is the way in which *Prisoner* is most comprehensively remembered as part of television's archive. More than a decade after it finished broadcasting, *Prisoner* is still an item of daily discussion on its own mailing list. The '*Prisoner Cell Block H*' Mailing List (the program's title was changed when it was screened in Britain, in order to avoid confusion with the 1960s British science fiction program *The Prisoner*) provides an active site for continuing public discussion of *Prisoner* episodes (and can be subscribed to by emailing pcbh-request@pcbh.freeuk.com). Every day, a new email contains details of repeat screenings, detailed discussions of the content of episodes, and other pieces of *Prisoner*-related information. Similarly, the 'PCGB Ring' is a series of linked Internet sites dedicated to *Prisoner*. (This can be accessed through Frida's *Prisoner* Page: http://members.xoom.com/mumsbums/kf.htm). This brings together dozens of websites from around the world, dedicated to the discussion and dissemination of this program. To return to one of the central concerns of this book, it is difficult to argue that television programming consists of an ephemeral flow when a program such as this resolutely refuses to vanish, but survives as an important part of culture, not only in viewers' memories, but also as a focus for the daily production of new cultural texts (such as emails and websites). These are 'cult programs': according to Lewis and Stempel's definition, cult programs can be identified by the 'fervour' of fans. They are objects of 'special devotion', give birth to 'merchandising, a fan club, a fanzine, conventions [and] a secret language' (Lewis & Stempel 1993: 8). Prisoner is, they say, an 'indisputable qualifier' for the category.

In Jon Lewis and Penny Stempel's collection *Cult Television*, *Prisoner* is the only Australian television program to be named as an indisputable cult program. On the criteria they define, it has undoubtedly reached such a status. This can be seen in the often-cited example of Franky Doyle's death. Chris Keating names this as a 'seminal moment in Australian drama' (Keating 1999a). It certainly has cult potential:

> Los Angeles, 10 January 1980. Around fifty leather clad women bikers congregate outside TV station KTLA-5 ... The night before, TV character Franky Doyle, lesbian bikie inmate of the fictitious Wentworth Jail ... has been killed by a police bullet while trying to escape. In total across Los Angeles more than 3000 Doyle fans assembled to pay homage.
>
> (Lewis & Stempel 1993: 202)

> *Prisoner* ... was exported to the USA and was second in the ratings only to *Charlie's Angels* ... when the lesbian character Frankie died in the series, women bikers in San Francisco held a wake.
>
> (Zalcock & Robinson 1996: 88–9)

> When *Prisoner* was sold to America ... Los Angeles lesbians picketed the studio protesting at the portrayal. Later they adopted Frankie as a champion. When she died they held a wake.
>
> (Kingsley 1989: 274)

Even though the geography may be uncertain—Los Angeles, or San Francisco, or both?—the importance of remembering this moment is clear. *Prisoner* is a cult success, a program that is remembered and still survives as an object of viewing pleasure.

The Internet has revolutionised fan audiences, making it possible for virtual communities of fans to be established around cult television programs with greater ease and disregard for geographical distance than has ever previously been the case (when fan publishing relied on photocopiers and paper, for example). It has also made it easier for the researcher to participate in the fan community. This makes it possible to trace the ways in which *Prisoner* has survived: the elements that are celebrated, and the discourses that circulate around it. Given this access, it is interesting to compare the different ways in which *Prisoner* is understood in various cultural arenas.

Realism

For a researcher such as myself, who first encountered *Prisoner* in the United Kingdom as a cult phenomenon rather than in Australia as a mainstream television success, it is bizarre to find that part of the program's public image in Australia has been one of 'realism'. Lewis and Stempel note that 'From the start the series was radically different, with the emphasis on realism: Australia's longest serving female prisoner, murderess Sandra Willson, acted as series advisor' (Lewis & Stempel 1993: 202). Albert Moran has suggested several times that the program should be interpreted in such a way: '*Prisoner* ... is significant for a number of reasons ... [including] a shift ... towards a greater "dramatic realism" ' (Moran 1985: 154–5; Moran 1989: 154). In his account of the program, Moran quotes Michael Horhensee, who suggests that,

> With *Prisoner*, we're going more for realism. All the situations are things that have happened, or could have happened ... For dramatic emphasis, the producers have used more bars and grilles—all of which are steel—normally associated with a prison.
>
> (Moran 1989: 154)

Although not using the term 'realism', Idato suggests something similar in his terminology when he remembers the program as 'a benchmark in the industry for ... the brutal honesty of the storylines it portrayed' (Idato 1995: 13).

The term 'realism' is one that has been much contested in film theory. Ongoing debates ask whether 'realism' can be a progressive mode or if it is necessarily reactionary; whether 'documentary realism' is an acceptable form of political filmmaking; how it differs from 'classical realism'; and so on (see, for example, McCabe 1974; Fiske 1987). But the writers quoted here are not engaging with the complexities of film theory. Rather, by using the term 'realism' they seem to be implying a grittiness, an unflinching look at the unpleasant facts of life, a serious attempt to discuss difficult issues (a kind of 'social realism').

As I mentioned, it strikes me as odd to describe *Prisoner* in terms of such gritty realism: this is not how the program is understood when it is circulated as a cult phenomenon. 'Matt', describing the program's appeal, writes: 'Realistic? No idea since I've never been in a women's prison. If you try to explain why *Prisoner Cell Block H* is so superb, it comes out sounding kitsch' (Matt's *Prisoner Cell Block H* Quotes Page: http://www.aubreyco.demon.co.uk/prisoner.htm).

The program's public image now—an image that seems to sustain its cult appeal—is rather a camp one: wobbly sets, over-acting, and unbelievable storylines. It is remembered more as an excessive and melodramatic text than as a gritty realist one (see http://home.swipnet.se/wentworthweb/). The fan sites engage with such concerns, not wishing to attack the program but still insisting that it is not gritty realism. On the site 'Who's Who in Wentworth', answering the question 'Why *Prisoner*?', the program is defended in the following terms:

> It's classic TV—the idea that it's total dross with moving scenery, terrible dialogue and worse acting really won't stand up to examination ... but it's probably true that most fans simply could not believe their eyes and ears when confronted with their first episode.
>
> (http://www.zen.co.uk/home/page/zahid.john/prisoner/intro.htm)

The phrase 'couldn't believe their eyes and ears' suggests something of the program's appealing excess. 'Rachel's Unofficial *Prisoner Cell Block H* Website' negotiates between the claims for gritty realism and melodramatic excess in the program's appeal: '*Prisoner* is sometimes brutal, sometimes touching and often hilarious. At times it is gritty, at others it borders on the fantastical—but it is always entertaining' (http://www.geocities.com/TelevisionCity/Studio/8118/).

It can be 'gritty' and 'brutal', it seems, but also 'hilarious' and 'fantastical', and throughout all it is 'entertaining'. It survives as a cult program not because of its breakthroughs in presenting the gritty realism of life in a woman's prison but because it is entertaining.

The melodramatic tendencies of the program have also been acknowledged in other sites. Docker notes that it is 'a classic of serial melodrama' (Docker & Curthoys 1997: 1293) and suggests that it 'does not aim at realism' (Docker 1983: 58). Certainly, watching the early episodes of the program now, it is the melodramatic effects that are the most immediately apparent aesthetic strategy rather than a realist desire to present social problems in a convincing way. In the first episode, Sally escapes from her cell (*Prisoner* 1979a). The series opens with a chase scene through the dark, shadow-ridden corridors of Wentworth. When she is recaptured and locked back up in her cell, she gives a scream that is reminiscent of a horror film. Later in the episode, as new prisoner Karen (Peta Toppano) is walked to her cell, she walks past Sally's cell. An arm suddenly bursts through the grating in the door, and Sally's voice hysterically sobs, 'Please, Miss Bennett, please'. The shock tactics, the hysteria, and the shadows all make this seem like something from a Gothic horror. Vera shoves the arm back into the cell and slams the door shut on the grate; harsh music—almost reminiscent of *Psycho*—plays over the scene.

Indeed, there are more explicit allusions to that film in the first episode of *Prisoner*. Karen has to have a shower when she arrives at the prison. As soon as she sees the water, we cut to a flashback scene: she sees her husband covered in blood in a shower and goes into hysterics. Later in the episode she has another flashback in which we see her husband beating her up. We find out that while Karen was out having an abortion, her husband was in bed with another woman. As she runs into the kitchen and grabs a knife, there is grand music playing on the soundtrack. We hear dialogue echoing over the music—her husband's voice saying 'Trust me'—and the 'me ... me ... me ... ' echoes over the scene. Her husband is in the shower, and we see the scene from her point of view as she stabs him. There follows a shot of him, in slow motion, keeling over, blood pumping out from under the hand that he is clutching to his chest. The flashback ends with a shot of him lying on the shower floor. Even the final low chord that ends the scene is reminiscent of *Psycho*. It is hard to read this in terms of the brutal, harsh 'realism' mentioned by some commentators on the program.

Similarly melodramatic aesthetics occur throughout the first few episodes. One of the inmates of Wentworth, Lynn (Kerry Armstrong), has been imprisoned for kidnapping the baby she was supposed to be nannying and burying it alive in the garden. We know that she is innocent. We are shown a scene in which the baby's mother, Mrs Bentley, is talking to the baby. It is shot from the baby's point of view, inside the crib. Mrs Bentley's face looms hugely into the camera as she says, 'Now be quiet, or I'll put you back into that big hole'. The performance is one of twitching madness. In the scene that ends the second episode of the program—when 'Queen' Bea Smith (Val Lehman), finally finishing her term of imprisonment, leaves Wentworth only to return to her home and shoot her husband dead—melodramatic aesthetics are also employed. Bea rings the doorbell and has a desultory conversation with her husband in a medium two-shot: 'When the hell did you get out?', he asks. 'Yesterday', she says. 'Don't think you're coming back.' 'I don't want to come back—I just brought you a present.' Bea pulls a gun out of her handbag. There is a close-up of his face—overacting fear, eyes goggling—then a close-up of the gun. It fires. Another close-up of his face, as his eyes roll back in his head and he falls. Throughout these shots, music swells to a crescendo. The camera swings around to his new girlfriend, cutting to a big close-up as she screams.

Throughout these early episodes, melodramatic codes are employed for moments of high tension: twitching performances, big close-ups, zooms, and crashing music.

Prisoner survives in the public archive both as 'realistic' and as 'melodramatic'. In its cult success, it is the second aspect that is emphasised. Watching the episodes now, this is certainly the element that is most obvious.

Female roles

Apart from aesthetic considerations, though, the single most important element of *Prisoner*—both in fan accounts of this cult program, and in the popular archive—is what the program did with gender roles.[1] At the time of its first production, it was described in these terms: 'Elspeth Ballantyne, who plays warder Meg Jackson ... claims *Prisoner* is a breakthrough for actresses. "The series has proved that women can handle a show on their own ... "' ('Prisoner's Key Women' 1979: 11). This account of the program's importance has lasted. Jacka and Johnson note that '*Prisoner* ... provided strong character roles for actresses' (Jacka & Johnson 1998: 214), and according to Terry Blake

> It turned out to be a milestone for Australian TV serials and did much to awaken female audience participation. Until then, local TV was all *Homicide* and *Division 4*. Now, few would dare to make a show without strong parts for women.
>
> (Blake 1991: 13)

Fan accounts of the series also point to such concerns: 'I love *Prisoner* for its gripping storylines, its humour and its strong female characters' (Rachel's Unofficial *Prisoner: Cell Block H* Website, http://www.geocities.com/TelevisionCity/Studio/8118/). 'Token male notwithstanding, one of *Prisoner's* biggest claims to fame was its mostly female cast ... [and] strong female characters' (Wentworth Web, http://home.swipnet.se/wentworth-web/). In a conversation for this book with a fan of the program, it was interesting that when asked what it had that other programs did not, the reply was instantaneous. It did not require contemplation: 'strong women'. But what does this mean?

Female agency

In terms of characters, it is certainly true that many of the inmates in *Prisoner* possess characteristics that are not traditionally understood to be 'feminine'.

In the first episodes, one character plays out a traditionally feminine role: the new inmate Lynn. She has, the program makes clear, been wrongly accused. Her reaction to this situation is to weep, sob, and be helpless. She is introduced crying, sitting in the prison van beside Karen, sobbing that 'they won't believe me. I keep trying to tell them, I haven't done anything ... I'm innocent'. She continues to cry throughout the whole of the first episode.

But the other characters in Wentworth do not behave in this way. They have agency. Given an undesirable situation, they can take control of it and of the narrative. They can make plans and carry them out. They do not have to cry, or wait for someone else to sort things out for them.

Patricia Palmer's research on schoolgirls' perceptions of the program suggests that its popularity is based on what she calls 'strong characterization'. Bea 'was particularly admired for her toughness and shrewdness and lack of respect for authority' (Palmer 1986a: 17–18). Indeed, one of the girls she interviewed aspired to be like Bea, stating that 'She's a leader, she always does everything right' (Palmer 1986a: 17–18).

It is possible to aspire to be like these characters. Their control and leadership are desirable qualities. As one commentator suggests, 'Haven't we all at one time or another wanted to be down and dirty like Frieda (Franky) Doyle?' (Howes 1993: 641)—or 'calm and capable', like Judy Bryant? Or '[i]ntuitive and crafty'—like Bea. Or even, Howes suggests, '[j]ust plain nasty (and cruel and powerful)'—like 'the Freak'? There is a range of female characters here that are available for identification and that are attractive enough to encourage aspirational viewing (Howes 1993: 641).

These characteristics are indeed desirable. Bea makes plans, and makes them happen. When she is (briefly) leaving the prison—and knowing that, as soon as she has murdered her husband, she will be returning—she puts in place plans to deal with the period while she is away. She even organises for

Marilyn (Margaret Laurence) to leave the room as she plans, so that she can brief Doreen on the fact that she will not be gone long.

Franky (Carol Burns) can similarly make plans and take control. She organises a series of sit-ins in the canteen—organised political activity of which women are not usually shown to be capable in soap operas. Marilyn can also make plans. Although her plans have different ends—sexual gratification with the electrician who services the detention centre—they are no less efficacious. She gets Lizzie (Sheila Florance) to pick the lock on the prison's fuse box, so she can rewire it, causing a short circuit, so that the electrician will have to be called out (*Prisoner* 1979c). How many female characters has television presented who not only possess basic electrical skills, but are also able to employ these in the service of a plan they have developed for themselves?

However, the characters are not simple binary reversals, presenting women playing roles that are traditionally masculine. In some (admittedly quite limited) ways, the female characters in *Prisoner* do partake of traditional gender roles. In terms of occupations, we see the women often working in the laundry, engaged in a traditionally feminine occupation: washing clothes. Even this, as we have seen, can be twisted in perverse ways (for example, using the steam press not to care for another's clothing, but to crush and burn someone's hand). When one beloved character—'Mum' (Mary Ward)—leaves Wentworth, she is presented with a gift of a quilt. 'Every girl made a square for it', she's told (*Prisoner* 1979b). Perhaps the most important way that the female characters in *Prisoner* retain something of traditional feminine characteristics is in a sense of kinship and networks of caring for each other. Quoting one character in the program, who says that 'the thing about Rita is she's tough, but she cares about people', Gleitzman suggests that 'the series was like that too'. The characters are not simply strong: 'When they'd finished calling each other names, the characters were capable of expressing their vulnerabilities in a particularly rough-edged ... way' (Gleitzman 1992: 22).

The structures of support and caring are inflected in a particular way: this is a prison 'family', as one of the warder's sons puts it (*Prisoner* 1979c), with a matriarch called 'Mum' who cares for the others. But, as a prison family, it has to follow prison rules. When Lynn first comes into the laundry room, Bea treats her nicely, as a new inmate. After introducing her to the steam press, she says, 'Sit down for a minute love and I'll finish these'. However, when she finds out that Lynn has broken the strict rules of this prison family—committed a crime against a baby—she then crushes her hand in the steam press. The prison lifestyle is based on rules and hierarchies that must be obeyed, but within which, caring and support is possible. When Franky starts a riot, it is thrown off course by the fact that one of the prisoners—Rosie—is heavily pregnant. This brings the unwritten rules of the prison back into play. Lynn tells Franky that she must let Rosie out to see a doctor. 'Nobody tells me what to do', says Franky. Lizzie intervenes: 'She's right. This fight between you and Bea's one thing, but if anything happens to Rosie's baby, your life won't be worth living'.

These women, then, are capable, in control, and able to execute a plan and organise a narrative. There are glimpses of traditionally feminine characteristics, but these are presented within a context of prison rules and hierarchies.

But these are not simply 'positive images' in the sense that is still current in much popular and governmental discourse (National Working Party on the Portrayal of Women in the Media 1993: 1). It is certainly true that these characters are quite different from the majority of television programs at that time, which tended to show women as 'happy wives and mothers ... vulnerable and in need of protection, as irrational and over-emotional' (Palmer 1986a: 3, 4). But it is difficult, within the vocabulary of 'positive images', to see criminals, with many socially undesirable characteristics (loud, selfish, pushy, violent), as a 'positive image'. (Indeed, this reveals the problems with the very terminology: who gets to decide what is 'positive'?) Thus, writers such as Palmer, while recognising the distinctiveness of these characters, can still dismiss them for not being positive enough:

> Even the few programs such as *Prisoner* which portray women not as glamorous, happy and dependent, but as active, ordinary-looking and even angry, nevertheless often 'punish' them for not being the usual TV types. The women on *Prisoner*, because of their social context, do not have much control over their own lives, nor are they allowed to mix in 'normal society'. There is a very strong negative message in this for girls who are so attuned to the consequences of social behaviour for women
>
> (Palmer 1986a: 31)

In a way, such comments are unsurprising: as cultural critics, we often have a tendency to want to criticise everything. We want to prove that everything on television is bad. And it is always possible to argue the case that any given representation is bad because there is something it *doesn't* do (here, show women outside of the prison situation, with socially desirable characteristics). In the case of *Prisoner*, it is surely more useful to note what the program *does* do, which is different from what has gone before.

Unglamorous

However, the fact that many of *Prisoner*'s characters have narrative agency, and are capable of organising both plans and other people, is only one aspect of the program's importance in terms of the representation of female characters. Another fan, writing on the PCBH mailing list, suggests that '*Prisoner* was something different. At last, women could be seen in something for their acting ability instead of being a glamorous star. There were no sexually inviting flashy dresses, make-up and hair dos' (Peter Criddle, pers. comm. 21 August 1999). And this must be counted as one of *Prisoner*'s great contributions to Australian television. It is what makes it unique, not just in Australian television history, but in Western television more generally. In examining the Australian public archive, it is interesting how often one word turns up to describe *Prisoner*: 'unglamorous'.

Prisoner was not the first program to feature female characters who were able to fight, shoot guns, and have narrative agency. Early examples are *Honey West*, the secret agent and crime fighter who appeared on American television in 1965 (D'Acci 1997) and Honor Blackman and Diana Rigg in *The Avengers* (Miller 1997). But until *Prisoner*, these women—although they could be centred in the narratives—still had to purchase such centrality by glamour and sexiness. They had to be looked at while they fought. Sherrie Inness discusses at length the phenomenon of 'tough women' in television programming, from *The Bionic Woman* and *Wonder Woman* to *Charlie's Angels* and *Xena: Warrior Princess*, and argues that all of them had to be glamorous as well as 'tough' (Inness 1999). By contrast, *Prisoner* was unique in Western soap operas—as Darren Gray expresses this distinctiveness, there were 'No gorgeous young models, no sun-drenched beaches—just the grim walls of Wentworth Detention Centre and a selection of decidedly unglamorous inmates and warders' (Gray 1994: 36).

To cite another author making much the same point—in order precisely to show how commonly employed is this discourse about the program, and how detailed it can be—John Docker describes the characters thus:

> The women in *Prisoner* [are not] in the least glamorised. They are usually dressed in shabby prison uniforms, or for those on remand usually in fairly ordinary clothes. Their faces suggest no make-up, and they range in bodily shape from the skinny wizened old Lizzie ... to the big girls like Bea, Doreen and Judy. Their faces ... are shown as grainy and interesting, faces full of character,

of signs of hardship and suffering, alternately soft and hard, happy and depressed, angry or bored.

(Docker & Curthoys 1997: 1295)

Beverley Zalcock and Jocelyn Robinson agree that the characters are 'distinctly unglamorous ... they sweat, they have wrinkles, some of them are overweight' (Zalcock & Robinson 1996: 89).

The fact that the term 'unglamorous' recurs so often suggests just how unique *Prisoner* is in this respect. It is particularly interesting if we compare the program with earlier examples of media texts with the same setting.

Prisoner's generic roots are in what Zalcock and Robinson refer to as the 'Women in Prison' sub-genre—exemplified by films such as *Caged* [1950] and *Caged Heat* [1974] (Zalcock & Robinson 1996: 90). Indeed, it is interesting that when *Prisoner* was aired in Canada, its name was changed to *Caged Women* (Lewis & Stempel 1993: 204). The links identified by Zalcock and Robinson between *Prisoner* and these precedents include such 'stock characters ... [as] the butch, corrupt and repressed warden ... the innocent newcomer ... [and] the mad/bad con' (Zalcock & Robinson 1996: 90–1). Representatives of these types in *Prisoner* would be, respectively, 'Vinegar Tits', Lynne, and Frankie.

However, as Zalcock and Robinson note, although the characters might be similar, in the 'Women in Prison' films the characters are also presented as visually appealing bodies: 'The Women in Prison film caters to the expectations of a predominantly male audience. It addresses the male gaze through its use of overt sexuality [and] female nudity' (Zalcock & Robinson 1996: 91). They note that a stock element in many of these films is 'the shower scene'—a soft-porn sequence that allows us to see the bodies of these 'strong women' in a sexualised way. *Prisoner* offers nothing similar. The one shower scene that appears in the first few episodes serves as a flashback to a scene of Karen slaughtering her husband. We see nothing of her body in the sequence.

The way that the women's bodies in *Prisoner* are presented gives little hope for visual pleasure. There is a notable scene in the first episode when Karen arrives at Wentworth for the first time. The dress she wears when she arrives is very thin; in fact, you can see her nipples through it. By the next scene, she has been changed into prison uniform. This is a thick, shapeless blue smock, worn over a yellow or dark green shirt. There is no chance of seeing a nipple through these, or even the shape of a breast. In order to enter Wentworth, Karen must be desexualised.

The uniforms of the prison officers are not revealing either. They may be sexy to some viewers, but only for reasons other than visual pleasure. In this, the women's bodies are like the rest of the program. As with several of the programs discussed in this book, *Prisoner* does not offer up visual pleasure as one of its central qualities: the sets and costumes are all drab and simple.

There are, of course, degrees of deglamorisation in the inmate population. In the first episode, the two newly arrived inmates, Karen and Lynn, are both pretty young women, and even though they change into their uniforms, their hairstyles and makeup remain traditionally feminine. Marilyn is the most extreme version of this: her archetype is a 'dolly bird', and she wears big eighties hair and glamourous make-up. Even she, though—as she flirts with the doctor—is trapped in the uniform of the blue smock. (It is true that she does briefly escape it, while making out with a visiting electrician in a roof cavity, but even then we see nothing more risqué than her shoulders.)

Most of the characters are not traditionally attractive, and do not display any elements of traditional femininity. As Docker notes, Lizzy's body is wizened and skinny. Franky is butch and burly. And 'Queen' Bea is larger than traditional feminine ideals would allow. When Bea complains that her meal is late ('I thought you were gonna starve me to death'), the Freak replies, 'Now, that would take years, Smith'.

In this context, it is fascinating to note that in the end credits for *Prisoner* a full-screen credit is given to 'Hairdressing by Gilbert Broadway', giving this man equal importance, in accreditation terms, to the Executive Producer Reg Watson. Obviously, to appear 'not glamorous' takes a lot of make-up and hairdressing skill.

This lack of glamour is important. It frees up the female characters in *Prisoner* to use their bodies in quite different ways from those prescribed by traditional gender roles.

Strong bodies

As Germaine Greer points out in *The Female Eunuch*, many of the accoutrements of traditional femininity—tight skirts, high-heeled shoes, long fingernails, and even make-up—help to render women physically inactive. You cannot run in high-heeled shoes, fight with long fingernails, or eat pizza without smudging your lipstick (Greer 1970). Women's bodies in *Prisoner*, freed from the constraints of looking glamorous, can do things that traditionally they should not be capable of. They are not fragile. These women are not constrained by thinking of themselves as helpless, and their bodies as being in need of protection.

Again, it is through the induction of one of the new inmates that we see this in the first episode of the program. Karen is initially put in a cell with Franky. Franky makes it clear that she has sexual intentions towards Karen: 'I love beautiful things', she says. 'We're going to have a happy time together.' When Karen replies 'I'm not like that', Franky goes on: 'You're gonna have to be. And anything you don't know, I'll teach ya!' She touches Karen on the arm, and Karen shakes her off—'Don't touch me!' Karen then goes to see the Governor, and demands to be moved. She tells the Governor that Franky has made a pass at her. 'Did she hurt you?' demands the Governor. When Karen says no, she asks, 'Did she touch you?' 'Yes.' 'Where?' 'On the arm.' The Governor removes her spectacles, and angrily explains to Karen how she must regard her body in the world of Wentworth: 'Young woman, let me give you a word of advice ... if you run trying to report prisoners every time one of them touches you on the arm, you'll make a lot of enemies'. This is not telling her that she must accept being raped or treated badly—the Governor has already asked: 'Did she hurt you?' Rather, it is the lesson that female bodies in Wentworth are not fragile, delicate, precious things. Women here are corporeal beings, who must get used to physical contact. When someone touches you, you do not run to an authority figure to seek protection; rather, you must deal with it for yourself.

Similarly, when we get our only glimpse of female flesh in the first episode—Karen strips off for her medical examination and we see her back—the scene does not present the female body as a site of voyeuristic pleasure. Rather, it is presented to the audience so they can see the scars on it. They come from cigarette burns.

On a related theme, when Franky is shown in her cell in solitary, the shot includes the toilet in the corner. Not many television programs show toilets. This is a more upfront attitude towards bodies than that of most television programming: the women in Wentworth are embodied and corporeal. They lead physical lives.

Uncouth sluts

And the women can use these bodies for violent ends. They can speak in an aggressive and violent way. Lorraine Bayley, the mother-goddess of *The Sullivans* (still running at this time) was a member of 'God's police'. She could not even bear to hear the phrase 'rough as guts' spoken in her house. This would not bother any of the characters in *Prisoner*. Even within the bounds of acceptable prime-time television language, *Prisoner* manages to provide its female characters with a rich, aggressive, demotic vocabulary. The women are—as Vera Bennett puts it to Franky with a poetic eloquence—'uncouth sluts'. Frankie calls Doreen a 'stupid cow', and refers to Vera as 'vinegar tits'. The language promises physical aggression. When Franky confronts Karen over the latter's failure to hold ranks at a sit-in Franky had organised in the canteen, she promises her that 'if you so much as move a finger … [She gives Karen the middle-finger] You saw what happened to your friend Lynn [her hand was put in the steam press]. I won't just stick your hand in the press—I'll stick your pretty face in' (*Prisoner* 1979c). When Bea is enjoying her one night of freedom before killing her husband and returning to Wentworth, she is unhappy with the attitude of the porter in the posh hotel she has chosen: 'I'll give you a tip: you look down your nose one more time at me and I'll chuck you through that bloody window. Now get out' (*Prisoner* 1979b).

These women are foul-mouthed and direct, promising violence. And they follow up on that promise.

Top fights

The moments in *Prisoner* in which physical violence breaks out are also an important part of its public archive. In its cult manifestation, the fights in *Prisoner* are an important reference point. When I posted an email to the PCBH mailing list asking for suggestions for the best fight in the program, this was understood to be a sensible question: 'What a thoroughly brilliant idea for a poll! I'd have to go for the obvious one (during the fire), where Bea throttles Joanie with a chair leg. TOP FIGHT!!! Nice one Alan!' (Bettridge 1999).

In the first few episodes of the program, we see many examples of physical violence. When Doreen (Franky's lover) is moved from their shared cell, Franky smashes up the recreation room. She picks up furniture and throws it around the set with some conviction. Franky later destroys Lynn's garden, and Lynn goes for her with a shovel. They end up rolling around in the dirt (*Prisoner* 1979b). In the laundry, when Franky has threatened Karen (see above), she grabs Karen's face. Her fingers dig into her skin and push her head back harshly; it is convincing physical contact (*Prisoner* 1979c). After she has had her temporary position as 'Top Dog' in the prison overthrown by Bea returning to Wentworth after one day of freedom, Franky again demonstrates violence, throwing tables over in the canteen and chucking chairs (*Prisoner* 1979c). When this leads to a riot, Franky seizes the warder, Meg Jackson (Elspeth Ballantyne), and grabs her by the neck—again, we see the fingers digging into the flesh. When Bea and Franky end up fighting during this riot, we see Bea give Franky a two-handed swing to the stomach, smashing her on the back of the neck on the way down.

And, of course—to return to the memorable moment that opened this chapter—we see Bea crush Lynn's hand in the steam press. This scene is underplayed. It is not shot melodramatically as some others are; there are no huge close-ups of overacted screaming. Rather, it is played mostly in a mid-shot, showing Bea, Lynn, and the press. Bea gets Lynn to smooth the clothes out and then crushes her hand. Lynn screams. In the background, Lizzie laughs. There is no emotive music. This example of a woman physically attacking another woman is almost throw-away. This casual abuse and cruelty continues. In the next episode, when Bea is convincing Lynn not to tell the Governor about what happened, she sneaks into her cell at night: 'You're going to be quiet. If you don't, I'll punch your face in', and she reaches out and roughly squeezes Lynn's burnt hand (*Prisoner* 1979b).

This violence is not exactly performed as 'gritty realism'. There are melodramatic codes in some of the scenes. But what is noticeable is the conviction with which the physical movements are performed. The actresses do not look as though they are scared of physical contact. They do not pull away from it. They actually engage with each other in physical and violent ways.

The importance of this fact—that it is not just fighting, but fighting as though the women involved are not scared of physical contact—is obvious when comparing *Prisoner*'s fight scenes with other examples of women fighting in television series.

Diana Rigg's Emma Peel (in *The Avengers*) is a famous 1960s example of a woman who was able to fight and take care of herself. In one well-known episode of the program—'A Touch of Brimstone'—there is an example of her fighting. Emma has gone undercover into a sadomasochistic venue called the Hellfire Club, and thus has ended up dressed in a leather dominatrix outfit with studded collar. In order to fight, she must dress up in a sexy and provocative manner. But when we watch Rigg's famed fighting, it seems very staged. The actor does karate chops and kicks, but with a lack of conviction. She seems to be scared of actually touching anyone. When she does touch another actor, she pulls back quickly. She always tries to keep her body out of harm's way, reaching out at arm's length to deliver her attacks.

The epitome of this traditionally female form of fighting—reaching out to hit without committing the body to the possibility of physical contact—is the catfight. Jami Bernard suggests that 'Men enjoy seeing the kind of physical "catfight" in which there's hair pulling: they either find it hilarious, or a turn on' (Bernard 1997: 125). Roughly contemporaneous with *Prisoner*'s success was that of the American soap opera *Dynasty*. This program also presented women fighting, but in quite a different way. Jane Feuer describes the popularity of *Dynasty*'s catfights among its cult gay male audience: '*Dynasty* night is an inviolable ritual in gay bars across the country; at one in Los Angeles, tapes of epic catfights between Alexis and Krystle are played over and over in an endless loop' (Feuer 1995: 132).

Prisoner's women do not indulge in catfights. They punch each other in the stomach. They grab each other's throats (not hair). They show no reluctance to make physical contact. They are not scared of smearing their make-up. This is an important aspect of *Prisoner*'s place in the Australian public archive.

Transgressive women

It is interesting to note just how transgressive it could be during the 1970s for television to show women who were unashamedly physical. In the late 1960s and early 1970s the Australian Broadcasting Control Board had stepped in several times in order to stop images of violent women being broadcast. The controversy centred on women in sporting programs:

> The programme *The Roller Game* had for a considerable period caused the Board concern because of the display of violent action, particularly on the part of female contestants ... an undertaking was given by the stations that displays of violence by female skaters would be eliminated from future programmes.
>
> (ABCB 1967: 101)

Similarly,

> A professional wrestling programme televised by a metropolitan station included a bout between two females ... this type of entertainment had been the subject of some public concern ... the Board decided that the presentation of female wrestling on television was contrary to the fundamental principles of the Standards. Stations were informed to this effect.
>
> (ABCB 1969: 112)

Women's violence is not acceptable. Why not? Two years later, the Board explains why it will not ban (male) boxing, even though it has received complaints from viewers about this 'undesirable form of violence':

> The Board took the view that it would not be justified in intervening in the arrangements between the stations and the boxing organisations governing the conduct of such programmes in that boxing, which is a widely accepted form of sport in Australia, is permitted by law and is conducted under accepted rules.
>
> (ABCB 1971: 139)

Male violence is 'widely accepted', so the Board cannot intervene. Female violence is unacceptable, therefore the Board can demand its removal.

Other snippets of evidence suggest the transgressive potential of *Prisoner*, or at least its ability to annoy those who see themselves as guardians of morality. The Festival of Light—a Christian wowser organisation that exists in order to condemn publicly things it does not like—hated the program:

> The Festival of Light stated that *Prisoner* does a great disservice to the Department of Corrective Services: 'Staff appear no better than the prisoners. This program breaks down respect for law and order—especially young people still watching at 8.30 p.m. It includes excessive violence and crude language'.
>
> (Curthoys & Docker 1989: 52)

One of my favourite responses to my calls for viewers to supply me with details of their great moments in Australian television for this book was that which condemned *Prisoner*. It appeared in a story in a community newspaper discussing the project. One reader cut out a copy of the article and defaced it with comments scribbled aggressively in red pen. Over my thoughts on *Number 96* was written, diagonally in firm capitals, 'RUBBISH PROGRAM'. Scribbled across my mention of *Prisoner* was 'MORE RUBBISH'. In the margin was written: 'We should have better quality programs, that promote the well being of society instead of undermining it and family life'. In so annoying this viewer—in convincing her or him that the program was undermining society and family life—*Prisoner*'s violent women, lack of respect for traditional gender roles, and scenes such as Bea carelessly crushing Lynn's hand in the steam press were doing their job. The program is remembered for these characterisations, to the extent that, for many viewers, remembering the program means keeping it in the present through archiving, rewatching, and discussing it. It is cult, transgressive, and an important part of the public archive of Australian television programs.

Availability

Prisoner is one of the most comprehensively archived programs in the history of Australian television—not officially by Screensound (which does hold a few, mainly early, episodes for public viewing), but by viewers. Many fans of the series have complete, or nearly complete, runs of the series held in private collections.

A complete summary of the content of every episode is also available. Again, it is not officially produced, but is the work of a fan. It can be found at http://www.zen.co.uk/hom/page/zahid.john/prisoner/intro.htm.

Note

1 However, from an academic point of view, *Prisoner* has mostly been of interest in terms of its audience. It is, I think, the program about which most ethnographic work has been done in the history of Australian television (see Thomas 1980; Palmer 1986b: 16; Fiske 1987; Hodge & Tripp 1986; Turnbull 1984; Docker & Curthoys 1997: 1295).

11

Sale of the Century: 'And the Ladies Look Beautiful Too'

1980–99; Sale of the New Century, 2000–

On 8 February 1997, Nicky Buckley made the front cover of *TV Week* magazine. The reason was simple: she was pregnant. And she was a game show hostess on Australian television. This combination led to a headline, in the vocabulary of *TV Week*'s cover stories: 'PREGNANT NICKY'S SALE SHOCK'. And it is indeed a 'shock', for not only is Nicky pregnant, but she intends (this is the 'shock') to keep working during her pregnancy!

Why should this be shocking? What is so inconceivable about the fact that a woman might continue to work while pregnant? After all, working in television—although we are often assured in interviews with stars that it involves long hours and is, really, very hard work—does not actually involve much heavy lifting. What then makes Nicky's decision such a 'shock'? And why is it remembered in Australia? For it is remembered.

When *Woman's Day* in 1999 comes to write on the roles of women in game shows, Nicky's pregnant body is called to mind as an iconic moment:

> Nicky … who has six years at the helm of *Sale*, caused a stir when she slipped her very pregnant body into some slinky dresses, not once but twice, to host the show … looking pregnant and glamorous. Despite looking radiant, the Nine Network was inundated with calls of both complaint and support for Nicky. She was one of television's first personalities to defy convention and work through pregnancy on screen. Even now, after the much publicised births of her two children, two year old Cooper and Jasper, 10 months, Nicky doesn't see what all the fuss was about … 'I was no different to anyone else who was pregnant, except that I was going to work and had people to help me get dressed. In the Nineties, so many women work … '.
>
> (Williams 1999: 17)

Similarly, an interview with Nicky introduces her and summarises her lasting contribution to the Australian public sphere: she got pregnant.

> Nicky's two very public pregnancies—during which she outraged a vocal minority by continuing to work on *Sale* and wear figure-hugging dresses almost until the births—have shaped her image as a popular homemaker and working mother.
>
> (Stanley 1999: 8)

Continued discussion ensures that Nicky's pregnancies, and discussions about what they mean, continue in the public sphere:

> I thought she [Nicky] looked beautiful ... it was great to see a high-profile woman working to the end of her pregnancy. Her actions send out a message that says if you want to work through your pregnancy, and you're healthy enough, it's OK to do so. A lot of people still think that once you're pregnant you can't work any more, and it's so cool that Nicky disproved that.
>
> (Weiniger 1997: 24)

John Berger, in a statement typical of the delightful simplicity of more abstract forms of cultural theory, once suggested that in terms of dominant forms of representation 'Men act. Women appear' (Berger 1973). This has never been *entirely* true, although as a generalisation, it works rather well. And in some specific genres, the statement fits with a disturbing exactitude. The case of the game show hostess is one of these. Three previous chapters have traced the way in which representations of women on Australian television became important and interesting objects of public debate: in the sex of Abigail on *Number 96*, the restrained and nostalgic motherhood of Grace Sullivan, and the unglamorous physicality of *Prisoner*. This chapter looks at the way in which a similar debate was taking place in another genre, what happens to men and women in the game show format, and why it is memorable when the rules for gendered appearance are broken.

The success of *Sale*

Sale of the Century is

> the most successful game show ever produced and shown on Australian television. The series began on the Nine Network in early 1980, and apart from the

> short four-week summer break each year, has been transmitted in the same prime-time access slot of 7.00 p.m. five nights a week ever since.
>
> (Moran 1997b: 1427)

Sale has been an immensely successful part of the Australian media. By 1980, it was the number one program in both Sydney and Melbourne, rating almost two million viewers in these two markets alone (ABT 1981b: 70). Although it did not long retain this premier position, in 1982 it was still the number two program in these markets (ABT 1982: 58), and by 1986 it was still in the top ten in both cities (number three in Sydney and number seven in Melbourne) (ABT 1986: 71). According to the work of Peter Beilby, *Sale of the Century* is the number-three highest rating Australian television program up until 1981 (Beilby 1981: 185). In a 1990 newspaper article on successful television programs, *Sale* is included: '*Sale of the Century*: Achievements: On July 14, the show turns 10 years of age. That longevity is probably its greatest achievement. An estimated weeknight Australian audience of 3.5 million' (Bowring 1990: 46).

Sale is based on an earlier program, *Temptation*, which had many similarities, including the 'same format' and the 'same host'. *Temptation* started as a daytime quiz show, airing five days a week, in 1971, hosted by Tony Barber. Its popularity in that slot led it to move to the evening schedule, as *The Great Temptation*, in 1972. It was the most successful quiz show in Australia up to that point (Murphy 1981: 80).

Grundy then remade the program in 1980, using the title and format of a similar American program, *Sale of the Century*:

> *Sale of the Century* originally ran on NBC, the American television network from 1969 to 1973 … Grundy bought the format for *Sale of the Century* in 1979 … The outstanding rating success of *Sale* in the Australian television market made it easier to sell the format elsewhere. Since 1982 the company has reversioned *Sale of the Century* in five other territories: Hong Kong … the United States … the United Kingdom … New Zealand … and Germany.
>
> (Moran 1997b: 1427–8)

In the years since 1980, *Sale* has had only two hosts: Tony Barber left in 1991, to be replaced by Glenn Ridge. In that period, there have been six regular 'co-hosts': Victoria Nicholls, Delvene Delaney, Alyce Platt, Jo Bailey, Nicky Buckley, and Karina Brown. And the relationship between these 'hosts' and their 'co-hosts' is a fascinating example of the politics of gender representation.

We must be careful, as academics writing about popular culture, not to attempt to read into, or out of, texts interpretations that are neither obvious nor important to the audiences watching them in situ in the mediasphere. It is one of the failings of theory-driven work that it can often end up producing readings of texts that bear little relation to those texts as they are experienced by audiences. This is not to say that these readings are 'wrong'—simply that they bear little relation to the programs most of the audience experience.

In the case of *Sale of the Century*, this is not a problem. Indeed, the program seems deliberately to set itself up as a demonstration of those problems of gender representation in popular culture that were identified by feminist cultural theory in the 1970s.

Nicky's body

Nicky's body, and her decision to present it to the viewing public in its pregnant form, was certainly a popular topic of media discussion in the weeks following the first announcement of her intentions. As is the case in many chapters of this book, although the public attention appears to have been national, it was undeniably more excitable and more obvious in the media of Melbourne, the city where *Sale* is produced. The public coverage consists of two kinds of material: first, letters (for and against) commenting on Nicky's body, and second, editorial coverage of this issue. The letters, opening the controversy, insist that Nicky is breaking an unspoken rule of *Sale*'s genre by appearing on screen while pregnant. 'Nicky Buckley,' says one, 'why don't you dress with more decorum, instead of flaunting your pregnancy in skin tight clothes?' (Clarke 1997: 18). Another asks, 'Couldn't Nicky Buckley wear more suitable clothing and give her on-camera appearance more dignity? Grandpa, Brighton'. One viewer wishes 'Glenn [would] stop telling her she looks great—she doesn't. Disgusted, Reservoir' (as quoted in Hooks 1997: 3). She is 'flaunting' herself (Goeschel 1997: 24), and making a 'sideshow' of her pregnancy (Grant 1997: 20). Her body should not appear on television when it is pregnant.

There follows public discussion about this issue. It includes editorial comment on Nicky's body (Squires 1997: 22), interviews (Hooks 1997: 3), and television stories on *A Current Affair* (28 April 1997). Nicky's body is used as way to discuss issues of body image for women (Tom 1997: 13) and maternity wear (Deveny 1997: 1). '[W]hat's wrong with a pregnant woman continuing to work for as long as she wishes to, and for as long as it is safe to do so? What's wrong with a woman being proud of the fact that she's pregnant? She can still do the job' (Warneke 1997: 16), says one article. Another comments that 'A pregnant woman is apparently public property. Strangers touch her tummy on the tram and start intimate conversations' (Brady 1997: 3). Another article uses Buckley's pregnancy as a way to discuss the issue of women's bodies more generally:

> Suddenly, because of Nicky's shameless pride in her pregnancy, and uncompromising devotion to fashion frocks, all the nitpicky little controversies about pregnancy have merged into one shocked, rip-snorter of a nationwide bunfight about what is beautiful and what is not ... The whole vexed limbo-like state of pregnancy, the 'not virgin, not mother' confusion has polarised us into opposing 'Monster!' and 'Masterpiece!' camps, with poor Nicky smack in the middle.
>
> (Burns 1997: 5)

But in a way these comments are misguided. When one letter asks, in an exasperated way, 'Why are so many people disgusted with Nicky Buckley?' or another wants to know 'what is wrong with a pregnant woman continuing to work?' they are missing the point. Nicky Buckley is not simply a 'woman'. Rather, she is a game show hostess, which is quite a different thing. Or rather, it involves more of being a 'woman' (in the traditional sense) than most female members of the Australian population have to bear.

In the flurry of press interest that followed Nicky's decision, one interview provides a particularly interesting comparison. A journalist, interested in the brouhaha that is emerging, questions a variety of television personalities on their feelings about Nicky's pregnancy. Mary Delahunty, then a newsreader in Victoria (before becoming a member of parliament for that state) proves to be an interesting case. She declares that she remained in her news-reading job throughout her pregnancy, and nobody even noticed:

> She says the key to the Buckley controversy is her role on the show. 'She's drawing attention to her shape by the clothes she's wearing. Nicky is an entertainer and a component of her job is highlighting her beautiful body, and she's continuing to do that ... '.
>
> (Hooks 1997: 3)

Nicky's body is so interesting precisely because the format of the game show works so hard to insist that women are bodies, to be looked at. And again, the public discussion of Nicky's role that takes place around this controversy makes very clear what a game show hostess is for:

> Buckley says that while she feels no compulsion to conceal her changing profile, she has had problems finding suitable clothes ... 'There's not a lot of evening wear in the maternity line ... how hard do you think it is for the wardrobe department here to find me five outfits a week for six months?'
>
> (Hooks 1997: 3; see also James 1997: 18)

Nicky's primary problem is finding a different designer frock for her pregnant body five nights a week, and this is why her pregnancy is so different from Mary Delahunty's. By the 1990s, it was acceptable for newsreaders to be female, and although there may be gendered guidelines for their acceptable appearance and age, their primary role is to read news. This equity of narrative roles in the news is simply not true of game shows: Nicky Buckley is, we are told, there to be looked at. Her job is to be glamorous, taking on a traditionally feminine role. Should she challenge that in any way—for example, by becoming pregnant—controversy will ensue. After all, as one commentator notes, 'Within the television industry, the top-range coat-hanger to have your label modelled on is, undoubtedly, Nicky Buckley. Because, let's face it, how many of us only watch *Sale of the Century* to see what Nicky's wearing tonight' (Jellie 1997: 1). It is for this reason that Nicky's pregnancy is remembered as an important moment in the public archive of Australian television, and became the catalyst for a public debate that explicitly discussed and challenged the conventions of gendered representation at the heart of one of the most popular genres on Australian television.

The rules of the game

Writing about the role of the game show hostess, Brian Davies claims that 'feminist groups' in the early 1970s did not take 'kindly to afternoon television's masters of ceremony' (Davies 1981: 92). Although we must be wary of journalistic writing that makes claims about 'feminist groups' without specific evidence to back up these claims, Davies' account does point us to the possibility of some emerging public dissatisfaction with the strictly demarcated gender roles of game shows during the 1970s. Putting the game shows into a television context in which 'family comedy stereotyped women as home-makers whose roles and skills were both lesser and fewer than males', where female characters in other genres were dependent, with 'trivial' interests, Davies suggests that 'women's media action groups' attacked the game shows and their representations of gender (Davies 1981: 92).

With a text the size of *Sale of the Century* (literally thousands of hours of television), it is simply not possible to analyse the entire text in detail. To do this would, anyway, be to misunderstand the program: there will be very few viewers who have seen every single episode of the program since 1980. That is not how the program is designed to be watched. Rather, it is necessary, in attempting to make sense of it, to trace the ways in which it is placed in the mediasphere and the ways in which particular meanings of it are promoted. Buckley's pregnancy suggests that the question of gender representation in the program is of some importance. An analysis of the ways in which this occurs reveals a careful binary structuring of roles—a binary that is more explicit in *Sale of the Century*, and in game shows generally, than it is in almost any other genre on Australian television. Indeed, as I suggest above, the program is almost parodic in its careful attention to the various issues raised by feminist film theory in the 1970s—issues that are often taken too literally as a description of the whole of a culture, but that are completely appropriate for understanding *Sale of the Century*.

Positive and negative images

Linda Artel and Susan Wendgraf, writing in 1978, worry that there are no 'positive images' in the media: there are no 'independent, intelligent women; adventurous and resourceful girls ... [who] question the value and behaviour of the traditional male/female role division' (Artel & Wendgraf 1990 [1978]: 9). It is by now generally accepted that the division of representations into the simple binary of 'stereotypes' and 'positive images' is not a particularly useful way to analyse the media: it is too simplistic a taxonomy for understanding the complexity and messiness of representation (see chapter 10 and Waldman 1978). Yet, the roles played by men and woman in game shows fit perfectly into the concerns about 'stereotypes' and 'positive images' developed by feminist film theory in the 1970s.

Control

Sale of the Century is presented by men: the hosts (Barber and Ridge). Men run the program. Men manage it. Men ask the questions. Men are in control. There are, however, slight complications associated with this rule, even in this game show. The role of contestants, for example, is interesting. For game show contestants, gender really is not important. There is little distinction made between the way that male and female contestants are treated. Occasionally, Nicky Buckley might say something like: 'We have some very intelligent women on the show, don't we?' and Glenn might reply: 'We do, but we're still waiting for a female champ' (*SOTC* 1999c). But these are isolated moments, and do not structure the program. In general, the gender of the contestants is not an important part of the pleasure of *Sale of the Century*.

But for hosts, gender is vitally important. Game show hosts are men. This rule is so unbendable that the tiny number of exceptions that do exist in Australian television history appear as mutant offspring, unhealthy and doomed to die. I am aware of three quiz shows in the history of Australian television with female hosts: *Now You See It* (Sophie Formica), *Guess What* (Alison Brahe, then Jacquie Rindt), and *I Do I Do* (Lisa Treloar) (Keating 1999b). None of these was particularly successful, and at least one (*I Do I Do*) can be seen as a hybrid (game/lifestyle show), whose generic uncertainty allowed it to have a female host. Most tellingly, not a single one of these programs had a male co-host, dressed in revealing clothing, making small-talk while looking absolutely gorgeous (a sad loss to Australian television).[1]

It is overwhelmingly the case that the 'host' of a game show is male; and the 'co-host' is female. The terminology is important. In the descriptions both within the program itself and in secondary texts such as newspapers, Glenn Ridge is never the 'co-host' of *Sale*, and Nicky is never described as the 'host'. The very first episode of *Sale of the Century* begins with a voice-over (male) introducing the prize car, and then: 'And now, here is the star of the show: Tony Barber!' Tony then introduces Victoria Nicholls: 'Let me tell you who's going to help me on this show, a lovely lady, you may have met her before, the vivacious Victoria Nicholls' (*SOTC* 1980). She is the helper, not the star. This is the standard introduction for Tony Barber and, later, for Glenn Ridge.

This control is manifest in the program in the way that the speech of the 'star' and that of the 'co-host' are managed. Bob Dyer brought *Pick-a-Box* to television on 2 February 1957 and brought with him his sidekick and wife, Dolly. Asking, 'Who's our next contestant, Dolly?' (Davies 1981: 86), Bob placed Dolly in the role of one of Australian television's earliest game show hostesses. Bob was in charge: he told Dolly what to do, gave her permission to speak, and managed her performances. In the same way, Glenn allows Nicky to speak—'Who's up against the champion tonight, Nicky?' (*SOTC* 1999b)—before sending her from the set. Similarly, Tony Barber tells Victoria Nicholls what to do: 'Thank you, Victoria, we'll see you later'. He kisses her on the cheek and she leaves the set (*SOTC* 1981). He manages Delvene Delaney in the same way: 'Thanks for that, Delvene—I'm going to hop right into it', he says, dismissing her (*SOTC* 1983). The quiz is beginning, so she must leave the stage. It is his domain. At the end of a program, Tony must give Victoria permission to speak: 'Say goodbye, Victoria' (*SOTC* 1981). She says goodbye.

Of course, it is possible to suggest that this is reading too much into isolated moments in the text, but the point of this chapter is to suggest that such an interpretation of *Sale* is not awkward or wilful. Rather, this is the way the program—proudly—presents itself.

Stereotypical gender roles

The game-show assistant can be a very ditsy young woman. Victoria Nicholls' persona is certainly the most ditzy of the *Sale* co-hosts. Appearing in the gift shop, on a kids' bike that features as a prize, she is dressed like a child in tracksuit pants, ringing her bell and shouting 'Wheeeh!' (*SOTC* 1981). Although Delvene Delaney was more elegant and sophisticated, she also had her ditzy moments, such as when she appears in a gift shop, standing beside some bunk beds:

> Every kid loves bunks. Except for me. I used to have to sleep on the top bunk and there was a little frog in the rafters that used to keep me awake all night. That's got nothing to do with this prize ...
>
> (*SOTC* 1983)

Not only are the co-hosts helpers, being told what to do, but there is also a tendency for them to be dippy (although none of the later women were as explicitly ditzy as Nicholls). They also perform certain standard gendered behaviours, the most obvious example being Nicholls's insistence on giggling inanely at all of Tony's unfunny jokes—as all women should do in a heterosexual relationship (at least in the dating phase).

What is more, the show likes to suggest that there are gendered expectations of what women and men will like. As the male voice-over puts it, introducing some of the prizes in the gift shop, 'I'm sure that most women would love one of these fabulous furs', or, even better, 'Here is the answer to every woman's dream'—a fridge (*SOTC* 1980).

The only point at which the program directly challenges gender roles is in the male presenter's exclamation at the end of each show: 'Let's go shopping!' Shopping is gendered as a feminine activity—a delight in, and insistence on, going shopping even more so. In one episode, the winner is an ex-boxer who looks as rough as guts, and it is quite an odd moment when Tony says: 'Let's go shopping!' This gendered behaviour is rarely seen in other genres of Australian television.

The gaze: men act and women appear

> [P]leasure in looking has been split between active/male and passive/female. The determining male gaze projects its fantasy onto the female figure, which is styled accordingly.
>
> (Mulvey 1990 [1975]: 33)

Laura Mulvey's famous article on 'visual pleasure and the narrative cinema' argues that women are rendered passive in order to become objects for the sexual gaze of men. Again, this formulation is now generally realised to be simplistic and problematic in its use of psychoanalytic theory to describe a simple, empirically verifiable point (Gamman & Marshment 1988). But, once again, game shows seem to be deliberately setting out to prove that they can make themselves exactly fit this critique of popular culture.

Set moves

In the documentary *35 Years of Television* (1991), Tony Barber gets his own segment: a montage of clips of him running on to the set at the start of *Sale*. This is followed by a *Comedy Company* sketch, parodying his enthusiasm by having him wildly throwing himself about the set. Glenn, by contrast, is more restrained: he merely strides purposefully.

By comparison, the co-hosts move a lot less. Indeed, in the earlier episodes of *Sale*, they barely move at all. While Tony runs on, Victoria Nicholls is actually carried in on a rotating set. She doesn't have to move at all; she merely has to stand, smiling. When she is with him, he kisses her; she does not kiss him. Again, he acts and she is passive. Tony has much more freedom to explore all of the set. After Victoria, standing in the gift shop, has introduced the prize, Tony bounds in. He can go wherever he wants (*SOTC* 1981).

Providing the ultimate example of this motionless beauty are the models who show the contestants to their seats. In the early episodes, as the contestants are announced and take their seats, a blonde model in a very smart gold dress stands perfectly still and gestures her arms in a kind of 'Aloha' motion (the 'Adriana manoeuvre', perhaps) (*SOTC* 1981; 1983; 1980). These women do not move, apart from these hand gestures; they do not speak at all. They simply stand and look 'glamorous'.

By 1999, this has changed somewhat. Now, while male contestants continue to receive similar treatment from similar models, female contestants are shown to their seats by men in evening suits (*SOTC* 1999c). Still, the men do not wear revealing clothing, and we are not allowed glimpses of their pectoral muscles.

Lovely ladies

As we know from popular culture's own memory of game-show history, the co-hosts are more 'glamorous' than the hosts. In an article specifically on 'the game show girls' (not, of course, 'women'), Marina Williams discusses the figure of Barbie Rogers in the 1970s predecessor to *Sale of the Century*, *Temptation*. Known for her knee-high boots and hotpants, Barbie apparently (in standard journalistic terms) 'sent viewers into a frenzy', and created much media interest (Williams 1999: 17, 18).

And so Tony introduces Victoria Nicholls: 'Let me tell you who's going to help me on this show, a lovely lady, you may have met her before, the vivacious Victoria Nicholls' (*SOTC* 1981). Victoria is lovely; he is specifically telling us that we must judge her on her appearance. Tony is never referred to on the program as 'lovely'. Delvene Delaney is similarly 'my lovely lady—Delly' (*SOTC* 1983). And, of course, the co-hosts dress differently from Tony or Glenn. In part, this is pro-filmic logic: women dress differently from men in culture generally. But we know that there is a variety of clothing from which women can choose—female newsreaders, to return to the example of Mary Delahunty cited above, are not dressed to draw attention to their cleavages. But within the genre of game shows—and, as noted above, in contextual discourses—we are told that the women's clothing is worthy of attention; it is to be looked at. 'You're wearing leather tonight', Glenn comments. 'It's not really leather', Nicky reassures him. She says nothing about his suit: there is little to say (*SOTC* 1999b). Delvene Delaney gets to wear a gorgeous light-blue evening gown, draped over one shoulder and held in place by a clasp (*SOTC* 1983); Tony Barber wears a suit.

As noted above, the case of contestants is somewhat different. The pro-filmic codes that are part of wider cultural norms often mean that female contestants tend to wear more make-up than men, to have more complex hairstyles than men, and to wear more colourful clothes than men, just as women generally do in Australian culture. But this is not inescapable. The female contestants do not *have* to be glamorous—as is the case of the champ Barbara, for example (*SOTC* 1999), a stocky, grey-haired woman in a resolutely homely flowery blouse.

Visual pleasure and the narrative of the game show

Mulvey's article draws attention to the fact that many feature films are structured so that men drive the narrative, which is interrupted periodically so that women can be looked at (Mulvey 1990 [1975]). This is exactly how *Sale of the Century* is structured, with its gift shop segments standing in for the musical numbers of classical Hollywood cinema. The silent models discussed above appear at their most obviously glamorous in these segments.

Sit and stroke

The first gift shop in the first episode of *Sale of the Century* features 'This compact four-in-one unit: television, AM and FM radio, and alarm'. While Victoria describes this marvel of modern technology, another female model—in a blue evening dress, cleavage prominent, with long blonde hair and glamour lips—sits and strokes the appliance. The third gift shop of the same episode features a chair. Victoria sits on it and talks about it; another glamorous female model strokes it. In a later episode, when the prize is 'a luxurious kitchen', another model (in a glamorous metallic red dress) leans on a counter and strokes the oven (*SOTC* 1981). In the same episode, Victoria again gets to sit next to the prize—a hi-fi system—while a model with long blonde hair and a spangly metallic blue dress again strokes the back of the machine and the sides of the speakers. A close-up shows us her fingernails: very long and red, and impractical for working the buttons of the machine, but perfect for stroking it. Victoria even gets a chance for some stroking action at the end of the first episode of *Sale*: the big prize is a Mercedes. Victoria strokes it.

Men use lawnmowers

Men have appeared in the gift shop since the beginning of *Sale*; but they are used quite differently from the female models. In the first episode, a dining table has a chubby, big-bearded man sitting at it. Any confusion about why he is sitting here, interrupting our visual pleasure, is quickly resolved. 'This is Professor Sam Ball', says Tony. 'He sets the questions and adjudicates.' He is not simply there to be looked at. He does not show his cleavage. He is a brain, whose purpose on the show is to set questions—not to be looked at. And we do not, of course, learn the name of any of his fellow models in the episode—those who wear metallic evening dresses and stroke things.

Male models occasionally appear in early episodes, increasingly so in later years. They are often doing something. This can be gender-appropriate behaviour. For example, one gift shop features a man (fully dressed) using the lawnmover that is offered as a prize. ('I think this is the most amazing thing I've ever seen! ... this fantastic grass cutter', gushes Victoria.) It can also be gender-inappropriate, as when Nicky appears in a kitchen with a male model, dressed in jeans and a T-shirt, who is actually cooking. This, is should be noted, is still very different from leaning on the counter in an evening dress and stroking the oven (*SOTC* 1999a).

Sometimes, the male and female models do similar things, but dressed very differently. A swimming pool, for example, may feature both male and female models lounging beside it, but the woman wears a skimpy bikini that leaves no doubt that she has very large breasts. The man wears gym wear—not, as might be expected, a skimpy set of Speedos (*SOTC* 1999b). If the female model is looking through a telescope, she will still reveal her cleavage for the camera to linger on (*SOTC* 1999c).

The most spectacular example of the narrative break for visual pleasure in the episodes studied is the 'relocatable home' gift shop. This segment features a woman in *very* short shorts running around this mobile home, opening curtains. A second woman appears, in even shorter shorts, slit up the side to be more revealing still. Both models have the huge blonde hair and overdone make-up of porn stars in the 'lesbian' scene of a straight porn film, and low-cut tops to match. They frolic around the home together, looking delighted at kitchen appliances and doonas. It is as though *Sale of the Century* has briefly stopped in order to play some footage from a mid 1980s porn video (*Sale of the Century* 1983).

Please touch the merchandise

In the first episode of *Sale*, one of the prizes is a fur coat. The model who is displaying this prize wears no pants—just tights—and the fur barely covers her buttocks. Tony brings the contestant over and tells him, 'You can touch the merchandise' (*SOTC* 1980). It is unclear if he means the fur or the woman, and indeed, in the context of the program, the two are often collapsed. In a way that is simply not true for the male models, the female models become the prizes.

Nicky, for example, presents a variety of eveningwear as a prize. This is presented as a fashion parade. The models are all female. When Nicky has finished describing the frocks, Glenn comes in: 'And the ladies look beautiful too' (*Sale of the Century* 1999b). They are as much to be looked at as the clothes they are wearing.

During 1999, a film clip introduces the prize Alpha Romeo in many episodes of *Sale*. It features a model in a strapless red evening dress, which cups her breasts but in no way restrains them. She strokes the car; she leans against it; she is shot through the car window so that only her torso and breasts are visible. (We never see men in shorts leaning against a car.) As this performance takes place, the male voice-over suggests: 'If you've never felt passion for a car ... '. But what is creating the passion: the car, or the breasts of the woman leaning seductively against it? Never mind—it is all merchandise. You can touch it, it seems (*SOTC* 1999b).

Game-show developments

The format of game shows has changed in recent years on Australian television. Chris Keating notes that *Sale of the (New) Century* and *Wheel of Fortune*—the two longest running game shows on Australian television—are the only game shows of recent years to employ the traditional role of hostess, and are thus, to some degree, 'anachronistic' as the genre evolves (Chris Keating, pers. comm. 17 May 2000).

Indeed, he suggests, game shows themselves may currently be anachronistic. Adult game shows have declined in number (although, at the time of writing, the massive successes of *Who Wants to be a Millionaire* and *The Weakest Link* suggest that this cyclical favouring of forms is returning the game show to the central place in the Australian mediasphere it once held) (Keating, pers. comm. 17 May 2000).

It is only the two game shows that have survived from previous decades that maintain the strict division of labour whereby men act and women appear. But still, these programs remain an important part of the Australian mediasphere, and with the appointment of Karina Brown, the tradition of appointing female co-hosts on the basis of their physical appearance continues in the genre. And Nicky Buckley's body, as the quotations that opened this chapter suggest, will not go away. She broke the rules in the game show—cheated perhaps—and in doing so promoted public debate on the ways that masculinity and femininity are constructed in that genre. Not all game shows now feature an attractive female co-host, but the moment when one of these women had the temerity to appear pregnant is remembered as 'causing a stir' and 'defying convention'—and being an important moment in the public archive of Australian television.

Availability

Screensound holds a few episodes of *Sale of the Century* in its access archives. The program also broadcasts five nights a week during ratings periods, which presents a good way of developing an archive.

Notes

1 Popular culture, it often seems, takes a perverse pleasure in defeating academic generalisations. As this book was going to press, *The Weakest Link*, hosted by Cernelia Frances, had become one of the most popular game shows on Australian television.

12

A Country Practice: Making Issues Social

1981–94

On 12 February 1991, Wandin Valley was struck by the apocalyptic effects of decades of deforestation and environmental degradation, resulting in a desiccated landscape of ash and slurry. The regular characters of the soap opera *A Country Practice* were reduced to the status of scavengers: drinking stagnant water and fighting for food. In a dimly lit landscape of rubbish and industrial debris, underscored by a deep rumbling noise, central characters wandered around, lost, shouting for their friends. They wore rags, their faces covered in dirt, and crouched by a broken pipe, trying to collect the black sludge that spurted out. Dr Elliott, one of the central characters, found himself by the corpse of a young girl, sobbing, 'I can't save them'. This episode was the epitome of the program's desire to address 'social issues'—to inform its audience about the world in which they lived (*A Country Practice* 1991a; 1991b).

A Country Practice has been given a special regard in writing on Australian television, both academically and in popular culture. It is, as Albert Moran and John Tulloch call it, 'quality soap'. The program does indeed have many of the characteristics of a soap opera: a medical serial, based in a rural community, with a large cast; narratives often focusing on romantic and other interpersonal relationships; and ongoing storylines. But it is not for these reasons that the program is best known. What leads to the adjective 'quality' is another tendency in this series (a tendency that the environmental destruction in Wandin Valley pushes to its extreme): the inclusion of 'social issues' in the program.

Wherever one finds a description of *A Country Practice*, in journalistic or academic writing, it is likely to be remembered for its 'social issues' (McKay 1993: 227; Muecke 1989: 56; Burke, Wilson, & Agardy 1983: 4; Gibson 1997a: 438; O'Regan 1994: 28; Tulloch 1990: 32; McCamey 1984; Mcintyre 1984: 24; Schaffer 1993: 128). Indeed, the program explicitly sold itself using such terms (Tulloch & Moran 1986: 211). These 'issues' are the element that sets *A Country Practice* apart from other Australian television programs, and which guarantee its place in the public archive of Australian television. But what exactly are the 'social issues' for which it is remembered? And what part do such issues play in this Australian series?

Great moments

A Country Practice was 'one of Australia's longest-running and most successful drama series' (Gibson 1997: 436), and there are many moments from the program that are remembered in Australia. The death of Molly is a moment that has survived for many viewers (see chapter 9). The marriage of Simon Bowen and Vicky Dean also survives, remembered in *Who Weekly*'s list of 'Television's 100 Greatest Moments' (1999: 63). The appearance by the then prime minister, Bob Hawke, in an anti-nuclear episode was also notable (Wark 1999: 19; Muecke 1989).

The moment that is the focus of this chapter—the environmental destruction of the Wandin Valley community in the program's eight-hundredth episode, 'The Promised Land: Part 2'—is an important one, according to the production company's attempts to write the program's history in its promotional literature. *A Country Practice*'s souvenir tenth anniversary booklet emphasises once again that 'The folk at Wandin Valley tackle issues that count', noting that 'Over the years *A Country Practice* writers have dedicated themselves to many issues of public conscience, not the least of them being the preservation of the rainforests'. This is illustrated with photographs of the 'nightmare scene in which Wandin valley was treeless and waterless' (Tipping 1991: 61). The program's own publicity identifies this as the moment when *A Country Practice* reached its apotheosis in its presentation of 'social issues'.

A Country Practice is the Australian television drama that is most strongly associated with 'social issues'. But it is by no means the first to include such material as part of its entertainment. In the USA, the anthology drama series format in the 1950s 'attempt[ed] to deal with ... socially relevant subjects' (Spigel 1992: 144), while in the UK, dramas such as *Cathy Come Home* are well known for fictionalising social issues such as homelessness (MacMurraugh-Kavanagh 1997: 249). In Australia, many programs have laid claim to the same tradition. The Australian Broadcasting Control Board noticed such a tendency in the early 1960s:

> For some time it was possible to divide the bulk of television material into two clearly defined categories—pure entertainment and diversion [on the one hand]; and public affairs programmes in the form mainly of news services and documentaries [on the other]. The dividing line between the two categories has become less clear with the appearance on Australian television of several dramatic series (produced in the United States of America) in which matters of public interest are dealt with in the guise of entertainment. Episodes of these series use important and controversial issues as central themes and manage to convey a great deal of information about them as well as offering entertainment.
>
> (ABCB 1962: 45)

Homicide is a notable Australian example. By the seventh episode of the program, it was addressing domestic violence. In this episode, a son is accused of murdering his father. In court, the mother defends her son's actions by telling of the physical and emotional abuse she suffered at her husband's hands. The prosecuting counsel responds with disbelief: 'Is anybody else coming forward to give evidence about attacks? None of your neighbours?' The battered wife responds: 'He was a different man in public. He was only violent in the sanctity of his own home'. Indeed, by its twenty-first episode, *Homicide* was broadcasting introductions to some episodes, explaining that 'Many cases in *Homicide* carry a message. This one does'.

Jenni Gyffin makes similar claims for *Bellbird*: 'The issues raised in *Bellbird* ... extended to child abuse, under-age smoking and drinking, pangs of first loves and losses, sub-standard housing, the impact of death upon a close-knit community and many other aspects of individual and group conditions' (Gyffin 1988: 43).

Such claims—which undoubtedly confer a certain status on programs (as Tulloch and Moran's use of them to justify the description of *A Country Practice* as 'quality' drama demonstrates)—have been made for such unexpected programs as *Number 96* and *The Box*. Commenting on the script for episode 1000 of the former, Don Reid notes that 'In scene 7, through the characters of Lee and Grant, reference is made to a current social issue ['dropping out']' (Reid & Groen 1977: 118), while Hector Crawford, interviewed on *Four Corners* in 1977, defends *The Box* by stating that the episode 'had a very important social message which a lot of people have chosen to ignore' (Barr 1977: 137). Tom O'Regan uses the term 'social problems' to describe an element of Australian television programming, and lists *Flying Doctors*, *Bellbird*, *Certain Women*, *GP*, and *Homicide* as programs 'which treat social problems less sensationally than do some US programs, with their producers priding themselves on their social responsibility' (O'Regan 1994: 28).

Nevertheless, it is *A Country Practice* that has the most developed image of being about 'social issues' (or 'social problems'). And the program itself insists that this is a valuable thing.

Not just entertainment

As I mentioned in the Introduction, Thomas McLaughlin suggests that popular culture is engaged in what he calls 'vernacular theory'—questioning and working out what culture is for and how it operates—in ways that are similar to academic work, if not so insistently 'rigorous' (McLaughlin 1996). *A Country Practice* certainly does this in 'The Promised Land': the program's regular characters spend the majority of the first of this two-part episode formulating theories about what the media are for. In the first half of this story, a film crew has come to Wandin Valley in order to shoot an untitled post-apocalyptic action film—'2015—civilisation as we know it has ceased to exist'. Both this episode of *A Country Practice* and the film within the film open with a shot of a child's feet on volcanic ash, standing next to a dead body, pulling back to show a young boy carrying a fox, with several burnt corpses lying around. 'Gotta find food', he says, as the director yells 'Cut!' and the dead bodies start to get up; we are back in Wandin Valley.

Throughout the episode, both the regular characters and the members of the film crew argue about what this film should be doing—and, more generally, about what purpose the media should serve. The consensus is overwhelmingly that it should *not* simply entertain: it must have a serious message, otherwise it is worthless.

The two doctors (Shane Porteous and Michael Muntz) open the debate by discussing the film being made in Wandin Valley as they walk through hospital reception. Dr Elliott is railing against an unnamed filmmaker: 'he jams characters into situations for effect', he complains. Films should be for 'stimulating our senses, by challenging them—that's what films are for'. The debate is set up initially in terms of what might be aesthetics, but is quickly revealed to be pedagogy: films must teach something ('challenge'), otherwise they are not doing what films 'should'. Although *A Country Practice* is not a film, the terms of the debate as the episode continues are so self-serving and self-righteous that it is hard not to see this as the program setting out its own agenda for what it thinks it is contributing to the Australian mediasphere, and what all other programs (of any worth) *should* be doing.

The director of the film later gets into an argument with the stuntman on the project: 'the backers want an action flick; I'm giving them an action flick', she says. 'I just thought I was working on a film that had something worthwhile to say', replies the stuntman. (Later in the episode we will discover that he is working as the stuntman because of his relationship with the director, which explains the otherwise odd decision to place the voice of social conscience with a stuntman—not an obvious archetype for such concerns.) He later describes the film: it's a 'crummy futuristic action flick. It started off as this futuristic fable: man's destroyed the environment; a kid and a fox left; how do they survive?' The terms are obvious, claimed by *A County Practice* as a manifesto for entertainment: it must 'challenge' and include the didactic element of the 'fable' otherwise it is worthless.

This debate continues throughout the two parts of this story. The nurse Lucy (Georgie Parker) expresses her opinion: 'You know what? I think there should be more movies about the environment'. 'Yeh, but they're not box office', replies the stuntman. Lucy then turns on the director: 'How could you let them turn this film into one of those action-smash, thrills-and-spills kind of things, when enough of that stuff is being churned out anyway? Surely something that was educational and entertaining about the environment would have been more worthwhile?' 'Right or wrong', replies the director, 'the box office is the bottom line, full stop.' And so on and so forth until, at the end of the episode, the director quits the film. She tells her socially aware stuntman/boyfriend: 'the producer … can use all the rubber monsters and laser beams that he wants'. They hug and kiss, their love for each other and their love of the planet equally obvious.

The use of the 'film-within-the-program' allows *A Country Practice* to make its manifesto explicit: educational and entertaining—therefore 'worthwhile'. And that is indeed what the program offers.

What is a social issue anyway?

A Country Practice is remembered for its 'social issues'. But what is a 'social issue'? It is easy to produce a list of some of the topics covered by the program: 'drugs, alcoholism, unemployment and child abuse' (Laud 1988: 25); 'crime … conservation issues like kangaroo culling … strong social issues like pregnancy termination and wife bashing' (Clark 1988: 34); 'the abandoned child of heroin addicts ... an elderly homosexual couple' (Burke, Wilson, & Agardy 1983: 10); 'heart failure, leukaemia, epilepsy ... and leprosy' (Gibson 1997: 438); 'multiculturalism, inter-racial relationships, single parenthood, environmental destruction, unemployment ... glue sniffing heroes, marital breakups, AIDS, abortion, in vitro fertilisation and maternal surrogacy' (Schaffer 1993: 128); 'the problems of white–Aboriginal relationships, the exploitation of non-English-speaking migrant women ... the effects of radiation from A-bomb tests ... VD in schools; euthanasia' (Kingsley 1989: 93); 'sexual permissiveness [and] social conscience' (McKay 1993: 227). What links these topics?

Health is one obvious area of concern—the *Practice* of the title is a medical one, after all. The program disseminates, in a straightforwardly pedagogical way, information about health. Often this is simply about diseases: AIDS, epilepsy, and leprosy. In 'The Promised Land', the issue of deforestation and environmental destruction is brought to Wandin Valley when it is revealed that the stuntman on the film is actually an environmental activist, wanted by the police for destroying logging equipment in Malaysia. This is revealed when he ends up in the Wandin Valley Bush Nursing Hospital with malaria. As well as attending to environmental issues, this allows the program to pass on some handy information: 'I'm not all that familiar with malaria cases', says the nurse, Anne. 'Well, you should be', says Dr Elliott. 'Think of the countless number of Australians who go over to South-East Asia every year—without adequate precautions!' He goes on to pass on some statistics: 'We're talking about a disease which affects a hundred million people a year—and kills a million of them'. 'And we can expect a relapse', says Anne. 'Yes', agrees Shane. 'Until the body acquires an immunity to the parasite. And, as you know, that can take years.'

In the medical situations, the program simply has to pass on information and advice: here are the statistics, here are the effects (information), and here is what you should do, the practical outcomes (take 'adequate precautions', which your doctor, presumably, can advise you of). As one group of government researchers states of this straightforward pedagogical and informative practice: '*A Country Practice* and *GP* are by far the favourite programs [with his focus groups], because they deal with real life problems, like leukaemia and suicide and provide useful information and a contact number afterwards' (Coupe, Jakubowicz, & Randall 1992: 37).

It is interesting to note that the program also takes this opportunity to attack entertainment media—which are not 'worthwhile'—once again.

Dr Elliott goes on to rail against those who travel without 'adequate precautions':

> It's the Jungle Jim syndrome ... Jungle Jim was my hero ... in every movie there was always some white hunter lying on a camp bed, covered in sweat, groping for a couple of pills. It made malaria seem almost romantic—and certainly fictional!

Bad films. Not educational enough.

Diseases, then, can be dealt with in simple practical terms: information and advice. But the relationship between health and social issues is a complex one. Diseases are not exactly 'social issues', although various aspects of health can be. Neither sweated labour nor indigenous–settler relations are diseases—although health obviously features strongly as an aspect of each of these issues. But the program also addresses questions about social organisation—about 'unemployment', 'multiculturalism', and even, one commentator above suggests, 'social conscience'—which has little necessary relation to medicine or disease.

A history of 'the social'

The term 'social issues', or 'social problems'(the terms are often brought together), is one which, as well as circulating commonly in popular culture (as we have seen above in public discussions of *A Country Practice*), also has an academic existence. It is used in sociological disciplines to describe 'some aspect of society ... about which large numbers of people are concerned ... [which] lends itself to change as a result of people's effort' (Henslin 1990: 3). If a situation is seen as undesirable, if it is caused by social organisation (rather than, for example, natural forces such as earthquakes), and if it is solvable by means of changes in social organisation, then it is a 'social issue' or 'social problem' (Spector & Kitsuse 1987: 1–2, 96; (Rubington & Weinberg 1989: 4; Morgan 1992: 3). In contradistinction to 'personal' problems of the individual (Henslin 1990), these are problematic issues about the way in which 'society' is organised.

The term 'society'—a concept that Ien Ang (citing Ernesto Laclau) describes as a 'totality' that 'attempts to limit ... differences' by imagining a unified whole of a group of people (Ang 1996: 172)—unlike 'public' or 'citizenry', is one that allows us to think about large groups of people without implying, as these other terms do, political engagement, organisation, or management. This is important for understanding how *A Country Practice* works. When the program deals with issues that are also within the remit of the political sphere in Australia—unemployment, multiculturalism, the degradation of the environment, for example—it does not do so in party political terms (although its conclusions might be read in such a way). It must, rather, address these questions from the 'social' point of view: the area of the relationship between individuals and their experiences.

Recent cultural theory in Australia—particularly the work of Tony Bennett—has been interested in trying to trace the evolution of 'the social': When did the word emerge in its current usage? And what does it mean? Bennett uses the work of French historian and philosopher Michel Foucault to argue that, from the late nineteenth century onwards, social organisation significantly altered. The state began to take more responsibility for managing the lives of working-class citizens (Bennett, Emmison, & Frow 1999: 227). The distinction between the state (the institutions of government) and society (the lives and relationships of citizens) became increasingly important, with the former taking responsibility for managing the latter:

> these new forms of public culture both depended upon and worked to maintain a distinction between state and society, organising the latter—the social as a problematic set of conducts—as the surface on which culture was to act in order to produce the effects of social and moral improvement it was called on to perform.
>
> (Bennett, Emmison, & Frow 1999: 227)

'The social'—the conduct of groups of individuals—emerged as a separate sphere, to be managed and changed by 'culture'. *A Country Practice* is a cultural product, commenting on 'the social' (the non-state lives of citizens).

Bennett also notes that culture has created a variety of ways of studying, surveying, and commenting on 'the social', not least of which are academic disciplines such as sociology. The area of 'the social' is discursively 'talked into being' by such disciplines, and also by television programs throughout Australian broadcasting history, culminating in *A Country Practice*. 'The social' is the site of 'problems' and 'issues'. It is an area that is to be worked on and perfected. The relationships of human beings within a country are not to be accepted as they are; they are to be compared with a utopian ideal and continually found wanting, in need of rearrangement in some way. Over thirteen years, *A Country Practice* identified literally hundreds of ways in which 'society' in Australia was wanting. Of course, the program did not aspire to change the behaviours of its audience in relation to every single one of these in any significant way. Rather, it kept the imperfect field of 'the social' continually in play. And, as Toby Miller notes,

> the emergence of modern capitalism is connected to the rise of the sovereign state, which was concerned with delivering a docile and healthy labour force to business ... Cholera, sanitation and prostitution are figured as the business of government in the modern era.
>
> (Miller 1998: 17)

A Country Practice can be understood as a governmental (in a Foucauldian sense) project, which seeks to create a healthy society in Australia. Indeed, it is notable that so many successful television drama programs in Australia, as elsewhere, have centred around the institutions of the state and their intervention in the social lives of citizens: police (*Homicide, Matlock Police, Division 4, Cop Shop, Blue Heelers*), hospitals and medical practices (*A Country Practice, All Saints, GP*), courts (*Rafferty's Rules, Carson's Law, SeaChange*), and even prisons (*Prisoner*). It is only the soap operas (*Number 96, The Sullivans, Neighbours, Home and Away*) that have escaped the state, focusing rather on families and sexual relationships as the institutions through which citizens are managed.

And the place of television in the project of working out social problems is one of which the federal government approves. As the Australian Broadcasting Control Board noted in its 1964 *Report*, despite its desire to keep 'controversial' material off television (which, as we saw in chapter 2, meant anything that suggested the government or social life in Australia was anything less than consensually perfect), the Board would allow for the 'serious presentation of moral or social issues' (ABCB 1964: 72).

Individualising issues

One Marxist-informed tradition of cultural studies writing on the media—particularly British and British-derived work in the late 1970s and early 1980s—is very unhappy with the way that television news and current affairs programs personalise and emotionalise public issues. Such writing is also relevant to a discussion of Australian television drama—and *A Country Practice* in particular—as it condemns television's presentation of social issues and social problems more generally. Stuart Hall, for example, notes that 'There are very well-established ways in television of setting up a social problem and of handling it and it matters a hell of a lot whose social problem you think it is' (as quoted in King 1983: 43).

The charge of such writing is that the media propose merely individual solutions within an accepted social framework: they do not insist on the necessity of revolutionary change of the complete social structure. Hall, for example, insists that television presents 'radical and reactionary positions, but both within the reactionary framework ... [so that it] is extremely difficult ... not to contest the wrong positions within the framework, but to challenge the framework itself' (as quoted in King 1983: 49).

As Tulloch and Moran point out, 'It is often argued by media teachers that television cops out of its public responsibilities by individualising social problems' (Tulloch & Moran 1986: 189; see also Bell 1983: 108). By individualising and personalising social issues, so the argument runs, the media ignore the 'reality' of the situation: that it is in fact 'the system' that is the problem, and that must be changed in order to deal with these social issues:

> The media select anomalies of social actors and justice and render them into ... stories, which in their denouement, plump for a suitable aetiology (which does not threaten social order) and appropriate nemesis (which balances social accounts).
>
> (Young, as quoted in Bell 1983: 107,)

In relation to *A Country Practice*, Ien Ang and Jon Stratton state that:

> *A Country Practice* attempts to take account of ... Australian contemporary reality ... through its issue-based approach ... a new social concern is raised in *ACP* ... each week ... The concerns have ranged from alcoholism, unemployment, white–Aboriginal relationships, teenage abortion through to a wide range of illnesses ... as these threats are included in the program as 'issues', they are never a fundamental threat to the stability of the community.
>
> (Ang & Stratton 1995: 132–3)

Stephen Muecke addresses the second point—the resolution of these problems—in his comments on the appearance of the then prime minister, Bob Hawke, on the program:

> [H]ow do [the] issues [addressed on *ACP*] get resolved? Does the text incite, or do the issues get normalised by the narrative formula of the happy ending? ... After using the nuclear issue to intensify the audience's moral feelings about the rights of children—this is now a dominant way of narrativising the nuclear issue—the resolution is in terms of utter normalisation to the clichéd constructions of popular culture: a drink in the pub.
>
> (Muecke 1989: 56–7)

The traditions developed within cultural studies for addressing 'social issues' in the media allow very little space for positive readings of television programs that include such representations. Because issues tend to be personalised, not address systematic problems, and present 'happy endings' with easy (personalised) solutions, the media are not—many writers insist—addressing the 'reality' of these issues.

Such critical approaches to the media can be limiting, however (Bell 1983). Typically 'critical', in the sense of always seeking to find out what is 'bad' about mass media, they present a totalising account of the media in which no representation will ever be good enough, or revolutionary enough. Analysing the way in which a particular 'social issue'—that of environmental degradation and deforestation—is presented in *A Country Practice* allows for a more nuanced understanding of the way in which 'social issues' are presented in such a program. Such an analysis points to the importance of genre in considering representations of the social (Hartley & McKee 2000). While news and current affairs programs tend to insist on the control of deviance by mapping difference onto a 'they' community (for example, 'criminals') against which 'we' are pitted, television drama has traditionally been much more liberal and tolerant in allowing 'deviant' characters to be part of the 'we' community.

In these two episodes of *A Country Practice*, it is undoubtedly true that the problem of environmental degradation is personalised: it is mapped onto the body of an outsider (the stuntman on the film) visiting the community of Wandin Valley. Tom Masters (or Tom Grace—he uses a pseudonym) is an environmental activist who has been fighting logging in Malaysia by blowing up the equipment of the logging company. The film crew start off as traditional 'outsiders', disrupting the life of the regular community in the program (Geraghty 1991: 84). Young Luke (Matt Day), for example, has been seduced away from his job at the vet by delusions of getting into the starry world of film production. He can no longer help out with the Brownies because of his work on the film. Esme attacks him for this: 'Have you got no sense of loyalty? These are the Brownies who awarded you the honorary cooking badge!' He cannot be persuaded, however, and she laments that 'Luke's turned into a used-car salesman'.

However, the community quickly comes to accept Tom Grace. As we have already seen, there is general agreement among the regular characters with his belief that the film being shot in Wandin Valley should have a message about environmental degradation. And the issue of environmental management is personalised further, when it is taken up by the regular, familiar members of *A Country Practice*'s community. When the policeman

Frank tells his wife Shirl that Tom Masters must be deported to Malaysia for destroying logging equipment, she quickly makes it clear that she is on Tom's side:

Shirl So what? ... they're hacking down around eleven square kilometres of rainforest a day. Now, that's a greater rate of destruction than the Amazon.
Frank You're a walking *National Geographic.*
Shirl It costs nothing to be informed. He's fighting for something important. Anyway, it isn't long since we faced the bulldozers here in Wandin Valley.
Frank Not the same.
Shirl Why not?

Even Esme, the liminal character of the town gossip, helps to bring this issue into the community, making it one that personally affects the familiar characters of the program. Cookie claims that Tom, as an 'environmentalist', is 'a hairy lunatic'. Esme responds: 'Are you calling me a hairy lunatic? I stood up to be counted when Councillor Muldoon wanted to flood the valley'.

In this genre of programming, the issue must be personalised, it is true; it must be shown to affect characters who are liked and familiar, in directly personal ways. Tom Masters is the character who carries the burden of representing the issue in these episodes, and the program works to ensure that the regular and familiar characters show us that he is to be embraced and supported. What is more, the issue is tied directly to other issues that have directly affected the community of Wandin Valley.

Having personalised this issue, the program *visualises* it in order to create a greater impact. First, as Tom Masters is hospitalised with a malaria attack, he talks to Lucy about deforestation: 'Picture this,' he says, inviting Lucy and the audience to put the issue into visual terms, 'two football fields filled with full-grown trees. Now imagine chainsaws slashing through those trees, cutting them down. That's how much of the rainforest dies every minute of every day.' It is an emotive image, and Lucy reacts in an emotional way: 'That's terrifying'. Tom continues:

> Now, as the forest dies, erosion will start to accelerate. Every time a tree is cut down, carbon dioxide is released into the atmosphere. The world is going to get hotter, and the climate will start to form new, destructive patterns. And as the planet is stripped away, there won't be a country that doesn't have to deal with starvation. There will be no renewal. That's what Donna's film was supposed to show. Until she let them turn it into a B-Grade thriller.

As Lucy gets ready for bed later in the episode, she tells her husband Matthew that '[Tom] painted me a picture today, of what the world could be like if we don't act in time'. But simply to describe the picture is not good enough; the program must actually *show* it in order for such visualisation to have the best effect. As Lucy lies in bed, we see a close-up of her face, which fades into her dream landscape, making the move to the dream clear, and leaving no space for concern about what is going to follow. This visualisation is a fantasy space, but it must be shown nonetheless. The dreamscape opens with mists and blue light, a deep rumbling noise in the background, rubbish and industrial debris lying abandoned around the screen. Lucy wanders around this landscape, obviously lost, shouting for Matthew, framed through a piece of abandoned machinery. We see other regular characters—in rags, their faces blackened—crouching by a broken pipe, trying to collect the black sludge that spurts out. They cry out, 'We've got to find water'. Lucy then stumbles over Dr Elliott: he is also in rags, his hair messy and skin blackened, standing by the corpse of a young girl. 'I can't save them', he sobs.

Lucy wakes up with a start for a brief moment, only to fall back into the dream. Now she holds a seedling in a pot—'The last one'. As Matthew and Luke dig a hole in the background, Cookie and Bob wander across the nightmare landscape, dressed in surreal costumes. Cookie wears a top hat and a clown costume. He has already been established in the program as an unrepentant capitalist—he explicitly uses the term to describe himself—which is used to make fun of him, as his schemes to make money consistently backfire. In the dream, he is calling out, 'Water! Get it while it lasts!' Lucy rushes up to him: 'Spare some for a seedling?' 'No way', he says.

As he vanishes, Lucy is left wandering around, lost and confused. We are presented with close-ups of her feet on the smoking ruins, as she calls out, 'Where are we? Where is this place?' Finally, she finds the broken pieces of a sign saying 'Wandin Valley'. This is presented as a revelation (although it is easily guessed beforehand), with loud, clashing chords of music and a big close-up of her face. This is what will happen to the familiar and beloved place of Wandin Valley if environmental degradation is not addressed. Lucy digs further into the rubble and finds Tom Masters under the ash. As she pulls him out, the colour of the scene returns to normal. He smiles. He is the saviour who will prevent this from happening.

The abstract issue of deforestation, then, is individualised, made emotive, and visualised in *A Country Practice*, just as the writers cited above might have predicted. Later, I consider some positive ways of interpreting such an approach. First, though, it is worth noting that the program also presents this issue in ways that do not quite fit with the accounts presented by these critics.

The system is wrong

One character in *A Country Practice* continually refuses to side with Tom Masters: Frank, the policeman. And his reasons for this—and the other characters' refusal to agree with Frank—provide an interesting case study of the limits of what is possible in the 'social issues' of popular fictional media.

Lucy is talking to Frank about the fact that he is going to arrest Tom and help in his deportation to Malaysia: 'I don't believe he's done anything wrong morally. And don't shout about the law; the law picks and chooses who it protects'. The law, the state, the status quo, and the authority figure of Frank are not perfect. They are, Lucy insists, part of the problem. Frank is stung: 'I'm not the judge and jury. The law is the law', he insists. Lucy goes on, in a big close-up showing the shining sincerity in her eyes:

> Well I wish there were a hundred Tom Graces out there, because we can't start to hope that people will change the way they think unless you put your neck on the line. The logging companies aren't sending Tom Grace to an Asian prison because he blew up some of their equipment, Frank. They're doing it because a man like that might just make a difference.

There is a long pause, before Frank says very quietly, 'I'm just doing my job'. It is obvious from his performance that he realises that he is in the wrong and that nobody else in the regular community agrees with him. When Lucy leaves, his wife says, 'For what it's worth, Frank, I'm on Lucy's side 100 per cent'. Indeed, she expands on this later in the episode: 'While the law protects multinationals and greedy governments, the forests are dying … this is a problem for the whole world'. This is the end of the scene; there is no comeback to this. The law is the problem. In yet another scene, Frank tries to justify himself to his wife: 'I'm a policeman. I'm not doing anyone's dirty work'. 'She wasn't accusing you personally', Shirl reassures him. 'She was saying that the system is weighted against anyone who tries to change things.' This could have been written by a cultural studies critic disenchanted with social organisation in Australia but it is spoken in an entertainment program trying to deal with 'social issues'.

The program also offers a variety of practical steps for any viewers who might have been moved by its personalised, emotive, visualised account of deforestation. In a separate subplot, the farmer Stevie is installing a 'keyline cultivation system' on her farm. 'You can't replace soil', she explains. 'You can only protect it. I found this out from the Department of Ag [Agriculture] ... it's been around since the '40s.' 'How does it work, Stevie?' asks Bob Hatfield. Stevie explains: 'Well, the keyline is a contour that separates the flooded part of the valley from the steeper part ... There's a low-impact cultivation program as well, but what we have to do now is plant more trees'. Cookie interjects: 'Times have changed: time was farmers would clear all the trees'. 'Hmmm, yes', says Stevie. 'Cut down all your trees today and there'll be no land left tomorrow.'

As well as the practical advice to farmers, the program demonstrates the steps that other viewers can take. Shirl and Lucy start a campaign on the issues raised by Tom. Shirl converts her domestic space—the kitchen table—into a political office. She has a pile of paperwork there, offering viewers the possibility of seeing themselves as political activists in their own homes: 'We have to write letters and make phone calls', says Shirl. 'We have to pressure the federal government to stop the importing of tropical rainforest timber.' 'They'll just sell it somewhere else, won't they?' asks Lucy. 'Well, it works two ways', Shirl continues. 'A lot of these countries, they're in a trap, logging the forests is central to their economies. So we have to stop importing the timber, and use some of our overseas aid to help them develop new industries.' 'Would that work?' asks Lucy. 'Well, according to the experts, it's the best way to begin saving the forests.' Shirl is a maternal, sensible, middle-aged woman. She is a regular, familiar, central member of the community. She is 'us'. Lucy chimes in: 'Tom's lit the torch; it's up to the rest of us to carry it now. We've got a lot of work to do'.

Dr Elliott offers practical support from his position, offering to give evidence at the extradition hearing: 'I think the court should be aware of the state of your health—the possible consequences of imprisonment in a Malaysian jail'. At the end of the episode, Shirl is in the pub (the space that Muecke dismisses as 'clichéd'), organising another practical intervention in the issue of deforestation: 'We're going to involve the whole community in this, and it will be a yearly event—plant a tree, bring back the birds, and renew the land ... and I expect everybody to be involved'. The camera swings around the room, showing it to be crowded, and very supportive. Frank comments that 'I don't think you'll have any trouble getting volunteers'.

A Country Practice takes a large-scale abstract issue—environmental degradation—and it personalises and visualises it. It also offers a variety of practical interventions: changing farming practices, lobbying members of parliament, planting trees. What it does not support is violent action.[1] Tom has convinced Lucy that the forests need protection. 'Whose side are you on?' he asks. She looks pensive, then down at the hospital bed he is lying in. 'The rainforest's', she says quietly:

> But I'm not on your side. I don't like violence. I don't trust it. You say you had to blow that equipment up. Then why did you run for it? The only point in doing it was to draw attention to what the company was doing, but you behaved like a criminal.

And the episode goes on to make clear that Tom doesn't actually approve of violence either. It transpires that blowing up the logging equipment was, for him, an irrational act, emerging from his frustration at his powerlessness to stop the loggers blowing up a blockade by native people. He regrets the act: it has destroyed his life. The episode cannot end with Tom escaping the law and becoming a fugitive again: the demands of the state must be satisfied, even as its authority is fought by other means.

Personalised, emotive, visual communication

A Country Practice has the potential to suggest the systemic nature of social problems, even as it personalises them. A particularly important 'issue' from this perspective is unemployment. An episode of the program dealt with the health implications of unemployment, emerging from Australian Medical Association documentation on the issue. Tulloch and Moran note that 'Unemployment is a social problem, and not one easily handled within a framework built around the notion of "consensus" ' (Tulloch & Moran 1986: 174). Mark Gibson notes that the episode, although personalising the issues, did not leave responsibility with the individual. Rather, it insisted 'that unemployment cannot be blamed on a lack of motivation of the unemployed themselves' (Gibson 1997a: 438). Keith Windschuttle detects this tendency in the program more generally. He suggests that by showing the social dimension to problems that are often individualised in other parts of the media, soap operas such as *A Country Practice* (which he identifies by name) 'can perform valuable social therapy', showing the audience that 'such problems arise from much more than personal failings'. Indeed, such programs can point towards 'community solutions' for such issues (Windschuttle 1988: 187).

It is certainly the case that *A Country Practice* is involved in the construction and the management of this field known as 'the social'. And it is indeed true that in addressing this field, it personalises, visualises, and makes emotive certain 'issues'. But this need not be seen as a bad thing. Following the same argument as that presented in chapter 2, the democratisation and feminisation of the 'postmodern public sphere' described by John Hartley (1996; see also the related work of Livingstone & Lund 1994; Shattuc 1997) can allow us to see this tendency to present public debate in emotional, sexualised, and visual ways as a positive thing. If we do not condemn *A Country Practice* for this mode of address, but rather allow a more generous reading, other ways of interpreting its presentation of 'social issues' emerge. At the end of the episode, Lucy is planting a seedling. She explains, in a big, sympathetic, close-up, what she has learnt from the story:

> Those are two things we have to fight, Matthew: ignorance and despair … I had a dream last night … I dreamt that the whole valley had been destroyed … When I woke up, all I could think was—if we act now, it doesn't have to be like that. It is in our hands.

The program wants to address social issues from two perspectives. It wants to overcome ignorance, but also to avoid despair. It is in offering the possibility of individual agency, even in addressing systemic problems, that it attempts to do the latter:

> [W]e decided very early on … that we would reinforce the positive values of human existence. So in this program people like each other, they relate to each other … the News is full of negativism. I believe that people get enough in the newspapers and the News about the hard facts of life. We're not going for chocolate box stuff; we deal with really tough situations but in a very positive way.
>
> (Producer, James Davern, as quoted in Burke, Wilson, & Agardy 1983: 16)

The point is similarly emphasised in the program's tenth-anniversary souvenir booklet:

> [T]he reality of the news is so shocking so often that we have learned to 'turn off'—not the television but our emotional responses … That is why *A Country Practice* is such an important program. Its team of writers, producers and actors have taken it upon themselves to introduce important issues into our lives in a way that doesn't assault our senses. The important issues are part of the storylines of the everyday encounters about normal folk. *A Country Practice* goes even further. It raises the issues and shows how normal folk can rise to the occasion and deal with the problems. Many people don't act on important issues because

> they seem too big or too far away ... *A Country Practice* helps to remind us that if we all do a little bit in the realm of our everyday lives the big picture will improve.
>
> (Tipping 1991: 61)

From some political perspectives—for example, that of Marxism—the program can never be a success, because it does not emphasise collective action. The focus on individual agency is too much a classic bourgeois liberal ideal. The community will pull together, but always as a collection of disparate individuals, with their own, individual agency. Even the self-proclaimed capitalist of the program—Cookie—is brought into the community work of environmental protection in this episode. 'What's in it for me?' he asks, when Shirl tries to get him involved in the tree-planting scheme. His mate Bob replies, 'Without trees, the rivers get polluted. The oceans start to die. No more gemfish'. Cookie is shocked: 'No more gemfish? Count me in—there's some things a man's got to fight for'. Each person in the community, and each viewer, is appealed to at an individual, emotive—perhaps selfish—level to contribute to the practical management of 'social problems'. This is a form of public debate that moves away from abstract arguments about the greater good, and towards personal investment in social change.

The End

Hilary Kingsley does not agree that *A Country Practice* always provides 'happy endings'. The program, she claims, 'shows itself aware of real social problems which can't be solved between the opening music and the closing titles' (Kingsley 1989: 7). This may be the case, but 'The Promised Land' certainly attempts to provide closure. It is true that the problem is not solved: Tom will still go to court, and we do not know how his trial will turn out. Shirl has not yet started her lobbying campaign. The planting of trees will happen every year. But at the end of the episode, the issue vanishes. Tom Masters leaves and does not return. Shirl does not continue her lobbying in the next episode, and the tree-planting is not shown. The narrative is not concluded, but the community's involvement in the issue of environmental degradation is. The episode ends with the standard closing titles: shots of a wombat, a koala, a wallaby, an echidna. Nature is saved, returned after the apocalypse of Lucy's dream. The end credits return stability to the narrative.

A Country Practice ended in 1994, after being previously cancelled by Channel Seven and having a brief run on Channel Ten. 'Social issues' have continued to be an important part of Australian television drama since the program's demise: programs such as *Blue Heelers* and *All Saints* concern themselves with multiculturalism, wife-beating, and illicit drug use (Cunningham & Jacka 1996: 110; McKee 1999/2000). But *A Country Practice* is still remembered as a program that presented social issues, twice a week, to Australian audiences for over a decade.

Availability

Screensound holds episodes 1 and 2 of *A Country Practice* as access copies, copies of all episodes from 27 to 200, of which a few are access copies, and a small number of episodes from 200 onwards.

JNP Productions (Sydney) holds copies of every episode of the program, and has in the past proved to be friendly and helpful to researchers interested in the program.

Note

1 In this, *A Country Practice* accords with the principles of Amnesty International, which 'campaigns for the release of people imprisoned for their beliefs who have neither used nor advocated violence'.

13

Return to Eden: Australianising America

1983

On 27 September 1983, Rebecca Gilling was savaged by a crocodile. Importantly, not only did she survive this attack by Australian wildlife, but she went on to have major plastic surgery, secretly return as a supermodel, and gain the ultimate revenge on the lover and the best friend who had betrayed her. This is the story of the mini-series *Return to Eden* (1983).

At the time of its broadcast, the program was hugely successful. It was the top-rating mini-series of 1983, with an average rating in all cities of 39 (percentage of available audience in its time slot) and a 47 rating in its highest rating city (Melbourne) (ABT 1988: 12). Indeed, it was the third most successful mini-series in Australia during the entire decade. And both the crocodile attack and *Return to Eden* more generally are well remembered in Australia's public archive of television history. Correspondents for this book volunteered the 'crocodile attack in *Return to Eden*' as one of the great moments in Australian television. Channel Ten obviously agreed, given that, in their countdown of 'Ten's Top 10 Moments' (in the fortieth-anniversary documentary *Forty Fun Years of Television*), only one mini-series appears: at number eight on the list was 'The crocodile attacking Stephanie in *Return to Eden*'. When the documentary history series *35 Years of Television* addressed the genre of the mini-series, it did so by replaying the clip of the crocodile attack from 'this worldwide smash hit' (*35 Years of Television* 1991). And *Eden* is one of the very few mini-series to be repeated in prime time during the 1990s, scoring a rerun in February 1999, when it was promoted as 'the Australian classic'.

Difference in Eden

As Albert Moran has suggested, *Return to Eden* 'broke decisively with the pattern of Australian mini-series up to that point' (Moran & Pinne 1993: 381).

In the period from 1975, following the popular and critical success of *Against the Wind*, the mini-series format became an important part of Australia's mediasphere. The term 'mini-series' refers to a particular format. In terms of form, Moran describes it as 'large blocks of time over a short period ... [for example] two-hour episodes over eight consecutive nights'. In terms of content, Moran draws on Paul Kerr's description: 'The insertion of (sympathetic) fictional characters into "real" historical and/or institutional settings "in time of tremendous stress" '. Moran goes on to note that 'the bulk of [Australian] mini-series has been narrower than this and has gravitated to the historical end of the spectrum' (Moran 1985: 206). Indeed, more than this, the mini-series in Australia during its heyday became strongly associated not simply with historical content, but also with 'quality', historical, nation-building drama. The first Australian program generally recognised as a mini-series—*Against the Wind*—explicitly claims a national character for itself: its own publicity material described it as 'the story of Australia' (as quoted in Moran 1985: 208). And most of the mini-series that followed addressed similar material in a similar way. As Moran notes, 'The local mini-series have consciously engendered discourses about the nation, about the founding moment of settlement, about significant turning points in the nation's history and consciousness, and most especially, about Australian identity' (Moran 1989: 251–2; see also *The Australian Image* 1989e; Breen 1997: 128).

The bulk of Australian mini-series, then, have featured historical elements, laying claim to Australian national identity, and by doing so have been granted a 'quality' status (Cunningham 1989: 315). This combination of factors means that the mini-series format has been, with news and current affairs, one of the few areas of television's programming to receive a substantial amount of academic interest. Because of its claims to historical status, some work examines its role as historiography (see, for example, Cunningham 1983; Crofts & Craik 1983; Lawson 1983: 100; Bass 1984, on *The Dismissal* and *Bodyline*). Because of its claims to quality, it is one of the few televisual forms that has been discussed in the aesthetic terms usually reserved for film studies (Mayer 1985; Ryan 1977).

Return to Eden is not like this. It is not a historical piece; it does not deal with any moments of national import for Australia; nor does it lay any explicit claim to dramatising Australian identity. Although its production values are high, its melodramatic quality means that it is more likely to be described as 'trashy' than 'quality'. Several critics have noted *Eden*'s status as an exceptional mini-series (at least in the sense of being an 'exception' to most of the rules of the format) (O'Regan 1989: 140; Cunningham & Miller 1994: 140). And in the public archive, the series *35 Years of Television* explicitly places the series apart from other mini-series, suggesting that 'once we'd come to terms with some of the more serious strains of our history and national identity, we could have some fun. *Return to Eden* was a worldwide smash hit' (*35 Years of Television* 1991).

Return to Eden is certainly an exceptional mini-series. Looking at it now, one of the most interesting aspects of its presentation is the way in which it challenges the expectation that a mini-series will address the topic of Australian national identity. For, against the dozens of mini-series that sell themselves through explicit appeals to Australian history, events of national importance, and the Australian identity and character, *Return to Eden* succeeds by—and is remembered for—doing something quite different.

American melodrama

In 1999, when *Who Weekly* remembered *Return to Eden* and placed it at number 87 in its '100 Greatest Moments in Television', it described it thus: 'With its plastic surgery makeovers and dastardly double crosses, the *Dallas/Dynasty* inspired saga "got a pounding" by the critics, but was a success both at home and away" ('100 Greatest Moments in Television' 1999: 89).

Stuart Cunningham and Elizabeth Jacka similarly note that the program 'resembled US prime time soaps ... with its far-fetched plot of a glamorous and vengeful woman' (Cunningham & Jacka 1996: 173), while Ewan Burnett names *Eden* as the only Australian mini-series to resemble American productions of an 'epic, escapist nature' (Burnett 1984: 35). This accusation of an American identity is partially an accurate one: some aspects of *Eden* do indeed resemble an American prime-time soap opera. This is one reason that the program is so fascinating. It is a successful Australian mini-series, which is well remembered by commentators and viewers, and which negotiates, in an intelligent way, two imperatives: American melodrama, on the one hand, and Australian concerns with national identity on the other.

As I have emphasised throughout this book, it is important not to take cultural artefacts out of context—to make interpretations of them that have little relevance to the way they have circulated and continue to circulate in the mediasphere. In the case of *Return to Eden*—a highly successful mini-series in a country where mini-series have been explicitly concerned with Australian national identity, and a mini-series whose distinctiveness is publicly asserted to be linked to its American characteristics—a reading of national identity seems reasonable. And the program does open itself up wonderfully to such an approach.

As noted above, the mini-series format was, in 1983, one of the dominant televisual spaces of 'Australianness' and a format strongly identified with a project of Australian national identity. However, at the same time, *Eden*'s national identity is ambivalent. *Return to Eden* has a strongly melodramatic impulse. While there is nothing intrinsically American about melodrama—Stuart Cunningham points out that 'there are strong antecedents and parallels in theatre, literature and vaudeville for an Australian melodrama' (Cunningham 1991: 24)—in the early 1980s, melodramatic narratives were strongly identified with the USA. Indeed, at that time, the phrase 'wall-to-wall *Dallas*' was used to express worries about the international dominance of American television.

Plot elements

There are many recognisable elements of melodramatic narrative in *Return to Eden*. The story revolves around a family saga, including heroine Stephanie's (Rebecca Gilling's) children, and her father. Indeed, it is the absent figure of her (recently deceased) father who opens the mini-series, with Stephanie talking in voice-over about 'the day he died', and noting that 'If I knew then the nightmare to follow, I think I would have chosen to die with him'. The narrative follows her struggle, as her business manager puts it, to move out from under her father's 'shadow'—a typically melodramatic narrative element (Ang 1996: 88–91).

The reference to 'nightmares' points to another melodramatic element to the plot: fantasies, nightmares, and madness. Stephanie's revenge is an excessive one. She does not simply turn her attackers over to the police when she survives; rather, she spends months building a new identity, working herself back into their lives, and then attempting to drive them mad. At the end of the narrative, she traps Jilly in her country house and uses a secret broadcasting system to send her voice into every room in the house. She succeeds in pushing Jilly over the edge into gibbering alcoholic despair and helpless sobbing.

Anti-realism

This suggests another characteristic of melodrama: not only are plot points in *Eden* reminiscent of previous melodramatic narratives, but an ethos of anti-realist excess also informs the production (Feuer 1995: 116). This sustained anti-realism is best illustrated in the plot point whereby Stephanie undergoes plastic surgery in order to create her new life. At the start of the program, Rebecca Gilling is supposed to be plain; she becomes gorgeous in the course of the story (mirroring the storyline of another classic melodramatic narrative, the 1952 Bette Davis film *Now Voyager*). Much is made of this transformation. Stephanie does not simply want reconstructive surgery after the crocodile attack: 'I want more than just these scars covered up', she says. 'I want to look different. When I leave here, I want to be a completely different person.'

An entire episode of the program is devoted to her change (episode 2), and she spends much of this time wrapped in bandages, building the suspense for the revelation of her new face. Her plastic surgeon warns her that when she looks in the mirror after the bandages are unwrapped, she should prepare herself for a shock: 'They will be your eyes, but looking back from a stranger's face'. The removal of the bandages is presented as a moment of revelation. We are given a shot of the plastic surgeon looking at her face; there is no reverse shot to show us what she looks like. As we look on from behind, she lifts the mirror to her face, and we finally get a close-up that shows us her face in the mirror (almost identical to the sequence in another melodramatic narrative—*Dynasty*—where Stephen Carrington removes his bandages after plastic surgery). It therefore comes as something of a shock when the bandages are removed, and Stephanie looks exactly the same as she did before the crocodile attack and plastic surgery.

This may be a matter of changing fashions: to a viewer largely untutored in the nuances of early eighties fashion and make-up, the differences between pre- and post-operation Stephanie are not as obvious as they may have been to the first audience of the program. After several viewings, it becomes apparent that Stephanie's clothes at the start of the story are meant to signify 'frumpiness'. But even given this knowledge, it is still very obviously Rebecca Gilling playing the new Stephanie. It is the same actress, with the same face.

It is for this reason that the later twists of the narrative are so wildly anti-realist. Building a new life for herself, Stephanie (now called Tara) returns to Sydney. She visits her home, and watches her children. They do not recognise her—although they note her resemblance to their mother. When Greg meets Tara for the first time, his first comment is, 'I don't believe we've met'—this to a woman who is the twin of the woman he believes he has just murdered.

There is a moment that makes sense of this plot strand, at least in generic terms. When Stephanie/Tara first visits her old house, she almost bumps into one of her servants. Not confident as yet about her new face, she quickly puts on a pair of sunglasses, and he walks past, not noticing her. In this moment, *Eden* harks back directly to a melodramatic forebear. In the Victorian novel *East Lynne*, the heroine, Lady Isabel Carlyle, divorces her philandering husband. Not allowed by the laws or the mores of the time to see her own children after this, she disguises herself (by means no more drastic than wearing a pair of coloured spectacles) and returns to work with her family as a governess. No one sees through her deception (Wood 1984 [1861]). The sunglasses worn by Stephanie are only a part of her (diegetically) far more radical transformation, but they serve the same purpose for a similar, similarly melodramatic, narrative.

Other elements of the narrative are recognisably melodramatic: amnesia (Stephanie temporarily loses her memory after the crocodile attack, telling her bushman saviour that 'I don't even know who I am'); a character returning from the (presumed) dead; and the heroine who loves a man but cannot have him. (In episode 4, when Stephanie's new love interest—her plastic surgeon, Dr Marshall—proposes to her, she turns him down. 'I don't love you', she says. But we know that she does, and what she is really saying is, 'I love you, but we can never be together', a staple of romantic melodramatic fiction.)

Melodrama has traditionally been understood as a feminised form. And—unusually for the Australian mini-series—this is certainly another way in which *Eden* partakes in the melodramatic address.

Feminised address

Susan Dermody and Elizabeth Jacka note the 'gender bias' of the 'historical mini-series', with their 'all-male diorama approach to the re-staging of great sporting and military defeats from the hall of memory' (as quoted in Cunningham and Miller 1994: 144). *Return to Eden* is one of the first exceptions to the masculinity of Australian mini-series. Later examples include *Dirtwater Dynasty* (1988) (Cunningham 1988: 184), *Come in Spinner* (1990), and *Brides of Christ* (1991) (Cunningham & Miller 1994: 144).[1]

Apart from the concern of melodramatic narratives with traditionally 'feminine' areas (the family, romance, and love), *Eden* places Stephanie squarely at its centre. Not only is she the heroine, but she is also the only character granted a voice-over, which allows her to position the audience in relation to the narrative. Indeed, her voice-over is the first speech we hear in the program, introducing the whole situation to us: 'My name is Stephanie Harper, and this is Eden'.

Similarly, the melodramatic concern with taking on a new identity is inflected in a traditionally feminine way: as a concern with appearance. Stephanie undergoes cosmetic surgery, does aerobics to reshape her body, and teaches herself about fashion by reading from magazines: 'With a good collection of adaptable accessories, you can dress up or down with little fuss'.

At the climax of the mini-series, there is also an element of female solidarity in the narrative resolution: Greg, the lover, is killed, while Jilly, the treacherous best friend, is reconciled with Stephanie (and although she ultimately goes to jail for her part in the attempted murder, Jilly helps save Stephanie by shooting Greg while he attempts to strangle her in the swimming pool; they get to hold and look at each other before Jilly is carted off in the paddy wagon).

But what is most noticeable about the feminised address allowed by the melodramatic leanings of *Eden* is the amount of male flesh that is gratuitously presented for the delectation of the audience. Three male characters in particular benefit from this freedom to take their clothes off. Greg Marsden often removes his shirt, particularly when he is in bed with Stephanie, as on their honeymoon night, and the morning after she has come back as Tara and seduced him. He also shows off his body as he suns himself in a very skimpy pair of bathers. (Tara is stalking him at this point, and gets both to look at his flesh and to take photographs of it.)

Stephanie's new love interest, Dr Marsden, also has trouble keeping his shirt on when he is passionate. On the occasions when they almost manage to make love (Tara keeps breaking off), he usually takes it off.

Most spectacularly exhibitionist is the photographer with whom Tara works during her successful supermodel career, Jason Peebles (Chris Haywood). When one of the models won't take her clothes off during a shoot, Jason demonstrates how she should do it by leaping out of a cake, naked except for a sporran. He will only work when his shirt is open, revealing both pectorals and nipples.

Sundry other male characters reveal their flesh at different times during *Return to Eden*. The indigenous characters are consistently topless, although the conventions of Australian narrative seem to demand that this is read in ways other than sexual titification (see below) and, while we never get to see Tara's chest, she works with male models wearing only the briefest of briefs, who are required by the narrative to stand up, get a copy of their script, and look at it—all in a long shot that allows every curve and bulge to be seen.

Indigenising melodrama

Return to Eden is a melodramatic narrative and, in keeping with the traditions of this genre, a feminised one. As suggested above, this has particular implications for the nationalised address of this mini-series, given that in the early 1980s melodrama was understood to be an American form.

It has not always been so: as noted above, Australia has its own melodramatic tradition, and the citation of *East Lynne* in the narrative of *Eden* makes it clear that Victorian Britain also had a strong tradition of melodramatic novels and theatre. But by the time of *Eden*'s production, the USA's successful export of melodramatic television programs—principally *Dallas* and its clone *Dynasty*—almost defined that country in terms of global television. As Ien Ang notes:

> [the] very success and popularity [of *Dallas*] were fastened on for renewed expressions of concern over the steadily growing influence of American consumer capitalism on popular culture. *Dallas* was regarded as yet more evidence of the threat posed by American-style commercial culture against 'authentic' national cultures and identities ... prominent intellectuals [in Europe] ...had even proclaimed *Dallas* as the 'symbol of American cultural imperialism'.
>
> (Ang 1985: 2)

This is not unusual in Australia or, indeed, in any culture. As this book has shown, many of Australia's most successful and lasting programs have been based on imported examples. This does not make them any less 'Australian'. As we noted in chapter 7, there is no such thing as an 'authentic', untainted, pure Australian identity. All attempts to portray a national identity are necessarily constructions, and using forms that are imported from other countries is not necessarily a problem in projects of constructing a national identity (Martin 1994: 11; Jacka 1992: 189; Rowse & Moran 1984; Cunningham 1985). Some writers suggest that the mini-series format as we currently know it developed from the American example of *Roots* (Moran 1985: 206).[2] Stuart Cunningham suggests that 'the mini-series gives us back an Australian "history" and "culture" embedded in a masterful play within the "imported" genre conventions that have *become* part of that history and culture' (Cunningham 1988: 196).

It is interesting to examine the ways in which *Eden* uses an imported form and mode (the mini-series and the melodramatic) and then indigenises them. This occurs in a variety of ways.

There are elements of the program that remain impeccably Australian throughout. Most of the main players have Australian accents (the exception being love interest Dr Marshall, played by James Smilie with an English accent). There is an Australian vocabulary present throughout: 'mates' and 'bastards' recur. The use of already known Australian stars—Rebecca Gilling, Wendy Hughes, and James Reyne from the band Australian Crawl—adds to the perceived Australian authenticity of these characters (Dyer 1998).

But in other ways, the program moves into and out of 'Australianness'. For the storyline of *Return to Eden* explicitly deals with two worlds and two lives. When Stephanie has been rescued after the crocodile attack, and is being nursed back to health by a bushman, she is suffering from amnesia and can recall nothing about herself. The bushman gives her a new name: Tara. As the program makes explicit, the new name is not an innocent one. The bushman explains why he has given her this name. He has only had one love (not, apparently, his wife): a woman named Tara. 'Her mother only ever saw one film in her entire life,' he says, 'and that was *Gone With the Wind*.' The heroine of this mini-series is renamed for a fictional American place—indeed, for an American melodramatic setting. As the narrative progresses, Stephanie/Tara must learn to negotiate between the Australian life she has lost, and the American identity that is given to her as she recreates herself as a supermodel.

The narrative leads its heroine between a life in the bush (as Stephanie) and a life in the city (as Tara)—between a life of traditional Australian icons and a life of glamorous success. And the program explicitly codes each of these with a national identity. The bush—and the woman who lives there—is Australian. The city—and the lifestyle it entails—is coded in many ways as American. The story of the heroine learning to reconcile these two lives thus becomes a metaphorical narrative for the reconciliation of 'Australian' and 'American' elements in Australian television.

Eden as Australia

Landscape

It is a common observation that self-consciously nationalistic cinematic and televisual narratives in Australia have often turned to the landscape in order

Dynasty ...

... in the outback

to create an Australian identity (Thomas 1996). This is also the case in *Eden*, but in the shift from bush to city, a variety of landscapes are employed.

The story opens with shots of 'Eden'. This is the name of Stephanie's family house—centred in the narrative by its eponymous status in the program's title. As a location, it is an uneasy synthesis of the bush and the opulent lifestyle of American soap operas. It is a grand house—similar in style to something from *Dynasty* or *Dallas*—with columns, extensive gardens, and a swimming pool. It is green and sunny—Californian, even. These opening shots show us none of its surroundings. It is 'Eden'—a prelapsarian space—perhaps even a utopia ('no place').

In the next shots of the program, we see Stephanie galloping her horse away from the refinement of Eden and into the bush—a greenish brown landscape, stretching into the distance in every direction. The American opulence of the house is placed within a traditionally 'Australian' landscape. Already, the pull between different national spaces is obvious.

Stephanie then travels briefly to Sydney for her wedding, and returns to the bush for her honeymoon. As she travels back to Eden, we see lines of scrawny trees and a windmill pump in the background as the stockwoman Katy drives the newlyweds in a truck through the bush with a sheepdog on the back. Later in the first episode, when Greg puts his dastardly plan to kill his wife into action, he takes Stephanie out on a crocodile hunt. Here we are presented with a lot of Australian nature: glorious shots of the sunset and the river. Then, after Stephanie is rescued, we see her recovery take place in the swamp where she was discovered, before she goes off to the island of Dr

Marshall for her reconstructive surgery. A variety of landscapes is shown throughout these first two episodes.

Despite her mobility, Stephanie is strongly associated with the bush. She gets married in Sydney, surrounded by a socialite crowd but the program works hard to ensure that she does not really fit in here: she is too frumpy for this glamorous lifestyle, and is always keen to return to Eden. When she is in the bush, it is emphasised that she fits in and belongs there.

Characters

It is notable that all of the characters in the Eden scenes (until the very last scene of the mini-series, when Dr Marshall appears) are Australian. Unlike the city sections of the narrative, this is a space inhabited entirely by Australian accents and actors.

Indigenous Australians

Perhaps most telling, though, in an examination of national identity in this mini-series—and most disappointingly for a chapter that is examining *Eden* as an example of successful hybridisation of national forms—is the way in which indigenous Australians are used in this program.

The montage scene that opens the mini-series, as well as including shots of Eden, shows Stephanie riding past a line of indigenous women. Straight away, indigenous Australians are presented as part of the landscape of Eden. As the narrative progresses, we are regularly shown the stockhands of Eden: two indigenous men, Chris and Sam (Charles Lathalu Yunipingu and Steve Djati Yunipingu). These actors speak almost no lines during the entire mini-series. Rather, their role is to be *visual*. There are dozens of shots in *Return to Eden* in which a close-up of one of the indigenous characters shows him (there are no named female indigenous characters) watching white characters, and/or looking concerned. When Stephanie tells Chris that she is going on a crocodile hunt, we see a close-up of his face, looking concerned. If he suspects something, he says nothing. In a later scene, Jilly and Greg—having an affair before they try to kill Stephanie—have an assignation in the stables. Chris is present, and watches them make love. He stands in stillness and silence, watching but doing nothing. Later, as Greg and Jilly talk around the camp fire after they have thrown Stephanie to the crocodile, Chris stands—framed with the fire burning in front of him—silent and watching. Throughout this, Chris does not have a single line that consists of more than a single word (for example, 'yes').

And then the action moves to Sydney, and the indigenous characters vanish. There are no indigenous Australians in Sydney, according to the narrative of *Return to Eden*. They signify tradition, spirituality, the countryside. They are not part of the modernity of Australia (Miller 1995). They are associated with the bush, and with Australianness. They do not speak; they are mysterious, powerful, and silent (McKee 1997b). This is one of the important ways in which *Return to Eden* (literally) indigenises the landscape of *Eden*.

Coming to Sydney/coming to America?

At the end of the second episode of *Return to Eden*, Stephanie has become Tara. She has recovered from her plastic surgery and arrives in Sydney to create a new life for herself.

Landscape

The program continues to use landscape as a visual means of anchoring the place where the drama is taking place. Throughout the third, fourth, and fifth episodes, the program is obsessed with the icons of the Sydney skyline. A majority of the outdoor scenes take place against the Harbour, the Bridge, the Sydney tower, or the Opera House. The first scene of Tara's return to Sydney shows her walking in front of the Harbour Bridge. She visits her financial consultant, who has an office with a glass wall overlooking the Harbour Bridge. She then manages to find a room for rent with a harbour view (for $50 a week). In a later scene, she discusses with Jason how tired she is, while standing in front of the Bridge; the very next scene takes place the next morning, as Greg is being informed by the financial consultant that he has been cut out of the company—in front of the Harbour Bridge. When Tara becomes a successful supermodel in episode 3, she moves into a new flat, which overlooks the Opera House. Tara and Greg's first date is a romantic drive, over the Harbour Bridge. And so on and so forth.

As in the bush scenes, there is a visual insistence on the landscape within which the characters move, but this urban landscape is not rendered 'Australian' in the same way. It is, rather, Americanised.

American character

Literally, to begin with, there is an American character in the Sydney scenes: an assistant in the photographic agency. Then, as noted above, there are no indigenous characters in Sydney. The focus is on buildings, not the tamed nature of Sydney's parks or trees. This is a space of modernity—an Americanised space—for, in Australia, as David Bromfield notes, 'The modern is ... something that has already happened elsewhere' (as quoted in Morris 1998: 16).

Glamour and success

The Americanness of 'modernity' is most obvious in the glamour of the Sydney that we see in this mini-series. It is often observed that British soap operas are concerned with working-class characters, Australian with middle-class characters, and American with upper-class characters. The Sydney of *Eden* closely resembles the world of America's most popular 1980s melodramas: the soap operas. Stephanie's marriage—taking place at a garden party overlooking the harbour—is attended by paparazzi, who tell us that Stephanie is 'the richest woman in Australia'. This is not the story of the typical Aussie battler; it is a narrative of overtly conspicuous consumption. It is also a narrative of success. This emphasises its Americanness, for, as Graeme Turner has shown, Australian narratives tend to favour spectacular failure as an identifying characteristic of their heroes (Turner 1986).

The Sydney scenes are also Americanised in their iconography. At the end of episode 2, we see Tara's new look revealed. She strides into the office of a modelling agent, and throws back her head wrap. We have already seen her (diegetically) new face; now we see her new make-up, hair, and style. She has thick blue eye shadow, a shiny face, bright red lips, and short, styled hair. She enunciates clearly: 'I need an agent—someone who can get me on the front cover of *Vogue* in six months'. The episode ends with this spectacular, camp glamour—excessive not only in the makeup, but in the simplicity of notions as to how fashion works. Episode 3 opens with Tara on the catwalk, her modelling career already (elliptically) successful, shot against a series of international flags (including that of the USA). She has entered the international fashion sphere, which is full, again, of an iconography that is familiar from American melodramatic narratives (Jackie Collins's mini-series as much as *Dallas* and *Dynasty*). The plot points in these episodes could come from a standard episode of *Dynasty*: relationship break-ups, alcoholism, photo studios, the glamorous world of fashion, boardroom politics, very difficult goals achieved very quickly (Tara's career continues with a montage of photo shoots, and suddenly it is six months later and she is on the cover of *Vogue*).

Australian palimpsest

Throughout these ('American') episodes, recognisably Australian icons and motifs do recur to some extent. The presence of Australian accents and city landmarks has already been noted. Stephanie's wealth comes not from oil, but from uranium mining. There is also a nice moment that blends the glamorous melodrama with the female gaze and an 'Australian' touch: one of Tara's catwalk appearances features her flanked by two male models dressed as lifesavers, wearing little rubber caps, Speedos, and nothing else.

Another neat comment on an Australian identity is the fact that no matter how successful Tara becomes, she always drinks beer—out of the stubby if possible. When she and Dr Marshall go on a date to the Opera House, they decide not to go in, heading instead to a blokey, workingman's pub. She is comfortable here—and, indeed, it turns out that the English-accented up-market plastic surgeon she is dating also grew up around here, and this pub was his dad's local. 'Beers are on the house', says Dot, the barmaid, pouring the midis. The glamour of their American genre is replaced by a brief insistence on working-class Australian authenticity.

The return to Eden

The last segment of the narrative returns us—as the title suggests—to Eden. It is a return to the bush.

Stephanie/Tara has already worked out that, in the bush/city dichotomy, it is the bush that is necessary to her life and her identity. Sitting on a beach on the island where Dr Marshall runs his plastic surgery clinic—a space that is outside the country/city dichotomy—she is able to discuss this with her new paramour. The island, he tells her, is the ideal place for a clinic: 'It has its own healing properties'. When she tells him that she was 'born in the country' (Eden), he says, 'I envy you'. The country, the space of nature, is seen to be a healing, nurturing, desirable place. She must return there.

Stephanie/Tara's return to Eden is part of her elaborate plan for revenge. She persuades Greg—the man she married, who tried to kill her, whom she has now seduced under her new identity, and who still does not realise that she is his wife—to take her to Eden. She tricks Jilly—the best friend who betrayed her by having an affair with her husband, then by helping in an attempt to kill her—into coming too. The logic is that it must be at this place—the place where she was betrayed, died, and came back to life—that the climax of her revenge must occur.

In episode 6, when they fly back into Eden, we are presented with an aerial shot of this hybridised place: a glamorous home set in the middle of bush, the blue of the swimming pool out of place in the otherwise brown landscape.

Stephanie's affiliation with this countryside then becomes an important plot point. As she and Greg flirt in Eden, we are shown long shots of them in Akubras, on horseback, riding through the trees—shots that could have come from *The Man From Snowy River* or any of its filmic kin. A closer shot shows us that, under her Akubra, Stephanie is still 'Tara', wearing impractical supermodel gear, large collar, and vast metallic drop earrings. But now Katy—Eden's stockwoman and house servant—recognises Tara as Stephanie because 'She always had her own way of sitting on a horse'. Indeed, she is the only person who can ride the horse 'King'. It is her excellent horsemanship that gives away her identity as Stephanie.

And it is only in these final sequences that 'Stephanie' and 'Tara' become reconciled. Throughout, we have seen her keep the two identities, and the two worlds they inhabit, firmly apart. This is the reason that she cannot marry the man she loves (Dr Marshall), for Tara's life and Stephanie's cannot become mixed. We even see her, when he comes around to visit her as Tara, hiding a photograph of her children (that is, Stephanie's children). While she is Tara, Stephanie must remain a secret. But as she rides (like Stephanie) through the bush, while dressed like a supermodel (like Tara), a reconciliation begins. We see long shots of her galloping in slow motion through the trees. Watching her riding through the countryside, Greg says to her, 'You fit this landscape, you know—just like the fashion scene in Sydney'. She previously fitted in only in Eden. Now she has mastered the glamorous, modern world of Americanised Sydney as well.

The final scenes of the program take place entirely within Eden, the hybridised space that places *Dynasty* in the outback. After Stephanie/Tara has finally revealed herself to Greg and Jilly, Greg stalks her with a gun through Eden and its grounds.

The indigenous characters who have vanished during the modern Sydney phase of the story return to play an important part in its denouement. In episode 5, Chris gets his first line: 'Yoh' (yes). While Stephanie explores the house, she sees him watching her silently, with some 'spooky' music playing over the top. The stableman Sam gets to say 'Yes, Mr Marsden', and offers to saddle up Stephanie's horse, King: 'Nobody ever rode

King except Miss Harper. He was her horse'. Like the dogs at Stephanie's Sydney house (and the metaphor, insulting as it is, is offered by the program itself), the indigenous characters in Eden recognise that Tara is Stephanie, instinctively.

As Stephanie walks outside the house at night, she passes Chris; again, he is watching her. Later in the program, she enlists him as a sidekick: 'Chris, I need you to help me tonight'. Sam is sent to take a note to the police. Chris's part in Stephanie's revenge plan is, it turns out, to put on 'traditional' body paint, play the didgeridoo, and dance around a fire, in order to build tension for Stephanie's plan to drive Jilly mad. He also rushes in to save her when she first reveals herself and Greg tries to kill her, getting shot in the chest for his trouble. He is not dead, though. At the end of the narrative, as Greg tries to fly away with a wounded arm, he crashes his plane. As it goes down, we are given a sudden close-up of Chris's eyes flicking open. Why? The implication seems to be, at the very least, that Chris is supernaturally aware of what is happening outside—perhaps even that he has somehow caused it to happen.

Indigenous characters and landscape are used in the bush scenes to emphasise Australianness. When Stephanie returns here, she has negotiated a period of Americanisation and survived it. She took something of her Australian identity to Sydney (the accent, the beer, the history of Stephanie), and brought something American back (the hysterically melodramatic narrative). The narrative ends—as it should—with Stephanie's children flying in with Dr Marshall. She is, once again, in the perfect nuclear family, in the bush. The final shot shows Stephanie and Dr Marshall (the plastic surgeon who loves nature) shot against a bush sky, a straggly tree to the side of the shot.

Wildlife

It is the crocodile attack that is the single, best-remembered element of *Return to Eden*. The wildlife in the program is distributed in much the same way as indigenous Australians: it exists in the 'Australian' country scenes, but not in the 'American' city scenes. And in the country scenes, it is represented only by a crocodile; the series eschews more traditionally 'Australian' animals. This may be partly explained by narrative demands: although koalas can be bad-tempered creatures, they would be unlikely to murder a visiting tourist. The same can be said for kangaroos, emus, and platypuses.

Australian wildlife, American motives

However, this cannot be the entire explanation for the absence of other forms of wildlife. There is no reason, for example, why Stephanie should not have a pet wombat called 'Fatso' at Eden. The lack of symbolic wildlife represents one area in which Eden eschews standard ploys for claiming an 'Australian' national identity.

Nevertheless, the crocodile is an important part of *Return to Eden*'s lasting place in the public archive. This attack is also double-coded: it is an attack by a dangerous animal of the Australian bush (a typically Australian narrative), but it is organised by a scheming husband, and survived by plastic surgery (an 'American' melodramatic one). It brings together the different national strands in a single reptilian body. And, by a coincidence, it also allows us to discuss the way in which *Return to Eden* works by comparison with the national negotiations of another famous Australian Crocodile: Mick Dundee.

Meaghan Morris takes the success of *Crocodile Dundee* as an opportunity to think about questions of cultural forms and national identity. Addressing concerns that the film represents an 'Americanised' version of Australian culture, she dismisses such an analysis. Considering the history of Australian cultural production, she points out that neither a desire for 'positive authenticity' (the search for the 'real', 'genuine' Australian identity) nor a desire for 'positive unspecificity' (the production of texts that have no identifying features of their Australian production) has produced a success as great as *Crocodile Dundee*'s. She names the strategy whereby this film achieved its unique success—both within Australia and overseas (much as *Return to Eden* did)—as 'positive unoriginality' (Morris 1988: 246). Unoriginality, she argues, is not necessarily 'A Bad Thing' (Morris 1988: 46): 'a theory of positive unoriginality [provides] a context in which, for critics, the privileged metaphors of postmodernism can come into play—image-scavenging, borrowing, stealing, plundering' (Morris 1988: 247). And so, in the case of *Crocodile Dundee*: 'Its borrowings are as clearly displayed as Dundee's outback costume, with its comic mishmash of cowboy/western, bushman/jungle shreds—originating and imitating nothing but a late rural effort at vintage Bow-wow-wow' (Morris 1988: 248).

The same can be said of *Return to Eden*: with its crocodile, five years before Dundee's, it blatantly borrows from American forms but is unashamedly Australian in its iconography and concerns. Its unoriginality is unique, productive, and interesting.

Effects of *Return to Eden*

Return to Eden has survived in the Australian mediasphere, its crocodile attack repeated, remembered, and archived as an important moment in Australian television. However, it did not immediately change Australian television. True, the mini-series was popular enough to spin off a series, but this rated very poorly (17 in Melbourne, 14 in Sydney) and was quickly canned (ABT 1988: 49). Similarly, *Eden* did not herald a new era of contemporary mini-series. Even after its success had shown that modern myths of Australia could be created, 'The obsession with historical subjects [continued in] mini-series. Between 1984 and 1987, twenty-seven with a historical theme were made out of a total of thirty-four' (Jacka & Johnson 1998: 215).

There was a more general move to 'internationalisation' of mini-series in the years after 1985 (Cunningham & Miller 1994: 142). Commentators attribute this to economic factors (Moran & Pinne 1993: 26). But such factors do not necessarily explain either the production or the success of *Return to Eden*. This mini-series is produced well before the dates of supposed internationalisation, and it fits neither Albert Moran's nor Cunningham and Miller's description of the typically internationalised mini-series. Even if part of its form can be explained by economic factors, this is less interesting than tracing the ways in which the program negotiated with the elements of national identity it inherited, and the ways in which its success at that project have contributed to its enduring place in the Australian public archive of television. Stephanie Marsden is remembered because she was eaten by a crocodile; she survived to become a supermodel; and she survived that in order to return to the Australian landscape with an understanding of how the glamour of American culture might be experienced as an opportunity rather than a threat.

Availability

The mini-series of *Return to Eden* was released commercially on video. Although it has since been deleted, some commercial video stores hold copies. Screensound hold the first episode of this. The subsequent

22-episode series that appeared in 1986 (starring Peta Toppano) is not held by Screensound and has not been released on video.

Notes

1 It should be noted that the situation is quite different in the case of cinema, where the nationalistic and historical imperatives of the 'AFC genre' were often played out with female leads—for example, *Picnic at Hanging Rock*, *The Getting of Wisdom*, *The Mango Tree*, *We of the Never Never*, and so on (Dermody & Jacka 1987).

2 Although not everyone would agree with this assertion. One anonymous reader of this manuscript refers to this suggestion as a 'furphy'.

14

Neighbours: National Niceness

1985–

On 1 July 1987, Channel Ten screened the 'wedding of the decade'. Charlene Ramsay married Scott Robinson in an episode of *Neighbours* that was watched in Australia by over two million people: 'the highest rating episode of a soap on Australian TV' (Wark 1999: 83). This moment has subsequently been identified many times as one of Australian television's greatest moments. In Channel Ten's 'Top ten moments on Ten' (1996), it makes number two in the list (beaten only by the delicatessen bomb blast in *Number 96*) (http://www.magna.com.au/~lindsay/info/Preface4.html). The wedding makes John Hartley's international list of the fifty greatest television moments: '(the passport to international *ahh*dom)' (Hartley 1999a). It is collected in Channel Ten's documentary *ATV 30 Years of Television* (1994), and is number thirteen in *Who Weekly*'s 'The 100 Greatest Moments in Television' (1999: 54): ' "The hype was incredible", says *Neighbours* casting director Jan Russ. "We've never really had anything like that in Australia" … the wedding ballad, Angry Anderson's "Suddenly", shot to no. 2 in the charts'.

Several correspondents for this book also named this moment as a great one in Australian television. It was released as a video by Grundy's, and when *TV Week* was calling for readers' memories for an article on great moments in Australian television, the magazine's prompting began with 'What's you most memorable Australian television moment? Is it Charlene and Scott getting married in *Neighbours*?' ('What's Your Most Memorable Australian Television Moment?' 1999: 31). Screensound—the official Australian national archive of film, television, and radio history—keeps only one episode of the program: again, the wedding. It is a sanctioned part of Australia's cultural heritage.

But all of this is not necessarily what makes Scott and Charlene's wedding so important. What has made a greater impact on the Australian mediasphere is, bizarrely, the number of people who watched the episode when it screened somewhere else: in the United Kingdom on 8 November 1988, 19.4 million people, or over 80 per cent of the available viewing audience, watched the nuptials.[1] One of the most important aspects of *Neighbours* in the Australian public archive is how many people watched it in another country.

Success story

Neighbours is a soap opera in twenty-minute episodes, designed to be shown on a daily basis. Its original rationale, long since superseded, was to feature the tensions and trials of two historically rival families living in the same street: the Robinsons and the Ramsays. The cast has always included a large number of attractive young characters, and the setting and most of the storylines are resolutely suburban.

It was the first Australian television series to dominate the television ratings in the United Kingdom. The program was initially shown in the United Kingdom as a cheap daytime schedule-filler on BBC1, starting on 27 October 1986. Schoolteachers and headmasters soon began to make public complaints: class sizes were shrinking because children were staying at home to watch the program. It was then shifted to an early evening slot, where the ratings increased dramatically. At its high point, *Neighbours* was screening (the same episode) twice a day in the United Kingdom and rating over nineteen million viewers daily (Oram 1988: 51).[2] No Australian program had ever done this in the 'mother country'.

And as *Neighbours* became popular in the United Kingdom, Australia became obsessed with its overseas success. Endless newspaper items, magazine stories, and even academic articles were written, all asking, endlessly, the one question: 'Why is *Neighbours* so popular in Britain?'

It is obvious that the insistence with which this question was posed is evidence of cultural cringe; it is most unlikely, for example, that the success of a program such as *Friends* on Australian television leads to much concern in the United States press about why this sitcom is so popular overseas. It is the very fact that it is an Australian product succeeding overseas that causes so much fuss, and when we look at how *Neighbours*' success was publicly debated in Australia, we can see that writers continue to find ways to feel inferior, even as their national product is consistently defeating British television in the ratings of that country.

Overseas sales

The Australian media have long been obsessed with the possibility of exporting television programs. As far back as 1961, before Australian television production was even able to sustain its own popular drama series, the Australian Broadcasting Control Board hopefully noted that 'It is understood that at least one programme has already been sold overseas' (ABCB 1961: 46), and indeed both *The Terrific Adventures of the Terrible Ten* and *Consider Your Verdict* had been sold overseas in 1961 (Keating, pers. comm. 17 May 2000). From this starting point, concern with export grows in discussions of Australian television. This is not just an economic issue, of course; it is a matter of national pride. It is not just programs we should be exporting, it is culture.

By 1968, newspaper articles are already hopefully stating that

> Australia ... is on the verge of developing a substantial television export industry ... In the last few years Australia has exported 150 half hour episodes of *The Terrible Ten* ... *The Magic Boomerang* and *The Adventures of Seaspray* have had similar worldwide sales ... *The Stranger* [has been sold to] 11 overseas countries ... [and] *Skippy* has been extraordinarily successful already.
>
> (Jay 1968: 61)

Oh, and *Homicide* is selling to 'Scottish, Welsh and north of England networks' (Radic 1968: 4). Indeed, one commentator at this time notes (making fun of the whole phenomenon, it seems) that 'Perhaps there are already American mothers who are outraged because their children imitate Rolf Harris and talk like Australian policemen from *Homicide*' (Battersby 1968: 91).

This desire to map minutely the details of which Australian television programs have been sold overseas continues to the present day, both in the popular press and in academic writing on the media. It is not hard to see why: Australian film and television heartily partake in discourses of protectionism, the need to protect 'our' culture and 'our' industry from the imports of the United Kingdom and the USA. No wonder that every sale of an Australian television program to one of these countries—or anywhere else, for that matter—is so exciting. It is a matter of national pride: we are good enough to sell overseas.

Particularly interesting are the recurring articles on Australia's great breakthrough in international exporting, which is always *just about* to happen (as in the 1968 example cited above). In 1979, an article entitled 'The Australian Invasion' (1979: 7) appears in *TV Times*:

> Sales of major Australian TV series to the US are creating a new TV marketplace for quality local [Australian] productions—ending the past one-way traffic from the US ... The Seven Network's historical drama series *Against the Wind* was the first Australian drama series to sell in the US ... The highly successfully Ten network serial *Prisoner* has been sold to both American and Canadian TV networks ... Overseas distribution rights to the current series *Patrol Boat* have been sold to Paramount.

Every sale is proof of an 'invasion' on 'our' part and testament to the fact that we can do it just as well as the Yanks. Similarly, 1983 became 'Australia's year in the United States' as, among other things, 'it was possible to turn on the radio and hear Men At Work; switch to television and see *The Thorn Birds*; go to a cinema and see *The Year of Living Dangerously*' (Hamilton & Mathews 1986: 11).

It is possible, from reading the popular press, to be well schooled in the geography of Australia's television exports: the international travels of programs such as *Homicide*, *The Sullivans*, *The Paul Hogan Show*, *A Country Practice*, *The Flying Doctors*, *Richmond Hill*, *Prisoner*, *Sons and Daughters*, *The Young Doctors*, *Chances*, *Boney*, *Power Without Glory*, *Bluey*, *Ryan*, *Against the Wind*, and, of course, *Skippy, the Bush Kangaroo* (Rees 1978a: 386; Oram 1987: 124; Oliver n.d.; 'Homicide' n.d.; Hohensee 1978b: 36; Day 1981: 134).

Until the success of *Neighbours*, *Skippy* was Australia's sole champion export, the only really successful one. It was a televisual product that stormed the world's markets, and something that 'we' could be proud of. It was '[t]he most widely distributed series that's ever been made in Australia' (*The Australian Image* 1989d). In fact, 'There aren't many people in the world who haven't heard of Skippy'. By 1971,

> it was estimated that in Australia [*Skippy*] was being seen by 2 200 000 viewers weekly. But in eighty-four other countries the weekly audience was in the region of 300 000 000, including 164 channels in the United States ... On an Australian country tour, it was estimated that more people came to see Skippy than to see the Queen Mother and LBJ combined.
>
> (Rees 1978a: 391)

There is an implication of national pride here—that *our* Skippy could do better than *their* (the United Kingdom's) Queen Mother and *their* (the USA's) LBJ. This discourse for writing about television exports is developed further in another piece from the same year:

> [I]t's been said that Australian made TV shows and feature films could be our best ambassadors. If that's true, no one has done more for flying the flag than *Skippy*. Since Skippy came to life in the mid-1960s, the series has been sold to 130 countries. And she's still hopping up everywhere. No Australian TV product, or movie, can claim such a successful track record overseas.
>
> (Hohensee 1978b: 36; see also Courtis 1981: 128; Allen & Spencer 1983: 125)

Skippy was flying the flag for Australia.

And then along came the *Neighbours* 'phenomenon' in the United Kingdom (Cunningham & Jacka 1995: 207); its success was 'the most dramatic sign of the export successes of Australian television' (Cunningham & Jacka 1995: 192). And—not surprisingly, given Australia's history of obsession over television exports and the tendency to see this in terms of national pride—the success of *Neighbours* has been publicly interrogated in relation to one repeated question: 'What does this say about us as a nation?'

Postcolonial soap

In an article on the success of Australian soap operas in the UK, Lynette Cassells points to a fascinating example of reverse colonialism. In production company Granada's television studio in Manchester, she tells us, 'there is a replica of Sydney's Whale Beach kiosk. Complete with Streets' ice-cream posters, glass-fronted fridges and Violet Crumble bars'. Another set in the UK, of a house interior, is 'every inch Australian', including 'packets of Weetbix, and a Whirlpool fridge'. Set up to record a new UK–Australian soap co-production, the sets illustrate, she says, the maxim currently accepted in British television production: 'If you can't beat them, join them' (Cassells 1990: 28). Who is the 'them' that the UK cannot beat? Who must the UK 'join'? Why, Australia of course.

Richard Paterson notes that in an information age, unexpected things can happen to previously quite stable colonial relationships. He describes the case of Brazil and Portugal, where the 'phenomenal success' of Brazilian telenovellas (long-form soap operas) in overseas markets has led to a 'strange reverse colonization pattern', whereby Portugal, the country that previously invaded and colonised Brazil, is now dominated culturally by Brazil's television output (Paterson 1998: 62).

Comparing the above account with Toby Miller's writing on the desire to make Australia look like other places in television programs (Miller 1990), it is possible to build an attractive postcolonial—or reverse colonial—discourse about *Neighbours*' success in the United Kingdom. Now the United Kingdom is trying to make itself look like us. And concerns about the effect of a flood of imports on indigenous culture—so familiar in Australian public discourse—begin to emerge in the UK:

> As 1988 turned towards 1989 the serial seemed to be everywhere: swap stickers appeared at supermarket check-outs; performers featured on magazine covers, participated in live television phone-ins from Australia, presented awards and even functioned as prizes ... in viewer competitions.
>
> (Craven 1989: 3)

Indeed,

> 'England has gone *Neighbours*-mad', said Carol Millward of the BBC press office ... Early in 1988 the [London *Sunday Mirror*] ran a competition built around *Neighbours*, with winners given a trip to Melbourne to see the soap being made ... More than a million entries were received in the first three days.
>
> (Oram 1988: 51)

In such a context, it was not surprising that British drama producers 'held concerns that imports on this scale might stifle indigenous talent and compromise local production' (Craven 1989: 2). In another newspaper item that discusses the 'Aussie invasion', we discover that

> Britain's TV chiefs are worried the runaway success of Aussie soapie *Neighbours* has got out of hand. The show is outshining British made programs in the ratings battles ... [a UK TV executive says] '*Neighbours* success has taken us all by surprise ... it's now threatening the reputation of [BBC soap] *EastEnders*'.
>
> (Cho 1988: 28)

We are 'invading' and 'threatening' the United Kingdom. Indeed, even the ultimate sign of British colonial domination of Australia—the monarchy—has been taken over by this Australian television production. James Oram recounts the story of Colin Stanley-Hill—Australian court correspondent—receiving a phone call from the palace in the middle of the night, demanding to know the latest plot developments: '*Neighbours*, man, *Neighbours*. We all watch it here. The Queen's very interested to know what stage the serial has reached in Australia' (Oram 1988: 1).

It is interesting to note, given this possible interpretation, that the public furore in Australia over *Neighbours*' success in the United Kingdom does not generally take on such a triumphant tone. It is as though, when the export revolution predicted for so long in the press finally happens—when the 'invasion' actually succeeds—the media are not quite sure how to react to it. It is still too unexpected.

Invading or appropriated

Neighbours began in Australia in 1985, on Channel Seven. The program was not successful and was quickly cancelled. It moved to Channel Ten in 1986, with some changes—younger cast members, a more concerted campaign to sell to a younger audience—and became very successful, even before its British popularity became an issue in Australia (Keating 1999b). By 1987, most issues of *TV Week* in Australia had a *Neighbours* star on the cover, usually one of the 'big four' young stars of the series: Kylie Minogue, Jason Donovan, Guy Pearce, or Annie Jones. In March 1987, the show made the front page of Sydney newspapers, with stories about crowds coming out to meet cast members at the Sydney Royal Easter Show (Oram 1988).

And then, during 1987, the program's success in the United Kingdom hit the Australian public sphere. 'Britain adopts our *Neighbours*' runs one of the headlines (Rowbotham 1987: 26). '*Neighbours*—that dinky di slice of Aussie soap suburbia', states another, 'is now one of the big, big success stories on British TV' (Withers 1987: 27). These are not small columns on the television pages of newspapers; they are big news stories. And they continue throughout the next few years. Indeed, for almost a decade, the Australian public sphere—newspaper stories, magazine articles, and television current affairs shows such as *Page One*—keeps on returning to the fact that one of Australia's own television programs was successful in the United Kingdom. It was a fact so worrying it could not be left alone (Luck 1988; see also Ross 1988: 16; Harris 1990: 38; Gleitzman 1992: 5).

And similar themes returned throughout these stories, particularly a desperate concern to explain why *Neighbours* was popular in the United Kingdom and a concern about what this means for 'our' image overseas.

Explaining popularity

In 1989, yet another newspaper story carries the headline 'The Oz Invasion'. It is a typical example of this cycle of stories: 'why has this particular series been singled out among a sea of soapies from Australia?' (Solomon 1989: 23). But particularly interesting is the illustration that accompanies this story. A cartoon beside the headline shows a drawing of Great Britain, with a huge mouth in one side, just about to devour a sandwich in the shape of Australia. In this juxtaposition of the headline and the illustration, a great ambivalence about *Neighbours'* success can be seen. On the one hand—as the title suggests—we are successfully 'invading' the UK in a hostile takeover of their culture. But on the other hand—and at the same time—there is a worrying possibility that this might be a bad thing. Perhaps *we* are being devoured, appropriated by *them*? Perhaps they are still in control, and we are just fodder for their BBC television? A deep suspicion remains: the reaction to the United Kingdom's desire for *Neighbours* is less one of rejoicing than of a surly and suspicious 'Why do you want it?' So Les Solomon asks, 'why has this particular series been singled out?' Peter Luck asks, 'what is the appeal of *Neighbours*?' (Luck 1990: 13). Lynden Barber seeks the 'explanation for the success of *Neighbours* in the UK' (Barber 1990: 9). '[W]hy should something like *Neighbours* be such a runaway success?' asks another article (Blake 1991: 15), and '[*Neighbours* star] Peter O'Brien told the British press the popularity of the show was a mystery to him' (Rowbotham 1987: 26). Indeed, with a sense of explicit cultural cringe, 'The Australian *Sun-Herald* asked a number of [*British*] Fleet Street newspapers to explain the *Neighbours* phenomenon' (Oram 1988: 52).

As Stuart Cunningham has noted, the explanations that were provided in response to this obsessively asked question were formulaic and largely unenlightening: 'speculations about the mythological content and serial format of the programmes … [and] "slight foreignness"' (Cunningham & Jacka 1995: 208). Indeed, the question of why a given program succeeds, while another fails, is an unanswerable one (Ang 1996: 10). With the full benefit of 20/20 hindsight, explanations can always be produced, but of course they can never be tested or used to produce consistent theories that would then be useful for making predictions about which programs will be successful next. Most of the explanations found for *Neighbours'* success in the United Kingdom tend to banal, consisting of lists of characteristics of the series that are as true for dozens of failed programs as they are for the successful one:

- 'Its pleasant setting with pleasant neighbours … The kids are positive and tend to resolve their own problems' (Blake 1991: 15).

- 'It was the very first series in British television history that was strip-programmed' (Solomon 1989: 23).
- 'the fantasy element ... family atmosphere, the sense of community' (Solomon 1989: 23).
- 'the sunshine and swimming pools ... exotic ... comedy ... sexual attractiveness' (Solomon 1989: 24).
- 'its idealised depiction of the overwhelmingly white, suburban society for which most Britons secretly yearned' (Barber 1990: 9).
- 'that cheerful loving joie de vivre was certainly what made the show such a phenomenal success in its biggest overseas market, Britain ... [it features] overwhelmingly *nice* people' (Williams 1995: 48).
- '[It doesn't deal] with issues like AIDS and teenage pregnancy. [It is not] issue-based, like the old *A Country Practice* used to be' (Williams 1995: 48).
- 'British soap producers take themselves too seriously; they concentrate on slice of life scenarios, so reality is a major component of their soaps. Australia[n soaps] ... deal with major issues in an entertaining way' (Macken 1989: 23–4).
- 'It avoids "gratuitous violence" and uses "a lot situation comedy"' (Bowring 1990: 45).

What do they think about us?

Another recurring theme in newspaper coverage about the success of *Neighbours* in the United Kingdom is a niggling concern about what the British think about it: the worry of those unused to shipping their cultural product overseas that people might think badly of us because of it. This can be sensed in a story such as 'Ten Series is Junk, Says UK Soap Star':

> A British television soapie actress has slammed the Melbourne-made soap, *Neighbours*, after it scored a spot in the BBC's prime rating evening timeslot. According to a report from London today, one main cast member of the rival British soap *EastEnders*, Linda Davison has attacked *Neighbours* claiming the scripts, acting and sets were appalling, banal and dreadful.
>
> (Lee 1988: 26)

This is a story in an Australian newspaper that tells us nothing more than that a British actress does not like our biggest television export. Why on earth would such a story feature, with a large headline and a decent number of column inches, as news in Australia? Because, it seems, it really matters to us what *they* think of us. And because Australia does not have many television export successes on the scale of *Neighbours*, that program, of course, becomes representative. Public discourse worries about what *Neighbours* makes 'them' think of 'us'. We are thus concerned, for example, about the impact that *Neighbours* might have on tourism and on immigration. In a delightful example of the way that journalistic writing tends to generalise social change from a few isolated examples, we find in reading through newspaper stories about the program that *Neighbours* has hugely increased travel to Australia, and *for the same reasons*, it is threatening to stop people travelling to Australia. On the one hand, 'Oz soapie cleans up UK in TV ratings war ... the visa applications and immigration queries continue to flood into Australia House' (Smith 1988: 15; see also Macken 1989: 23–4). On the other, 'The success of Australian soaps such as *Neighbours* and *Home and Away* in the United Kingdom could be deterring Brits from holidaying down under—because they believe Australia is too much like home, according to the Australian Tourist Commission' (Collins 1996: 16).

This concern with tourism is linked to the possibility that what is seen by viewers in foreign countries is understood to be the *reality* of Australian life, leading to a desire to visit that reality (through tourism or immigration). The Tourist Commission is thus involved in working out whether these images of Australia are appropriate ones to be showing overseas, identifying 'the sort of Australia' that other countries would like to see (McCathie 1991: 32).

Again, such concerns are unimaginable for those countries that routinely export television programs. It is unlikely that public debate in the USA would address the issue of whether *Twin Peaks* presents the 'correct' image of the USA to overseas audiences. Yet, when only one program takes on such an international status, such concerns apparently become more reasonable. Jon Stratton suggests that '*Neighbours* ... could be misrecognized as actually representing real life in Australia' (Stratton & Ang 1994: 6). David Rowe comments that, 'In spite of the programmes' [*Neighbours* and *Home and Away*'s] status as drama and fantasy, they were sufficiently compelling portrayals of real life Down Under to stimulate an avalanche of emigration enquiries at Australia House in the late eighties' (Rowe 1994: 17). In less restrained terms, Pat Bowring suggests that *Neighbours* simply *is* Australian; simply *does* represent Australia: 'What could be more Australian than *Neighbours*? ... it [is] close to Australian reality' (Bowring 1990: 45).

As has been noted in several chapters of this book, such discourses are common in the Australian public sphere: claims that a particular representation (be it *Homicide*, Paul Hogan, or *Against the Wind*) is *authentically*, or *genuinely*, or *really* Australian. Such claims are interesting in terms of their importance in Australian public discourse, even as we continue to recognise that they are always somewhat mistaken. They try to *create*, rather than simply *recognise*, a sense of unified Australian national identity. Given that this has been an important part of *Neighbours*' public image in Australia, it is worth turning to the program itself in order to examine the images and narratives that Australia has been exporting to the United Kingdom.

An Australian image

James Oram claims of *Neighbours* that 'the script had to stay within the bounds of suburban credibility ... everyday problems confronting the average Australian family' (Oram 1988: 25). It is interesting that *Neighbours* can be read as 'everyday' and 'average'. The program lays claim to showing 'normality' and 'Australian reality' (Ang & Stratton 1995: 131). What kind of 'average', 'normal', 'real' Australia does, for example, the wedding of Scott and Charlene present?

One of the most obvious characteristics of *Neighbours*' version of Australia is—as has been noted many times —the fact that it is a white Australia. (Indeed, Germaine Greer suggests that this is one of the reasons for its success.[3]) As Ian Craven notes, '*Neighbours* has introduced no long-serving non-Anglo-Celtic character or family into Ramsay Street' (Craven 1992: 248; see also Coupe, Jakubowicz, & Randall 1992: 29; Jakubowicz 1994: 83; Barber 1990: 9).

It is not useful, however, to overstate this point, as though *Neighbours* were simply a racist text, presenting a racist account of Australian society. Such readings are simplistic and—as is often the case—take little account of the messy details of the texts themselves. As Ian Craven points out, for example,

> What is striking about the daily soaps ... is the fact that despite the economic and ideological pressures against the registration of fundamental social change ... this change [still becomes] apparent in the programmes ... In *Neighbours* the Joe Mangel character sports an Aboriginal land-rights sweat shirt whose striking motif is plainly visible as he walks around the set.
>
> (Craven 1992: 251)

Similarly, the program's gender politics are messier than might be expected if it were simply presenting the 'dominant ideology' of patriarchy. A good sign of its success in challenging patriarchal ideals is the fact it deeply annoys reactionary commentators. This can be seen, for example, in an article in the right-wing journal *Quadrant*, which condemns the program precisely for its lack of fit with dominant sexist ideologies, complaining that it is dominated by female characters (Conway 1988). This feminine address can be seen in the program's propensity to cast muscular young men who make a habit of taking their clothes off (see chapter 13). In the wedding episode, for example, we see Henry (Craig McLaughlin) wandering around with his shirt casually undone to reveal a very shapely pair of pectorals. Mike (Guy Pearce, a former body building champion) is also in the program at this point, as is the (much less visually spectacular, but still pleasing to some viewers) Scott (Jason Donovan). Many of *Neighbours*' finest moments have involved male characters taking their clothes off: Henry running around the Ramsay household, naked apart from a top hat clutched to his genitalia; Billy persuaded to strip naked for a life-drawing class by his girlfriend; or, in the most spectacular instance, the entire male cast going the 'Full Monty' for a diegetic charity performance in 1999.

It is also interesting, in terms of basic identity politics, to look at the way in which *Neighbours* presents class in Australia. Traditional notions of class identity, developed outside of Australia, do not map very well onto the Australian situation (see chapter 15). Suburbia, in Australia, is not easily described as a middle-class institution, as it might be in the United Kingdom. The suburbs in Australia are as much a working-class as a middle-class space (Bennett, Emmison, & Frow 1999). However, the suburban life presented by *Neighbours* is undoubtedly a middle-class one. There is no equivalent on Australian television of the insistently working-class cultures represented on the United Kingdom's most popular soap operas, *Coronation Street* and *EastEnders*.

In terms of aged identity, Australia is a young country according to *Neighbours*. In the early days of the program's success, it is focused around a group of young characters: Kylie Minogue's Charlene, Jason Donovan's Scott, Guy Pearce's Mike, Annie Jones's Jane, and Craig McLaughlin's Henry. In the wedding episode, the fact that Kylie is doing such a grown-up thing as getting married is worthy of comment. As Jane says to Charlene, 'How does it feel to be an old married woman?' Charlene replies, 'Your turn next', and Jane is shocked at the suggestion: 'No way—not for another ten years at least'. Australia is white, middle-class, and terribly, terribly young.

In episode 523—the *Neighbours*' wedding that makes it into so many lists of television's great moments in Australia—we see the program's community gathered together to celebrate this communal moment (*Neighbours* 1987). This is how soap operas work: creating a central community whose boundaries are carefully policed in order to demonstrate who belongs to the 'we' of the community, and who proposes a threat as 'them' (Geraghty 1991). In the church, as Jason and Kylie—or Scott and Charlene (the characters' and the actors' names at this point in the program's success were almost interchangeable)—prepare to exchange vows, we have a panning shot over the 'we' community who have gathered to celebrate this event. Indeed, everyone in the church is white. *Neighbours* has often included non-Anglo characters in the 'we' community, but rarely for any length of time (McKee 1997a).

A particularly interesting aspect of this episode is what does *not* happen during this wedding ceremony.

- Kylie Minogue does not appear in a dual role, bursting into the church at the climax of the ceremony to unveil the woman about to marry Scott as her evil twin sister.
- It does not turn out, half-way through the vows, that Scott has in fact been brainwashing Charlene with a mixture of drugs and subliminal tapes played while she was sleeping in order to make her think that she was in love with him.
- Terrorists do not break into the church, massacring many of the congregation.

That is to say, *Neighbours* is not an American soap opera.

Similarly,

- Charlene does not have to sell her only precious possessions in order to pay for her wedding dress.
- Her mother does not fail to turn up to the wedding because she has been unable to find anyone to cover for her in the small business she runs.
- Neither of the protagonists is HIV positive.

Which is merely to say that *Neighbours* is not a British soap opera. The mode of most American soap operas is a grandly melodramatic one, where any of the first three events could easily happen (and have, in *Sunset Beach*, *All My Children*, and *Dynasty* respectively). The mode of British soap operas tends towards gritty realism, dealing with the difficulties of living on the poverty line—in examples such as *EastEnders*, *Coronation Street*, and some aspects of *Brookside*. American soap operas do not require any commitment to the belief that they are showing the 'reality' of American life. With their generic affiliations, British soap operas seem to lay greater claim to being 'realistic'. What is interesting is that in both of them, large and important problems are addressed, whether they are melodramatic (gunmen massacring your family) or gritty realist (coping with the death of your HIV-positive girlfriend).

By contrast, the mode of *Neighbours* is a profoundly banal one. What distinguishes the program—and the picture of Australia it presents—from soap offerings in other countries is its absolute lack of anything *important* in the lives of its characters.

Often, weddings in soap operas will face some threat: an undiscovered secret about the past of one of the partners, perhaps; a speeding car killing the bride just as she takes her vows (as with Sydney in *Melrose Place*); or (as with *Dynasty*) a well-armed terrorist group standing around the glass church ready to rain bullets on the bride, groom, and guests. By contrast, there are only two threats of disruption to the joy of the community in this episode of *Neighbours*.

In the first of these, at the church, Scott turns to Mike and says, 'What if she doesn't turn up?' However, the audience already knows that she is going to turn up—we have just been watching her getting ready and know that she is running a few minutes late. And just as Scott finishes saying, 'What if she doesn't turn up?' the church door swings open and Charlene walks in. There is no tension, no threat, no real danger of disruption. This is a safe, supportive, and loving community. Everything will be fine. There will be continual small disruptions to the status quo (as in this example), but their threat is extremely limited. This is the community suggested by the original opening title sequence of the program. As we listen to the wonderfully supportive and hopeful lyrics—'Neighbours—everybody needs good neighbours, with a little understanding ... good neighbours become good friends'—we see everyone laughing together. Some of the lads are playing cricket in the street, and a cricket ball breaks a window. Everyone winces, but then they all start laughing again.

So there is very little build-up to the big moment of this wedding in *Neighbours*. Without notable disruptions to hold back the narrative drive, it is less than eight minutes into the episode before all of the preparations have been shown, everyone has turned up, and the ceremony has been completed. Charlene is shot to look like an angel (slightly blurry, appearing in the bright whiteness of the church door), while Angry Anderson's 1980s pop classic 'Suddenly' plays in the background: 'the only dream that I could find—a loving heart, an open mind. See the real me, and I hope that you would be—the one'. A series of pans and close-ups show us that everyone is smiling at everyone else. Interestingly, we do not even hear most of the ceremony. Unlike American examples—where it is important to hear every word so that, first of all, you can exhale when it is finished and relax in the knowledge that the ceremony is not going to be disrupted by a jealous ex-lover and, second, you know that the real ceremony has taken place, and that it was not carried out by a fake vicar employed by a jealous ex-lover who deliberately used a wrong version of the ceremony—here in *Neighbours*, the whole thing is just a nice experience. Narrative twists are less important than hearing Angry Anderson and watching Kylie looking radiant. We do hear Scott and Charlene starting on the 'will you have this man ...' lines, but these are rudely interrupted as well, less important than the emotive music. We see their lips move, but hear nothing of their voices as Angry Anderson is mixed up on the soundtrack. Then Scott lifts the veil and kisses Charlene, and we fade to the reception.

Here, the second major narrative threat is presented: Lucy has lost her mouse. Apart from this, there is little drama at the reception. Again, it is all 'we-dom' (Hartley 1992a: 206), with people welcoming and loving each other: 'I'm really proud of you'; 'Welcome to our family'.

But then—and just as Des says, 'Everything's gone without a hitch'—with perfect comedy timing, and comic music, the program presents a close-up of the mouse running around under the table. As Henry tries to get it out from under the table, the older female character Mrs Mangle shrieks, 'You were groping my leg'. A few seconds of general shouting follows, until Henry emerges with the mouse, all of the women shriek, and we zoom to a close-up of Scott and Charlene, laughing. The scene ends with their kiss.

With these as the major narrative threats in the episode, it is not surprising that the tone of *Neighbours*—if it is taken to be a representation of Australia—suggests most importantly that nothing important happens in Australia. It is a land of small jokes, lack of disruption to relationships, and basic happiness. There is even a lack of any threatening 'liminal' characters within the community of *Neighbours*. Christine Geraghty describes liminal characters as those who sit on the boundary of the soap community, not quite embraced by it, but occasionally included—character types such as the 'gossip' and the 'tart' (Geraghty 1991: 100). In *Neighbours*, the liminal characters are particularly non-threatening. The early episodes of the program feature Mrs Mangel (Vivien Gray); by the time of the wedding, she has been joined by Hilary. In this episode, we see that the gossips are amusing, but not vindictive. They do not plan, or scheme, or aim to cause difficulties for other characters (as might be the case in the British soaps). And they are completely unlike the characters in American soap operas, who often plan to destroy each other's marriages or break up families. The worst that Mrs Mangel does here is to pass on incorrect gossip: 'I don't want to be the bearer of bad news, but ... Paul and Gail had an argument last night'.

This is a safe and happy community, whose threats are of the most banal kind (lost mouse). It is also a world seemingly unthreatened by the more passionate versions of sexuality. As noted above, *Neighbours* has a tendency to show the pectorals of well-developed young men. But this seems to be quite an innocent form of sexuality. The program presents us with neither simulated love-making nor post-coital bliss. Scott and Charlene's honeymoon night is an unerotic affair. They spend it in the Robinson household. Charlene is more excited by her wedding presents than she is by the body of her new husband—'I don't believe it! It's a four-year apprenticeship at the garage, indenture papers and everything! This makes everything extra perfect. Now I've got everything'. Scott says, 'So have I', and the scene fades to the pair of them lying on the bed the next morning, still in their wedding clothes. When Scott's sister Lucy enters the room, he rushes to reassure her that 'We weren't pashing'. And they weren't.

This is the Australia of *Neighbours*. In a way, it seems odd to be assessing the program in terms of the image it presents of Australia: it is obviously not a genre that makes any claims, on its own terms, to realism or representativeness. However, given the context of its initial distribution, the frenzied worry about 'what they think of us', the concern with the image of Australia that the program was projecting, the program is called upon to bear such representations. And if the question is 'What kind of Australia does *Neighbours* present?', then this is the answer: a safe, community-oriented, non-passionate, and non-threatening community. White, suburban, working–middle class, and with plenty of muscular young men to look at. This is 'Australia'.

Debating on

As a footnote, it is interesting to observe that public debate about *Neighbours* and the 'image of Australia' continued in a tangential way, through another television program entirely. *Sylvania Waters* (1994) was a BBC-produced 'soapumentary' that showed the 'real lives' of a Sydney family, and attracted possibly even more public attention than *Neighbours* did. The debate about *Sylvania Waters* was not distinct from that about *Neighbours*: the two were explicitly linked at many points. When *A Current Affair* did an item on the worrying reception of *Sylvania Waters* in the United Kingdom, one British viewer complained that 'It's straight off bloody *Neighbours*!' However, most comparisons of the programs emphasised the differences between them. As Turnbull notes, '*Neighbours* was hardly like *Sylvania Waters* at all' (Turnbull

1994: 10). The BBC explicitly sold *Sylvania Waters* as an investigation of Australian life, prompted by the success of *Neighbours*. It was a 'new, REAL LIFE version of *Neighbours*' (Stratton & Ang 1994: 7), and 'Many reviews assessed *Sylvania Waters* with reference to *Neighbours*' (Rowe 1994: 16). McKenzie Wark suggests the program was perceived to be 'unveiling the quotidian Australian "reality" behind the public face presented by *Neighbours*' (Wark 1999: 173).

With such claims to represent reality (it was, after all, a documentary, and thus its generic status regarded as much closer to 'truth'), *Sylvania Waters* prompted much discussion about 'our' image in the BBC. And the vehemence with which this discussion was conducted suggests the degree to which *Neighbours* had become an acceptable version of 'our' Australian image overseas. To the extent that *Sylvania Waters* was publicly excoriated for being the wrong image, we can see that the relative lack of such vehemence in discussions of *Neighbours*' success suggests that it was the 'right' image:

> The public and critical reaction of *Sylvania Waters* is a lot like that which surrounded *The Adventures of Barry McKenzie*. Critics, eminent personages, writers of letters to the editor and the like have made quite a fuss, objecting to the image of Australians presented in the program and to the effect it might have on 'what people overseas' think of us.
>
> (Turner 1992: 37; see also Stratton & Ang 1994: 8; Rowe 1994: 14; O'Regan 1996: 256)

Sylvania Waters presented a documentary account of the life of a wealthy suburban Australian family. The family members fought with each other; many were proudly materialistic and enjoyed the pleasures of alcohol. This image was, as one newspaper declared, a 'national embarrassment' (Rowe 1994: 15): 'Millions of open-mouthed Britons tuned in to the BBC last night to confirm their impression that Australia is a nation of materialistic vulgarians with drinking problems' (Rowe 1994: 16). By contrast, as David Rowe notes, 'The view of Australia that is gained from [*Neighbours* and *Home and Away*] does ... constitute an attractive and benign image which is not easily accommodated within the ... colonialist "frontier" conception of Australia' (Rowe 1994: 16).

An attractive and benign image. The wedding of Scott and Charlene on *Neighbours* is a great moment in Australian television, one that is well remembered as an important part of television's heritage. It was the most watched single episode of an Australian television program in the United Kingdom. The success of the program led to public discussion about 'our' image, about how Australia should be seen overseas. It reopened debates about cultural imperialism, with the delightful twist that Australia was now colonising the United Kingdom. And it presented to the world—if we are worried about national image—a resounding and convincing representation of just how *nice* Australian reality 'really' is.

Availability

The wedding episode of *Neighbours* was released commercially on video, but has since been deleted. It is the only episode of the program that is available for viewing at Screensound. Production company Grundy's holds a complete run of the series, but tends to refuse access for researchers. Repeats of early episodes occasionally appear on Channel Ten, as during 1999 and 2000. New episodes continue to be produced at the time of writing.

Notes

1 This information is supplied by Grundy's Productions, Publicity Office.
2 Although it should be noted that this figure was gained by adding together the figures for the two separate showings each day.
3 Again, it is worth noting that, as an explanation of the program's success, this is deeply unconvincing. *EastEnders*, which has been one of the few British programs to beat *Neighbours* consistently in the United Kingdom ratings, sells itself as being precisely the opposite of this, regularly presenting Afro-Carribean and Pakistani families as part of its central community.

15

Burke's Backyard: Neighbourly Communities

1987–

The '*E! News* board game' is based on the Channel Ten entertainment news program of the same name. Play progresses by answering Australian-focused, entertainment-based questions, which tend towards the blindingly easy. Representative questions include 'Which city is *Water Rats* set in?' and 'What street do Madge and Harold live on?' One question reveals the degree to which Don Burke's place in collective memories about Australian television is certain and commonsensical: 'Which TV host credits himself with creating "Lifestyle Television" in Australia?' The answer—of course—is 'Don Burke'. The game is not willing to claim, as a simple fact, that Burke did, in fact, create the genre—such judgments do not suit the straightforwardly factual emphasis of the game—but his own claim to that status is familiar enough to make its way into a game that celebrates the familiar and the well known. *Burke's Backyard* is the lifestyle program upon which this claim to originative status in the lifestyle genre can be based.

It is not appropriate for this chapter to open, as others have done, with a 'great moment' that is well remembered and that suggests the importance of this program within a genealogy of Australian television programs. The lifestyle and infotainment program *Burke's Backyard* is undoubtedly an important program in Australia's television history. But it does not lend itself, as other programs do, to public controversies or spectacular images, the moments that are remembered and added to the public archive, and that provide a way into talking about what makes these programs important. Indeed, part of what makes *Burke's Backyard* so interesting is its position in a genre of 'newslessness' (Medhurst 1997: 244; see below). It succeeds without controversy, scandal, or any attempt to present the qualities that characterise 'good' programming in other television genres.

Rather than presenting a 'great moment' that has survived in the public archive, it is more appropriate to begin this chapter with a 'telling example'—one that is not widely and publicly archived, remembered and discussed, but that illustrates the ways in which *Burke's Backyard* functions in Australia's mediasphere.

On 3 September 1999, Don Burke interviewed Jeff Kennett—then Premier of Victoria—on *Burke's Backyard*. This was two weeks before a Victorian state election. The interview was a very friendly one, and this disturbed some viewers:

> After a seven year absence, how timely of Don Burke to choose the middle of an election campaign to screen a return visit to Jeff Kennett's garden. The Liberal Party must have been delighted with Don not only promoting Jeff Kennett, the gardener, but also Jeff, the most admired Premier in the land, the Premier who has put a smile on everyone's face, and so on. Indirect political advertising that money could not buy. If Channel 9 believes in fair play, can we look forward to seeing Steve Bracks' garden before Saturday?
>
> (Holten 1999: 9)

The timing of this interview was undoubtedly notable. However, the fact that the interview was an uncritical and friendly one is not evidence of any particular political inclination on Don Burke's part. Rather, it is emblematic: a moment that demonstrates just how *Burke's Backyard* works as it sets out to construct a sense of Australian community, and to work out what it means to be a part of such a thing.

The importance of *Burke's Backyard*

Don Burke is one of only a very few television personalities to make the list of 'Famous Australians' presented in Penguin's *Pocket Aussie Fact Book*, along with such luminaries as Hector Crawford, Bert Newton, and Lisa McCune (Nicholson 1999: 85). Such an honour seems only fitting. *Burke's Backyard* is, after all, remembered in both the journalistic and the academic enclaves of the public sphere as 'the grandfather of ... infotainment programming' (Woods 1996: 48; see also Johnson & Smiedt 1999: 355) and 'the first of the lifestyle wave' (Bonner 1999a: 1). The program is 'one of the local media success stories of the 1980s and 1990s' (Malor 1991: 59) and 'the trend setter' (Turnbull 1993: 17) for infotainment programming in Australia.

There are, of course, alternative histories that could be written of the lifestyle genre in the Australian mediasphere. The documentary *35 Years of Television* (1991) presents *Burke's Backyard* as the *endpoint* of the evolution of the infotainment genre, rather than its genesis, tracing earlier examples back to 1958 and the program *Home Hints*: 'In 35 years, we've managed to get from Elaine White's home to Don Burke's backyard' (*35 Years of Television* 1991). Similarly, Frances Bonner notes that 'prior to the arrival of the category of lifestyle programming in the late 1980s, related programs were hidden in a category called "information" ', identifying examples from the 1970s such as the ABC's *The Inventors* (Bonner 1999: 1).

Nevertheless, despite such messy histories, it is obvious that *Burke's Backyard* has now assumed an originative status. When the program first appeared, there were few comparable programs in prime time. During the 1990s, this situation changed to the point where several of the top-ten rating programs in Australia were regularly infotainment programs (during 1999 and 2000, *Burke's Backyard*, *Good Medicine*, *Our House*, *Better Homes and Gardens*, *Harry's Practice*, *Backyard Blitz*, and *Money* all regularly appeared in the top ten). Indeed, in many weeks of 1999 and 2000, there are more infotainment programs in the top-ten listings of programs than any other genre (often two or three dramas, two or three sitcoms, and two news or current affairs programs). The genre was 'the boom program type of the 1990s (as the mini-series was for the 1980s)' (Bonner 1999: 1), to the point where Channel Nine's Director of News could confidently affirm that 'infotainment is what audiences want [and] they should get it … Infotainment programmes are the most popular programmes in the country; people want to watch them' (Tuohy 1994: 13). The germinal status of *Burke's Backyard* can be seen in the number of presenters from the program who have gone on to present other infotainment programs, including Reg Livermore, Kay Stammers, Dr Harry Cooper, Peter Harris, John Stower, Bruce Samazan, Peter Brock, and Noni Hazlehurst (*Burke's Backyard: 10th Anniversary Special* 1997).

There are many interesting aspects of the program, as evidenced by previous academic writing on it (Malor 1991; Turnbull 1996a; Neumann 1999; Bonner 1999; Benn 1999). The aspect on which this chapter focuses is that suggested by the moment of Jeff Kennett's appearance: the way in which *Burke's Backyard* creates a community for itself. What are the parameters of the community *Burke's Backyard* addresses? And how does the program speak to it?

Don's community

The community of Don Burke is insistently characterised by terms connoting lack of exceptionality. A typical program opens with the camera panning through the undergrowth to find Don shovelling compost: 'If you've not caught the program before, this is what it's about: the chooks, the kids, the dogs, the cats, the plants, the whole lot, in the average Australian back yard' (*Burke's Backyard* 1987). Another episode has Don explaining the rationale of the program: 'created for the ordinary Australian family a bit like mine, one which lives in their backyard' (as quoted in Bonner 1999: 5).

Don is speaking to the 'ordinary' Australian, or, rather, Don is creating such a community by addressing it, and thus talking it into existence. Which begs the question, what do you have to do to be 'ordinary'? What are the limits of ordinariness? Who does the program think it is talking to when it imagines such an audience?

The 'ordinary' Australian

As is already obvious from the above quotations, there is a strong nationalistic impulse in Don's community-building project. He is talking to not just 'ordinary' *people*, but ordinary *Australians* (see chapter 7). The program consistently reminds us that 'we' (the 'we' who are watching the program) call Australia home. As the theme song for the program (unchanged for its lifetime) puts it:

> I've been around the world a couple of times or maybe more.
> I've seen the sights; I've had delights
> on every foreign shore.
> But when my friends all ask me the place that I adore
> I tell them right away:
> Give me a home among the gum trees …

In much the same way, the program has travelled abroad but always returns 'home'. In his 1997 tenth-anniversary episode, Don notes that 'we've visited France, England, Bali, Greece, Spain, New Guinea, New Zealand … Mexico and America'. But this has always been 'visiting'; the home to which the program returns is Australia. Within Australia, the program travels to every state and territory, but without the need to make these into 'visits' in the same way, and without the need to establish a 'home state' (which would be New South Wales) to which it returns.

The program does recognise state identities: in the program's interviews with state premiers and territory chief ministers (discussed in more detail below), Don always allows time for them to promote their own states as the best in Australia. And he has publicly stated his lack of commitment—from a horticultural perspective—to a unified national ideal, explaining that he is not simply committed to the planting of native Australian plants,

> because a thing from Western Australia doesn't belong in Sydney. Indigenous plants [are] from your suburb or area ... The feel of the suburb is pivotal to living there and I push this hard through the program and the things I write.
>
> (as quoted in Weaver 1990: 91)

Nevertheless, it is clear that the nation of Australia is 'home'—even if it consists of different states. The idea of Australian national identity slips continually into the program and its publicity. It is the 'home among the gum trees', and after all, 'What is more Australian than the good ol' summer barbecue—the friends are round, the beers flowing, the salads are made, and the steaks are ready to go' (Channel Nine Publicity 1999). 'Nothing sums up the laid back, unpretentious nature of Australia better than the backyard barbie'—or so say 'ordinary backyard barbecue lovers' and 'average Aussies' (Burke 1999a: 35). The program even shows how you can decorate your Christmas tree with 'Green and gold Aussie spirit', 'gumnuts and gum leaves' and 'Koala ... candy canes' (Walter 1999: 50).

Fiona MacDonald suggests in an item on garden ornaments that viewers should 'Think about featuring one or two items—like these good old Aussie lizards' (*Burke's Backyard* 1987). Other countries are places from which one might bring back something for one's own backyard—a concrete Buddha perhaps ('a Chinese takeaway', as Fiona puts it—*Burke's Backyard* 1987)—or to which one might be 'transported' by décor: 'You can sit in the spa bath [in your Australian backyard] and be transported to Bali' (Burke 1999b: 11). Too strong an affiliation overseas can bring Don's gentle disparagement, as when he presents a segment on an English-style cottage garden with the comment that 'some people ... yearn for the old country' (*Burke's Backyard* 1990).

The program addresses the 'ordinary' 'Australian' community, but what does this community look like?

Geography

The 'backyard' of *Burke's Backyard* connotes a variety of elements. It has been read as a distinctively Australian organisation of domestic space. Bonner argues that 'the program's focus on the backyard gives it a distinctive Australianness' (Bonner 1999: 5). Don himself claims that 'Australians have the highest rate of backyard ownership on earth' (as quoted in Weaver 1990: 91).

The backyard is also a private space: 'The front garden was public in display ... the backyard was private' (Fiske, Hodge, and Turner 1987: 49). It is utilitarian rather than aesthetic, traditionally containing such items as 'a woodheap ... a wash-tub ... clothes line ... mint or parsley ... a dunny ... There might be chooks ... A lemon tree was nearly universal' (Seddon 1997: 155): 'the front garden was determined by canons of middle-class decency and taste, the backyard seemed to effortlessly disregard them in the name of practicality' (Fiske, Hodge, & Turner 1987: 49).

More difficult to pin down is the geographic space of the backyard. For some writers, it is an icon of suburbia: 'the iconography of the suburb', argues Lucas, includes 'Hill's hoists, [and] backyards' (Lucas 1994: 114). For other writers, though, 'the front garden was urban or suburban, the backyard was closer to the rural ... . The front garden was carefully cultured, the backyard was naturally neglected' (Fiske, Hodge, &A Turner 1987: 49).

It is interesting that much writing on *Burke's Backyard* assumes that it is a suburban program, as with McKenzie Wark's comment that 'What I found curious about *Burke's Backyard* was the way a gardening show could express so much about the suburban ideal of the good life' (Wark 1999: 151).

It may indeed be addressing an audience who are concerned with their gardens and homes—as in, for example, Fiona MacDonald's comments on what 'you' can do with 'your basic suburban block' (*Burke's Backyard* 1987)—but the suburbs are by no means the only space presented in the program. Burke more often takes us to the urban and inner-city homes of 'celebrity gardeners' or the rural vistas of 'exceptional' gardens. Sue Turnbull has argued that, 'Although the focus of the program is suburban, the touchstone is the bush—or, more accurately, the Bush ... [the] "mythologising of Australia ..." ... simultaneously domesticating it' (as quoted in Bonner 1999a: 6).

In fact, I would go so far as to argue that *Burke's Backyard* is not very suburban. The program works to show that its central interests—the garden, the family, the home—are common ones that cut across a variety of boundaries (the urban/suburban and rural, the working class and the middle class, genders, ethnicities, and sexualities) in one 'ordinary' Australian community.

Gardening and DIY

Burke's Backyard—unsurprisingly—includes items on gardening. It also includes do it yourself (DIY), pets, and household hints. This is a program for people who are interested in thinking about their domestic spaces as places in which to work and play. This might lead one to suggest that Burke is addressing a community of home-owners. After all, as a press release for the program tells us, 'the Great Australian Dream' is to own your own home (Channel Nine Publicity 1999), and according to Chris McAuliffe, the nineteenth-century boom in suburban growth in Australia 'consolidated a peculiarly Australian faith in home ownership as the key to the good life' (McAuliffe 1996: 14).

It is important to note, though, that the program does not only address home-owners. As another of the program's own press releases notes, 'Although it is seen as the "Great Australian Dream", a large proportion don't own their own' (Channel Nine Publicity 1999), and Don sometimes refers to those viewers who do not have gardens and who may not be home owners. An item on growing strawberries includes explicit advice to viewers who live in flats (*Burke's Backyard* 1989). In a 1990 episode, he notes that 'Many of you have complained that you don't have a backyard—what you have is a flat or a home unit. So we're going to look at what to do with the balcony' (*Burke's Backyard* 1990). So, although the ideal of the program is indeed a garden, with which one lives for an extended period of time—Don tells us that it will 'probably take ten years' for a garden to become fully established (*Burke's Backyard* 1992)—the program also allows for those who do not have gardens. The condition of belonging to the community of Burke is an *interest* in homes and gardens, rather than the *ownership* of them. It is expected that the audience will understand the address when Don states that 'everyone has plant problems' (*Burke's Backyard* 1987) (in fact, I don't), or when Kay Stammers introduces an item on home safety with the question 'How many times you have walked around your home in bare feet with a drill?' (*Burke's Backyard* 1990). (Well, never actually, but thanks for asking.)

Family

More insistent is the program's construction of the traditional nuclear family as a necessary component of its community. As noted above, Don quickly characterises 'the kids' as an important part of the 'average' Australian life.

Children rarely appear in the program—usually in the background during a pet 'road test'—but they are often invoked. Introducing a segment on pergolas, Don lays out as a basic requirement: 'Does it allow the children to play table tennis when it's raining?' (*Burke's Backyard* 1987). Road-testing dogs, he asks, 'So you're thinking of buying a dog for the kids?' and recommends a dalmatian (*Burke's Backyard* 1988). More than simply invoking children, Don even polices the limits of the good family while talking to the guests in his 'celebrity gardener' spot. He asks Angry Anderson, 'How does being a family man go with being a rock and roller?' and commenting on Anderson's own childhood—which he characterises as 'hardly regulation'—asks, 'Are you surprised that you're as normal as you are? Into gardens and kids and home life?' (*Burke's Backyard* 1987). Similarly, he notes that Gai Waterhouse, racehorse trainer, has a hectic schedule and spends little time with her children. He asks her, 'The kids—when they grow up, are they going to say you're a good mum?' (*Burke's Backyard* 1991).

These, then, are the central terms of Don's community—backyard, home, and family, although ownership of any of these is less necessary than a commitment to, and an interest in, these ideals.

Burke's consensual community

But how is this community managed? As I noted in chapter 12, John Hartley has noted that different television genres have different approaches to managing the community they address. News and current affairs focus on a 'they' community: the bad guys who 'we' do not like, and who threaten 'us' and 'our' lifestyle (criminals, immigrants, anyone who might deviate from given social ideals). By contrast, 'softer' news and genres such as infotainment and lifestyle programming focus on 'we' communities: who we are, what 'we' like, what 'we' do. They aim to build up a picture of a community without picturing the bad guys (Hartley 1992a: 206). So programs like *Burke's Backyard* focus on 'us', identifying the points at which 'we' are similar. As Deborah Malor notes, 'Very rarely do the problems of boundaries come up—encroachments, trespass, lack of privacy and other threats to property and wellbeing' (Malor 1991: 66). Rather, 'the fantasies on offer are structured to be inclusive wherever possible' (Bonner 1999: 4). Catharine Lumby notes that the infotainment genre avoids the typical tactics of creating bad guys to reinforce community feeling: 'growing media literacy has … resulted in cynicism and contempt for media arrogance. Invasion of privacy, foot-in-the-door journalism and journalistic high-handedness have all come under attack in recent years' (Lumby 1999: 51).

It is true that *Burke's Backyard* has occasionally constructed itself as a source of crusading investigative journalism. For example, Don surveys his forays into this field in the program's 1997 tenth-anniversary special: 'We took a very strong stand against cats and the way they affect our environment ... The program we did on that played a major role in changing the laws in relation to cats'. And after an item on mulching machines—which resulted, Don tells us, in one company going out of business—'we became the first television program to be sued in the Federal Court' (*Burke's Backyard: 10th Anniversary Special* 1997).

But this is not the typical tone of the program. An interest in families, home, garden—these are the central elements in Burke's community. But the boundaries are not policed rigidly. Bad guys are rarely created: indeed, as Don says of the cats he has campaigned to have controlled, 'It's not the cats that are the problem—it's us'. Don's community formation is a consensual process and not an adversarial one. And this is expressed in his personal politics:

> I think I was the ultimate rebel. To me, it's only the pseudo-rebels that fight against everyone else. I feel, if you are a real rebel—not an anarchist, but somebody who wants to do his own thing his own way—why fight with anyone? Why not quietly do it your own way? And that's what I did.
>
> (as quoted in Weaver 1990: 90)

So, given this ethos of intense consensus, a letter of complaint to the program must be addressed: 'We've got our first complaint letter at *Burke's Backyard*, a matter we take very seriously', Don states. Apparently, an item on making compost showed a teddy-bear being thrown onto a pile. 'Don't worry,' says Don, 'we only ever use stunt teddies.' And indeed, in the studio, a teddy-bear in a harness abseils into shot (*Burke's Backyard* 1987).

Then and now: the lack of change over ten years suggests the stability of Burke and his community

Andy Medhurst has noted that in British cinema history 'newsreels ... neglect suburbia ... that is one of the founding attractions of the suburbs ... the *newslessness* of suburbia' (Medhurst 1997:

244). *Burke's Backyard* is not entirely suburban, but it is similarly newsless. Avoiding the techniques of adversarial journalism, little changes in *Burke's Backyard*. Don still dresses the same as he did in 1987. His hairstyle is the same (if slightly greyer), as is his beard. The theme music is exactly the same; the opening credits have hardly changed at all (give or take slight colour variations).

Don's open community

Frances Bonner has said of *Burke's Backyard* that it is 'where the camp males get air time, the non-Anglos are the folks next door (maybe quaint, but at least on-air) and the working class are taught how to adopt middle class(ish) decorating values' (Frances Bonner, pers. comm., 28 July 1999). There are undoubtedly particular structures of representation on the program, but as Bonner suggests, it presents a range of Australians as part of Don's community, all of whom are 'at least on air'.

Gender and sexuality

Don may be the centre of the program—and he is undoubtedly male—but gardening is a peculiarly ungendered pastime in Australia, practised equally by men and women, and Don's presenters promote this (Bennett, Emmison, & Frow 1999: 251). He has both male and female experts on a variety of plants and gardening techniques, although men retain the right to be handymen and speak about DIY. And the program can even cope with homosexuality. There is no sex on *Burke's Backyard*—except with one glorious, pornographic, and fully explicit exception, between slugs (*Burke's Backyard* 1988)—so gay men do not have sex on the program. But it can happily present two men, who live together and have developed their garden together, both interior designers, stylishly dressed and rather camp. Once again, if you're willing to evince an interest in gardening, you can join this community (*Burke's Backyard* 1997).

Ethnicity

Writers on the program have celebrated Don's mix of presenters:

> The reporters on the show are as unconventional a mix as the topics that are covered. Burke defied Channel 9's attempts to fit it into a classic mould and

> proudly claims the show is a mixture of all the wrong people. 'All the wrong people' include naturalist Densey Clyne (whom Burke says makes a mockery of the myth that women are finished in television at 30), veterinarian Harry Cooper ... Jim Pike (whom Burke fought to get on air although he looks like a benign bikie) and Reg Livermore (formerly a flamboyant star of the stage). The only 'normal' person appears to be Kay Stammers, who has 15 years in the industry as a reporter/presenter/writer.
>
> (Weaver 1990: 92)

Richard Glover similarly notes that, 'In the Ken-doll world of television, Burke's "reporters" are a pleasingly eccentric mix—a middle-aged naturalist ... a one-time drag and theatre star, a plump vet' (Glover 1991: 13). However, despite this heterogeneity, all presenters are white Australians. There are no Asian or even (until recently) non Anglo-Celtic Europeans.

Anne Neumann has claimed that '*Burke's Backyard* promotes multiculturalism ... achieving new syntheses *happily* ... or happily accepting the impossibility of synthesis' (Neumann 1999: 199). This seems to be overstating the case. Placing whiteness at the centre of the program certainly has an effect. However, in another way she is absolutely correct: it is indeed possible for other ethnicities to appear in the program in other capacities. Shoppers of Asian descent appear in an item on garage sales (*Burke's Backyard* 1989); the garage sale is hosted by a couple who appear to be of Italian descent. This is not stated: the program demonstrates no desire to label. It is, perhaps, ethnocentric and anti-racist: everyone who is willing to demonstrate an interest in its topics (family, garden, home) can become an 'ordinary' Australian.

Class

Class has not been a favoured term for cultural analysis in Australia (compared with, for example, the tradition of cultural studies in the United Kingdom). Certainly, in a society only so recently created in its current form, much of the tradition that goes with class positions in countries such as the United Kingdom simply does not apply in Australia. Nevertheless, a recent survey suggests that Australians are very aware of their class identities: 'about a third of the Australian population claim a working-class identity, about half choose the category of middle-class, with the remainder selecting upper-middle- or upper-class identities' (Bennett, Emmison, & Frow 1999: 22).

Given these statistics, it is notable that Australian television does not have—as the United Kingdom does with its soap operas—a televisual site devoted to representing working-class Australians (see chapter 14). Sue Turnbull has suggested of *Burke's Backyard* that 'the obviously middle-class Australian way of life is demonstrated for us in its ideal form by very middle-class Australians' (Turnbull 1996a: 5). As with the geographical imagery of the program, I'm not sure that a class analysis of the program can be performed so easily. Indeed, lacking the signifiers of class familiar in a mediasphere such as the United Kingdom's, it is difficult to know how one would go about analysing representations of class in terms that do not immediately begin to sound stereotypical or patronising. It is perhaps possible to look at differing accents: broader Australian accents tend to be associated with more working-class representations on Australian television, as we have noted as far back as *Homicide* (chapter 3). Or perhaps class could be read through signifiers such as clothes, make-up, and hairstyles, where more obviously expensive looks should be read as middle-class. Such attempts to read class on Australian television are necessarily tentative. The Australian mediasphere has not concentrated on class in the way that British television has. In the United Kingdom, much television is obsessed with the class origins of its protagonists. In the repetitive playing out of class clashes in sitcoms (*To the Manor Born*, *The Good Life*, *On the Up*, *Keeping Up Appearances*, *Birds of a Feather*, *Class Act*, etc.) and the insistent working-class habitus of soap operas (*Coronation Street*, *EastEnders*), British television has developed a familiar and simple language for denoting class difference that continues to insist on the availability, relevance, and visibility of class in that country. Australian television has never developed such a comprehensive vocabulary for representing class. It has tended to focus strongly on middle-class characters, exnominating other classes to the extent that they feel almost unrepresentable.

Given such a context, readings of class in *Burke's Backyard* must be exploratory rather than definitive. With such a caveat, it is possible to say that *Burke's Backyard* is, indeed, as Sue Turnbull suggests, full of middle-class Australians, but it is also full of working-class Australians. The program makes no systematic attempt to distinguish between these class positions in its representations of the 'Australian' community. It is true that different segments on the program tend to be classed differently. In the 'funny pets videos', or in the stories on road testing dogs, or in Don's 'plant roadshow', where women bring their sick plants for his advice, working-class Australians commonly appear on the program, while the celebrity gardeners and many of the 'spectacular' show gardens that Don visits are presented by middle-class Australians. But class does not exist for the program; it is simply not aware of it. Once again, everyone is welcome, so long as they are willing to commit to home, garden, and family.

Ordinary experts

Don's community is not exclusive: you need no special characteristics to join. When you are in, you are 'ordinary'. And Don, himself, therefore, cannot be special. As David Lyle, Director of Program Development at Channel Nine, puts it, '90s viewers don't like being patronised or lectured and reject programs in which journalists assume tones of priestlike authority. They want information, they want a touch of passion, they want programs to speak to them in their language' (Lumby 1999: 51; see also Cunningham & Miller 1994: 39). As we saw at the start of this chapter, Don explicitly names himself 'ordinary'. Of course, he is not. He is the star of one of Australia's most popular and longest-running shows. But he is determined to appear to be so, and in the program, his (mostly successful) struggle to be exactly like the audience he addresses—to the point of having no specialist expertise—can be seen.

This is necessarily an ambivalent project—for Don must give advice, and be, in some way, the expert on gardening. But he is rarely 'priestlike', and he attempts to minimise his difference:

> Colloquial language wasn't a living language in the media when I started ... so I was determined about it from the 'G'Day' at the beginning to the final 'Hooroo'. It's got to be conversational because we're about recreation. Most of the gardening blokes before me used a lot of technical words ... I'm far better at them than they are, but I don't feel any need to use jargon to impress. Gardening had a horrible image of being both boring and technical. I set out to turn that upside down, and I think we've been successful.
>
> (as quoted in Weaver 1990: 92)

Don's language is colloquial. More than this, he uses phrases such as 'As I'm sure you know' before imparting information—seeking not to establish his own superiority, but to draw the audience into identification around shared knowledge (*Burke's Backyard* 1987). Early in the program's history, some segments were explicitly based on debunking popular knowledge and demonstrating Don's superior access to 'truth'. In the 1987 season, 'Old husband's tales' was a segment where popular truths—for example, 'Australian native plants are low maintenance plants'—were debunked (*Burke's Backyard* 1987). However, this item does not survive into later series. It sets up too rigid a boundary between expertise and the ordinary viewer.

Don calls upon a diverse range of experts in the program. The 'Garden advisory panel' of 1991—composed of four middle-aged, white men offering sage advice—has also vanished (*Burke's Backyard* 1991) and a more varied range of people are now called in to take their place. The program does call, quite happily, on traditionally institutionalised expertise—for example, a museum scientist commenting on wildlife (*Burke's Backyard* 1991)—but such institutionalised knowledge is not placed at the top of any hierarchy of expertise: the museum expert is simply one of the range of experts upon which the program draws. Many of the others are 'ordinary people'. Many of the experts on *Burke's Backyard* are dog-owners. The pet road-testing section each week usually includes two or three interviews, often with members of the appropriate dog-breed society. Certainly, their expertise is institutionalised in the societies to which they belong (sometimes a president or secretary of these organisations), but these are not traditionally members of 'the knowledge classes' (Frow 1995). They are 'ordinary people', talking about their 'ordinary expertise'. This allows those who are not traditionally regarded as having worthwhile knowledge to speak on the program. So, for instance, to provide expert commentary on show bags at the Royal Show, Don naturally turns to a group of Australians who have some expertise in this area: children, who give their advice on which are the best show bags (*Burke's Backyard* 1992).

Don does still have moments where he does claim specialist expertise. For example, in 1997 he claims that

> We are also prepared ... to flout the opinions of you, the viewer ... we have supported sustainable development ... when we had Dr Graham Webb, and I think people like him will determine the salvation of the planet, we had our largest-ever response in the negative. Sorry, but we stand by that opinion.
>
> (*Burke's Backyard* 1997)

But this is unusual. Mostly, as in other areas of the program, Don strives to create an open community—one where specialised knowledge is not unequally distributed, but everyone is acknowledged to have expertise in their own area. A good example of the way in which the program attempts to ensure that Don's expertise does not get in the way of an open community can be seen in an item on roadside nurseries. Don interviews the two owners of one of these roadside operations, and it is possible to detect from his tone of voice and his questions that he is not entirely happy with the practice of untrained people running such a nursery: 'Do you feel that not having studied horticulture impairs the service you offer to customers?' he asks. The camera shows a close-up of money changing hands. If this were a current affairs program, such a shot would signify 'shoddy dealing', but the consensual, non-adversarial world of *Burke's Backyard* cannot suggest this, even if these dealers are indeed practising without any appropriate horticultural training. Don approaches two customers and points out that the palms they are about to buy are mislabelled. 'That doesn't worry you?' he asks. 'No. Not at all', they reply. Don is dissatisfied with this answer, and presses the point: 'Wouldn't worry you that the labels might be a bit wrong?' 'I don't think so—as long as they grow nicely', the customers insist. Eventually Don has to give up: he will not claim the position of expertise, condemning these people for their ignorant approach to gardens. His final summing up is:

> A lot of people are very satisfied ... You'll pay say $15 for a palm, a nursery will charge $38 dollars for the same plant ... On average, you pay 112% more for a plant in a nursery. But in a nursery, you've got qualified staff, maybe child-minding staff, a much better range of products, and some of them have a money-back guarantee in case the plant dies, so there are some advantages. But you can come here [and] buy a lot of plants very cheaply.

Aesthetic expertise

One area in which Don's claims to open community and non-hierarchical membership are pushed to ambivalent extremes is that of aesthetics and value judgments. John Hartley has named Don 'an electronic visual artist if ever there was one' (Hartley 1992b: 226), whereas Anne Neumann sees the program as avoiding questions of aesthetics and value:

> Don Burke claims—and given his inclusiveness, I believe him—to present a gardening show that is as value-free as possible ... [including only] *implied* value judgements when he asks proud owners on his regular 'Come and see my garden' segment, 'So you did *all* this your*self*?'
>
> (Neumann 1999: 124)

Once again, viewing the program suggests that this area is more ambivalent than Neumann suggests. Don does indeed occasionally position himself entirely outside of aesthetic discourses: 'This is what gardening is really about—not so much about plants and trees and flowers, as much as it is about having fun in your own backyard'. Such a position again removes him from the position of being the expert, for, after all, everybody is their own expert on whether or not they are having fun. But more often, Don takes quite a different stance. Having removed himself from the position of being the scientific expert, he is placed in another position of expertise: in making aesthetic judgments.

And such judgments do occur in *Burke's Backyard*, quite regularly. Graeme Greenhalgh—'in my [Don's] view ... our best garden designer'—appears several times on the program, employing a discourse of traditional aesthetics to describe, for example, how he has ' taken the straight lines from the swimming pool' to inspire the design of one of his gardens (*Burke's Backyard* 1988; *Burke's Backyard* 1991). Because this is *Burke's Backyard*, though, and a desire for aesthetics really cannot be allowed to interfere with the promotion of an open community, even this aesthete offers open and non-judgmental advice at the end of his segment:

> make a list of what you want the garden to do—you might need the space for children, you might want to work on your car, you might want to start a collection of prize winning begonias ... know what you want to do.

But the fact remains that if you do want to work on the car in your garden, then your relationship to Don's open community may be ambivalent. Don regularly visits particularly spectacular gardens: the first segment of his retrospective tenth-anniversary show presents 'some of the best gardens in Australia'. These are huge gardens, with winding paths, pergolas, acres of grass, flowers and trees, ornamental ponds and fountains, many open to the public with visitors walking through them (*Burke's Backyard: 10th Anniversary Special* 1997). These are not the 'ordinary' gardens that Burke lays claim to in his 1987 episode. As the owner of one of the these gardens—'Foxglove Spires'—claims, 'I like to feel when I step into my garden that I might just get lost'. This is something that few 'ordinary' Australians can hope for. (Indeed, how many 'ordinary' Australians have *names* for their gardens?)

In the same special episode, Don introduces a variety of gardens that are much more ordinary, but the rationale linking these is a very different one: 'Not all of the gardens we have in Australia are all that good', he says: 'some are absolute horrors. So we celebrated that fact'. The program 'celebrates' ordinary gardens in a segment entitled 'Australia's worst gardens'. The gardens in this section feature piles of rubbish, disused car parts, and sand. The owners are working-class, as opposed to the powerfully middle-class owners of 'Foxglove Spires'. And—although Don might be 'celebrating' the worst gardens—the owners of them are ambivalent about appearing on the program: they are shy; they laugh (with the presenter) at their gardens and at their own lack of skill and aesthetic pretence.

It is in the space of aesthetic judgments that Burke's open community falters. Bennett, Emisson and Frow's research work suggests that the desire to beautify the home and garden is largely a middle-class one. Those Australians who nominate themselves as working-class, they suggest,

> speak of [the home] more as a place to *be* and *do* in rather than as a stage that has to be prepared ... expressing a conception of the home as being primarily for the benefit of those who live there ... terms suggesting that a home should be valued for how it might appear to outsiders are rejected.
>
> (Bennett, Emmison, & Frow 1999: 31)

Burke's Backyard commonly suggests that viewers might care to worry about how the home and garden 'might appear to outsiders'. 'As soon as you put some ornaments in the garden, you will immediately polarise your friends: some will love them, and some will loathe them', says Don, introducing an item on garden ornaments (*Burke's Backyard* 1987), although here he still insists that the choice is yours and there is no final right or wrong decision. Meanwhile, Fiona MacDonald appeals to viewers who are 'into impressing your friends with antiques' (*Burke's Backyard* 1987). The gardens shown on this program tend to support Bennett, Emmison, and Frow's findings: the 'best' gardens are large, rural, aesthetically pleasing, and owned by the upper-middle classes; the 'worst' are suburban, utilitarian, and working-class. The latter enjoy only the most ambivalent membership of Burke's open community.

But again, ownership of a suitably aesthetic garden is not a requirement of joining the community: only the *desire* to have one (which, again, Bennett et al. suggest is a middle-class characteristic in Australia). Don can offer to move you from being 'worst' to 'best'. As Don himself describes it,

> One of the really satisfying bits of *Burke's Backyard* for me is where we take a fairly ordinary sort of a garden and create a flight of fantasy ... we turned a fairly ordinary house into this wonderful Mexican makeover.
>
> (*Burke's Backyard: 10th Anniversary Special* 1997)

This is a very odd practice, given the stated desire of the program to address the 'ordinary'. Ordinary here is obviously a bad thing; fantasy is better.

But Don also includes the price of each makeover: $300, or $800, or $1600 (*Burke's Backyard: 10th Anniversary Special* 1997). This is presented as something that the 'ordinary' family could do. Once again, Don's community is open: you can be an 'ordinary' Australian if you fantasise about having an interesting garden. Again, it is an ethnocentric openness, insofar as such fantasies are predominantly a middle-class pastime, but the community is open to anyone—of whatever class—who wishes to fantasise with Don.

Interviewing pollies

All of which brings us back to Jeff Kennett, and the reason that Don told him he was 'the most admired premier in Australia' and the man 'who has put a smile on everyone's face'. This was not political partisanship, and it was not simple sycophancy. It was not an attempt to get Kennett re-elected. It was, rather, a perfect example of Don's open, consensual, non-adversarial construction of an 'Australian' community through we-dom.

In 1988, Don presents the program from Western Australia. His celebrity gardener is Peter Dowding, Labor premier of the state. Don's questions are neither adversarial nor political. He comments on the garden: 'the use of colours is exceptional'. Peter talks about his cage of finches and the operation his dog has just had, before explicitly going on to distance the garden from politics: 'Politics is a really hype thing, and the point of having something lovely as this is that you get away from it'. Don's questions are flattering ones: 'You're no Methuselah', he points out, asking how Peter copes with being so young and so successful. Peter responds by emphasising the private sphere: 'You really need to be able to just touch it down, relax, read the paper, talk to the family, and enjoy the lifestyle'. Peter is easily brought into Don's community: loving home, family, and garden (*Burke's Backyard* 1988). As Wark points out, 'the stress [is] on creating a private world behind the fence ... an image of a public life composed of private places and passions' (Wark 1999: 152). The public sphere is outside of the house; traditionally this is where politics takes place. Siting his interviews—even with public

Open community—even Paul Keating is welcome in Burke's backyard

figures —in the private space allows Burke to put them outside of politics. And as a member of what John Hartley has named 'the smiling professions' (Hartley 1992a: 119)—those media figures whose address is friendly, community-building, and accessible—Don can smile and laugh and ask flattering questions. It is his space and his genre.

So when he moves from the Labor Premier of Western Australia to the Liberal–National Party Chief Minister of the Northern Territory, Don's address need not change. Meeting Marshall Perron, Don's questions are similarly friendly: 'after a rugged day in parliament, it [the garden]'s therapeutic, eh, Marshall?', once again separating the garden from the parliament. He congratulates Marshall on his 'variegated pandanus'. Marshall comments that 'There is something wonderful about growing your own coconuts' (*Burke's Background* 1990). All of the politicians on the program come across as being human. They wear short-sleeved shirts and slacks. All resist the desire to pontificate on public issues.

Of course, the desire not to talk party politics is a political one in a more general sense. Don's consensual politics of open community does not favour opposition leaders. They are, by virtue of their status, a little too adversarial.

Other guests—those who are not politicians—are allowed more latitude in speaking on public issues. Within the community of 'ordinary' Australians, they are allowed to have 'ordinary' opinions on issues. When Archbishop Peter Hollingworth appears on the program as a celebrity gardener, the conversation does not mention gardening at all (although Don is impressed by 'your own little chapel in your own backyard'). Most of the conversation, however, is about political—or, perhaps, 'social'—issues (see chapter 12). Once again, Don's questions are flattering and friendly: 'You're the best-known priest in Australia', he says. 'Did you make a conscious decision to stick your head up?' The Archbishop replies: 'We had a clear social-action role, an advocate for the poor. I kept on doing that, and the media kept coming back for comment.' 'You're very much guilty of getting your hands dirty by meddling in the real world', Don goes on—again, a very nice question. Peter replies, 'We've got to formulate a good political and social structure that enhances people's lives and their dignity, and if that's not happening, you've got to speak up and say how it might change.' As he speaks, we get a big close-up of his face, looking concerned:

> the issue of unemployment—it's not getting any better, in fact it's getting worse ... there's major issues there, not only for government, but for the whole community—we're going to have a whole lost generation if we're not careful.
>
> (*Burke's Backyard* 1990)

From Jeff Kennett to Mandawuy Yunupingu: a variety of viewpoints are allowed on the program

Similarly, Mandawuy Yunupingu appears on the program, stating that 'What we're trying to do is enrich our culture by getting those certain elements that make *your* world work. Those little bits and pieces that is not gonna destroy our culture, but we can use to enrich and strengthen our culture' (*Burke's Backyard: 10th Anniversary Special* 1997). Social comment, even political comment, is allowed, but adversarial party politics is not. *Burke's Backyard* is a consensual community, a we-dom that is open to all who are interested in its area, and that does not construct itself by creating bad guys and policing boundaries.

Jeff Kennett's appearance on *Burke's Backyard* is a classic moment. He is flattered and befriended by Burke because that it how Don Burke's journalism works. As a forum for the smiling professions, busily constructing a we-dom, *Burke's Backyard* offers the possibility of a community of 'ordinary Australians' marked by an interest in gardens, homes, and family, where other issues (party political preference, race, religion, gender, sexuality, and even, perhaps, class) are not relevant. If guests are willing to accept the terms of the fantasy, and the proscriptions on what can be said, then all are welcome in the ordinary Australia of *Burke's Backyard*.

And this was resoundingly demonstrated when Kennett lost that Victorian election, to be replaced as premier by Labor's Steve Bracks. Despite the concerns of Diana Holten, *Burke's Backyard* proved itself not to be partisan in its presentation of successful political leaders. Episode 6/2000 of the program, broadcast on 17 March 2000, featured Bracks as the celebrity gardener. As the program's press release puts it:

> Having been in Parliament for only 5 years, Steve Bracks took over leadership of the Labour Party in Victoria only 7 months prior to the last election. He defeated the undefeatable Jeff Kennett and is now Premier of Victoria. Don catches up with Steve and his wife Terry in their recently renovated home.

Bracks is heroic—he 'defeated the undefeatable'—but more importantly, he has recently renovated his home. So Don 'catches up' with him, exactly as he did with Kennett. For, as we know, Burke is remembered—in board games, journalism, academic writing, and lists of Australian facts—as the grandfather of the lifestyle genre in Australia. And this is how the lifestyle genre functions.

Availability

Burke's Backyard is not held by Screensound. CTC Productions holds all episodes, but have no formal facilities for viewing them. Researchers can contact them directly to negotiate access.

16

Live and Sweaty: 'When is Nudity Acceptable in Sport?'

1991–94

On 19 March 1993, Elle McFeast took over as the host of *Live and Sweaty*.

This ABC sports–comedy–variety program had, for its previous two seasons, been hosted by Andrew Denton (Nicklin 1993: 44). McFeast—a loud, vulgar, excessive (fictional) character played by ex-lawyer Libby Gore—changed the nature of the show. With this icon of femininity at the helm, the program became a feminist commentary on sports culture in Australia.

This moment is not a strongly remembered part of Australian television. During the program's four-year run, its ratings were never spectacular, hovering around '3% of the potential viewing audience' (Cook & Jennings 1995: 5), and McFeast's ascendancy to the captain's chair did not thrust the program into the limelight 'the ratings remained stable' when she took over (Ricketson 1994: 69). The reason for including McFeast's *Live and Sweaty* in this book is simply this: she is the only woman to have hosted a sports panel program in the history of Australian television. And, given the centrality of sports to Australian television, this is certainly worth noting as an interesting part of Australia's cultural heritage. This chapter is my own memory of Australian television, and my attempt to place a new moment in the public archive of Australian television rather than mapping the presence of an existing one.

Sport and television

'Sport holds a privileged status in Australian culture' (Poynton & Hartley 1990: 146), and it 'has always been a critical component in our television history' (Cunningham & Miller 1994: 73). Indeed, it was sport that first brought television to Australia, when 'The 1956 Olympics were a catalyst for its introduction' (Cunningham & Miller 1994: 73). Cate Rayson argues that the 1956 Melbourne Olympic Games stands as 'the earliest television memor[y]' for most first generation Australian television viewers. She suggests that 'the TV set itself came to symbolise Australian success, power and a burgeoning feeling of connection with the rest of the world' (Rayson 1998: 15; see also Hall 1976: 33).

After the initial importance of the Olympics, sport has continued to provide Australian television with momentous events:

> The three top-rating programs through the 1980s in Brisbane were the opening of the Brisbane Commonwealth Games in 1982 and the 1987 and 1989 State of Origin rugby league fixtures. The eleven-day period of the 1990 Commonwealth Games saw the Nine Network gain 70 per cent of national advertising expenditure ... In Melbourne, Seven scored a rating of 53 during the 1989 Australian Rules grand final. No other station reached double figures.
>
> (Cunningham & Miller 1994: 73)

This important link between Australian television and sport continues with a disproportionate amount of sports coverage on the country's television: 'Today, broadcast TV in Australia carries about 4000 hours of sport per annum ... This compares with some 2500 hours in Britain' (Cunningham & Miller 1994: 73). It is interesting that even the 'news' in Australia is more about sport than it is about any other subject: 'content analysis shows that the most important part of news in Australia is ... sport' (Bell, Boehringer, & Crofts 1982a: 14).

And this sport—so central to Australian television—is resolutely masculine. For the media, sport is something that men do, and that men watch.

This is not the case when one looks at general Australian participation in sport. In fact, women play many sports, representing the majority of participants in two of Australia's top ten most popular sports—tennis and netball. In three of those top ten sports, women are more likely than men to be regular participants themselves. And yet, it is men's sport that is overwhelmingly shown on television (National Working Party on the Portrayal of Women in the Media 1993: 14).

On the sports field, women are important players of sport in Australia. But on Australian television, this is not the case: the medium carefully constructs the area as something practised by—and only of interest to—men:

> Women's sporting events and achievements receive little public recognition or media coverage. For example, in 1992 women's sport coverage occupied

> approximately 4.2% of total sports coverage in Australian print media and only 1.2% of total sports coverage on television.
>
> (Cook & Jennings 1995: 6)

Similar findings suggest that 'Over the 1993 Easter break, approximately 67 hours were dedicated to male sports on TV and one hour to female sports' (Toby Miller, as quoted in Yeates 1995: 37).

As well as covering men's rather than women's sports, the coverage of sport on television tends to presents itself in ways that are regarded as traditionally 'masculine'. Helen Yeates argues that, 'In the nineties, Australian ... sporting programs have constructed a particularly shrill and insistent form of brash, heterosexual sporting masculinity in football reporting' (Yeates 1995: 35). Bill Bonney argues that cricket coverage relies on 'a certain image of masculinity' (Bonney 1992: 132), while for Beverley Poynton and John Hartley, football coverage relies on 'the systematic exclusion of [the] fact [of women's interest]' (Poynton & Hartley 1990: 144).

Given these tendencies, it not surprising that statistics show that women are not greatly interested in sport on television: 'One in three men nominate sport as their number one TV program choice compared with one in ten women' (National Working Party on the Portrayal of Women in the Media 1993: 14). In even more telling figures 8.9 per cent of respondents who nominated sport as their favourite programming were men; 52 per cent of women said there were too many sports programs on television, and only 6 per cent wanted more (the figures for men were quite different— 26 per cent and 21 per cent respectively) (Nugent and others 1992).

Only 6 per cent of women would like to see more sport on television. And despite the fact that Australia broadcasts almost twice as much sport as comparable countries, 21 per cent of men would still like to see more. Sport is a supremely gendered genre on television.

Which brings us back to Elle McFeast, presenting a sports entertainment program that deals mainly with men's sports but which suggests both that women might be interested in these sports and that they might be so for reasons other than those proposed by most sporting programs.

Firsts

Elle McFeast was not the first woman to be involved in the broadcasting of sport in Australia. From the mid-1980s in Australia, women had been involved in a minor way with television sports coverage. Dixie Marshall on

Sportsworld caused some controversy by entering the locker rooms of sportsmen to interview players; Joanna Griggs and Debbie Spillane were both sports reporters during the 1980s; and Kate Fitzpatrick provided cricket commentary (although she seemed to be employed more for her aesthetic interests, and ability to comment on uniforms, than on her detailed sporting expertise) (Keating 1999b). The first two seasons of *Live and Sweaty*, hosted by Andrew Denton, also featured Elle McFeast, Karen Tighe, and Debbie Spillane as reporters. However, in the genre of the sports panel show, Elle was the first woman to be put in control and given the hosting position. The sports panel–variety–entertainment program had previously been hosted by men. For example, *World of Sport* (1958–87), hosted by Ron Casey, evolved into a five-hour Sunday-afternoon marathon, involving reporting on sports matches, studio panel discussions, handball contests, and so on (Keating 1999b). The ABC's *The Winners* was a 'slick, pacy production, professionally presented and institutionalised within national television broadcasting' (Poynton & Hartley 1990: 152). The ABC's *This Sporting Life* 'translated the inner-city cult duo of H. G. Nelson and "Rampaging" Roy Slaven from alternative radio to national television' (Cunningham & Miller 1994: 70). These programs did not simply replay sports matches, but provided sports coverage in a more general sense, mixing commentary on matches with panel discussions of sports culture.

Generically, *Live and Sweaty* mixes sports coverage and commentary with other entertainment items that have nothing to do with sport. This was not an innovation introduced by McFeast; during Denton's reign, the show had bands playing in the studio and tenuously 'sport-related' material such as Denton going ten-pin bowling with the then-leader of the Opposition, John Hewson (O'Donnell 1992). This tendency continued in McFeast's version of *Live and Sweaty*. For example, in McFeast's first episode, the Screaming Jets play two songs live in the studio; no attempt is made to make this relevant to sports culture. Similarly, an item on the Logie Awards makes no sports references. Some items, such as an interview with singer Margaret Ulrich, are linked to sport only tangentially—she used to be, we are told, involved with gymnastics when she was younger. An interview with Bob Geldof takes place as he and Elle play darts.

It is not surprising to note that the program was produced by the ABC's comedy department rather than its sports department (Nicklin 1993: 44). In public discussions of the program it is variously named 'a weekly hour of Australian sports comedy chaos' (Cook & Jennings 1995: 5), an 'eccentric ABC-TV sports/comedy show' (Nicklin 1993: 44), and a 'wacky late Friday night sports show' (Ricketson 1994: 69). As Karen Jennings and Jackie

Cook note, the program generically mixes the 'closed authority ... of the sports report ... with the openness of television review-comedy' (Cook & Jennings 1995: 6). Perhaps it is this generic mixing that allows the program to do the unthinkable: to have a woman in charge of a sports-oriented program.

Evening dress and cricket bat

In a genre as relentlessly masculine as television sports, any woman taking over a sports program would demand attention in terms of gender representation. But in the case of *Live and Sweaty*, this is even more noticeably the case. The program under McFeast does not play a postfeminist game of pretending that gender doesn't matter. From the first McFeast episode, it is explicitly about gender roles in relation to sport.

The title sequence of the program opens with a female diva-style voice singing 'Live ... and sweaty!', while McFeast appears in an evening dress, punting a football. This sets up immediately the program's project in relation to gender roles: bringing traditional codes of femininity together with sport, in a conjunction that distorts them both. At the end of the title sequence, still in the same gorgeous peach satin evening dress, McFeast swings a cricket bat and hits the ball into the camera: aggressive, sporting, and yet at the same time stereotypically feminine. Her appearance plays up traditional feminine accoutrements. She is 'the buxom, vampy host of ABC TV's *Live and Sweaty*', who 'flaunts her sexuality' (Ricketson 1994: 67, 70).

At the opening of this first episode, McFeast appears at the top of a set of stairs in another evening dress (this time, hot pink with a black belt and diamanté buckle), wearing black satin gloves and shouting in a broad Australian accent and a very loud voice (not traditionally 'ladylike'), 'Welcome to the 1993 premiership season'. Throughout the episode, McFeast's insistently exaggerates stereotypical femininity, making it a part of the sports that she is discussing.

A single case exemplifies this tendency. On a location sequence, before going into a National Rugby League (NRL) meeting, McFeast (in yet another evening dress) stops to check her reflection in a car windscreen, demonstrating stereotypically feminine concern about her (stereotypically feminine) appearance. But the windscreen is, she says, 'A bit grubby', so she spits on it and rubs it clean. It is not often that you see a woman gobbing on television, far less a woman in evening dress. (My research suggests that Nicky Buckley has *never* done this on *Sale of the Century*.) Satisfied—once again, in a stereotypically feminine manner—that her appearance is perfect, she goes into the meeting. The behaviour associated with sports—crude, physical, 'masculine'—deforms that of stereotypical femininity, producing a persona that mixes the excesses of both.

Similarly, McFeast performs sexual attraction towards men (as a good 'vampy' woman should), but in a way that takes on blokey physicality and, as a result, appears to terrify the objects of her affection. At the NRL meeting, she buttonholes a player and asks him how to get conversation going with people at the NRL function. (She isn't sure because, as she tells us, she is more of an AFL woman herself.) She wonders if she should just go up to them and say, 'Hi, feel like a bonk?' Her gender is obviously relevant, but the expected behaviour is again mutated. While she is speaking to another man at the event, he suggests that she 'intimidates people'. 'What do you mean?' she demands, before grabbing his shirtfront and starting to head-butt him. He looks distinctly nonplussed by the whole experience. This woman is invading his personal space, in a physical, jokey way. This is not what somebody in an evening dress should be doing.

In a later item, Bob Geldof makes a joke about McFeast's size. Discussing the skill of playing darts, he notes that 'You have to get your stomach as big as possible—which in your case ...'. She kicks him, and he ends up running away from her, shouting 'Stop it!' This is the second man she's terrified with a physical attack in one episode. She then dips Geldof's hair in Guinness (good for its condition, apparently), before putting his locks in her mouth and sucking the beer out of them. She finishes the segment by putting a photograph of Elle McPherson on the dartboard and throwing darts at it: a pointed comment, as it were, on traditional images of desirable femininity. Laddishness and femininity in one aggressive and well-cleavaged package.

Other femininities

McFeast is not the only female presenter on the program, and so she does not have to take on the burden of being 'representative' of all women—an obligation that can arise if only a single character comes from a particular group. The line-up of *Live and Sweaty* at this point included two other women: Karen Tighe and Debbie Spillane. Together, respectively, they were 'the brunette, the blonde and the redhead' (Cook & Jennings 1995: 6) of *Live and Sweaty*. And each demonstrated a different relationship between femininity and sport.

Karen Tighe presents the 'sports news' items of the program, from the 'World Sports Desk'. These are very traditional sports news segments, with a presenter who 'just happens' to be female. Like the archetypal female newsreader, she has neat, long hair and wears a smart suit jacket as she does her pieces to camera. She offers the news, but little in the way of analysis.

Debbie Spillane, by contrast, presents sports analysis and discussion with Elle. She is presented as 'Debbie "Skull of Rust" Spillane'. The nickname is interesting—a strong tradition among men involved in sports, but an honour that is rarely bestowed upon women. This suggests yet another articulation of femininity and sport: Spillane is presented as much more of a tomboy than Elle. she wears a check shirt and a denim skirt (a combo that will be familiar to any client of gay or lesbian bars, or bootscooting events). Spillane demonstrates considerable expertise in her discussion of the week's sports, inflected with a concern for the traditionally feminine: of the world youth soccer cup, she notes that 'The England defence is tougher to crack than a Bronwyn Bishop hairdo'. McFeast, in comparison, is given the position of an interested observer, commenting on the difference in supporting styles at the match rather than the skills of the players: 'All the English fans are going [she puts on an effect upper-class English accent] "Support him! Challenge him!" and the Aussie ones are going [in a broad Aussie accent] "Kill 'im ya bastard!"' This segment finishes with another hybridised performance that deforms both traditional femininity and masculinity. Elle asks, 'Shall we do a high five?' Debbie replies, 'I think high fives are a bit blokey'. 'Let's do our own', suggests Elle. They flick their hair, touch their lipstick, and then do cat claws at each other: 'Miaow!' This is a program with a quite conscious agenda of examining masculinity and femininity in relation to sport.

Idiots and jokers

Meanwhile, the men who appear on the program serve as distractions and entertainment. The way they are presented is a 'blatant destabilisation of the male expert and a consistent assertion of female expertise' (Cook & Jennings 1995: 7). In short, the men are presented as idiots.

Claiming that they are going to get some soccer analysis, Karen Tighe passes to 'our roving soccer expert, Lex Marinos'. This is a comedy item, supposedly covering the opening of the seventh World Youth Soccer Cup. It consists of a series of amateur-style snapshots of people's feet, the sky, hands, with Lex's voice-over talking comic gibberish: the players on the pitch, apparently, 'formed two words—Welco and Me—which in Esperanto means Here we go, here we go, here we go'. At the end of the segment, Karen gets to cut him off: 'That's enough of that, Lex'. She is in control, the source of serious information. Lex is the amusing bimbo.

Similarly, the Melbourne report from Peter 'Crackers' Keenan involves an interview with one Bill Lawry, ex-cricketer and pigeon-fancier. Crackers asks ludicrous questions—'Do you get pigeon groupies' and Bill is not entirely happy that his interviewer is refusing to take the sport seriously: 'it's a worldwide sport, but I think it's a bit too complicated for you'.

Neither of these men is appearing for their sports expertise. Karen and Debbie have that. The men will give us a bit of a laugh.

Looking at sports

Perhaps the most interesting part of *Live and Sweaty*'s project of bringing femininity and sport together is what happens to sportsmen's bodies when this conjunction takes place.

Film theory suggests that our culture is set up to encourage looking at women's bodies: the 'masculine gaze'. Chapter 11 suggests that this is very much the case in genres such as the game show. But sport is quite a different, and more ambivalent, case. For many sports present men's bodies—and attractive, firm, muscular men's bodies at that—as things to be looked at. And yet, these are not meant to be the *objects* of a lustful gaze. The audience is not encouraged to think of these as potential sexual partners. Presented as active, skilful, powerful, these bodies are supposed to be for awe and identification in television sports coverage.

The fact remains, though, that these bodies are *there*, on the television screen, and the possibilities of what might be done with those images are, ultimately, open. They are not filmed to *encourage* sexual looking—they don't stand still long enough for us to get detailed, loving shots of their legs and buttocks, for example, as game show models do. But sexual looking is still a distinct possibility.

Given this, it should be acknowledged that an important part of ensuring that men in television sports are not looked at as sex objects is simply convention: making sure that we know that we are not *supposed* to look at them in that way. As was noted above, women do not watch as much television sport as men. Yet it is *possible* to watch sport from a position that views the players as sex objects. Beverley Poynton notes that

> what attracted my interest [to AFL] were the images of male bodies. Here were barely clad, eyeable Aussie males in top anatomical nick. The cameras follow their rough and tumble disport with relentless precision … [presenting] choreographed spectacle: lyrical, flagrantly masculine, erotic.
>
> (Poynton & Hartley 1990: 151)

And it is not simply the bodies on display, but the way in which they are represented that can lead to such eroticism of the men involved: 'the use of slow-motion, close ups and freeze-frame intensifies the representation of masculinity as bodily display … the pleasure of the image' (Yeates 1995: 39). And yet, despite all this, Poynton doesn't feel that 'television footy is designed for the gratification of voyeuristic women' (Poynton & Hartley 1990: 151).

It should be noted that it is entirely possible for women to watch sport as it is intended to be watched: identifying with the players rather than considering their bodies as erotic objects. And it is, of course, possible for men to see the sexual potential of the male bodies that are playing. And—as queer theory has suggested—any viewer can be involved in any combination of these different kinds of watching at any given moment in the viewing experience, identifying with the erotic body. It is a gross simplification to suggest only two kinds of viewing: a male gaze that identifies with players, and a female gaze that turns them into sex objects. Nevertheless, it is with just such grossly simplified binaries that culture works, and with which *Live and Sweaty* plays: 'In her ethnographic research, Nightingale found that women do enjoy watching League, but as one of her interviewees states: "[Women] aren't supporters like us guys …" ' (Yeates 1995: 39).

Women who watch sport are not offered obvious viewing positions; the discourse of 'the supporter' is an insistently masculine one, offered primarily to men. Women who attempt to move into that space are somehow not doing the right thing. Looking at sportsmen's bodies as sex objects is not a public thing: watching men's bodies in such a way allows female viewers to 'keep their gaze within bounds while allowing them secret, pleasurable experiences which are often denied' (Yeates 1995: 39).

What *Live and Sweaty* does is offer a loud and public identity for a woman who is interested in sport. As Cook and Jennings suggest, it does this by making 'an overt claim for the female gaze' and showing 'the covert eroticism of sports television itself' (Cook & Jennings 1995: 10, 11).

Moving bodies

Poynton and Hartley suggest that we must

> Pity the footballer whose public image strays from his position and function in the team and on the field, to be singled out by the media as a showpiece of sex-object speculation. Sydney Swan's talented full-forward Warwick Capper, of the short, tight shorts, flowing blond locks and pout is a prime example of the media's unease in dealing with masculine sex-objectification. Capper had the dubious privilege of being the object of media promotion by his club's advertising agency, not for his obvious, match-winning skills, but for his good looks, his sex appeal.
>
> (Poynton & Hartley 1990: 151)

For Capper, the position may have been an uneasy one: he was one of the first sportsmen whose body was publicly circulated in such a way. But other writers suggest that since the mid-1990s, the public acknowledgement of sportsmen's bodies as sex objects has become more apparent in Australia.

Toby Miller notes that: 'The increased appeal by sportscasters to single women and gay men, because they fall into cohorts with high discretionary income, means that a formerly exclusive address to straight men has been deflected towards other communities' (Cunningham & Miller 1994: 69). Helen Yeates suggests that activities such as the 'annual Men of League calendars' (Yeates 1995: 39) attempt to attract women to the game. These black-and-white photographic collections present muscular, topless footballers shot in artistic and erotic poses. It is hard to see how they could be looked at any other way than sexually.

In April 1991, a major event had taken place in the representation of sportsmen's bodies in Australia: a photograph of Andrew Ettinghausen's penis was published in *HQ* magazine. Ettinghausen sued the publishers (and won $350 000). But it was predictable that this magazine would want to publish such a photograph. After all,

> Ettinghausen ... was the first glamour boy star of League, becoming a superstar model off the field ... In the late eighties, and into the nineties, his good looks leapt out from many a magazine, poster, and of course the Men of League calendar ... His role as a sex object for women and, more interestingly, for men, is very deliberately cultivated through the Rugby League marketing machine.
>
> (Yeates 1995: 43)

The controversy of Ettinghausen's penis marks a turning point in public discourses about sportsmen's bodies. Miller discusses in detail its contribution to the 'commodification' of the 'penis', and the sexualisation of sportsmen's bodies (Miller 1998: 103). Ettinghausen wanted to control the availability of his body to the sports audience—to insist that the erotic possibilities of sport (including the after-sport shower) should not be part of his public image. *HQ* wanted to make Ettinghausen explicitly into a sex object. He did not want to go all the way. *Live and Sweaty* picks up on precisely this moment in order to present its own feminine position: that sportsmen's bodies can be for fantasising about, as much as they are for identifying with.

Each episode of *Live and Sweaty* includes 'Controversy Corner', a panel discussion of some issue associated (however loosely) with sport. Elle introduces her first Corner as host:

> When is nudity acceptable in sport? We've already had this year the big Andrew Ettinghausen court case where he wasn't very happy about having his, albeit blurry and flaccid, member exposed in a magazine that published a photograph of him.

This leads in to a prerecorded section about naked sporting bodies. A woman in the street is vox popped: 'Do you reckon these sporting figures demean themselves by baring all in magazines?' She is enthusiastic about such bodies: 'I think it's fantastic'. The precursor of Ettinghausen then appears. Warwick Capper, famous for posing nude with his wife for *Playboy*, is interviewed: 'Semi-erotic's the way to go', he says, acknowledging that these bodies can indeed be erotic objects. His wife chips in: 'If people are going to pose naked, why not sports people, 'cos they've got the best bodies'. The program then goes on to interview one Sam Kekovich: 'You were the first to do it—but did you do it tastefully?' *Live and Sweaty* is presenting us with a cultural history of nude sports bodies.

This leads to a studio interview with Brett Cochrane—the photographer 'behind the most famous shower scene since *Psycho*'. Brett explains that the photograph of Ettinghausen in the shower was taken as part of a project to document a football tour: 'I wasn't interested in the games themselves. I was more interested in capturing the culture ... What it's like when you get thirty big boofy blokes ... away on tour'. This was not a photograph trying to be erotic or pornographic; it was a document of sporting culture. Again, it becomes obvious that sport is *already* erotic. *Live and Sweaty* simply validates these erotic possibilities for looking. Elle, Brett, and the audience then look at some of his sporting photographs. All of these explicitly make men's bodies 'to-be-looked-at': a study of Mal Meninga, topless; another player, topless; a third, bending over in the shower. We are presented with a variety of objects to look at.

As noted above, this is not really a 'female gaze'; anybody can look at Mal Meninga's body in a sexual way. Elle speaks as a woman, but when she asks (in a later episode of the program) 'When you do dream about footballers, have you ever noticed how they're never playing football?' (Cook & Jennings 1995: 11), the 'you' she addresses is not necessarily female. She is asking this of all the audience. In a primarily heterosexual society, though, it will appear to be common sense that it is women who might take up such a viewing position. And it is notable that in the studio panel discussion of the topic of sport and nudity, it is the male panellists who object most strongly: Crackers Keenan insists that sports fans do not want to see their stars naked, while another panellist argues that 'There's no place for nudity in sport in the same way that there's no place for nudity in opera. There's certain things you don't have to see'. Here, 'you' is the male sports fan, while Elle's 'you' seems to be the woman dreaming of naked footballers.

In this first episode, McFeast's *Live and Sweaty* insists that sporting bodies can be looked at. This was not a one-off aberration. In a later episode, 'she convinced West Coast Eagles footballer Karl Langdon that everybody who was anyone on the East Coast had stripped off for the cameras. Langdon obliged' (Nicklin 1993: 45). And the set of the program proclaims the continuing interest in these bodies: it is decorated with classical Greek statues—naked sporting men, to be looked at for their aesthetic beauty as much as admired for their athletic skills. When Debbie comments that the set 'indicates your interest in philosophy', Elle replies that her interest is really in 'Sport as art': bodies to be looked at. Elle proclaims that such looking need not be, as Yeates notes, 'secret': it can be proudly announced on national television. It authorises and makes public the practice of looking at sportsmen's bodies as something to be dreamt about and fantasised over.

The good, the bad, the ambivalent

No question in cultural politics has a single, definitive answer. What is the best way to deal with the strong connection between sports, men, and masculine culture in Australian television? McFeast's *Live and Sweaty* suggests one answer: that both women and feminine culture might be introduced to television's sports coverage. But for some women involved in television sports, this might be the wrong answer.

Sports journalist Nicole Jeffrey complains that female sports journalists are not taken seriously enough. Recent sociological research, she claims, has found that 'readers regard female sports writers as far less credible than their male colleagues'. Female sports journalists have been accused, she goes on to argue, 'of rating players on sex appeal rather than on football performance' (Jeffrey 1999). This is indeed what McFeast does. Unhappy with this, Jeffrey seems to be arguing that only the sex of the journalists needs to be changed; the culture itself should remain untouched. From this point of view, McFeast's attempts to provide a woman's gaze of sports bodies are a retrograde step, encouraging viewers again not to take women seriously. It is Karen Tighe who is Jeffrey's ideal: a woman presenting sports news in exactly the same way that a male journalist might.

On the other hand, even Jeffrey is uncertain about her ideal. She goes on to argue that 'female writers do … provid[e] a different insight into men's sport', citing a female sports journalist who claims that 'I think being female does mean that you have a different perspective' (Jeffrey 1999). That perspective is about presenting 'the more human stuff'. She is arguing for two changes simultaneously: that women sports journalists should be able to write in a different way about sport, and that this form of 'feminine writing' should be accorded as much credibility as the 'masculine' approach to sports writing. However, there is no place in this 'feminine' writing for the sexualising of sportsmen's bodies.

Perhaps the greatest achievement of *Live and Sweaty* is that it does not present a single 'feminine' viewpoint. Tighe, Spillane, and McFeast all approach sport quite differently. There is a range of possible articulations of the female and sport. However, it must be acknowledged that the format of the program, and McFeast's presence at the centre of it, operates in such a way that *Live and Sweaty* fails to promote the 'credibility' of female sports journalists. Part of its feminisation of sport involves not taking it too seriously. This is not exactly what Jeffrey wants. But no representation can fulfil every political desire; no representation can be everything at once.

After *Live and Sweaty*

Live and Sweaty did not change the mediasphere in Australia. McFeast lasted only two seasons as the host of the program, which was then cancelled. During the 1990s, the genre of sport–comedy programs became an important one on Australian television. Melbourne's intensely masculine *The Footy Show* became a ratings hit, and spawned a flurry of poorly received imitators such as *Four Quarters*. On the ABC, Roy Slaven and H. G. Nelson's *Club Buggery* carried on the tradition of irreverent sport comedy, vulgar humour, and musical entertainment, which reached its apotheosis in their wildly popular Olympics program, *The Dream* (2000). But none of these thought about the gender roles of sport in quite the same way. (None had female hosts, to start with.) Men's bodies in *The Footy Show* reverted to blokey traditions: the men might dress up in drag (and indeed did, with alarming regularity), but the show rarely showed us photographs of naked men for our viewing pleasure.

Elle McFeast went on to host her own political comedy variety show—*McFeast Live*—which lasted until 1998, and a series of documentary–comedy specials on topics such as 'Men, Love and Marriage' (Hooks 1999).

And *Live and Sweaty* stands as a unique moment in Australian television. It was the first and only program to seriously challenge the ways in which gender is constructed in this most central part of Australian television: sports coverage.

Availability

All episodes of *Live and Sweaty* are available for purchase from the ABC's Archives and Library Services in Sydney.

17

Frontline: Media Studies Media[1]

1994–97

On 16 May 1994, the ABC broadcast an episode of the comedy program *Frontline* entitled 'Desert Angel'. This featured a story about a woman who had been lost in the desert, and the ways in which a team of journalists (on a fictional current affairs program) created stories about her experience, alternatively celebrating or demonising her depending on commercial imperatives (*Frontline* 1994b).

Five years later, on 24 August 1999, Robert Bogucki—an American tourist who had wandered into the desert of Western Australia six weeks before and had been lost, presumed dead, for that time—was found.[2] He was discovered—after the Australian experts had given up and American trackers had been brought in to help—by the crew of a Channel Nine helicopter. A video tape that was leaked to the media showed that the *A Current Affair* (*ACA*) crew on the helicopter had waited 'at least 17 minutes' to give the man fresh water, while they got good shots of him walking around (Fyfe 1999: 6). Once they had picked him up, they gave him a banana. When he started retching, they set him down again to be sick—and then filmed it. It was then used in *ACA* as though this was how they had found him. Commenting on the questionable ethics of this event, Melissa Fyfe states that 'The antics of both Nine and Seven's current affairs programs provided plenty of inspiration for the ABC's satirical comedy *Frontline*' (Fyfe 1999: 6), and quotes Anthony McLellan, Executive Producer of Current Affairs for Seven: 'I think *Frontline* did have an effect on people's attitudes to what we do and there's a degree of cynicism ...' (Fyfe 1999: 6). The fact that *Front-*

line survives as a code-word for communicating unethical journalistic practices is the starting point for this chapter.

Frontline was a half-hour comedy program, made by erstwhile members of comedy team the D-Generation, set in the newsroom of the eponymous (and fictional) television current affairs program. Three seasons, each of thirteen episodes, were broadcast on the ABC, to high ratings and immense critical acclaim. The program is well remembered as part of Australian television's archive. The viewers who were correspondents for this book mention it as a 'great moment in Australian television', but even more notable is the program's place in journalistic accounts of television's great moments. It is number two in the *Sydney Morning Herald*'s list of 'The 25 All-Time Best Australian TV Shows' (Elder 1995) and made the *Age*'s list of 'television shows that really mattered' (Sedorkin & Schirato 1998: 110).

An important part of *Frontline*'s survival in Australia's mediasphere has been its ability to enable debate about how television current affairs do, and should, work. It has continued to fulfil that role, and is constantly called to mind as a reference point, even though it is no longer in production. Five years after its initial broadcast, the name *Frontline* can still be used in the Bogucki story in full confidence that readers of the *Sunday Age* will remember the program, and remember the points it made about the construction of television news and current affairs stories. In both the popular media and in more scholarly forms of academic writing, *Frontline* has become a common cultural reference point. Use of the program's title has functioned as a way to communicate quickly and efficiently the fact that the media construct stories for us, and that these stories are not simply 'truth'.

More than this, the program has challenged the distinctions between the work of scholarly research and the creation of popular culture to such a degree that it might have rendered obsolete the teaching of university media studies courses about current affairs television.

Self-reflexive prehistories

A tradition exists of Australian television programs parodying other shows. Indeed, this has been a popular pastime for the medium. As the documentary *35 Years of Television* (1991) notes, 'many comedy shows send up TV. Paul Hogan was one of the first'. Indeed, Paul Hogan's sketch *A Casual Affair* (which appeared in his *The Paul Hogan Show*), in which he parodies *A Current Affair*, has some characteristics similar to Mike Moore's *Frontline*. But even before Paul Hogan, many of the programs already discussed in this book parodied television: *The Graham Kennedy Show* included pastiches of Western series, and *Mavis Bramston* made fun of *Pick-a-Box*. Later television series such as *Fast Forward* and *Full Frontal* have devoted themselves almost exclusively to pastiche (Harris 1994: 136; *Fast Forward, the Book* 1990).

On a separate but related topic, many television programs have deconstructed television production in a variety of ways. The soap opera *The Box* interrogated the production of television drama, revealing the amount of adultery and lesbianism that went into producing a single hour of television. Many of the variety shows on Australian television still regularly call the researchers and producers before the cameras and give shots of the studio: *Hey Hey It's Saturday* did until it was axed, and *Good Morning Australia* and *Denise* still do at the time of writing. The ABC soapie *Something in the Air* in 2000 included a storyline in which a current affairs television crew came to a small town, showing how their stories were constructed and ethics compromised. In the USA, Rob Owen suggests that this has become the dominant subject matter for sitcoms and drama series (Owen 1997: 124). Catharine Lumby suggests that an increasing number of programs are involved in this process: 'The media is full of send-ups of the media. In Australia, these include *Frontline, Full Frontal, Good News Week, Martin-Molloy, The Footy Show* ... the popularity of such shows ... illustrates the way audiences have become increasingly media literate' (Lumby 1999: 7).

Even the genre of current affairs was involved in self-reflexivity before *Frontline* got involved. As Santo Cilauro mentions in the documentary *Behind the Frontline*, the program itself was inspired by a televised debate: 'Has the media gone too far?' (*Behind the Frontline* 1995). That debate included public discussion of several problematic issues in Australian current affairs television:

> In the year before *Frontline* went to air, Australian current affairs shows were plagued with controversy ... media practices which had caused public concern ... included a *60 Minutes* interview with John Hewson's children in which they were prompted to criticise their father, the graphic re-enactment of a shark attack on the nightly news, footage of journalists interviewing gunmen holding hostages, and numerous clips of journalists aggressively hassling people about their alleged wrongdoings.
>
> (Lumby 1999: 52–3)

Frontline's contribution to Australian television, then, was not simply to parody television production, or to take a self-reflexive approach to the medium. It was, perhaps, the dedication with which this was done—allowing the program to become a catalyst for discussing current affairs television—which was new. In this, I would suggest, it bears a disconcerting resemblance to academic writing on the genre.

Disseminating *Frontline*

At the time of its first broadcast, *Frontline* was the focus of much writing in the popular press. It is interesting that, right from the start, many journalists did not want to write about *Frontline*, per se. They were not particularly interested in analysing the program; rather, *Frontline* provided a pretext for discussing *current affairs television* itself.

For example, in the episode entitled 'The Siege', Mike Moore (Rob Sitch)—the host of the fictional program *Frontline*—manages, through a combination of vaguely unethical practices and outright stupidity, to have a member of the public murdered by a publicity hungry killer. Journalists were very taken by the episode, and used it to discuss not *Frontline* itself, but the ethics of current affairs production in Australia:

> While the industry stalls on an agreement for guidelines on the reportage of events such as the Cangrai siege … tonight's issue of *Frontline* brings the issue into focus … A year after the infamous siege of Hanging Rock … . [it asks] should *A Current Affair*'s Mike Munro have broken the police's exclusion zone? … Should Mike Willesee have spoken on the phone to killer Leonard Leadbeater and one of the children he was holding hostage?
>
> (Williams 1994a: 12)

Similarly, Wendy Tuohy uses *Frontline* to talk about 'the cliches and predictability of … the traditional anchor-taped story form of current affairs TV' (Tuohy 1994: 13). Lawrie Zion points out that many media used the first episode of the program to discuss the public persona of Dr John Hewson (Zion 1995: 10). Les Carylon uses *Frontline* in order to discuss *Sixty Minutes* (Zion 1995: 14). Corrie Perkin uses Brooke Vandenberg (*Frontline*'s female reporter and presenter) to discuss 'the reality … [for] many women on Australian television today' (Perkin 1994: 7). Phillip Adams wants to discuss the nature of television news as a manufactured commodity, so he does so through *Frontline* (Adams 1994). Tony Squires wants to discuss the ethics of *A Current Affair*, so he talks about *Frontline* (Squires 1995). Paul Chadwick's topic of interest is the legislation of media ethics. What does he talk about? *Frontline* (Chadwick n.d.). Sue Williams discusses guidelines for ethical practice in current affairs—by talking about *Frontline* (Williams 1994a).

In one sense, this is entirely usual for writing on television programs. Because of the lack of traditional aesthetic discourses for writing on the medium, many journalists writing on television prefer to focus on documentaries and then discuss the topic of the documentary rather than the program itself. Like academic work (see the Conclusion to this book), much journalistic writing about television programs is not interested in the television programs themselves but, rather, in the issues raised by those programs.

Because the issues raised by *Frontline* concern the production of the television program *Frontline* (and by extension, of *A Current Affair*, *Real Life*, *Sixty Minutes*, and so on), the program becomes a meta-text: a text commenting on a text. *Frontline* has allowed popular culture to discuss the production of popular culture. This trend continues as this book is being written: in a humourless article condemning the Channel Nine *Today* show, and the fact that the presenters indulge in badinage, Susan Mitchell asks, 'Where is *Frontline* when we need it?' (Mitchell 1999: 13). Still on media ethics, Amanda Meade notes that '*Frontline* exposed viewers to the duplicity and fakery that is part of the business, and the reality of modern-day tabloid television' (Meade 1999: 3).

As well as surviving as a meta-text, *Frontline* may well have bequeathed a genre to Australian television: the comedy that uses parody in order to discuss current affairs—not necessarily satire, but more a mixture of current affairs and entertainment. Again, *Frontline* was not the first (*Mavis Bramston*, of course; *The Gillies Report*; *Graham Kennedy's Coast to Coast*). But in the late 1990s, this genre flourished. Indeed, Phillip Adams suggests that it became the dominant form of television variety in this period, pointing to shows such as *The Panel*, *Good News Week* and *GNW Nite Lite*, and the short-lived *The Big News* and *The Late Report*.

Scholarly *Frontline*

Frontline, then, is an important text in popular culture's continual self-interrogation. But it is not simply a part of popular culture. *Frontline* has crossed over into academia as well, and in many ways, the program is, in fact, a *scholarly* investigation of current affairs television very much in the tradition of media studies and journalism education.

I was talking to a colleague at Edith Cowan University, who was required to give a lecture on media ownership. He was aware of how boring this subject can be for undergraduate students, and was looking for some related television program or film he could show the lecture to stall possible tedium. I suggested the *Frontline* episode 'Give 'Em Enough Rope'. He was most unenthusiastic. 'Not *Frontline*', he said. 'They get that every week in every course'. And indeed, *Frontline* has proven particularly handy for lecturers of media studies, for it makes most of the points about television current affairs that they might want to make, but does so in a more entertaining way than they can manage.

At high-school level, *Frontline* is now an approved academic text:

> Three episodes of the ABC's *Frontline* have been included in the 1998 VCE reading list by the Board of Studies. The show, according to the Board's study guide 'provides an extraordinarily telling critique of current affairs television and of news media in general'.
>
> (Curtis 1997: 3)

As the Board's study guide suggests, the program is not to be studied for itself—not for an appreciation of its aesthetic merits, for example. Rather, it is to be a 'text-program', in the sense of a textbook—again, a meta-text, that will teach students about current affairs television.

Many of us in media studies at university are doing the same thing as the Board of Studies. This can also be seen in the tendency of academics writing on current affairs television to use *Frontline* as their key text, just as journalistic writing about the media does.

Geoff Turner (at the University of Queensland)—writing in *Australian Studies in Journalism* in 1994 on '*Frontline* Ethics: The Australian Media's Siege Mentality', an article about guidelines for siege coverage proposed by the Society of Professional Journalists—starts his article with, of course, *Frontline*:

> Anyone who has seen the Australian Broadcasting Corporation television series *Frontline* will know just how powerful a tool a well-crafted satire can be in demonstrating the absurdity of commonplace things, like current affairs television. In particular, an episode which tackled the subject of media coverage of a hostage drama ... may have said more in 30 minutes than even the best-intentioned media commentators had in 12 months of careful analysis.
>
> (Turner 1994)

This exemplifies the tone of much academic work in this area: *Frontline* has already made this point for you, it seems to say. We will repeat it. If indeed the episode about the siege has 'already said more in 30 minutes than ... media commentators had in 12 months of careful analysis', one might wonder then what need we have of academic writing to make the same point. Similarly, in their chapter on 'Theory and Current Affairs Television' in the book *Journalism: Theory and Practice*, Gail Sedorkin and Tony Schirato (at Central Queensland University) want to 'give examples of some of the more central issues currently characterising the field' of current affairs television production. How will they approach this? '[T]hrough a description and analysis using the television series *Frontline*'. But why use *Frontline*, rather than performing their analysis on their proposed object of study, current affairs television? 'We have chosen to use *Frontline*, a dramatised series, rather than factual material ... because the series very clearly takes the field ... as its primary object of study', they reason (Sedorkin & Schirato 1998: 104–5). *Frontline* has already made the 'study', made the points; let us repeat them for you. These academic writers acknowledge that *Frontline* can be recognised as scholarly work. For Turner, it 'said more in 30 minutes' than any other site of analysis; for Sedorkin and Schirato, it is a 'study' that takes current affairs television as its 'object'.

For Warwick Mules (also at Central Queensland University), in his article 'Media Evolution: *Frontline* and the Media' in *AQ: Journal of Contemporary Analysis*, the topic of interest is the need for new codes of ethics for the media. Again, the article uses *Frontline* in order to examine this question. The illustration that accompanies the article is interesting. It shows three figures, lined up from left to right. On the far right, a press cameraman is taking a photograph. In the centre, a TV news cameraman films the press cameraman taking a photograph. On the left, another cameraman, in a mortarboard, films both of them. The caption on his camera reads 'Media Theory TV'. But in Mules's article, it is not the writer himself who is put in the position of this mythical cameraman; it is *Frontline* ('Media Theory TV'—a perfect label for the program, perhaps). If Mules were to be present, he would perhaps be a fourth figure, to the left of *Frontline*, watching it watching television news watching the press:

> A fundamental blind spot exists in Australian journalism practice and education. It concerns reluctance to come to grips with the changing nature of the realities confronting journalism today amid the emergence of tabloid media as a mainstream force in contemporary culture. The highly successful ABC television satire on the media, *Frontline*, has drawn attention to this blind spot. Through its portrayal of the day-to-day operations of a commercially-based television current affairs unit, *Frontline* has exposed what most of us have known for some time. Mainstream journalistic practice is compromised by the market imperative and that television—and, by implication, newspapers—does not so

> much accurately reflect the world out there as shape it to fit the media's obsession with ratings and marketshare ... *Frontline* shows how the traditional values of the press, including those of truth, objectivity and disinterest, are not so much discarded as reconfigured within a context of disingenuous moralising, sensationalism, stereotyping, and the cult of personality ... What does *Frontline* say about journalism and ethics?
>
> (Mules 1998: 28)

'What does *Frontline* say about journalism and ethics?' Once again, a relevant question might be, 'Why is Mules writing this article, if *Frontline* is already doing the work?' The program is already, for him, 'Media Theory TV'. It is not simply a meta-text of popular culture; it is acknowledged by academics as scholarly work. Indeed, for Mules, '*Frontline* suggests a number of ways in which we might rethink Media Studies' (Mules 1998: 32). It may indeed be *ahead* of the academic discipline in thinking about current affairs television: 'Taking our cue from *Frontline*, the question we should be asking of the media isn't "Is it true?". Rather "How is its truthfulness a condition of the power of simulation?"' (Mules 1998: 33). 'We' are media studies academics; 'we' should learn from *Frontline*.

Time after time

The view of current affairs presented in *Frontline* fits well with that practised in an academic discipline such as media studies for several reasons. The ways in which the two sites imagine their objects of study are remarkably similar.

To start with, both *Frontline* and much of the work done under the rubric of media studies are very interested in the production of programs, but largely uninterested in audiences and what they might do with the programs they watch.

The program also seems to hold some sense of the distinction between the ABC and commercial journalism that informs so much media studies: all we know about the provenance of the mythical current affairs program *Frontline* is that it is broadcast on an unnamed commercial channel. While we often find elements in stories that suggest that commercial channels are involved in the same dirty tricks as the *Frontline* crew, it is never suggested that the ABC is playing the same games. This reverence for traditional forms of public broadcasting also fits in well with much writing in media studies.

There are also interesting elements in the *form* of *Frontline* that make it particularly accessible to academia. Several scholarly writers have recently suggested that one of the important differences between various kinds of knowledge production in the late twentieth century—between journalism and academic research, for example—is one of speed:

> Modes of public communication, ranging from journalism to architecture, can be understood not only in relation to space (their geographical setting) but also in relation to time. 'Public address' of different kinds has a frequency, from the (high-frequency) instant to the (low-frequency) millennium ... journalism [is] high frequency, academic and scholarly writing [is] mid frequency and public architecture [is] low frequency.
>
> (Hartley 1999c)

It is interesting that *Frontline* bridges the time scales of daily news production and the much slower knowledge production of academia. In each of its three seasons, *Frontline* produced thirteen episodes. This is 'boutique production' (McKie & Natt 1996), whereby only small numbers of episodes are produced rather than fully embracing a production-line set-up. While *Frontline* produced thirteen episodes a year in each of its three seasons—more than a program like *Mother and Son*, which produced only six in each season—it is still far short of the daily output of *A Current Affair* or *Today Tonight*. At five shows a week, these programs produce as much material in three weeks as *Frontline* did in a year. Santo Cilauro suggests that the production team for *Frontline* 'just sit on the sidelines and toss stones' (*Behind the Frontline* 1995). They are not taking part in the race of current affairs journalism. They are sitting—stationary—and 'throwing stones' (not a bad description of much media studies work). More explicitly, Rob Sitch states that

> We never base a big subplot or a whole episode on something topical, 'cos in three or four weeks it dates a bit ... we really wanted these series to be able to be watched three or four years down the track.
>
> (*Behind the Frontline* 1995)

Current affairs journalism, by contrast, is specifically designed to be outdated in three or four weeks. (As far as I am aware, no news or current affairs programs have ever been the subject of retrospective seasons of repeats on Australian television, and none have been released on video.) Like academic writing, *Frontline*'s lifespan is designed to be measured in years rather than days.

One of the odd aspects of *Frontline* is that the name refers to two quite different programs: the mythical daily current affairs program presented by the fictional Mike Moore and Brooke Vandenberg, and the program about the making of this program, starring Rob Sitch and Jane Kennedy. Both are *Frontline*. And while the *Frontline* that most writers cite is the second of these—the 'behind the scenes' program—the mythical current affairs show *Frontline* reveals the speed of daily current affairs journalism. The title sequence is a masterpiece of speed and timing, featuring driving and aggressive music and editing.

Frontline, then, has been taken up as a scholarly meta text, produced more in the timescale of academia than that of current affairs television. And it serves this purpose well. To return to the articles mentioned above, it is interesting to see the points that they wish to make, and the degree to which those points have already been made for them by the academic work of the television program *Frontline*.

Every episode of *Frontline* confronts these issues from a variety of perspectives and in a range of ways. The following list provides only some examples of the program's work—it is certainly not exhaustive.

> **1** *Frontline* has shown how dangerous it can be to pander to the publicity demands of already unstable people in violent, precipitous situations.
>
> (Turner 1994: 27)

'The Siege' is one of the darkest episodes of the program, showing a murder that is the direct result of *Frontline*'s editorial practices (*Frontline* 1994e). This episode makes most of the points that Geoff Turner wishes to argue for in his article. In particular, it insists that a simple credo of 'the public's right to know' cannot be invoked to cover every instance equally.

Brian, the executive producer, is delighted to hear about the siege: 'We want to get the whole half hour out of this!' The *Frontline* team break the police's air exclusion zone around the besieged farmhouse, leading the police to claim that they are 'jeopardising negotiations'. They then manage to get the telephone number for the farmhouse where the siege is taking place and interview the gunman for the program. The police state that 'negotiations with the gunman have been halted as we are now unable to get through to him'. After the interview, in order to ensure that their interview remains an exclusive, producer Emma says to the gunman: 'You're obviously a little stressed at the moment, so why don't you take your phone off the hook, so nobody else bothers you?'

This does not lead to disaster: the gunman gives himself up without any shots being fired. The ratings for the episode are spectacular, but the next day, the host is accused of being 'irresponsible' and 'putting the lives of those children at risk' by the press and by radio talkback host Neil Mitchell. Mike Moore denies the charge, claiming that 'I believe I had a calming effect'. The episode spends five minutes discussing the ethics of the situation, but the *Frontline* line is simply to repeat publicly that 'no one got hurt', and privately that the ratings and publicity garnered were fantastic.

The episode ends 'Two weeks later'. 'In the studio—now!' Brian orders Mike. 'You're not going to believe this, but we've got another siege. He's asked for you.' Mike interviews him live on air. 'You've specifically asked to speak with me. Well, you've got the whole of Australia watching and listening: what do you want?' 'I want you to hear this', the gunman answers. Gunshots sound, as he shoots his hostages. The episode ends (*Frontline* 1994e).

> 2 *Frontline* shows how the traditional values of the press, including those of truth, objectivity and disinterest, are not so much discarded as reconfigured within a context of disingenuous moralising.
>
> (Mules 1998: 28)

In the episode 'This Night of Nights', a charity has had money stolen by an employee (*Frontline* 1994f). The money has been recovered and the employee charged. At a press conference, the charity asks the media not to cover this story, as they rely on donations in order to perform their work. Such revelations would damage public confidence in the charity, thus lowering donations. Marty, the *Frontline* journalist at the press conference, is willing to accept this. However, Brian, the executive producer, disagrees. In tones of the highest moral platitude, he explains his position to Marty:

> Let me tell you a story—a true story. About ten years ago I was working at a radio station, and we agreed not to run a story—about a guy who was threatening to poison the water supply. Cops reckoned people would panic. All right, a few days later he got arrested, and of course the story comes out. You should have heard the flak we copped from the talkback callers—what gives you the right to withhold information? Who do you think you are playing god with our lives? And you know what Marty? They were right.

Marty points out, 'But there's no lives being threatened'. Brian goes on:

> Lives, money, it's the same principle—we as the media have a duty to report what we learn. Not sit back and decide what people should or should not know ... the public has a right to know what happens to their money ... it's our duty.
>
> (*Frontline* 1994f)

The use of a story that will rate well but serve little 'public interest' is justified in the highest moral terms. The episode shows the way in which such discourses are used simply for moral effect, rather than because of any commitment to such principles on the part of those who use them. Later in the episode, when Marty justifies running the story to the dissatisfied host, he tells exactly the same anecdote, claiming it as his own 'true story—eight years ago, I was working on radio …'. Later again, Mike tries to claim the same anecdote as his own when justifying the story on talkback radio.

Frontline repeatedly presents examples in which actions taken by television current affairs journalists are obviously self-serving and selfish, yet justified in terms of moral duty. In 'Smaller Fish to Fry' (*Frontline* 1994d), the *Frontline* team is attacked for always chasing 'shonky repairmen', rather than going after the big businessmen who are involved in frauds worth millions of dollars. Justifying this, the characters ignore the charge and fall back on moralistic discourse: 'Do you realise how much these people [shonky fridge repairmen] cheat people out of?' A talent for claiming the moral high ground is presented as a requisite for working in television current affairs.

In smaller examples, the characters are shown to justify everything they do in terms of the higher good, even when it is obviously petty and selfish. Mike wants to get upgraded to business class on a flight: 'Not for me, for the show' (*Frontline* 1994c); arguing that he should present a Logie Award, he makes the same argument (*Frontline* 1994f).

> **3** *Frontline* shows how the traditional values of the press … are not so much discarded as reconfigured within a context of … stereotyping.
>
> (Mules 1998: 38)

Brian is adamant that a story on women's sport will not be run, until he finds out that it is about 'lezzos'. Emma argues, 'This is not about lesbians. It's about unfair dismissal'. 'Yeah,' says Brian, 'with lesbians … This is not a women's sport story; it's a lezzo story' (*Frontline* 1994a). The story runs, with a dramatised section that looks like a 'women in prison' movie (see chapter 9): three women in a shower area with towels wrapped around them; a butch woman with a clipboard enters the shower; one of the women's towels fall off, landing around her feet. When Brian voices his desire to stretch the story out for another night, Emma chips in: 'Yeah, add a little Mardi Gras footage, put some k. d. lang music under it' (*Frontline* 1994a).

> **4** *Frontline* shows how the traditional values of the press … are not so much discarded as reconfigured within a context of … the cult of personality.
>
> (Mules 1998: 28)

Is this what lesbians look like?

In 'Playing the Ego Card', the network's public relations people discover that Brooke is doing well with focus groups, proving particularly popular. Brian sends Mike overseas for a week, planning to dump him when he returns if Brooke rates well. Marty is mightily pissed off by this development: 'Here I sit with twenty-one years of experience, and I'm playing second fiddle to some show pony' (*Frontline* 1994c). The program repeatedly shows us that the presenters are employed for their looks and ratings appeal rather than their journalistic ability.

The role of the reporter, the executive producer insists, is to make stories friendly and appealing. As Brian asks, 'What's vision without a reporter? It's a documentary, that's what it is' (his tone making clear that this is his idea of an insult) (*Frontline* 1994c). The program emphasises the construction of identities for the presenters in the promos that are shot for them. Brooke Vanderberg's runs: 'she's the woman with the stories, the names, and the courage to tell it like it is' (*Frontline* 1994c).

> **5** One of the most interesting aspects of *Frontline* is the way in which characters such as Mike and Emma consistently 'speak' [of] ... disinterestedness, ethical conduct, the public interest, while their executive producer ... and Marty are 'doing something else' [that is, chasing ratings].
>
> (Sedorkin & Schirato 1998: 113)

In 'Divide the Community, Multiply the Ratings', Executive Producer Sam is determined to use violence to attract viewers. He deliberately inflames tension between two ethnic groups in order to create the violence that—his overnight ratings show—the audience wishes to see.

The episode starts with a tip-off that Croatian demonstrators are about to attack a Serbian consulate. Sam sends a camera crew, but deliberately does not tip-off the police; he wants footage of violence. He gets it, and it rates well. He wants to show the footage again, but needs an excuse, so he decides to organise a debate between members of the two communities. Mike Moore is delighted by this: 'A debate! Great! A chance to flesh out the issues!' When the debate happens, Mike tries to ensure that rationality dominates the discussion: 'This is a debate, and as long as I'm in control, there will be no inflammatory remarks'. ('Shit', says Sam in the control room; he wants violence.) Mike is delighted with the debate: 'We brought two people together ... I think they learned something'. Sam sums it up (behind Mike's back) as 'What a fizzer'.

Sam tries again: the next night will feature a forum, with fifty studio guests from the communities. Again, Mike is delighted. 'The whole idea of this forum is to resolve the issue, not inflame it.' Sam plants journalist Marty in the audience, because he is a 'professional shit stirrer'. He stands up at a tense moment and delivers one of the series most spectacular lines: 'The Serbs say it was the Croatians' fault. The Croatians blame the Serbs. My opinion—it's the Serbs' fault'. 'Go Marty', says Sam, as a riot erupts in the studio, the violence that will guarantee his ratings (*Frontline* 1995a).

> **6** [A] media culture ... redeploys the notion of truth as a function of simulation rather than adequate representation. *Frontline* is the perfect example of this.
>
> (Mules 1998: 33)

In most episodes of *Frontline*, the executive producer tells the journalists that they cannot run a story without 'vision':

> For an overseas story to be worth running, it's got to have three things: good vision, good vision, and good vision. It's important. A pub brawl in Manly is better than a massacre of millions if you've got the pictures. And if you haven't got the pictures, it sure as hell better have Australians in it.
>
> (*Frontline* 1994c)

Visualising rebel warfare

Frontline shows us how important it is that the visuals of a television current affairs story tell the right story—that they communicate the 'truth' of a situation. It also demonstrates that such images of truth must always be constructed: framed, shot, and edited in the right way in order to make sense to viewers. Brooke's endless 'noddies' make this point explicitly, as do Mike's attempts to get 'vision' of a civil war in Papua New Guinea. He crouches in front of two soldiers, who are pointing their guns out of frame. His line is: 'The soldiers are under constant attack from the secessionist rebels', but he has to keep breaking off, in take after take, in order to tell the soldiers how to behave—'Guys, you've got to fire when I talk'—in order for the visuals to tell the 'truth' about the situation. Similarly, in order to show the fact that there are armed rebels involved, he has to hand guns to a family: 'No, you hold it like this' (*Frontline* 1994c).

> 7 *Frontline* ... highlighted the cowboy antics of some current affairs television programs.
>
> (Turner 1994: 28)

It is not immediately clear what specific unethical practices Turner is suggesting here, but in such a category one could certainly include the practices of chequebook journalism and the intrusion on grief that are shown in the episode 'The Siege'. Interviewing the woman whose son is holding her grandchildren hostage, Brooke has her sign an exclusivity clause. 'Some other current affairs programmes can be quite unscrupulous', she explains, going on to lie that 'It's not so much to protect us as to protect you' (*Frontline* 1994e).

She displays similar tactics when interviewing a whistleblower in 'Add Sex and Stir': 'I'm sure you realise we have a policy on the show of not paying people for interviews. But what we do have is two tickets to the Gold Coast, accommodation included' (*Frontline* 1994a).

> 8 *Frontline* suggests ... [that] claims of truth are always made within contexts not of their own making.
>
> (Mules 1998: 32)

An example of this tendency dramatised by *Frontline* appears in the episode 'Keeping Up Appearances' (*Frontline* 1995b). The network chief refuses to allow a story on a woman whose face has been hideously scarred following an acid attack. 'I don't want that face on my network', he insists: 'People are trying to eat their dinner.' Any journalistic desires, or stories that could be told around this event, are rejected, in favour of a discourse of perceived audience desires. Characters in the program keep expressing the limits within which they work. Brian claims that 'it's not my job to listen to myself; it's to listen to those above me' (*Frontline* 1994d), as he is told by his superiors not to run a story on a merchant bank. Similarly, 'This Night of Nights' sees a story about Telstra, of which Brian is fond, canned because of the management's desire: 'They're big sponsors' (*Frontline* 1994f). Marty explains to a fellow journalist why he ran the Streetaid charity story (see above): 'What could I do? My editor put the hard word on me' (*Frontline* 1994f).

These articles, using *Frontline* to discuss current affairs television, are not interrogating, critiquing, or thinking about the program *Frontline*. Rather, they are citing it with approval, in the way that academics cite each other's work. The program has already made all of the points that it wishes to make about public affairs television; this is the reason it cites it.

Mutual movement

Frontline works both as an entertaining part of popular culture and as scholarly comment on popular culture. It is possible to suggest that academia is moving to meet *Frontline* as well, as it travels towards the arena of popular culture. Increasing demands for 'relevance' and 'vocationalism' in media studies courses at university promote a need to leave behind some of the 'slow time' of traditional academia, and to keep 'up to date' with the 'change'—metaphors of time—of the practice of media production. On the student feedback forms that are now a requirement for units taught at many universities, it is not unusual to come across comments about university courses such as 'not entertaining enough'. And demands for production components in media studies courses, and for the recognition of theses produced in audio-visual as well as more traditional written forms, are also increasing. As we move within universities to offer faster production of information, more entertainment, and the recognition of audio-visual scholarly work, it is not unreasonable to suggest that *Frontline* itself could be submitted as a PhD thesis in media studies. It bridges perfectly the spheres of popular culture and an increasingly speedy academia.

Having made this argument, it is also worth noting that there are points at which *Frontline* differs markedly from some work in media studies. The program, for example, manages to resist quite strongly any obvious authorial position. There is no character with whom we are asked to identify as embodying correct journalistic procedure. The closest we get is Emma, but she is often seduced—or more often blackmailed—into taking part in unethical practices herself. The most exact recitation of traditional journalistic principles comes from Mike Moore himself; the only problem is that he is too vacuous to realise that those principles are completely unworkable in his situation. (Indeed, Emma does not really embody 'traditional' journalistic principles so much as an ethically comported wiliness.) The executive producers (particularly Brian, played in the first season by Bruno Lawrence)—the most amoral and commercially oriented characters in the program—are also often the most likeable: funny, intelligent, and very definitely in charge. With Brian being a more attractive character than Mike, and more capable of enforcing his will than Emma, the idea of 'journalistic integrity' is presented with a certain ambivalence in the program. This bears little relation to the often very certain championing of easily listed (but practically impossible) ethical behaviours in some media studies writing.

Another strange aspect of the program—from the perspective of media studies—is the exemption of talkback radio from the investigations of unethical behaviour. In the first season, Melbourne talkback host Neil Mitchell is presented as a contrasting voice of good journalism, compared with the work of the television current affairs crews, as in 'The Siege', where he attacks Mike Moore with: 'I believe, and many of my callers believe, that it was totally irresponsible ... you are not a professional negotiator'. Media studies are unlikely to exempt talkback radio from charges of unethical practice in such a way; indeed, it often finds it to be the most unethical of the journalistic genres (Mickler 1998).

Frontline is strongly associated only with that work in media studies that is largely uninterested in audiences, as opposed to research that finds audiences interesting. As the Conclusion to this book will suggest, it is true that much media studies work on television falls into the former category: it is production and legislation that is the focus of most writing on the medium, and *Frontline* follows the same pattern. It has little interest in the audiences of these programs. The most interesting character from this point of view is Domenika, the receptionist. In many episodes of the program, she is the character who is representative of the audience. While everyone in the office mocks a 'lost dog' story, she says 'I think it's a cute story' (*Frontline* 1995b); in 'Give 'Em Enough Rope', she and Mike are the only characters who are familiar with the plots of the teen soapies *Sunshine Beach* and *Rainbow Island* (*Frontline* 1995c); and

The *Frontline* audience, represented by a woman with umbrellas in her head

she is the representative viewer whose reaction to a woman's disfigurement—'I wish I could do something to help her'—leads Sam to establish an appeal for that women (*Frontline* 1995b). This character—who likes and watches the television that *Frontline* produces—is relentlessly mocked by the program. Over the course of the series, she has different, increasingly outrageous hairstyles (cocktail umbrellas stuck into buns, or even a completely shaved head). Although her character is obviously meant to be sweet, she is equally obviously meant to be ditzy to the point of idiocy. This is the audience as imagined by *Frontline*, and it fits in well with much media studies writing on television.

But I have listed this as a difference from media studies because there exist other traditions in the discipline—particularly ethnographic work such as that of David Morley (1980), Ien Ang (1985), and theoretical accounts such as those of John Hartley (1992a; 1992b)—that do not imagine audiences in such a way. *Frontline* differs from these forms of media studies.

Finally, *Frontline* differs from the work of those media studies writers who are not so disturbed by the way in which television current affairs conducts its business (Lumby 1999). As Graeme Turner has recently argued, there is a major difference between unethical behaviour and 'tabloidisation' (that is, the move to entertainment and popular stories) in current affairs media. The former he finds unacceptable; the latter is much less worrying (Turner 1999). As was noted in chapter 15, John Hartley has argued that the promotion of the smiling professions such as newsreaders can be understood in a positive way, presenting public affairs in a non-confrontational and community-building way (Hartley 1992a: 119). Indeed, *Frontline* itself is a good argument for this point: it is entertaining, funny, and popular, while making serious points. It intelligently addresses very complex issues, turning them into tightly constructed narratives that illustrate those points by personalising them. Seemingly against its explicit intentions, *Frontline* demonstrates that the move to entertainment in current affairs television is not, in itself, a bad thing. In its explicit arguments, the program can be aligned with the more traditional, highly critical, high moral ground of media studies criticism; in its format and presentation, it supports arguments for less puritanical approaches to the media.

Frontline is remembered particularly in the academic sections of the public archive, but also in the public sphere more generally. It survives as a commentary on television's current affairs news practice. It is more media studies than much media studies, and it is much more entertaining.

Availability

It is also very accessible. Many episodes of the program have been released commercially and are available both at ABC Shops and in local video libraries.

Notes

1 The opinions expressed in this chapter are not necessarily those of the producers of *Frontline*.
2 An identical story occurred again in April 2001—with the commercial current affairs program that didn't secure an interview with the man going on to demonise him for wasting taxpayer's money—exactly as the *Frontline* crew do.

CONCLUSION
TELEVISION CHOICES

Objects of study

> The history of Australian television must inevitably be that of government policy and legislation.
>
> (Bailey 1979: 1).

As I suggested in the Introduction, writing on Australian television has tended to avoid its programs. This explains why Tom O'Regan's two magisterial accounts of media cultures—*Australian Television Culture* (1993) and *Australian National Cinema* (1996)—are so very different. The first offers (according to its cover blurb) 'a picture of Australian television'; the second analyses 'the distinct and diverse nature of Australian cinema'. Despite similar concerns, and a shared author, their objects of study are constituted very differently. O'Regan's analysis of Australian cinema is replete with examples of particular films, analyses of their representational strategies, and links to the social context of production. His account of television, by contrast, addresses almost no programs, and those that are mentioned appear only in passing. There is no analysis of any particular television text.

The difference between these books cannot be explained in terms of authorial fickleness; rather, it represents the different ways in which television and film have been constructed as objects of study. While film has a recognised canon and a tradition of close textual analysis, in the study of television the programs themselves have tended to vanish, as they do in *Australian Television Culture*. From this perspective, Bailey's 'must' is useful, for it makes clear what is so often implicitly assumed in academic writing about television: television is to be studied from the point of view of industry, policy, and production. That is, we assume, what it is *for*. This book has demonstrated that this need not be the case: that it is at least *possible* to write an account of Australian television that is interested in programs.

But still the book will seem fundamentally misconceived to many researchers on television. An anecdote may suggest why this is the case, and why it has not been attempted before in Australia, despite the publication of dozens of books, reports, and monographs on the medium. While I was researching this book, many academics to whom I spoke, upon hearing the title, gave a little laugh and said jokingly, 'Must be a very short book'. The number of times I heard this joke made it clear that this was not an aberrant response. I did not get the same response from people who do work outside the academy (except, strangely, from taxi drivers). The idea that Australian television programs might be worthy of study is still, a quarter of a century after media and cultural studies entered the Australian academy in significant ways, strange enough to inspire jokes. A brief account of writing on the medium in Australia suggests how this has remained the case.

Defining television

Political economy

Julie James Bailey's monograph on the history of Australian television (1979) proposes as an object of study a television that involves no broadcasting, no programs, and no audiences, focusing rather on government policy and legislation. And this approach—political economy—has been the most popular one in academic writing about the medium in Australia. Work from a variety of disciplines—politics, sociology, mass communications, media studies, and even textbooks for secondary school children—has made this the most visible model of what Australian television is, and how it should be studied. Dozens of books and reports have been published that provide a detailed history of these elements of the medium.[1] Particularly important for research that takes this approach is the Australian public broadcaster—the ABC. This institution, beloved of many media studies academics and journalists, sustains a disproportionate amount of historical research, again ensuring that the history of this institution, and the legislation that has governed it, have been recorded in detail in a number of books, reports, and articles.[2]

Public affairs

Such work generally finds the party politics that surround and enable broadcasting—rather than television itself—to be particularly interesting, devoting much time and energy to writing histories of government policy and institutional practice. Bearing this in mind, it is interesting to note that a second approach to the medium of television does address one genre of television programs, but again in order to discuss party politics and the workings of government. Thus, some writers have turned their attention to news and current affairs programming, which also sustains a substantial amount of research.[3] As with accounts of the political economy of the medium, politics is more interesting than television programs for much of the academic research into news and current affairs: for political economy researchers, it is the politics of television that is interesting; for researchers on news and current affairs, it is the televising of politics. Appropriate questions to ask of this version of 'television' include: How does television represent politics? How can television best serve a democratic society? What kind of public service remit should television be fulfilling, and what political and institutional structures can best support it in that service?

Medium theory

After political economy, and an interest in news, a third approach to the study of television—although one that is less prominent in Australia than in other countries—is medium theory. Such an approach is very different from industrial accounts, tending towards more abstract and theoretical ways of thinking about the medium. This approach considers the ways in which media alter perceptions and uses of space and time, irrespective of the programs that might be broadcast on them. This approach has been a particularly important one in Canada (Innis 1991 [1951]) and the USA (Meyrowitz 1985; Caldwell 1995: 19). Indeed, David Marc suggests that issues common in film studies—authorship and genre, for example—have been 'almost completely ignored' by studies of the mass media. As he notes, 'seminal television' studies works such as Macdonald's *A Theory of Mass Culture*, or Marcuse's *One-Dimensional Man* (and, I would add, McLuhan's *Understanding Media*) do not mention a single television program in their discussion of the medium (Marc 1995: 89; see also McLuhan 1964; Spigel 1992).

This tendency does have some purchase in Australia: witness, for example, Meaghan Morris's statement that 'I am less interested in music or TV than I am in how these cut across and organize the various time/spaces in which the labour, as well as the pleasure, of everyday living is carried out by Australian women' (Morris 1998: 114). Again, for academic work in this tradition, programs vanish from the consideration of what television is and how it functions. This approach to television is related—though not identical to—a position in cultural studies that draws upon the seminal work of Raymond Williams in *Television: Technology and Cultural Form*. Here, he takes a medium-wide view of television in order to suggest that it is characterised by 'a flow series of differently related units' (Williams 1990 [1975]: 93). Williams is careful to insist that this is only one possible aesthetic of television, and that different national systems organise their material differently (that is, this is a cultural rather than an ontological imperative). It should also be remembered that he uses the term as a way into making detailed analyses of particular examples of television programming. Nevertheless, the characterisation of television's programming as 'flow' suggests a lack of importance for individual programs, subsumed into a never-ending wash of 'programming', where nothing is outstanding or distinctive. Taking such an approach to Australian television leaves little space for interest in particular programs that might not be part of a 'flow' and that survive in various ways.

Audience research

A fourth approach to Australian television avoids discussing programs by addressing television's 'effects': through large-scale audience surveying, through small-scale psychological studies, or—in one memorable example—by wiring children into machines and measuring their reactions to visual stimuli, as in Richard Silberstein's 1983 paper on *Electroencephalographic Responses of Children to Television* (Silberstein 1983). Much (though not all) of this work is sponsored by the Australian Broadcasting Control Board/Tribunal/Authority, and it has a history as long as television's in Australia.[4] It is notable that most of these studies, interested in the 'effects' of television rarely mention programs; it is consumption of the medium in general that is the object of study.

Program production

A fifth approach discusses the production of programs, and is more interested in the industrial and institutional constraints of what is made than in the texts that are finally broadcast.[5]

Programs

None of these approaches to the study of television is logically incompatible with research into the history of television's programs. It is possible to acknowledge the importance of studying legislation and policy about television, and ownership and institution and production, and still allow that research into the history of television programs might also be worthwhile. Indeed, I would argue that there are advantages to including television programs in our study of the history of Australian television. Not least of these is the possibility of an interesting change of perspective on our object of study.

The back cover of Stuart Cunningham and Graeme Turner's book *The Media in Australia* (Cunningham & Turner 1993)—a standard undergraduate textbook for teaching media studies in Australia—states that 'Over the past decade the Australian media has undergone so many changes that most people are bewildered'. Such a description of the medium makes sense in the academic context, where 'changes' in regulation, ownership, and technology are of paramount importance. But it is not necessarily true that the majority of television's audience feels this way. For many of the viewers of Australian television—and I confess that this is an underresearched part of my project, and one that would repay further work—I suspect that ownership is actually of less interest than what is showing this evening. This does not make the experience of television audiences any less valuable or correct as an understanding of the medium; it is simply a *different* understanding of this cultural object. It is true that television's programs do occasionally make questions of media ownership and legislation relevant to the medium's content (a *Frontline* episode or a news story on a contentious issue, for example), but there is no evidence this is at the centre of the television experience for its audiences. Rather, there is much evidence (as this book has shown) that the public circulation and discussion of television puts *programs* at the centre of its functions and pleasures. From the perspective of most viewers, I suspect, television is a medium that presents programs.

Bits and pieces

Even within its own terms, though, this book must remain incomplete. From the day that the final draft was completed, the mediasphere continued with the ongoing, daily project of remembering, reworking, and reshaping the public archive of Australian television history ('Why Australians Love to Laugh' 2000; Blundell 2000; Este 2000). Every time a chapter seemed to be complete, a new documentary about Graham Kennedy would appear, or a series of repeats of *Number 96* would begin. The book is necessarily limited, for its object of study is not static.

But this ongoing nature of television does not mean that the medium does not have an archive. It is true that new texts contribute to public debate about which programs and which moments should be remembered and archived, but there is a consistency in the programs that are named and discussed that belies the image of an ephemeral medium promoted by so much academic writing. Television does not have to be dead for its archive to be discussed, as all of the newspaper, magazine, board game, Internet, fan publishing, and academic writings discussed in this book make clear. Indeed, all academic work on popular culture faces similar problems: the object of study inevitably changes. This need not be a debilitating realisation. As chapter 17 suggests, different forms of knowledge production in the mediasphere—including journalism and academic publication—work at different speeds. These forms are not hermetically sealed, but mix and communicate with each other. As an academic snapshot of the public archive of Australian television programming at one time—the end of the twentieth century and the beginning of the twenty-first—I hope that this piece of cultural history will remain of some interest to historians and theorists interested in television in Australia.

Archival tendencies

Looking through the 'moments' that make up the genealogy of collectively remembered programs in this book, it is obvious that it has been written by a media studies academic creating his own object of study. Questions of national identity, gender, public affairs, and democracy are all familiar issues within that academic discipline. Other approaches would probably notice quite different moments, and find them more important. Nevertheless, it is interesting to note how congruent the concerns of academia and popular culture prove to be when it comes to television.

Australianness

Many of the programs I have discussed survive in collective memory for their perceived relationship to Australianness. *Homicide* ('the first successful

Australian drama series'); Paul Hogan (the ultimate 'ordinary Australian'); *Neighbours* ('showing the UK what Australia's really like'); *Burke's Backyard* (insisting on the 'ordinary Australian'). The desire to represent 'Australianness' remains strong in the mediasphere, and many of the 'great moments' are related to this desire. The elements that have been brought under this rubric have been diverse: the suits and restrained accents of the *Homicide* detectives, the broad ocker performance of Hogan, the brightly banal suburban lives of *Neighbours*. As dominant discourses of what a 'real' Australian should look like change, so too do the television moments that are coopted into this desire. But the desire to struggle towards a representation of this ineffable identity remains strong throughout Australia's television history.

Identity politics

Questions of identity politics, now popular in many media studies, cultural studies, and English literature courses in academia, also figure in the archiving of many of the great moments of Australian television. *Number 96,* as I suggested, is strongly remembered in the public archive for introducing Australia not only to sex, but also to sexuality. The representation of Don Finlayson is strongly tied to the program's survival in the Australian public archive. Similarly, *Prisoner* survives as a cult program largely because of its unusual representations of female characters; *Sale of the Century* and other game shows promote strongly conformist representations of gender. *Countdown* is 'about' age as well as nation; the identity it promoted through a mixture of music, drugs, youth, and Australianness marks its continuing position in Australia's mediasphere. The work of the public archive in maintaining these great moments draws on such discourses for placing these programs in the history of Australian television.

Public affairs and democracy

Four Corners survives for its contribution to public debate in Australia; *Mavis Bramston* and *Frontline* for their satire; *A Country Practice* for the social issues it presented. It is not only academics and critical writers who are concerned about the function the media serve in a democracy: the public archive also addresses such issues as it picks its moments from such television programs to enable debate about what the media do, and what the media should be doing.

These three aspects of Australian television—Australianness, identity politics, and public affairs and democracy—demonstrate that media studies are not, as popular discourses often insist, an ivory tower, cut off from the rest of culture. A dissemination of ideas moves from popular culture to academia and back again.

Death

Moving outside of academic concerns, it is the deaths of characters in soap operas that have proven to be some of the best remembered moments of Australian television. Molly and Grace, between them, accounted for much of the personal memory of Australian television that was contributed to this book. This is perhaps the area where previous academic writing on Australian television has most obviously failed to find any commonality with collective memories of the medium.

Multiple archives

I suggested in the Introduction to this book that the collectively remembered programs of Australian television form a 'public archive' of great moments. The term 'public archive' must be approached with some caution. As with all discussions of 'the public'—whether it is 'the public sphere' or 'public opinion'—the use of a singular form is somewhat misleading. It suggests an imaginary totality that allows us to think about society as a whole, even though we know that in fact there are many different publics, many spheres, many opinions. There are also a number of public archives of Australian television. The forms of collective memory I have detailed throughout this book are brought together here as a totality—a single archive of great moments—that is necessarily a fiction. But it might be a useful one nonetheless. Some moments and programs are primarily remembered within the media industries themselves—the fondness for recalling the glory days of *Four Corners*, for example. Some are particularly well remembered by academic writing—as in the case of *Frontline*, which is not only remembered but continues to be described and discussed in great detail in academic writing. Other programs are recalled by those viewers whose feedback can be accessed (as was the case for this book) through calls for information in mainstream publications—the deaths in *The Sullivans*, for example fit into this category. Some moments seem to be part of a folk memory that only occasionally enters the mediated texts of popular culture—as with the sexual pleasures of *Playschool*, largely unspeakable on television itself, but 'known' and remembered by a large number of viewers nevertheless. Others are archived by passionate subcultures—the work that loyal fans put into remembering *Prisoner* being a case in point. Others can be accessed through particular identity groups in Australia—the importance of Don's homosexuality in *Number 96*, for example, being remembered by gay viewers and gay writers alike.

I do not wish to overstate this heterogeneity, however. The last of these examples is also a useful one for demonstrating that these enclaves of collective-memory production are not hermetically sealed, for Don's coming out is remembered by mainstream journalists and some academics, and by heterosexual viewers, as well as by members of Australia's gay community. Collective remembering is not spread equally across all sites in culture so that each great moment in equally remembered by all viewers, and in all public pronouncements, or in the same way. But there is, as this book makes obvious, enough consensus across various sites of Australian public discourse (including the 'publishing' of letters and similar texts from viewers, which I have placed in the category of 'public discourse' here for the sake of convenience) to make it sensible, at least to some degree, to discuss 'the' collectively remembered public archive of Australian television.

Watch more television

This book has presented case studies of seventeen programs that have an important place in the archive of Australian television—programs that are remembered by audiences and are part of 'our cultural heritage'. Of course there are many others that could be included. Indeed, as I suggested in the Introduction, the very incompleteness of the project is, for me, part of its charm. I invite anyone who is interested in Australian television and convinced that a program presented in this book does not really belong therein, or that another is more deserving of a place, to write more about Australian television programs. I would like to read what they have to say.

In the meantime, for anyone interested in studying the medium in Australia, I have no better advice to offer than that offered by John Hartley as the final sentence in his book *Uses of Television*: 'Watch a lot of television' (Hartley 1998: 234). By getting to know what is shown on the medium, and trying to understand the relative importance of different programs, we better understand how television works, what is shown on it, and what survives in the public archive as part of our cultural, television heritage. This strikes me not only as a project that is worthwhile, but also one that I personally find very interesting. I hope that others do too.

Notes

1 See National Library of Australia and National Film Archive 1981; Sgro 1974; Mayer 1976; McQueen 1977; Johnson & Armstrong 1977; Bailey 1978; Kippax & Murray 1979; Elder 1979; Boehringer & others 1980; Bonney 1981; Schou 1982; Armstrong, Blakeney, & Watterson 1983; Barr 1985; Brown 1986; Curthoys 1986; Bonney 1987; Wheelwright & Buckley 1987; Bonney 1988; Tribunal 1988b; Toshner 1988; Chadwick 1989; Hand 1990; Jones 1991; More & Smith 1992; Molloy & Burgan 1993; Cunningham & Turner 1993; Mayer 1994; Craik, Bailey, & Moran 1995; Osborne & Lewis 1995; Jacka & Johnson 1998.

2 See Ashbolt 1974; Dixon 1975; Harding 1979; Petersen 1993; Semmler 1981; Inglis 1983; Ashbolt 1987b; Ashbolt 1987a; Whitehead 1988; Peach 1992; Littlemore 1996.

3 See Hughes & Western 1966; Edgar 1980; Duffell 1980; Windschuttle & Windschuttle 1981; Bell, Boehringer, & Crofts 1982b; Gerdes 1982; Bell, Boehringer, & Crofts 1982a; Western & Hughes 1983; Gerdes & Charlier 1985; Lloyd 1988; Overton 1989; Langer 1989; Tiffen 1989; Masterson & Patching 1990; Rodney Weaver 1990; Mason & McLean 1993; Mayer 1994; Hurst & White 1994; Marshall & Kingsbury 1996; Bowd 1997; Stone 2000.

4 See Thompson 1959; ABCB 1970; ABCB 1971; Hammond & Glasser 1971; Blizard 1972; Powell 1974; ABT 1979c; Bednall & Hannaford 1980; Nugent & others 1992; Nugent, Loncar, & Aisbett 1993; Sheldon, Aisbett, & Herd 1993; Sheldon, Ramsay, & Loncar 1995; Cupitt 1998.

5 See Moran 1982; Burke 1984; Tulloch & Moran 1986.

REFERENCES

'ABC Axes Parody on Politicians' 1977, *Sydney Morning Herald*, 16 February, ABC clippings archive, file 'ABC - Television—General, 1976–1978'.

ABCB. See Australian Broadcasting Control Board.

ABS. See Australian Bureau of Statistics.

ABT. See Australian Broadcasting Tribunal.

Adams, Chris 1990, 'Life after Hoges', *B + T Advertising, Marketing and Media Weekly*, 7 December, pp. 22–3.

Adams, Phillip 1987, 'Beneath the Lino', in Mimmo Cozzolino & Fysh Rutherford, *Symbols of Australia*, Penguin, Melbourne.

Adams, Phillip 1994, 'Real-Life Portrait of Public Affairs', *Weekend Australian*, 14–15 May.

Adams, Phillip 1999, 'Bin There, Dunny That', *Weekend Australian*, 24–5 July, p. 29.

Advertising Standards Council 1978, *Third Report*, Advertising Standards Council, Sydney.

Advertising Standards Council 1981, *Advertising Standards Council: Fourth Report*, Advertising Standards Council, Sydney.

Aitken, Don 1972, 'Why We All Want to Know about the Government's Bungling', *The National Times*, 28 August–2 September, p. 14.

Allen, Yolanda, & Susan Spencer 1983, *The Broadcasting Chronology 1809–1980*, Australian Film and Television School, Sydney.

Altman, Dennis 1973, 'Gays Abandoned', *New Journalist*, June, pp. 6–7.

Anderson, Don 1972a, 'Coming Out', *Bulletin*, 11 November, p. 39.

Anderson, Don 1972b, 'Rotten Forbidden Fruit', *Bulletin*, 25 March, p. 40.

Anderson, Don 1972c, 'National Styles in Cops and Robbers', *Bulletin*, 5 February, 36.

Ang, Ien 1985, *Watching Dallas: Soap Opera and the Melodramatic Imagination*, Methuen, London.

Ang, Ien 1996, *Living Room Wars: Rethinking Media Audiences for a Postmodern World*, Routledge, London.

Ang, Ien, & Jon Stratton 1995, 'The End of Civilisation as We Knew It: Chances and the Postrealist Soap Opera', in Robert C. Allen (ed.), *To Be Continued: Soap Operas Around the World*, Routledge, London, pp. 122–44.

Appleton, Gillian 1988, *How Australia Sees Itself: The Role of Commercial Television*, Australian Broadcasting Tribunal, Sydney.

Aries, Philippe 1973, *Centuries of Childhood*, Penguin Books, Harmondsworth.

Armstrong, Mark, Michael Blakeney, & Ray Watterson 1983, *Media Law in Australia: A Manual*, Oxford University Press, Melbourne.

Arndt, H.W. 1986, 'The "Impartiality" of Four Corners', *IPA Review*, spring, pp. 42–3.

Artel, Linda, & Susan Wendgraf 1990 (1978), 'Positive Images: Screening Women's Films', in Patricia Erens (ed.), *Issues in Feminist Film Criticism*, Indiana University Press, Bloomington, pp. 9–12.

Ashbolt, Allan 1974, *An Australian Experience: Words from the Vietnam Years*, Australasian Book Society, Sydney.

Ashbolt, Allan 1987a, 'The ABC in Civil Society: The Relationships with Institutions and Audiences', in Ted Wheelwright & Ken Buckley (eds), *Communications and the Media in Australia*, Allen & Unwin, Sydney, pp. 97-116.

Ashbolt, Allan 1987b, 'The ABC in Political Society: The Relationship with Government', in Ted Wheelwright & Ken Buckley (eds), *Communications and the Media in Australia*, Allen & Unwin, Sydney, pp. 78–96.

ATV 30 Years of Television 1994, produced by Niki Wilton, directed by Bob Loxton, & written by Mal Walden, Channel Ten, Melbourne.

'Aunty Dares to Be Scandalous' 1985, *Canberra Times*, 27 December, held in ABC clippings library, 'ABC—Television—General 1979–1985'.

Australian Broadcasting Control Board 1957, *The Ninth Annual Report of the Australian Broadcasting Control Board*, L. G. Shea, Government Printer, Tasmania.

Australian Broadcasting Control Board 1958, *Tenth Annual Report of the Australian Broadcasting Control Board*, A. J. Arthur, Commonwealth Government Printer, Canberra.

Australian Broadcasting Control Board 1960, *Twelfth Annual Report of the Australian Broadcasting Control Board*, A. J. Arthur, Commonwealth Government Printer, Canberra.

Australian Broadcasting Control Board 1961, *Thirteenth Annual Report of the Australian Broadcasting Control Board*, A. J. Arthur, Commonwealth Government Printer, Canberra.

Australian Broadcasting Control Board 1962, *Fourteenth Annual Report of the Australian Broadcasting Control Board*, A. J. Arthur, Commonwealth Government Printer, Canberra.

Australian Broadcasting Control Board 1963, *Fifteenth Annual Report of the Australian Broadcasting Control Board*, A. J. Arthur, Commonwealth Government Printer, Canberra.

Australian Broadcasting Control Board 1964, *Sixteenth Annual Report of the Australian Broadcasting Control Board*, A. J. Arthur, Commonwealth Government Printer, Canberra.

Australian Broadcasting Control Board 1965, *Seventeenth Annual Report of the Australian Broadcasting Control Board*, A. J. Arthur, Commonwealth Government Printer, Canberra.

Australian Broadcasting Control Board 1966, *Eighteenth Annual Report of the Australian Broadcasting Control Board*, A. J. Arthur, Commonwealth Government Printer, Canberra.

Australian Broadcasting Control Board 1967, *Nineteenth Annual Report*, A. J. Arthur, Commonwealth Government Printer, Canberra.

Australian Broadcasting Control Board 1968, *Twentieth Annual Report*, A. J. Arthur, Commonwealth Government Printer, Canberra.

Australian Broadcasting Control Board 1969, *Twenty-First Annual Report*, Commonwealth Government Printing Office, Canberra.

Australian Broadcasting Control Board 1970, *Attitudes to Television—A Report Based on Surveys Made in Sydney and Melbourne During 1968 and 1969*, Australian Broadcasting Control Board, Melbourne.

Australian Broadcasting Control Board 1971, *Twenty-Third Annual Report*, Australian Government Publishing Service, Canberra .

Australian Broadcasting Control Board 1972, *Twenty-Fourth Annual Report*, Australian Government Publishing Service, Canberra.

Australian Broadcasting Control Board 1973, *Twenty-Fifth Annual Report*, Australian Government Publishing Service, Canberra.

Australian Broadcasting Control Board 1974, *Twenty-Sixth Annual Report*, Australian Government Publishing Service, Canberra.

Australian Broadcasting Control Board 1975, *Twenty-Seventh Annual Report*, Australian Government Publishing Service, Canberra.

Australian Broadcasting Control Board 1976, *Twenty-Eighth Annual Report*, Australian Government Publishing Service, Canberra.

Australian Broadcasting Tribunal 1979a, *Annual Report, Australian Broadcasting Tribunal 1978–79*, Australian Government Publishing Service, Canberra.

Australian Broadcasting Tribunal 1979b, *Annual Report, Australian Broadcasting Tribunal, 1977–78*, Australian Government Publishing Service, Canberra.

Australian Broadcasting Tribunal 1979c, *Television and the Public: A Decade of Research, 1968–1977*, Australian Government Publishing Service, Canberra.

Australian Broadcasting Tribunal 1981a, *Annual Report, Australian Broadcasting Tribunal, 1979–80*, Australian Government Publishing Service, Canberra.

Australian Broadcasting Tribunal 1981b, *Annual Report, Australian Broadcasting Tribunal, 1980–81*, Australian Government Publishing Service, Canberra.

Australian Broadcasting Tribunal 1982, *Annual Report, Australian Broadcasting Tribunal, 1981–82*, Australian Government Publishing Service, Canberra.

Australian Broadcasting Tribunal 1986, *Australian Broadcasting Tribunal, Annual Report, 1985–86*, Australian Government Publishing Service, Canberra.

Australian Broadcasting Tribunal 1988a, *The Price of Being Australian: Report of the Proceedings of a Conference Held to Mark the Tenth Anniversary of the Australian Broadcasting Tribunal and to Coincide with the International Institute of Communications Conference*, Australian Broadcasting Tribunal, Sydney.

Australian Broadcasting Tribunal 1988b, *Ratings of Australian Drama Series, Mini-Series, Films and Telemovies*, Australian Broadcasting Tribunal, Melbourne.

Australian Broadcasting Tribunal 1991, *Australian Broadcasting Tribunal Annual Report, 1990–1991*, Australian Government Publishing Service, Canberra.

Australian Bureau of Statistics 1995, *Australian Social Trends*, Australian Bureau of Statistics, Canberra.

Australian Image, The 1989a, episode 3, 'It's on the Record', written by Albie Thoms, directed by Christina Hunniford, & produced by Nick Hildyard & Ray Edmondson, Australian Capital Television and the National Film and Sound Archive.

Australian Image, The 1989b, episode 5, 'Stop Laughing—This is Serious', written by Wendy Thompson, directed by Christina Hunniford, & produced by Nick Hildyard & Ray Edmondson, Capital Television/National Film and Sound Archive, Canberra.

Australian Image, The 1989c, episode 6, 'Hooray for the Radio', written by Jacqueline Kent, directed by Christina Hunniford, & produced by Nick Hildyard & Ray Edmondson, Capital Television/National Film and Sound Archive, Canberra.

Australian Image, The 1989d, episode 8, 'You've Got to Be Kidding', written by Wendy Thompson, directed by Christina Hunniford, & produced by Nick Hildyard & Ray Edmonson, Capital Television/National Film and Sound Archive, Canberra.

Australian Image, The 1989e, episode 11, 'The One Eyed Monster', written by Catherine Brookman, directed by Christina Hunniford, & produced by Nick Hildyard & Ron Edmondson, Capital Television/National Film and Sound Archive, Canberra.

'Australian Invasion, The' 1979, *TV Times, Melbourne*, 28 July, p. 7.

Bailey, Julie James 1978, 'The Size and Structure of the Australian Film and Television Industry', *Australian Journal of Screen Theory*, no. 5/6, pp. 5–13.

Bailey, Julie James 1979, *Australian Television: Historical Overview*, no publication details, monograph reprinted from *Cinema Papers*, no. 23, September–October.

Baker, Glenn A. 1989, 'The Molly Resurgence', *Australian Magazine*, 20–21 May, pp. 18–22, 24.

Barber, Lynden 1990, 'Waiting for "Colour" TV', *Sydney Morning Herald*, 29 September, p. 9.

Barr, Trevor 1977, *Reflections of Reality: The Media in Australia*, Rigby, Adelaide.

Barr, Trevor 1985, *The Electronic Estate: New Communications Media and Australia*, Penguin, Melbourne.

Bass, Marco 1984, *Bodyline: A Study Guide*, Australian Children's Television Foundation, Melbourne.

Battersby, Jean 1968, 'Teenagers', in Mungo MacCallum (ed.), *Ten Years of Television*, Sun Books, Melbourne, pp. 86–110.

Bednall, David, & Marie Hannaford 1980, *Television and Children: Recall of Television Advertising and Programs by Children*, Australian Broadcasting Tribunal, Melbourne.

Behind the Frontline 1995, produced and directed by John Tabbagh, Frontline Productions, and Australian Broadcasting Corporation, Melbourne.

Beilby, Peter (ed.) 1981, *Australian TV: The First 25 Years*, Thomas Nelson, Melbourne.

Bell, Glennys 1972, 'Is the Taste of the Television Viewer Really So Bad?', *National Times*, 8–13 May, p. 3.

Bell, Philip 1983, 'Drugs as News: Defining the Social', *Australian Journal of Cultural Studies*, vol. 1, no. 2, pp. 101–19.

Bell, Philip, & Roger Bell 1993, *Implicated: The United States in Australia*, Oxford University Press, Melbourne.

Bell, Philip, & Theo van Leeuwen 1994, *Media Interview: Confession, Contest, Conversation, Communication and Culture*, ed. Gunther Kress, University of New South Wales Press, Sydney.

Bell, Philip, Kathe Boehringer, & Stephen Crofts 1982a, *Programmed Politics: A Study of Australian Television*, Sable Publishing, Sydney.

Bell, Philip, Kathe Boehringer, & Stephen Crofts 1982b, 'Willesee at Sixes and Sevens', *Australian Journal of Screen Theory*, no. 11/12, pp. 28–57.

Bell, Sharon 1998, 'Reinventing Chatwin's *The Songlines* for the Screen: Scholarly or Creative Process', in John Bigelow (ed.), *Our Cultural Heritage: Papers from the 1997 Symposium of the Australian Academy of the Humanities*, Australian Academy of the Humanities, Canberra, pp. 329–36

Benn, Jill 1999, 'Culture as Commodity: The Home as Spectacle in Popular Culture' Honours Thesis, School of Communication and Multimedia, Edith Cowan University, Perth.

Bennett, Tony, Michael Emmison, & John Frow 1999, *Accounting for Tastes: Australian Everyday Cultures*, Cambridge University Press, Cambridge.

Berger, John 1973, *Ways of Seeing*, Viking, New York.

Bernard, Jami 1997, *Chick Flicks: A Movie Lover's Guide to the Movies Women Love*, Citadel Press, Secaucus, NJ.

Bettridge, Gareth 1999, 'Prisoner', *PCBH Digest V2*, Edition 985.

Bianculli, David 1996, *Dictionary of Teleliteracy: Television's 500 Biggest Hits, Misses and Events*, The Television Series, ed. Robert J. Thompson, Syracuse University Press, New York.

Bigelow, John 1998, 'Introduction', in John Bigelow (ed.), *Our Cultural Heritage: Papers from the 1997 Symposium of the Australian Academy of the Humanities*, Australian Academy of the Humanities, Canberra, pp. vii–xii.

Black, Gregory D. 1997, *The Catholic Crusade Against the Movies, 1940–1975*, Cambridge University Press, Cambridge.

Blain, Ellis 1977, *Life with Aunty: Forty Years with the ABC*, Methuen of Australia, Sydney.

Blake, Terry 1991, 'Grundy's Gambling Man', *Weekend Australian*, 17–18 August, p. 15.

Blanch, Kirsten 1976, 'The Great Ocker Ad Debate', *Cleo*, September, pp. 130–3.

Blizard, John 1972, *Individual Differences and Television Viewing Behaviour*, Hedges & Bell, Maryborough, Victoria.

Blundell, Graeme 2000, 'Talk of the Town', *Australian, Media Section*, 13 July, p. 28.

Boddy, William 1999, Television in Transit, unpublished paper delivered at the Media in Transition conference, MIT, Boston, October 1999.

Boehringer, Kathe, Bill Bonney, Tim Rowse, & Helen Wilson (eds) 1980, *Media in Crisis: Proceedings of the Third Communication Technology and Control Conference*, Communication, Technology and Control Foundation, Sydney.

Bolton, Clive 1978, 'The Conscience of the King', *Australian*, 30 January, p. 8.

Bonner, Frances 1999, Lifestyle Television, unpublished draft.

Bonney, William (Bill) 1981, *Australian Media Ownership and Control*, Media Interventions, Intervention Publications, Sydney.

Bonney, Bill 1987, 'Commercial Television: Regulation, Technology and Market Forces', in Ted Wheelwright & Ken Buckley (eds), *Communications and the Media in Australia*, Allen & Unwin, Sydney, pp. 40–57.

Bonney, Bill 1988, 'Media and the People', in Verity Burgman & Jenny Lee (eds), *Constructing a Culture: A People's History of Australia Since 1788*, McPhee Gribble/Penguin, Melbourne, pp. 136–55.

Bonney, Bill 1992, 'Television and the Reconstruction of Cricket', in Albert Moran (ed.), *Stay Tuned: An Australian Broadcasting Reader*, Allen & Unwin, Sydney, pp. 124–34.

Bowd, Kathryn 1997, 'The New News Media—Do They Have a Future?', *Australian Journalism Review*, vol. 19, no. 1, June, pp. 57–68.

Bowden, Tim 1990, *The Backchat Book*, ABC Enterprises, Sydney.

Bowring, Pat 1990, 'How to Win in Television', *Herald*, 31 May, pp. 45–6.

Boyd, D. 1979, 'Sullivans Fan', *TV Times, Melbourne*, 11 August, p. 40.

Brady, Nicole 1997, 'Swelling Public Opinion', *Age, Metro Magazine*, 2 May, p. 3.

Breen, Myles P. 1997, 'Australian Programming', in Horace Newcomb (ed.), *Museum of Broadcast Communications Encyclopedia of Television*, Fitzroy Dearborn Publishers, Chicago, pp. 126–31.

Brown, Allan 1986, *Commercial Media in Australia*, University of Queensland Press, St Lucia.

Bryden-Brown, John 1981, *Ads That Made Australia: How Advertising Has Shaped Our History and Lifestyle*, Doubleday Australia, Sydney.

Burke, Don 1999a, 'Buying a Barbie', *Burke's Backyard*, December, pp. 34–9.

Burke, Don 1999b, 'Tropical Garden', *Burke's Backyard*, December, pp. 8–12.

Burke, Jacinta 1984, *Survey of Australian Television Program Production*, Australian Broadcasting Tribunal Research Branch, Melbourne.

Burke, Jacinta, Helen Wilson, & Susanna Agardy 1983, *A Country Practice and the Child Audience: A Case Study*, Australian Broadcasting Tribunal, Melbourne.

Burke's Backyard 1987, episode 10/87, tx (transmitted) 14.11.1987, produced by Don Burke & directed by Steve Wood, CTC Productions and Channel Nine, Sydney.

Burke's Backyard 1988, episode 9/88, tx 9.4.1988, executive produced and directed by Steve Wood, CTC Productions and Channel Nine, Sydney.

Burke's Backyard 1989, episode 10/89, tx 14.4.1989, executive produced and directed by Steve Wood, CTC Productions and Channel Nine, Sydney.

Burke's Backyard 1990, episode 10/90, tx 20.4.1990, executive produced and directed by Steve Wood, CTC Productions and Channel Nine, Sydney.

Burke's Backyard 1991, episode 11/91, tx 26.04.1991, produced & directed by Greg Beness, CTC Productions and Channel Nine, Sydney.

Burke's Backyard 1992, episode 10/92, tx 17.04.1992, produced by Greg Beness, CTC Productions and Channel Nine, Sydney.

'Burke's Backyard Press Release' 1999, Channel Nine, Perth.

Burke's Backyard: 10th Anniversary Special 1997, produced by Andy Simon and Chris Burke, CTC Productions and Channel Nine, Sydney.

Burnett, Ewan 1984, 'Mini-series', *Cinema Papers*, no. 44/45, pp. 32–6.

Burns, Janice Breen 1997, 'Maternity Masterpiece', *Age, Metro Magazine*, 7 May, p. 5.

Byrell, John 1995, *Bandstand and All That!*, Kangaroo Press, Sydney.

Caffrey, M. A. 1979, 'Sickened', *TV Times, Melbourne*, 8 September, p. 40.

Caldwell, John Thornton 1995, *Televisuality: Style, Crisis and Authority in American Television*, Communications, Media and Culture series, ed. George F. Custen, Rutgers University Press, New Brunswick, NJ.

Cassells, Lynnette 1990, 'Brits Spend Big to Give TV Soap a Sydney Scent', *Sun-Herald*, 18 March, p. 28.

Casson, John 1959, 'Vision in Television', *Walkabout*, November, pp. 23–6.

Chadwick, Paul n.d., 'Licensing Journalists is Fraught with Risk', *Australian*.

Chadwick, Paul 1989, *Media Mates: Carving up Australia*, Sun Books, Melbourne.

Channel Nine Publicity 1999, 'Burke's Backyard, Press Release, Ep. 41, 26.11.1999', Channel Nine, Sydney.

'Channel 7: 40 Years of Television', *West Australian*, supplement, October, pp. 3–17.

'Children Not Fond of Quota TV' 1976, *Canberra Times*, held in ABC, file, 'Children's TV', n.d.

Children's Television Advisory Committee 1974, *Production Guidelines for Children's Television Programmes, First Report of the Children's Television Advisory Committee to the Australian Broadcasting Control Board*, Australian Government Publishing Service, Canberra.

Cho, Judy 1988, 'Crazy for Kylie: TV Chiefs Sweat over Aussie Invasion', *Sun*, 23 February, p. 28 .

Clark, Lucy 1988, 'What Does Make a Successful Drama?', *Sun-Herald*, 4 September, p. 34.

Clarke, G. 1997, 'What a Fast, Oops, Farce', *Age*, 24 April, p. 18.

'Closeup' 1979, *TV Times, Melbourne*, 21 July, p. 7.

Cole, Michael 1990, 'Preface', in David Middleton & Derek Edwards (eds), *Collective Remembering*, Sage Publications, London, pp. vii–ix.

Collins, Carolyn 1996, 'Soaps' Success Puts Brits off the Tourism Track', *Weekend Australian*, 24 February, p. 16.

Connery, Brian A., & Kirk Combe 1995, 'Theorizing Satire: A Retrospective and Introduction', in Brian A. Connery & Kirk Combe (eds), *Theorizing Satire: Essays in Literary Criticism*, St Martin's Press, New York, pp. 1–15

Conway, Ronald 1988, 'Neighbours', *Quadrant*, June, pp. 50–2.

Cook, Jackie, & Karen Jennings 1995, 'Live and Sweaty: Australian Women Re-cast Australian Sports Television', *Media Information Australia*, no. 75, pp. 5–12.

Corner, John 1991, 'General Introduction: Television and British Society in the 1950s', in John Corner (ed.), *Popular Television in Britain: Studies in Cultural History*, BFI Publishing, London, pp. 1–21.

Countdown 1979, episode 201, executive produced by Michael Shrimpton, and produced & directed by Ted Emery, Australian Broadcasting Corporation, Sydney.

Country Practice, A 1991a, episode 799, 'The Promised Land: Part 1', written by Graeme Koetsveld, produced by Denny Lawrence & Robyn Sinclair, & directed by Richard Sarell, JNP Productions and Channel Seven, Sydney.

Country Practice, A 1991b, episode 800, 'The Promised Land: Part 2', written by David Phillips & directed by Richard Sarell, JNP Productions and Channel Seven, Sydney.

Coupe, Bronwyn, Andrew Jakubowicz, & Lois Randall 1992, *Nextdoor Neighbours: A Report for the Office of Multicultural Affairs on Ethnic Group Discussions of the Australian Media*, Australian Government Publishing Service, Canberra.

Courtis, Brian 1981, 'News and Documentaries', in Peter Beilby (ed.), *Australian TV: The First 25 Years*, Thomas Nelson, Melbourne, pp. 90–109.

Cozzolino, Mimmo & Fysh Rutherford (eds), *Symbols of Australia*, Penguin, Melbourne.

Craik, Jennifer, Julie James Bailey, & Albert Moran 1995, *Public Voices, Private Interests: Australia's Media Policy*, Allen & Unwin, Sydney.

Craven, Ian 1989, 'Distant Neighbours: Notes on Some Australian Soap Operas', *Australian Studies: Journal of the British Australian Studies Association*, no. 3, pp. 1–35.

Craven, Ian 1992, 'Race and Ethnicity in the Drip Dramas', in Werner Senn & Giovanna Capone (eds), *The Making of a Pluralist Australia 1950–1990: Selected Papers from the Inaugural EASA Conference, 1991*, Peter Lang, Bern, pp. 241–56.

Crawford, Hector 1959, *Commercial Television Programs in Australia*, Hector Crawford, Melbourne.

Crisp, Lyndall 1984, 'Molly's Finger on the Pulse', *National Times*, 9–15 November, pp. 29–30.

Crofts, Stephen, & Jennifer Craik 1983, 'Constructing the Political in *The Dismissal*', *Australian Journal of Cultural Studies*, vol. 1, no. 2, pp. 91–6.

'Crowning Glory' 1980, *TV Times*, 2–8 February, p. 17.

Cunningham, Stuart 1983, 'The Dismissal and Australian Television', *Australian Journal of Cultural Studies*, vol. 1, no. 2, pp. 83–90.

Cunningham, Stuart 1985, 'Hollywood Genres, Australian Movies', in Albert Moran & Tom O'Regan (eds), *An Australian Film Reader*, Currency Press, Sydney, pp. 235–41.

Cunningham, Stuart 1988, 'Kennedy Miller: "House Style" in Australian Television', in Susan Dermody & Elizabeth Jacka (eds), *The Imaginary Industry: Australian Film in the Late '80s*, special edn, Media Information Australia, no. 50, November, Australian Film, Television and Radio School, Sydney, pp. 178–99.

Cunningham, Stuart 1989, 'Style, Form and History in Australian Mini-series', *Southern Review*, vol. 22, no. 3, pp. 315–30.

Cunningham, Stuart 1991, *Featuring Australia: The Cinema of Charles Chauvel*, Allen & Unwin, Sydney.

Cunningham, Stuart 1992, *Framing Culture: Criticism and Policy in Australia*, Allen & Unwin, Sydney.

Cunningham, Stuart 1993, 'Cultural Studies from the Viewpoint of Cultural Policy', in Graeme Turner (ed.), *Nation, Culture, Text: Australian Cultural and Media Studies*, Routledge, London, pp. 126–39.

Cunningham, Stuart, & Elizabeth Jacka 1995, 'Australian Television in World Markets', in John Sinclair, Elizabeth Jacka & Stuart Cunningham (eds), *New Patterns in Global Television: Peripheral Vision*, Oxford University Press, Oxford, pp. 192–225.

Cunningham, Stuart, & Elizabeth Jacka 1996, *Australian Television and International Mediascapes*, Cambridge University Press, Cambridge.

Cunningham, Stuart, & Graeme Turner (eds) 1993, *The Media in Australia: Industries, Texts, Audiences*, Allen & Unwin, Sydney.

Cunningham, Stuart, & Toby Miller 1994, *Contemporary Australian Television*, University of New South Wales Press, Sydney.

Cupitt, Margaret 1998, *Infants and Television*, Australian Broadcasting Authority, Sydney.

Curthoys, Ann 1986, 'The Getting of Television: Dilemmas in Ownership, Control and Culture: 1941–1956', in Ann Curthoys & John Merritt (ed.), *Better Dead Than Red: Australia's First Cold War*, vol. 2, *1945–1959*, Allen & Unwin, Sydney, pp. 123–54.

Curthoys, Ann, & John Docker 1989, 'In Praise of *Prisoner*', in John Tulloch & Graeme Turner (eds), *Australian Television: Programs, Politics, Pleasures*, Allen & Unwin, Sydney.

Curtis, Maree 1997, 'Shakespeare or Mike Moore in VCE English? Hmmmmm … Disturbing Stuff', *Sunday Age*, 24 August, p. 3.

D'Acci, Julie 1997, 'Nobody's Woman? Honey West and the New Sexuality', in Lynn Spigel & Michael Curtin (eds), *The Revolution Wasn't Televised: Sixties Television and Social Conflict*, Routledge, London, pp. 73–94.

Dale, David 1998, 'The 50 Most Influential Shows in Australian Television History', *Sydney Morning Herald, The Guide Magazine*, 25–31 May, pp. 4–5.

Dale, David 1999, 'Give Us a Break', *The West Magazine [West Australian]*, 13 March, pp. 25–6.

Davies, Brian 1981, *Those Fabulous TV Years*, Casell Australia, Sydney.

Davies, Maire Messenger, & David Machin 1999, Children's Demon TV: Reality, Freedom, Panic: Children's Discussions of The Demon Headmaster, unpublished draft manuscript.

Dawson, Jonathan 1990, 'Our Beer', in Jonathan Dawson & Bruce Molloy (eds), *Queensland Images in Film and Television*, University of Queensland Press, St Lucia, pp. 93–103.

Day, Christopher 1981, 'Drama', in Peter Beilby (ed.), *Australian TV: The First 25 Years*, Thomas Nelson, Melbourne, pp. 134–59.

Day, Christopher (ed.) 1991, *A Country Practice: 10th Birthday Souvenir*, Express Publications with Georgie Broan Publicity, Sydney.

Dean, Peter 1978, 'The Sullivans' Amazing Grace', *TV Times*, 2 December, pp. 10–11.

Dearn, Alan 1972, 'Wallop for Homicide 2', *Herald*, 12 October.

Denton, Kit 1968, 'Public Affairs', in Mungo MacCallum (ed.), *Ten Years of Television*, Sun Books, Melbourne, pp. 44–66.

Dermody, Susan, & Elizabeth Jacka 1987, *The Screening of Australia: Anatomy of a Film Industry*, vol. 1, Currency Press, Sydney.

Deveny, Catherine 1997, 'At Large in the Bra Department', *Age, Metro Magazine*, 1 October, p. 1.

Dixon, Frank 1975, *Inside the ABC: A Piece of Australian History*, The Hawthorn Press, Melbourne.

Docker, John 1983, 'Unprecedented in History: Drama and the Dramatic in Television', *Australasian Drama Studies*, vol. 1, no. 2, pp. 47–62.

Docker, John 1988, 'Popular Culture and Bourgeois Values', in Verity Burgman & Jenny Lee (eds), *Constructing a Culture: A People's History of Australia Since 1788*, McPhee Gribble/Penguin, Melbourne, pp. 241–58.

Docker, John 1997, 'Kennedy, Graham', in Horace Newcomb (ed.), *Museum of Broadcast Communications Encyclopedia of Television*, Fitzroy Dearborn Publishers, Chicago, pp. 878–9.

Docker, John, & Ann Curthoys 1997, 'Prisoner', in Horace Newcomb (ed.), *Museum of Broadcast Communications Encyclopedia of Television*, Fitzroy Dearborn Publishers, Chicago, pp. 1293–7.

Dudding, Howard 1977, 'TV's Rock Coverage—Too Much, Too Soon?', *TV Times* 7 January 1977, pp. 11.

Duffell, C. 1980, *Bias and Television Coverage of the 1977 Election*, Media Papers no. 5, NSW Institute of Technology, Sydney.

Dyer, Richard 1998, *Stars*, revised edn, BFI Publishing, London.

Edgar, Patricia 1980, *The News in Focus*, Macmillan, Melbourne.

Edgar, Patricia, & Ursula Callus 1979, *The Unknown Audience: A Study of Children's Responses to Television Programs*, Centre for the Study of Educational Communication and Media, La Trobe University, Melbourne.

Edgar, Patricia, Don Edgar, Millicent Poole, Tom Roper, & Margaret Higgs 1973, *Under 5 in Australia*, William Heinemann Australia, Melbourne.

Elder, Bruce 1979, *Mass Media in Australia*, Making Australian Society, ed. D. O'Keefe, Thomas Nelson, Melbourne.

Elder, Bruce 1995, 'The 25 All-time Best Australian TV Shows', *Sydney Morning Herald, The Guide Magazine*, 26 June, p. 6S.

Elkin, P. K. 1973, *The Augustan Defence of Satire*, The Clarendon Press, Oxford.

Ellis, Eric 1996, 'Hasham Happy to Come Out in KL', *Financial Review*, 3 January, p. 41.

Este, Jonathon 2000, 'Bigwigs Put Playschool Together Again', *Australian*, 4 February, p. 2.

'Fake Cop Caper, The' 1964, *TV Times, Melbourne*, 11 November, pp. 12–13.

Fast Forward, the Book: The Complete Guide to 3000 Years of Television 1990, Penguin, Melbourne.

Felsenthal, Norman 1997, 'Sexual Orientation and Television', in Horace Newcomb (ed.), *Museum of Broadcast Communications Encyclopedia of Television*, Fitzroy Dearborn Publishers, Chicago, pp. 1477–82.

Feuer, Jane 1995, *Seeing Through the Eighties*, BFI Publishing, London.

Fiske, John 1987, *Television Culture*, Methuen, London.

Fiske, John, Bob Hodge, & Graeme Turner 1987, *Myths of Oz: Reading Australian Popular Culture*, Allen & Unwin, Sydney.

Fitzgerald, Justice Tony 1999, 'Telling the Truth, Laughing', *Media International Australia, Incorporating Culture and Policy*, no. 92, pp. 11–18.

'Flash of the Old Gra-Gra' 1988, *Sydney Daily Telegraph*, 26 September, p. 18.

Flew, Terry 1997, 'Homicide', in Horace Newcomb (ed.), *Museum of Broadcast Communications Encyclopedia of Television*, Fitzroy Dearborn Publishers, Chicago, pp. 786–7.

40 Years of Channel Nine Unplugged 1999, broadcast 19 November, Channel Nine, Sydney.

Foucault, Michel 1991(1971), 'Nietzsche, Genealogy, History', in Paul Rabinow (ed.), *The Foucault Reader: An Introduction to Foucault's Thought*, Penguin, London, pp. 76–100.

Four Corners 1963, executive produced by Allan Ashbolt, Australian Broadcasting Corporation, Sydney, tx 31.8.1963.

Four Corners: 25 Years 1987, executive produced by Peter Manning, Australian Broadcasting Corporation, Sydney.

Freeman, Jane 1999, 'Out and About', *Sydney Morning Herald, Guide*, 17–23 May, pp. 4–5.

Frith, Simon, & Jon Savage 1997, 'Pearls and Swine: Intellectuals and the Mass Media', in Steve Redhead (ed.), *The Clubcultures Reader*, Blackwell, Oxford.

Frontline 1994a, 'Add Sex and Stir', written, produced, & directed by Jane Kennedy, Rob Sitch, Tom Gleisner, & Santo Cilauro, Frontline Productions and Australian Broadcasting Corporation, Melbourne.

Frontline 1994b, 'Desert Angel', written, produced, & directed by Jane Kennedy, Rob Sitch, Tom Gleisner, & Santo Cilauro, Frontline Productions and Australian Broadcasting Corporation, Melbourne.

Frontline 1994c, 'Playing the Ego Card', written, produced, & directed by Jane Kennedy, Rob Sitch, Tom Gleisner, & Santo Cilauro, Frontline Productions and Australian Broadcasting Corporation, Melbourne.

Frontline 1994d, 'Smaller Fish to Fry', written, produced, & directed by Jane Kennedy, Rob Sitch, Tom Gleisner, & Santo Cilauro, Frontline Productions and Australian Broadcasting Corporation, Melbourne.

Frontline 1994e, 'The Siege', written, produced, & directed by Jane Kennedy, Rob Sitch, Tom Gleisner, & Santo Cilauro, Frontline Productions and Australian Broadcasting Corporation, Melbourne.

Frontline 1994f, 'This Night of Nights', written, produced, & directed by Jane Kennedy, Rob Sitch, Tom Gleisner, & Santo Cilauro, Frontline Productions and Australian Broadcasting Corporation, Melbourne.

Frontline 1995a, 'Divide the Community, Multiply the Ratings', written, produced, & directed by Jane Kennedy, Rob Sitch, Tom Gleisner, & Santo Cilauro, Frontline Productions and Australian Broadcasting Corporation, Melbourne.

Frontline 1995b, 'Keeping Up Appearances', written, produced, & directed by Jane Kennedy, Rob Sitch, Tom Gleisner, & Santo Cilauro, Frontline Productions and Australian Broadcasting Corporation, Melbourne.

Frontline 1995c, 'Give 'Em Enough Rope', written, produced, & directed by Jane Kennedy, Rob Sitch, Tom Gleisner, & Santo Cilauro, Frontline Productions and Australian Broadcasting Corporation, Melbourne.

Frow, John 1995, *Cultural Studies and Cultural Value*, Clarendon Press, Oxford.

Fyfe, Melissa 1999, 'Gourmet News Hounds Leave a Nasty Taste', *Sunday Age*, 5 September, p. 6.

Gamman, Lorraine & Margaret Marshment (eds) 1988, *The Female Gaze: Women as Viewers of Popular Culture*, The Women's Press, London.

Gawenda, Michael 1983, 'Molly: Pop of the Pops,' *Age Saturday Extra*, 25 June, pp. 1–2.

Geraghty, Christine 1991, *Women and Soap Opera*, Polity Press, Cambridge.

Gerdes, Peter R. 1982, 'A Content Analysis of Australian Television News', *Australian Journal of Screen Theory*, no. 11/12, pp. 58–85.

Gerdes, Peter R., & Paul Charlier 1985, *TV News—That's the Way it Was … A Comparative Analysis of Sydney's Television News, August 1978 and August 1983*, Resources Unit, Australian Film and Television School, Sydney.

Gerster, Robin, & Jan Bassett 1991, *Seizures of Youth: The Sixties and Australia*, Hyland House, Melbourne.

Gibson, Mark 1997a, 'A Country Practice', in Horace Newcomb (ed.), *Museum of Broadcast Communications Encyclopedia of Television*, Fitzroy Dearborn Publishers, Chicago, pp. 436–8.

Gibson, Mark 1997b, 'Four Corners', in Horace Newcomb (ed.), *Museum of Broadcast Communications Encyclopedia of Television*, Fitzroy Dearborn Publishers, Chicago, pp. 627–9.

Gifford, Graham 1976, 'Ocker and Out', *Sydney Morning Herald*, 12 July, p. 7.

Gitter, Michael, Sylvie Anapol, & Erika Glazer 1999, *Do You Remember TV?*, Chronicle Books, San Francisco.

GKC9S. See *The Graham Kennedy Channel Nine Show*.

Gleitzman, Morris 1992, *Gleitzman on Television: Just Looking*, Sun/ Macmillan, Sydney.

Glover, Richard 1991, 'They Love Him, They Love Him Not', *Sydney Morning Herald, Good Weekend Magazine*, 27 April, pp. 10–17.

Goddard, Martyn 1990, 'The Electronic Closet', *Outrage*, September, pp. 40–5.

Goeschel, K. 1997, 'Anything but …', *Age Green Guide*, 1 May, p. 24.

Goldman, Ronald, & Juliette Goldman 1988, *Show Me Yours! Understanding Children's Sexuality*, Penguin, Melbourne.

Graham Kennedy Channel Nine Show, The 1960, directed by Ron Davis & produced by Tom Miller, GTV 9, Melbourne.

Graham Kennedy: King of Television 2000, produced and directed by Tony Sattler, Wintergreen Productions and Channel Nine, Sydney.

Graham Kennedy Show, The n.d., no. 8/2, held at Screensound, Melbourne, accession no. AVC007738(1).

Grant, A. F. 1997, 'Buckley's Painful Pregnancy', *Age*, 4 May, p. 20.

Gray, Darren 1994, 'Soaps in Oz', *Wire TV Soap Special*, August, pp. 30–42.

Greer, Germaine 1970, *The Female Eunuch*, MacGibbon & Kee, London.

Gripsrud, Jostein 1998, 'Television, Broadcasting, Flow: Key Metaphors in TV Theory', in Christine Geraghty & David Lusted (eds), *The Television Studies Book*, Arnold, London, pp. 17–32.

Gutfield, Greg 1999, '30 Chores to Ignore', *New Woman*, August, pp. 100–5.

Gyffin, Jenni 1988, 'Australia's First Great TV Soapie', *Australian Listener*, 27 August–2 September, pp. 42–3.

Hall, Sandra 1972, 'Changing Fads in Ads', *Bulletin*, 12 February, pp. 47–9.

Hall, Sandra 1973, '*Number 96* and All That', *Australian Theatre Review*, no. 1, September, pp. 12–13.

Hall, Sandra 1976, *Supertoy: 20 Years of Australian Television*, Sun Books, Melbourne.

Hamilton, Peter, & Sue Mathews 1986, *American Dreams: Australian Movies*, Currency Press, Sydney.

Hammond, S. B., & Helen Glasser 1971, *Mass Media Preference in Adolescents: A Report*, Australian Broadcasting Control Board, Canberra.

Hand, Tim 1990, *Australian Mass Media Through 200 Years*, Kangaroo Press, Sydney.

Harding, Richard 1979, *Outside Interference: The Politics of Australian Broadcasting*, Sun Books, Melbourne.

Harding, Ann 1980, 'Anyhow, After Hogan the Admen Are Still Stunned', *National Times*, 20–26 July, p. 59.

Harris, Margaret 1990, 'Soap Sparks British Love Affair with Australia', *Sun-Herald*, 22 April, p. 38.

Harris, Richard 1994, *Punch Lines: Twenty Years of Australian Comedy*, ABC Books, Sydney.

Harris, Tina, & Jenny Irvine 1976, 'Is Television Really Bad for Kids?', *Woman's Day*, 22 November, pp. 76–7.

Harrison, Tony 1994, *The Australian Film and Television Companion*, Simon & Schuster, Sydney.

'Harry's Golden Night', *TV Times*, 22 October 1977, p. 5.

Hartley, John 1992a, *The Politics of Pictures: The Creation of the Public in the Age of Popular Media*, Routledge, London.

Hartley, John 1992b, *Tele-ology*, Routledge, London.

Hartley, John 1996, *Popular Reality: Journalism, Modernity, Popular Culture*, Arnold, London.

Hartley, John 1998, *Uses of Television*, Routledge, London.

Hartley, John 1999a, 50 Greatest Moments in Television, unpublished manuscript.

Hartley, John 2000, Public Address and the 'Frequencies' of Writing, unpublished paper, presented at the Media in Transition Conference, MIT, Cambridge, Mass., 8–10 October.

Hartley, John 1999c, The Television Live Event: From the 'Wandering Booby' to the 'Death of History', unpublished draft chapter.

Hartley, John, & Alan McKee 2000, *The Indigenous Public Sphere*, Oxford University Press, Oxford.

Hawkins, Trevor 1974, '*Number 96* Struck Paydirt: Now There's Another Series to Mine It', *National Times*, 14–19 January, p. 7.

Heading, Rex, & Trevor Jones 1996, *Miracle on Tynte Street: The Channel Nine Story*, Wakefield Press, Adelaide.

Henslin, James M. 1990, *Social Problems Today: Coping with the Challenges of a Changing Society*, Prentice Hall, Englewood Cliffs, NJ.

Herd, Nick 1988, *Variety Programs on Commercial Television*, Australian Broadcasting Tribunal Australian Content Inquiry, Australian Broadcasting Tribunal, Sydney.

Hewison, Robert 1986, *Too Much: Art and Society in the Sixties, 1960–75*, Methuen, London.

Hey Hey It's Saturday 1999, broadcast 20 November, Channel Nine, Melbourne.

Higham, Charles 1967, 'Tiniest Films in the World: Making Australian TV Commercials', *Bulletin*, 11 February, pp. 24–6.

Hill, John 1991, 'Television and Pop: The Case of the 1950s', in John Corner (ed.), *Popular Television in Britain: Studies in Cultural History*, BFI, London, pp. 90–107.

Hodge, Robert, & David Tripp 1986, *Children and Television: A Semiotic Approach*, Polity Press, Cambridge.

Hohensee, Michael 1978a, 'TV's Success Story—the Soaps', *TV Times, Melbourne*, pp. 24–5.

Hohensee, Mike 1978b, 'It's Lucky Skippy Doesn't Talk …', *TV Times, Melbourne*, 4 March, pp. 36, 38–9.

Holten, Diana 1999, 'Grassroots Campaign', *Age Green Guide*, 16 September, p. 9.

Homicide 1964a, episode 1, 'The Stunt', directed by Ian Jones & Bruce Ross Smith, written by Phil Freedman & Ian Jones, & produced by Ian Crawford, Crawfords Australia and Channel Seven, Melbourne.

Homicide 1964b, episode 5, 'The Man in the Suede Jacket', directed by Bruce Ross-Smith & Ian Jones, writtten by Phil Freedman, & produced by Ian Crawford, Crawfords Australia and Channel Seven, Melbourne.

Homicide 1964c, episode 7, 'Scent of Death', directed by Bruce Ross-Smith & Ian Jones, written by Della Foss Paine, & produced by Ian Crawford, Crawfords Australia and Channel Seven, Melbourne.

'Homicide' n.d., held in file 'Reference: Crawfords Australia Production Details—H', Crawfords Australia.

'*Homicide* Cop in Nude TV Role' 1972, publication details not given, kept in *Homicide* scrapbook, Crawfords Australia, Melbourne.

'*Homicide* Gets Off to a Good Start' 1964, *Listener In-TV*, 24 October, p. 9.

'*Homicide*—New Local Series Bows in on HSV' 1964, *TV Times*, 14 October, p. 3.

Homicide Story, The 1970, Crawfords Australia and Channel Seven, Melbourne.

'*Homicide* Strips Melbourne Naked' 1964, *TV Week*, 17 October, pp. 76–9.

'*Homicide*—Sudden Death to New Show Hopes' 1964, *TV Week*, 31 October, p. 24.

Homicide: 30 Years On 1994, written, produced, & directed by Jan Bladier & David Lee, Crawfords Australia, Melbourne.

Hood, Daryl 1964, 'They Are All in the Act', *Herald*, 3 November, p. 20.

Hooks, Barbara 1997, 'Star Learns Facts of Life About TV Pregnancy,' *Age Green Guide*, 27 April, p. 3.

Hooks, Barbara 1999, 'To Elle and Back', *Age Green Guide*, 18 November, p. 3.

'How the Ocker Prince Learned to Straddle the World' 1983, *Video Age*, January, pp. 6–7.

Howes, Keith 1993, *Broadcasting It: An Encyclopedia of Homosexuality on Film, Radio and Television in the UK 1923–1993*, Cassell, London.

Hughes, Colin, & John S. Western 1966, *The Prime Minister's Policy Speech: A Case Study in Televised Politics*, Australian National University Press, Canberra.

Hunt, Leon 1998, *British Low Culture: From Safari Suits to Sexploitation*, 1st edn, Routledge, London.

Hurst, John, & Sally A. White 1994, *Ethics and the Australian News Media*, Macmillan Education, Melbourne.

Hutchinson, Garrie 1986, 'The Funny Melbourne Television Phenomenon', *Meanjin*, vol. 46, no. 2, pp. 254–66.

Idato, Michael 1995, 'Cell Door Opens for Return of Prisoner', *Sunday Telegraph*, 27 August, p. 13.

Inglis, Ken 1983, *This Is the ABC: The Australian Broadcasting Corporation 1932–1983*, Melbourne University Press, Melbourne.

Inness, Sherrie A. 1999, *Tough Girls: Women, Warriors and Wonder Women in Popular Culture*, University of Pennsylvania Press, Philadelphia.

Innis, Harold 1991 (1951), *The Bias of Communication*, University of Toronto Press, Toronto.

Jacka, Elizabeth 1991, *The ABC of Drama, 1975–1990*, Australian Film, Television and Radio School, Sydney.

Jacka, Elizabeth 1992, 'Globalisation and Australian Film and Television', in Albert Moran (ed.), *Stay Tuned: An Australian Broadcasting Reader*, Allen & Unwin, Sydney, pp. 185–91.

Jacka, Elizabeth, & Lesley Johnson 1998, 'Australia', in Elizabeth Jacka, Lesley Johnson, Richard Paterson, & Anthony Smith (eds), *Television: An International History*, 2nd edn, Oxford University Press, Oxford, pp. 208 23.

Jackson, Stevi 1982, *Childhood and Sexuality*, Blackwell, Oxford.

Jakubowicz, Andrew (ed.) 1994, *Racism, Ethnicity and the Media*, Allen & Unwin, Sydney.

James, Caron 1997, 'Pregnant Nicky Stays on Sale', *TV Week*, 8 February, pp. 18–19.

Jancovich, Mark 1996, *Rational Fears: American Horror in the 1950s*, Manchester University Press, Manchester.

Jay, C. M. 1968, 'Australia's Surprise Export', *New Commonwealth*, February, p. 61.

Jeffrey, Nicole 1999, 'The Bias of the By-line', *Australian, Media Section*, 18 November, p. 9.

Jellie, Dugald 1997, 'Here's Your Free Stuff—Mind the Strings', *Age, Metro Magazine*, 11 April, p. 1.

Johnson, Patricia 1975, 'Paul Hogan Is Having the Last Laugh', *Cleo*, August, pp. 32–4.

Johnson, Nicholas, & Mark Armstrong 1977, *Two Reflections on Australian Broadcasting*, Media Centre Papers, Centre for the Study of Educational Communication and the Media, La Trobe University, Melbourne.

Johnson, Rob, & David Smiedt 1999, *Boom-Boom: A Century of Australian Comedy*, Hodder & Stoughton, Sydney.

Jones, Colin, & David Bednall 1980, *Television in Australia: Its History through Ratings*, Australian Broadcasting Tribunal, Sydney.

Jones, Dorothy, & Barry Andrews 1988, 'Australian Humour', in Laurie Hergenhan (ed.), *The Penguin New Literary History of Australia*, Penguin, Melbourne, pp. 60–76.

Jones, Mike McColl 1999, *And Now Here's … Four Decades of Behind the Scenes Fun in Australian Television*, Aerospace Publications, Canberra.

Jones, Ross 1991, *Cut! Protection of Australia's Film and Television Industries*, Centre for Independent Studies, Sydney.

Keating, Chris 1993, 'Australian Television Drama: A Brief Overview', *TV Eye: Journal of the Australian Television Appreciation Society*, no. 1, pp. 24–6.

Keating, Chris 1999a, personal communication, 27 March.

Keating, Chris 1999b, Interview with Alan McKee, September.

Kemp, Kevon 1971, 'Many Nice Guys but Where are the Stars', *National Times*, 26–31 July, pp. 22–3.

Kennedy, F. C. 1978, 'Looking in with the Viewer', *TV Times, Melbourne*, 29 April, p. 18.

Keys, Wendy 1999, 'Children's Television: A Barometer of the Australian Media Policy Climate', *Media International Australia*, no. 93, pp. 9–25.

'Kids Switch to Adult Night TV' 1976, *Telegraph*, 30 October.

King, Noel 1983, 'Current Affairs Television: Social Problems and the Problem of Representation', *Australian Journal of Screen Theory*, no. 13/14, pp. 43–58.

Kingsley, Hilary 1989, *Soap Box: The Australian Guide to Television Soap Operas*, Sun Books, Melbourne.

Kippax, Susan, & John P. Murray 1979, *Small Screen, Big Business: The Great Australian TV Robbery*, Angus & Robertson, London.

Kristianson, G. L. 1964, 'The RSL and Four Corners', *Australian Quarterly*, vol. 36, no. 1, pp. 20–30.

Kristianson, G. L. 1966, *The Politics of Patriotism: The Pressure Group Activities of the Returned Servicemen's League*, Australian National University Press, Canberra.

Langer, John 1989, 'Television News: "Shocking Me Right Outta My Brain"', *Media Information Australia*, no. 52, May, pp. 42–5.

Laud, Peter 1988, 'Practice—It Must Make Perfect Telly', *Sunday Times*, 21 August, p. 25.

Lawson, Sylvia 1983, 'An Audience for *The Dismissal*', *Australian Journal of Cultural Studies*, vol. 1, no. 2, pp. 97–100.

Lee, Sandra 1988, 'Ten Series is Junk, Says UK Soap Star', *Herald*, 5 January, p. 26.

Levett, J. 1979, 'Manners, Please', *TV Times, Melbourne*, 21 July, p. 40.

Lewis, Jon E., & Penny Stempel 1993, *Cult TV: The Essential Critical Guide*, Pavilion Books, London.

Lipitz, George 1990, *Time Passages: Collective Memory and American Popular Culture*, University of Minnesota Press, Minneapolis.

Littlemore, Stuart 1996, *The Media and Me*, ABC Books, Sydney.

Livingstone, Sonia, & Peter Lund 1994, *Talk on Television: Audience Participation and Public Debate*, Routledge, London.

Lloyd, Clement John 1988, *Parliament and the Press: The Federal Parliamentary Press Gallery 1901–88*, Melbourne University Press, Melbourne.

Lockwood, Kim 1980a, 'Non-celebrity Tattle-teller', *Herald*, 18 February, p. 2.

Lockwood, Kim 1980b, 'Quick Change Artist ... That's Jock', *Herald*, 19 February, p. 2.

Lopez, Rex 1972, 'How Will Cops Get the Bullet?', *Sun*, 13 October.

Lucas, Rose 1994, ' "Round the Block": Back to the Suburb in Return Home', in Chris Healy, Sarah Ferber & Chris McAuliffe (eds), *Beasts of Suburbia: Reinterpreting Cultures in Australian Suburbs*, Melbourne University Press, Melbourne, pp. 111–26.

Luck, Peter 1988, 'Luck on Soap', *Sydney Morning Herald*, 5 September.

Luck, Peter 1990, 'Relative Values', *The Listener*, 13 September, pp. 13, 16.

Lumby, Catharine 1999, *Gotcha: Life in a Tabloid World*, Allen & Unwin, Sydney.

McAuliffe, Chris 1996, *Art and Suburbia*, Craftsman House, Sydney.

McCabe, Colin 1974, 'Realism and the Cinema: Notes on Some Brechtian Theses', *Screen*, vol. 15, no. 1, pp. 7–27.

McCallum, John 1998, 'Cringe and Strut: Comedy and National Identity in Post-war Australia', in Stephen Wagg (ed.), *Because I Tell a Joke or Two: Comedy, Politics and Social Difference*, Routledge, London, pp. 202– 20.

MacCallum, Mungo 1968, 'Drama', in Mungo MacCallum (ed.), *Ten Years of Television*, Sun Books, Melbourne, pp. 67–85.

McCamey, David 1984, 'Top Series on TV Carries a Message', *Sunday Telegraph*, 24 April.

McCarthy, Phillip 1978, 'How Aunty Controls the Pop Game', *National Times*, 24–30 December, p. 7.

McCathie, Andrew 1991, 'Europe Tunes in to "New-look" Australia', *Financial Review*, 3 September, p. 32.

McClymont, Kate 1986, 'Will the Real Hoges/Hogan Stand Up?', *National Times*, 25–31 July, p. 10.

MacDonald, Marion 1973, 'TV Creates the Gold-plated Ocker', *Bulletin*, 24 February, pp. 53–5.

McGuigan, Jim 1997, 'Review, Popular Reality', *European Journal of Communication*, vol. 12, no. 2.

Mcintyre, Jan 1984, 'More Than Soap and Tears: A Closer Look at *A Country Practice*', *Metro*, no. 65, pp. 24–6.

McKay, Hugh 1993, *Reinventing Australia: The Mind and Mood of Australia in the 90s*, Angus & Robertson, Sydney.

McKee, Alan 1996, 'A Kiss is Just', *Australian Journal of Communication*, vol. 23, no. 2, pp. 51–72.

McKee, Alan 1997a 'Marking the Liminal for True Blue Aussies: The Generic Placement of Aboriginality in Australian Soap Opera', *Australian Journal of Communication*, vol. 24, no. 1, pp. 42–57.
McKee, Alan 1997b, 'The Aboriginal Version of Ken Done: Banal Aboriginal Identities in Australia', *Cultural Studies*, vol. 11, no. 2, pp. 191–206.
McKee, Alan 1999a, 'Australian Gay Porn Videos: The National Identity of Despised Cultural Objects', *International Journal of Cultural Studies*, vol. 2, no. 2, pp. 178–98.
McKee, Alan 1999b, 'Researching the "Reception" of Indigenous Affairs in Australia', *Screen*, winter, vol. 40, no. 4, pp. 451–4.
McKee, Alan 1999/2000, 'Must See TV', *Metro*, winter, nos 121/122, pp. 55–9.
Macken, Deirdre 1989, 'Invasion of the Aussie Soaps', *Sydney Morning Herald*, 8 April, pp. 23–4.
McKie, David & Hilaire Natt 1996, 'Rereading the ABC of Comedy: British Influences, Middle Class Mores and Boutique Quality', *Continuum*, vol. 10, no. 2, pp. 141–56.
McKinnon, Andrew 1979, 'Kids Spring TV Surprise', *Age Green Guide*, 21 June.
McLaughlin, Thomas 1996, *Street Smarts and Critical Theory: Listening to the Vernacular*, University of Wisconsin Press, Madison, Wisconsin.
McLuhan, Marshall 1964, *Understanding Media: The Extensions of Man*, Routledge & Kegan Paul, London.
MacMurraugh-Kavanagh, M. K. 1997, ' "Drama" into "News": Strategies of Intervention in *The Wednesday Play*', *Screen*, vol. 38, no. 3, autumn, pp. 247–59.
McQueen, Humphrey 1977, *Australia's Media Monopolies*, Visa, Melbourne.
MacSween, Prue 1980, ' "I've More to Offer Than Just One Role" ', *TV Week*, 8 March, pp. 5, 26.
Malor, Deborah 1991, 'From the Sublime to the Ridiculous: Edmund Burke's Bucolia—Don Burke's Backyard', *Not My Department*, vol. 1, pp. 57–70.
Manning, Peter 1988, 'Peter Manning Defends *Four Corners*', *Gerard Henderson's Media Watch*, August/September, pp. 17–21.
Marc, David 1995, *Bonfire of the Humanities: Television, Subliteracy and Long Term Memory Loss*, The Television Series, ed. Robert Thompson, Syracuse University Press, New York.
Marsha 1964, 'Marsha Says', *TV Times*, 9 December, p. 8.
Marshall, Ian & Damien Kingsbury 1996, *Media Realities: The News Media and Power in Australian Society*, Longman, Melbourne.

Martin, Adrian 1994, *Phantasms*, McPhee Gribble, Melbourne.

Martin, Hugh 1999, 'Kennedy Swears by F-word', *Sunday Age*, 19 September, p. 6.

Martinson, Floyd M. 1994, *The Sexual Life of Children*, Bergin & Garvey, Westpoint, Conneticut.

Mason, Mary & Kathy McLean 1993, *Here is the News: How the Media Present Issues in Current Affairs*, HarperCollins, Melbourne.

Masterson, Murray & Roger Patching 1990, *Now the News in Detail: A Guide to Broadcast Journalism in Australia*, Deakin University Press, Geelong, Victoria.

Matheson, Judith 1984, 'Workin' Flat Out', *B + T Advertising, Marketing and Media Weekly*, 14 December, pp. 28, 31, 49, 52.

Mavis Bramston Show, The 1964, episode 64/06, directed by David Cahill & produced by James Fishburn, ATN Channel Seven, Sydney.

Mavis Bramston Show, The 1965, episode 65/01, directed by David Cahill & produced by James Fishburn, ATN Channel Seven, Sydney.

Mayer, Geoff 1985, 'The Last Bastion: History or Drama?', *Cinema Papers*, no. 50, pp. 38–41, 87.

Mayer, Henry 1976, *Media Policies of Australian Political Parties*, Department of Government, University of Sydney, Sydney.

Mayer, Henry 1994, *Mayer on the Media: Issues and Arguments*, Allen & Unwin, Sydney.

Maynes, Mary Jo 1982, 'Foreword', in Richard Johnson, Gregor McLennan, Bill Schwarz, & David Sutton (eds), *Making Histories: Studies in History-Writing and Politics*, University of Minnesota Press, Minneapolis, pp. 4–7.

Meade, Amanda 1999, '"TV's Tawdry Affairs"', *Australian Media Section*, 22–28 April, pp. 2–3.

Medhurst, Andy 1997, 'Negotiating the Gnome Zone: Versions of Suburbia in British Popular Culture', in Roger Silverston (ed.), *Visions of Suburbia*, Routledge, London, pp. 240–68.

'Melbourne Challenge to TV Detective Imports' 1964, *Age TV Guide*, 16 October, p. 3.

Meldrum, Molly 1987, 'It's the Final Countdown', *TV Week, Brisbane*, 11 July, pp. 6–7, 11.

Melloy, Neil & Des Partridge 2000, 'Bloopers Put Careers Off Air', *Courier Mail*, 24 June, p. 5.

Mencinsky, Nadia & Belinda Mullen 1999, 'Regulation of Children's Television in Australia: Past and Present', *Media International Australia*, no. 93, pp. 27–40.

'Menzies Called for Script of "Four Corners"' 1963, *Sydney Morning Herald*, 4 September, p. 10.

Meyrowitz, Joshua 1985, *No Sense of Place: The Impact of Electronic Media on Social Behaviour*, Oxford University Press, New York.

Mickler, Steve 1998, *The Myth of Privilege: Aboriginal Status, Media Visions, Public Ideas*, Fremantle Arts Centre Press, Fremantle, WA.

Middleton, David & Derek Edwards, 'Introduction', in David Middleton & Derek Edwards, *Collective Remembering*, Sage, London, pp. 1–22.

Miller, Toby 1990, 'Mission Impossible: How Do You Turn Indooroopilly into Africa?', in Jonathan Dawson & Bruce Molloy (eds), *Queensland Images in Film and Television*, University of Queensland Press, St Lucia, pp. 122–31.

Miller, Toby 1995, 'Exporting Truth from Aboriginal Australia: "Portions of our Past Become Present Again, Where Only the Melancholy Light of Origin Shines" ', *Media Information Australia*, no. 76, pp. 7–17.

Miller, Toby 1997, *The Avengers*, BFI Publishing, London.

Miller, Toby 1998, *Technologies of Truth: Cultural Citizenship and the Popular Media*, University of Minnesota Press, Minneapolis.

Mills, Ian 1978, 'An Australian Mining Ad', *Australian Journal of Screen Theory*, no. 5/6, pp. 82–104.

Mitchell, Susan 1999, 'A Pile of Laundry on our Doorstep', *Australian*, 13 September, p. 13.

Moffit, Ian 1977, ' "Gay" Community Has a *Campaign* to Gain Respect', *Bulletin*, 2 July, pp. 89–90.

Molloy, Simon & Barry Burgan 1993, *The Economics of Film and Television in Australia*, Australian Film Commission, Sydney.

Moran, Albert 1982, *Making a Television Series: The Bellamy Project*, Currency Press, Sydney.

Moran, Albert 1982, 'Localism and Australian Television', in John Docker, Drusilla Modjeska, & Susan Dermody (eds), *Nellie Melba, Ginger Meggs and Friends: Essays in Australian Cultural History*, Kibble Books, Malmsbury, Victoria, pp. 89–102.

Moran, Albert 1985, *Images and Industry: Television Drama Production in Australia*, Currency Press, Sydney.

Moran, Albert 1989, 'Crime, History, Romance: Television Drama', in Albert Moran & Tom O'Regan (eds), *The Australian Screen*, Penguin, Melbourne, pp. 236–54.

Moran, Albert 1997a, 'Australia', in Horace Newcomb (ed.), *Museum of Broadcast Communications Encyclopedia of Television*, Fitzroy Dearborn Publishers, Chicago, pp. 114–21.

Moran, Albert 1997b, '*Sale of the Century*', in Horace Newcomb (ed.), *Museum of Broadcast Communications Encyclopedia of Television*, Fitzroy Dearborn Publishers, Chicago, pp. 1427–8.

Moran, Albert & Peter Pinne 1993, *Moran's Guide to Australian TV Series*, Australian Film, Television and Radio School, with Allen & Unwin, Sydney.

More, Elizabeth & Keith Smith (eds) 1992, *Case Studies in Australian Media Management*, Macquarie University Graduate School of Management, Sydney.

Morgan, George (ed.) 1992, *Social Problems: An Australian Perspective*, Social Science Press, Wentworth Falls, NSW.

Morley, David 1980, *The Nationwide Audience: Structure and Decoding*, British Film Institute, London.

Morris, Meaghan 1988, *The Pirate's Fiancee: Feminism, Reading, Postmodernism*, Verso, London.

Morris, Meaghan 1990, 'Banality in Cultural Studies', in Patricia Mellencamp (ed.), *Logics of Television: Essays in Cultural Criticism*, Indiana University Press, Bloomington, pp. 14–43.

Morris, Meaghan 1998, *Too Soon Too Late: History in Popular Culture*, Indiana University Press, Bloomington.

'MP Complains of Bad Manners of TV Interviewers' n.d., publication details not given, held in the ABC clippings library file '*Four Corners*'.

'Mr Television', *TV Times*, 1958, vol. 7, no. 1, p. 1.

Muecke, Stephen 1989, 'Bob Hawke's Country Practice: A Deconstruction', *Intervention*, no. 21/22, pp. 54–7.

Mules, Warwick 1998, 'Media Evolution: Frontline and the Media', *AQ: Journal of Contemporary Analysis*, July/August, pp. 29–35.

Mulvey, Laura 1990 (1975), 'Visual Pleasure and the Narrative Cinema', in Patricia Erens (ed.), *Issues in Feminist Film Criticism*, Indiana University Press, Bloomington, pp. 28–40.

Murphy, Jim 1981, 'Light Entertainment', in Peter Beilby (ed.), *Australian TV: The First 25 Years*, Thomas Nelson, Melbourne, pp. 60–89.

Murray, John 1969, *The Box in the Corner*, Georgian House, Melbourne.

Murray, John C. 1973 'Defending the Defenders', *Lumiere*, April, pp. 16–19.

Murray, John C. 1984, 'Bodyline', *Cinema Papers*, no. 48, pp. 330–3.

Naismith, Gaye 1997, 'The Soft-core Sex Films of the Australian Film Industry Revival', unpublished Honours thesis, Department of Visual Arts, Faculty of Arts, Monash University, Melbourne.

National Library of Australia and National Film Archive 1981, *Australian Film and Television Reading List*, National Library of Australia and National Film Archive, Canberra.

National Working Party on the Portrayal of Women in the Media 1993, *Women and the Media*, Department of the Prime Minister and Cabinet, Office of the Status of Women, Canberra.

'Near Nude Scene in ABC-TV Play' 1964, *TV Times*, 4 November, p. 8.
Neighbours 1987, executive produced by Reg Watson, Grundy Television and Channel Ten, Melbourne.
Nerone, John 1989, 'Professional History and Social Memory', *Communication*, vol. 11, pp. 89–104.
Nerone, John & Ellen Wartella 1989, 'Introduction: Studying Social Memory', *Communication*, vol. 11, pp. 85–8.
Neumann, Anne Waldron 1999, *Should You Read Shakespeare? Literature, Popular Culture and Morality*, University of New South Wales Press, Sydney.
Nicholson, Margaret 1999, *The Pocket Aussie Fact Book*, Penguin, Melbourne.
Nicklin, Lenore 1993, 'Live on Settee', *Bulletin*, 13 July, pp. 44–5.
Nixon, Margaret 1998, 'Home and Away: Australian Television's Recontextualisation of Foreign Programs', *Metro*, vol. 115, pp. 73–6.
Norman, Harvey 1999, 'Great Moments in Television: Featuring *A Country Practice*', advertisement, *TV Week*, 10–16 April, p. 29.
Number 96 1972a, episode 1, written by David Sale, directed by Brian Philips, & produced by Bill Harmon, Cash Harmon and Channel Ten, Sydney.
Number 96 1972b, episode 3, written by David Sale, directed by Ted Gregory, & produced by Don Cash, Cash Harmon and Channel Ten, Sydney.
Number 96 1972c, episode 4, written by David Sale, directed by Peter Bernardos, & produced by Don Cash, Cash Harmon and Channel Ten, Sydney.
Number 96 1972d, episode 6, written by David Sale, directed by Peter Benardos, & produced by Don Cash, Cash Harmon and Channel Ten, Sydney.
Nugent, Stephen, Milica Loncar, & Kate Aisbett 1993, *The People We See on TV: Cultural Diversity on Television, Australian Broadcasting Authority*, Monograph no. 3, Australian Broadcasting Authority, Sydney.
Nugent, Stephen, Linda Sheldon, Kate Aisbett, Cherie Harkess, & Nick Herd 1992, *What We Want From Our TVs*, Australian Broadcasting Tribunal, Sydney.
O'Donnell, John 1992, 'But Seriously', *Rolling Stone Australia*, September, pp. 50–3, 92.
OED. See *Oxford English Dictionary*.
O'Grady, Suellen 1989, 'Lone Star: The Private Life of King Gra-Gra', *Sydney Morning Herald*, *Good Weekend Magazine*, 1 April, pp. 22–6.

Oliver, Robin n.d., 'It's the End for *The Sullivans*', publication details unknown, kept in file of *The Sullivans* press clippings, Crawfords Productions.

'On the Street Where You Live' 1964, *Listener In-TV*, 17 October, p. 2.

'100 Greatest Moments in Television, The' 1999, *Who Weekly*, 12 April, pp. 44–94.

'One More Week' 1966, *Bulletin*, 17 September 1966, p. 30.

Oost, Victor 1993, 'Television Advertising: Iconography of a Mythic Australian Identity', in Don Grant & Graham Seal (eds), *Australia in the World: Perceptions and Possibilities: Papers from the 'Outside Images of Australia' Conference, Perth, 1992*, Black Swan Press, Perth, pp. 57–67.

Oram, James 1987, *Hogan: The Story of a Son of Oz*, Columbus Books, London.

Oram, James 1988, *Neighbours: Behind the Scenes*, Angus & Robertson Publishers, Sydney.

O'Regan, Tom 1989, 'The Enchantment with Cinema: Film in the 80s', in Albert Moran & Tom O'Regan (eds), *The Australian Screen*, Penguin, Melbourne, pp. 118–45.

O'Regan, Tom 1991, 'Inventing Australian TV', in Denise Corrigan & David Watson (eds), *TV Times: 35 Years of Watching Television in Austrlaia*, Museum of Contemporary Art, Sydney.

O'Regan, Tom 1993, *Australian Television Culture*, Allen & Unwin, Sydney.

O'Regan, Tom 1994, 'Situating Australia's Television Culture', *Metro*, no. 98, pp. 25–32.

O'Regan, Tom 1996, *Australian National Cinema*, National Cinemas Series, ed. Susan Hayward, Routledge, London.

Osborne, Graeme & Glen Lewis 1995, *Communications Tradition in Twentieth-Century Australia*, Oxford University Press, Melbourne.

O'Sullivan, Tim, John Hartley, Danny Saunders, Martin Montgomery, & John Fiske 1994, *Key Concepts in Communication and Cultural Studies*, 2nd edn, Routledge, London.

Our Century 1999, broadcast 18 April, Channel Nine, Sydney.

Overton, Derek 1989, 'Two Worlds: International Coverage on the ABC and SBS TV Evening News', *Media International Australia*, no. 52, May, pp. 36–41.

Owen, Rob 1997, *Gen X TV: The Brady Bunch to Melrose Place*, The Television Series, ed. Robert J. Thompson, Syracuse University Press, New York.

Oxford English Dictionary 1989, 2nd edn, J. A. Simpson and E.S.C. Weiner (eds), Clarendon Press, Oxford.

Page, Christopher 1986, 'Paul Hogan: Not So Much Born as Made', *National Times*, 25–31 July, pp. 8–9.

Page, Christopher 1992 (1986), 'Paul Hogan's Television Commercials', in Albert Moran (ed.), *Stay Tuned: An Australian Broadcasting Reader*, Allen & Unwin, Sydney, pp. 116–19.

Palmer, Patricia 1986a, *Girls and Television*, Social Policy Unit, Minister of Education, NSW, Sydney.

Palmer, Patricia 1986b, *The Lively Audience: A Study of Children Around the Television Set*, Allen & Unwin, Sydney.

Panel, The 1998, episode 10, Working Dog Productions and Channel Ten, Melbourne.

Pangallo, Frank 1979, 'Movie Bombing was Real Thing', *TV Times, Melbourne*, 13 October, p. 5.

Parsons, Joanna, Eric Scott, & Fred Robertson 1979, 'Graham Kennedy: The Man and the Myth', *TV Times, Melbourne*, 15 September, pp. 10–11, 37.

Paterson, Richard 1998, 'Drama and Entertainment', in Anthony Smith (ed.), *Television: An International History*, 2nd edn, Oxford University Press, Oxford, pp. 57–68.

Paulson, Ronald 1967, *The Fictions of Satire*, Johns Hopkins Press, Baltimore, Maryland.

Peach, Bill 1992, *This Day Tonight: How Australian Current Affairs TV Came of Age*, ABC Enterprises, Sydney.

Peach, Katrina 1990, 'Comedy Hero Looks Down the Barrel', *Sun News Pictorial*, 1 August, p. 19.

Pells, Richard 1997, *Not Like Us: How Europeans Have Loved, Hated and Transformed American Culture Since World War II*, Basic Books, New York.

Perkin, Corrie 1994, 'The Women Most Likely to Succeed', *Sunday Age View Magazine*, 25 July–31 July, pp. 6–8.

'Perth's Own TVW Channel Seven' 1999, Channel Seven, Perth.

Petersen, Neville 1993, *News, Not Views: The ABC, the Press and Politics 1932–1947*, Hale & Iremonger, Sydney.

Play School 1975a, episode 406, 24 April, Australian Broadcasting Corporation, Sydney.

Play School 1975b, episode 407, 30 April, Australian Broadcasting Corporation, Sydney.

Play School 1975c, episode 408, 1 May, Australian Broadcasting Corporation, Sydney.

Play School 1975d, episode 409, 14 May, Australian Broadcasting Corporation, Sydney.

Play School 1975e, episode 410, 15 May, Australian Broadcasting Corporation, Sydney.

Pollard, Arthur 1970, *Satire*, The Critical Idiom series, ed. John Jump, Methuen, London.

Popular Memory Group 1982, 'Popular Memory: Theory, Politics, Methods', in Richard Johnson, Gregor McLennan, Bill Schwartz, & David Sutton (eds), *Making Histories: Studies in History-writing and Politics*, University of Minnesota Press, Minneapolis, pp. 205–52.

Porter, Pip 1975, 'Soap Operas: Why Do We Watch?', *Cleo*, March, pp. 23–7.

Powell, R. J. 1974, *Television Viewing by Young Secondary Students: A Study of the Television Viewing Behaviour of Children at Form Two Level*, Australian Government Publishing Service, Canberra.

Poynton, Beverley, & John Hartley 1990, 'Male Gazing: Australian Rules Football, Gender and Television', in Mary Ellen Brown (ed.), *Television and Women's Culture: The Politics of the Popular*, Currency Press, Sydney, pp. 144–57.

Prisoner 1979a, episode 1, written by Reg Watson, produced by Ian Bradley, & directed by Graeme Arthur, Grundy Productions and Channel 0-10, Melbourne.

Prisoner 1979b, episode 2, written by Reg Watson, produced by Ian Bradley, & directed by Graeme Arthur, Channel Ten and Grundy Productions, Melbourne.

Prisoner 1979c, episode 3, written by Ian Bradley, produced by Ian Bradley, & directed by Rod Hardy, Grundy Productions, Melbourne.

'Prisoner's Key Women' 1979, *TV Times, Melbourne*, 14 July, pp. 10–11.

Pullan, Robert 1986, *Four Corners: Twenty Five Years*, ABC Enterprises, Sydney.

Radic, Leonard 1968 'Viewers (at Long Last) Make the Big Switch', *Age*, 7 February, p. 4.

Radic, Leonard 1973, 'Sex in the Suburbs Adds Up to Number 96', *Age*, 25 June, p. 8.

Rayson, Cate 1998, *Glued to the Telly*, Elgua Media, Redhill, Victoria.

Rees, Leslie 1978a, *A History of Australian Drama*, vol. 1, *The Making of Australian Drama, 1830s–1960s*, Angus & Robertson, Sydney.

Rees, Leslie 1978b, *A History of Australian Drama*, vol. 2, *Australian Drama in the 1970s*, Angus & Robertson, Sydney.

Reid, Don & Frances de Groen (eds) 1977, *Zoom In: Television Scripts of the Seventies*, Macmillan, Melbourne.

Return to Eden 1983, directed by Michael Laurence, written by Michael Laurence, & produced by Hal McElroy, Eden Productions, Sydney.

'Review of *Blankety Blanks, with Shane Bourne*' 1999, *Australian, Media Section*, 9 December, p. 26.

Richter, Christine 1980, 'Gracious!', *TV Week*, 16 February, pp. 2–3, 9.

Ricketson, Matthew 1994, 'Fantasy Figure', *Australian Magazine*, 10–11 December, pp. 66–70.

Robbins, Mikey 1999, 'Critic's Choice', *Who Weekly*, 12 April, p. 95.

Robertson, Fred 1972, 'A Chance to Solve Homicide Mystery', *TV Times*, 25 November 1972, p. 15.

Robertson, Fred 1979, 'The Sullivans Prepare for Peace', *TV Times, Melbourne*, 22 September, p. 6.

Ross, Teena 1988, 'There's More to Soap than Froth', *Sunday Times, TV Extra Magazine*, 6 March, p. 16.

Rowbotham, Jill 1987, 'Britain Adopts Our Neighbours', *Courier-Mail*, 15 December, p. 26.

Rowe, David 1994, 'The Federal Republic of Sylvania Waters', *Metro*, no. 98, pp. 14–24.

Rowse, Tim, & Albert Moran 1984, 'Peculiarly Australian—The Political Construction of Cultural Identity', in S. Encel & L. Bryson (eds), *Australian Society: Introductory Essays*, 4th edn, Longman Chesire, Melbourne.

'RSL, The' 1965, *Current Affairs Bulletin (Department of Adult Education, University of Sydney)*, vol. 35, no. 12, pp. 178–91.

Rubington, Earl, & Martin S. Weinberg 1989, *The Study of Social Problems*, 4th edn, Oxford University Press, New York.

Ryan, Tom 1977, 'Luke's Kingdom and Continuous Drama', *Cinema Papers*, no. 14, pp. 120–3, 189.

St John, Ed 1981, 'What the TV Rock Shows Think of Themselves and Each Other', *Rolling Stone Australia*, 6 August, pp. 82–5.

Sale of the Century 1980, episode 1, directed by Ray Punjer & produced by Garry Meadows, Melbourne: Grundy Productions and Channel Nine.

Sale of the Century 1981, episode 293, Grundy Productions and Channel Nine, Melbourne.

Sale of the Century 1983, episode 751, Grundy Productions and Channel Nine, Melbourne.

Sale of the Century 1999a, 15 September 1999, Grundy Productions and Channel Nine, Melbourne.

Sale of the Century 1999b, 16 September 1999, Grundy Productions and Channel Nine, Melbourne.

Sale of the Century 1999c, 17 September 1999, Grundy Productions and Channel Nine, Melbourne.

Salt, Jeremy 1964, 'Good Start to Homicide', *Herald*, 21 October, p. 30.

Sanders, Barry 1995, *Sudden Glory: Laughter as Subversive History*, Beacon Press, Boston.

Sanders, Noel 1982, 'Azaria Chamberlain and Popular Culture', *Interventions*, no. 16, pp. 53–69.

Satisfied Viewer 1964, 'Crime Series Shows We Have Talent', *Listener In-TV*, 5 December, p. 45.

Scannell, Paddy 1996, *Radio, Television and Modern Life: A Phenomenological Approach*, Blackwell, Oxford.

Schaffer, Kay 1988, *Women and the Bush: Forces of Desire in the Australian Cultural Tradition*, Cambridge University Press, Melbourne.

Schaffer, Kay 1993, '*A Country Practice*: Motherhood, Surrogacy and the Price of Love', *Hecate: A Women's Interdisciplinary Journal*, vol. 19, no. 2, pp. 128–39.

Schou, Kirsten 1982, *Structure and Operation of the Television Industry in Australia*, Australian Film, Radio and Television School, Sydney.

Schultz, Julianne 1998, *Reviving the Fourth Estate: Democracy, Accountability and the Media*, Cambridge University Press, Cambridge.

Scott, Eric 1979, 'Countdown—200 Not Out', *TV Times, Melbourne*, 30 June, pp. 10–11.

Searle, Samantha 1997, *Queer-ing the Screen: Sexuality and Australian Film and Television*, The Moving Image series, ed. James Sabine, Australian Teachers of Media, Melbourne.

Seddon, George 1997, *Landprints: Reflections on Place and Landscape*, Cambridge University Press, Cambridge.

Sedorkin, Gail, & Tony Schirato 1998, 'Theory and Current Affairs Television', in Myles Breen (ed.), *Journalism: Theory and Practice*, Macleay Press, Sydney, pp. 104–18.

Sekuless, Peter, & Jacqueline Rees 1986, *Lest We Forget: The History of the Returned Services League 1916–1986*, Rigby, Sydney.

Semmler, Clement 1981, *The ABC—Aunty Sally and Sacred Cow*, Melbourne University Press, Melbourne.

Sgro, Diane 1974, *Australian Research on Television: An Annotated Bibliography*, School of Social Sciences, La Trobe University, Melbourne.

Shattuc, Jane M. 1997, *The Talking Cure: TV Talk Shows and Women*, Routledge, New York.

Sheldon, Linda, Kate Aisbett, & Nick Herd 1993, *Living with Television*, Australian Broadcasting Authority Monograph no. 2, Australian Broadcasting Authority, Sydney.

Sheldon, Linda, Gillian Ramsay, & Milica Loncar 1995, *'Cool' or 'Gross': Children's Attitudes to Violence, Kissing and Swearing on Television*, Australian Broadcasting Authority, Sydney.

Shipp, George 1971, 'The Impartiality of TDT: Pretence or Reality?', *Quadrant*, May/June, pp. 26–33.

Shoebridge, Neil 1992, *Great Australian Advertising Campaigns*, McGraw-Hill, Sydney.

Shoemaker, Adam 1994, ' "Looking for Mr G'Day": Images of Australia in Canadian Magazines', in Don Grant & Graham Seal (eds), *Australia in the World: Possibilities and Perceptions*, Black Swan Press, Perth, pp. 187–94.

Silberstein, Richard 1983, *Electroencephalographic Responses of Children to Television*, Australian Broadcasting Tribunal, Melbourne.

'Simply the Best' 1999, *Woman's Day*, 25 October, pp. 114–15.

Smith, David 1998, 'Our Cultural Heritage: Parliament and the Constitution', in John Bigelow (ed.), *Our Cultural Heritage: Papers from the 1997 Symposium of the Australian Academy of the Humanities*, Australian Academy of the Humanities, Canberra, pp. 3–24.

Smith, Linda 1988, 'Oz Cleans up UK in TV Ratings War', *Sunday Times*, 7 Feburary, p. 15.

Smith, Michael George 1995, 'Ozrock: The State of Play', *Ozrock*, winter, pp. 32–6.

Solomon, Les 1989, 'The Oz Invasion', *Age*, 23 March, p. 23.

SOTC. See *Sale of the Century*.

Spector, Macolm, & John I. Kitsuse 1987, *Constructing Social Problems*, Aldine de Gruyter, New York.

Spigel, Lynn 1992, *Make Room for TV: Television and the Family Ideal in Postwar America*, University of Chicago Press, Chicago.

Spigel, Lynn 1995, 'From the Dark Ages to the Golden Age: Women's Memories and Television Reruns', *Screen*, vol. 36, no. 1, pp. 16–33.

Spigel, Lynn, & Henry Jenkins 1991, 'Same Bat Channel, Different Bat Times: Mass Culture and Popular Memory', in Roberta E. Pearson & William Uricchio (eds), *The Many Lives of Batman: Critical Approaches to a Superhero and his Media*, Routledge and BFI, New York and London, pp. 117–48.

Squires, Tony 1995, 'Rising to the Challenge', *Sydney Morning Herald, The Guide Magazine*, 28 August, p. 14S.

Squires, Tony 1997, 'Bravo, Nicky, for Declining to Take a Pregnant Pause from Sale', *Sydney Morning Herald*, 3 May, p. 22.

Stanley, Di 1999, 'Nicky Buckley: Super Mum, Super Model', *Woman's Day*, 25 October, pp. 8–9.

Stockbridge, Sally 1989, 'Programming Rock'n'roll: The Australian Version', *Cultural Studies*, vol. 3, no. 1, pp. 73–88.

Stockbridge, Sally 1992 (1989), 'Rock'n'roll and Television', in Albert Moran (ed.), *Stay Tuned: An Australian Broadcasting Reader*, Allen & Unwin, Sydney, pp. 135–42.

Stone, Gerald 2000, *Compulsive Viewing*, Viking, Melbourne.

Stratton, Jon 1992, *The Young Ones: Working Class Culture, Consumption and the Category of Youth*, Black Swan Press, Centre for Australian Studies, Curtin University of Technology, Perth.

Stratton, Jon, & Ien Ang 1994, 'Sylvania Waters and the Spectacular Exploding Family', *Screen*, vol. 35, no. 1, pp. 1–21.

Sullivan, Barbara 1997, *The Politics of Sex: Prostitution and Pornography in Australia Since 1945*, Cambridge University Press, Cambridge.

Sullivans, The 1976, episodes 1–4, written by Ian Blair & Jock Jones, directed by Ian Crawford & Ian Jones, & produced by Henry Crawford, Crawfords Australia, Melbourne.

Sullivans, The 1980, episode 598, written by Brian Wright, produced by John Barningham, & directed by John Dommett, Crawfords and Channel Nine, Melbourne.

'Sullivans on Kokoda Trail' 1978, *TV Times, Melbourne*, 26 August, p. 7.

Summers, Anne 1994, *Damned Whores and God's Police*, revised edn, Penguin, Melbourne.

'Supersonic' 2000, *Foxtel: The Magazine*, September, p. 24.

Sykes, Arlene 1994, 'Introduction', in Arlene Sykes (ed.), *Three Australian Plays*, Penguin, Melbourne, pp. 9–24.

Symons, Sandra 1977, 'Real Folk Oust the Ockers', *Bulletin*, 9 July, pp. 52–4.

Taylor, Ken 1994, 'Things We Want to Keep: Discovering Australia's Cultural Heritage', in Joy Hooton, Donald Horne & David Headon (eds), *The Abundant Culture: Meaning and Significance in Everyday Australia*, Allen & Unwin, Sydney, pp. 26–33.

The Graham Kennedy Story: From Birth to Stardom in Words and Pictures n.d., Southdown Press, Melbourne.

'The Sullivans: Award Winning Universal Appeal' n.d., publicity flyer, Crawfords Productions, Melbourne.

35 Years of Television 1991, directed by Magnus Vikingur, executive produced by David Lyle, Nine Network Australia, n.p.

Thomas, Allan James 1996, 'Camping Outback: Landscape, Masculinity and Performance in *The Adventures of Priscilla: Queen of the Desert*', *Continuum*, vol. 10, no. 2, pp. 97–110.

Thomas, Claire 1980, 'Girls and Counter-School Culture', in David McCallum & Uldis Ozolins (eds), *Melbourne Working Papers 1980*, University of Melbourne, Melbourne.

Thompson, R. J. 1959, *Television Crime Drama: Its Impact on Children and Adolescents*, Chesire, Melbourne.

Thring, Frank 1964, 'Money for Ham, and It's Murder, He Says', *TV Week*, 12 December, pp. 24–5.

Tiffen, Rod 1989, *News and Power*, Allen & Unwin, Sydney.

Tipping, Dee 1991, 'The Folk at Wandin Valley Tackle Issues that Count', in Christopher Day (ed.), *A Country Practice: 10th Birthday Souvenir*, Express Publications with Georgie Brown Publicity, Lismore, NSW, p. 61.

Tom, Emma 1997, 'Weighty Matters', *Sydney Morning Herald*, 28 May, p. 13.

Toshner, Linda 1988, *Arts Programs on Australian Television*, Australian Broadcasting Tribunal, Sydney.

'Tragic News!', *Sun*, 18 February, p. 23.

'Trapping Lorraine Was a Piece of Cake' 1979, *TV Times, Melbourne*, 3 November, p. 7.

Tulloch, John 1990, *Television Drama: Agency, Audience and Myth*, Routledge, London.

Tulloch, John, & Albert Moran 1986, *A Country Practice: Quality Soap*, Currency Press, Sydney.

Tulloch, John, & Graeme Turner (eds) 1989, *Australian Television: Programs, Politics, Pleasures*, Allen & Unwin, Sydney.

Tuohy, Wendy 1994, 'When Artifice Imitates Real Life', *Age*, 2 August, p. 13.

Turnbull, Sue 1984, '*Prisoner*: Patterns of Opposition and Identification', unpublished paper, Department of Media Studies, La Trobe University, Melbourne.

Turnbull, Sue 1993, 'The Great Australian Theme Park', *Melbourne Report*, vol. 8, no. 6, pp. 17–19.

Turnbull, Sue 1994, 'Noeline Donaher, This Is/n't your Life?', in Kate Bowles and Sue Turnbull (eds), *Tomorrow Never Knows: Soaps on Australian Television*, Australian Film Institute, Melbourne, pp. 8–24.

Turnbull, Sue 1996a, ' "The Australian Way" ', *The Melbournian*, vol. 11, no. 4, May/June, pp. 4–6.

Turnbull, Sue 1996b, 'A Cunning Array of Stunts: Women, Situation Comedy and Risky Performances on Australian Television', *Australian Screen Comedy, Continuum* vol. 10, no. 2, pp. 79–93.

Turner, Geoff 1994, 'Frontline Ethics: The Australian Media's Seige Mentality', *Australian Studies in Journalism*, no. 3, pp. 24–38.

Turner, Graeme 1986, *National Fictions: Literature, Film, and the Construction of Australian Narrative*, Allen & Unwin, Sydney.

Turner, Graeme 1987, 'Perfect Match: Ambiguity, Spectacle and the Popular' *Australian Journal of Cultural Studies*, vol. 4, no. 2, May, pp.: 79–93.

Turner, Graeme 1989, 'Transgressive TV: From *In Melbourne Tonight* to *Perfect Match*', in John Tulloch & Graeme Turner (eds), *Australian Television: Programs, Politics, Pleasures*, Allen & Unwin, Sydney, pp. 25–38.

Turner, Graeme 1992, 'Suburbia Verite', *Australian Left Review*, no. 144, pp. 37–9.

Turner, Graeme 1993, 'Media Texts and Messages', in Stuart Cunningham & Graeme Turner (eds), *The Media in Australia: Industries, Texts, Audiences*, Allen & Unwin, Sydney, 205–66.

Turner, Graeme 1999, 'Tabloidization, Journalism and the Possibility of Critique', *International Journal of Cultural Studies*, vol. 2, no. 1, pp. 59–76.

'TV's Top 100 Moments' 1999, *Today Tonight*, broadcast 16 April, Channel Seven, Perth.

'TV Trends of 1965' 1964, *TV Week*, 28 November, pp. 76–9.

Verhoeven, Deb (ed.) 1999, *Twin Peeks: Australian and New Zealand Film*, Damned Publishing, Melbourne.

Waldman, Diane 1978, 'There's More to a Positive Image than Meets the Eye', in Patricia Erens (ed.), *Issues in Feminist Film Criticism*, Indiana University Press, Bloomington, pp. 13–18.

Walter, Regina 1999, 'Trees to Please', *Burke's Backyard*, December, pp. 50–7.

Ward, Russel 1978, *The Australian Legend*, new illustrated edn, Oxford University Press, Melbourne.

Wark, McKenzie 1999, *Celebrities, Culture and Cyberspace: The Light on the Hill in a Postmodern World*, Pluto Press, Sydney.

Warneke, Ross 1997, 'It's Bin Night Tomorrow', *Age Green Guide*, 1 May, p. 16.

Waterhouse, Richard 1995, *Private Pleasures, Public Leisure: A History of Australian Popular Culture Since 1788*, Longman, Melbourne.

Weaver, Amanda 1990, 'Fearless Frontman in the Backyard', *Bulletin*, 18 December, pp. 90–3.

Weaver, Rodney 1990, 'The Politics of Storytelling: The Effects of Dramatic Structuring in Daily Current Affairs TV', *Media Information Australia*, no. 57, August, pp. 12–18.

Webb, Jeremy 1973, 'Puff Puff: It's Hogan the Magic Australian', *Bulletin*, 24 February, pp. 51–3.

Weiniger, Peter 1997, 'Three Women and No Baby', *Age Green Guide*, 26 June, P. 24.

Western, J., & Colin A. Hughes 1983, *The Mass Media in Australia*, 2nd edn, University of Queensland Press, St Lucia.

'What's Your Most Memorable Australian Television Moment?' 1999, *TV Week*, 30 October, p. 31.

Wheeler, C. 1979, 'Sullivans Wrong', *TV Times, Melbourne*, 21 July, p. 40.

Wheelwright, Ted, & Ken Buckley (eds) 1987, *Communications and the Media in Australia*, Allen & Unwin, Sydney.

White, Robert 1993, 'A Brief Cultural History of Vegemite', *Australian Popular Culture* (Special Issue of *Australian Studies*) no. 7, November, pp. 15–21.

Whitehead, Geoffrey 1988, *Inside the ABC: Geoffrey Whitehead's Personal Account*, Penguin, Melbourne.

'Who's Who in *The Sullivans*' 1977, *TV Times (Melbourne)*, pp. 10–11.

'Why Australians Love to Laugh' 2000, *TV Week*, 22 January, p. 11.

Wilgeosher 1964, 'Homicide Shows Courage', *Listener In-TV*, 7 November, p. 36.

Willey, Keith 1984, *You Might as Well Laugh Mate: Australian Humor in Hard Times*, Macmillan, Melbourne.

Willey, Keith 1988, 'A Hard, Dry Humour for a Hard, Dry Land', in Verity Burgman & Jenny Lee (eds), *Constructing a Culture: A People's History of Australia Since 1788*, McPhee Gribble/Penguin, Melbourne, pp. 156–69.

Williams, Marina 1999, 'The Game Show Girls', *TV Week*, 4 September, pp. 16–18.

Williams, Raymond 1990 (1975), *Television: Technology and Cultural Form*, Routledge, London.

Williams, Sue 1994a, 'Current Affairs Coverage Under Siege', *Australian*, 6 June, p. 12.

Williams, Sue 1994b, 'How Soap Lost its Virginity', *Australian*, 21 November.

Williams, Sue 1994c, 'Trailblazing Cops Put Accent on Local Talent', *Australian*, 17 October, p. 29.

Williams, Sue 1995, 'Viewers Back on Speaking Terms with Neighbours', *The Australian*, 2 January, p. 48.

Wilmoth, Peter 1983, 'Bye, Bye Sullivans', *Age, Green Guide*, 3 March.

Wilmoth, Peter 1987, 'The Day the Music Died', *Age, Saturday Extra*, 25 July, p. 8.

Wilmoth, Peter 1993, *Glad All Over: The Countdown Years 1974–1987*, McPhee Gribble, Melbourne.

Windschuttle, Keith 1988, *The Media: A New Analysis of the Press, Television, Radio and Advertising in Australia*, 3rd edn, Penguin, Melbourne.

Windschuttle, Keith, & Elizabeth Windschuttle 1981, *Fixing the News: Critical Perspectives on the Australian Media*, Penguin, Melbourne.

Withers, Helen 1987, 'Neighbours is Killing Them', *Sun*, 10 December, p. 27.

Wood, Mrs Henry 1984 (1861), *East Lynne*, Everyman's Press, London.

Woods, M 1996, 'Info Shows Go Strong', *Variety*, vol. 364, no. 6, p. 48.

Yeates, Helen 1995, 'The League of Men: Masculinity, the Media and Rugby League Football', *Media Information Australia*, no. 75, pp. 35–45.

Zalcock, Beverley, & Jocelyn Robinson 1996, 'Inside Cell Block H: Hard Steel and Soft Soap', *Continuum*, vol. 9, no. 1, pp. 88–97.

Zion, Lawrie 1995, 'Frontispiece', in *Frontline: The Story Behind the Story … Behind the Stories*, Penguin Books, Melbourne, pp. 1–16.

Index